THE FRONTIER OF LEISURE

THE FRONTIER OF LEISURE

Southern California and the
Shaping of Modern America

Lawrence Culver

OXFORD
UNIVERSITY PRESS
2010

OXFORD

UNIVERSITY PRESS

Oxford University Press, Inc., publishes works that further
Oxford University's objective of excellence
in research, scholarship, and education.

Oxford   New York

Auckland   Cape Town   Dar es Salaam   Hong Kong   Karachi
Kuala Lumpur   Madrid   Melbourne   Mexico City   Nairobi
New Delhi   Shanghai   Taipei   Toronto

With offices in

Argentina   Austria   Brazil   Chile   Czech Republic   France   Greece
Guatemala   Hungary   Italy   Japan   Poland   Portugal   Singapore
South Korea   Switzerland   Thailand   Turkey   Ukraine   Vietnam

Published by Oxford University Press, Inc.
198 Madison Avenue, New York, New York 10016

www.oup.com

Oxford is a registered trademark of Oxford University Press

Library of Congress Cataloging-in-Publication Data
Culver, Lawrence.
The frontier of leisure : Southern California and the shaping of modern America / Lawrence Culver.
p. cm.
Includes bibliographical references and index.
ISBN 978-0-19-538263-1
1. California, Southern—History.   2. Leisure—California, Southern—History.   3. Recreation—California,
Southern—History.   4. California, Southern—Social life and customs.   5. Leisure—Southwest, New—History.
6. Recreation—Southwest, New—History.   7. Southwest, New—Social life and customs.   I. Title.
F867.C79 2010
979.4'9—dc22   2009053932

1 3 5 7 9 8 6 4 2

Printed in the United States of America
on acid-free paper

Contents

ACKNOWLEDGMENTS

THIS IS a book about travel and tourism, among other things, and writing a book requires its own kind of travel. The long process through which this project became a book has at times been an arduous journey. Yet, as with all traveling, the greatest reward one can receive are the friends you make along the way. My first expression of gratitude must go to my dissertation committee at UCLA. My dissertation committee co-chairs, Stephen Aron and Thomas S. Hines, shaped this project more than anyone else. Steve consistently pushed my analysis, urging me to elucidate my ideas and understand why they mattered. Tom always urged me to conceptualize boldly and think broadly, and to think about how history has shaped—and been shaped by—natural and built environments.

The other members of my committee were of great assistance and support as well. Kevin Terraciano kept me attuned to Southern California's Native American, Spanish, and Mexican past. Denis Cosgrove, of the UCLA Department of Geography, introduced me to the literature of his discipline. If this book concerns itself with historical change over time, it also takes as a central focus change in place—how houses, resorts, cities, and landscapes changed over time. To Denis and Kevin, as to Steve and Tom, I offer my thanks. Denis died in 2008, and I deeply regret that I cannot thank him again.

I must also thank the skilled and resourceful tour guides who showed me the way through unfamiliar but rewarding terrain—the archivists, librarians, and staff at the institutions where I conducted my research. These institutions include Special Collections at the University of California, Los Angeles; the Archival Research Center at the University of Southern California; Special Collections at the University of California, Riverside; Special Collections at California State University, Northridge; the Huntington Library; the Institute for the Study of the American West at the Autry National Center; the Braun Research Library at the Southwest Museum of the American Indian, also at the Autry National Center; the Seaver Center for Western History Research at the Natural History Museum of Los Angeles County; Los Angeles City Archives; the City of Los Angeles Department of Recreation and Parks; the County of Los Angeles Department of Parks and Recreation; the History and Genealogy Department at Richard J. Riordan Los Angeles Central Library; the Catalina Island Museum; the Palm Springs Historical Society; the Palm Springs Public Library; the Agua Caliente Cultural Museum; Special Collections at the Hayden Library at Arizona State University; and the Arizona Historical Foundation, also at Arizona State University. I am deeply indebted to archivists and librarians at all of these institutions, but must express special thanks to Marva Felchlin and Manola Madrid at the Institute for the Study of the American West, Kim Walters of the Braun Library at the Southwest Museum, Peter Blodgett and Jennifer Watts at the Huntington Library, Jeri Vogelsang and Sally McManus at the Palm Springs Historical Society, Jeanine Pedersen at the Catalina Island Museum, John Cahoon at the Seaver Center, and Linda A. Whitaker at the Arizona Historical Foundation.

In the course of writing this book, I conducted a series of interviews and conversations with individuals. Of these, I must express special thanks to Frank Bogert, Elizabeth Coffman Kieley, and Thomas Kieley, all of Palm Springs, and all now deceased. At various stages I had conversations with many other individuals who contributed to the conceptualization of this book, read portions of the manuscript, or otherwise offered support along the way. This long list includes Annie Gilbert Coleman, William Deverell, Greg Hise, Alexis McCrossen, Jenny Price, and David Wrobel.

Portions of this book have been presented at numerous academic conferences, and I benefited greatly from the comments I received at each conference. As a graduate student, I also presented portions of it to the Los Angeles History Research Group at the Huntington Library and the U.S. Field Colloquium in the Department of History at UCLA. Two other venues in which my work was presented deserve special mention. First is the UCLA Interdisciplinary Environmental Studies Graduate Group (a.k.a. the Nature Nerds), a remarkable assemblage of individuals from across Los Angeles who shared a common intellectual interest in the environment, as well as in good intellectual and social company. Finally, WHEAT (Western Historians Eating and Talking), a dissertation reading group moderated by my co-chair Stephen Aron, provided the most generous forum of all. Steve and the graduate student members of WHEAT waded through much of this tome, and for that I proffer my thanks to Michael Bottoms, John Bowes, Cynthia Culver Prescott, Chris Gantner, Samantha Gervase, Wade Graham, Kelly Lytle-Hernandez, Arthur Rolston, Allison Varzally, Lissa Wadewitz, and other WHEATies. Their criticisms, however incisive, were always offered in a spirit of friendship and mutual intellectual endeavor, and for that I am profoundly grateful.

My editor at Oxford University Press, Susan Ferber, has been unfailingly patient and supportive with a first-time author. She has been enthusiastic about this book since we first met to talk about it on a sweltering patio at a resort in Phoenix. That setting was certainly appropriate, and all her advice and insights since have been as well. Susan's support meant that this book, though published by a large university press, received a remarkable degree of attention and care. I am deeply thankful for it. I also thank the anonymous readers for Oxford, who greatly strengthened this book. Jessica Ryan and the production and copyediting staff at Oxford also improved it in innumerable ways. The flaws that remain are my own.

This book has also benefitted from the support of many institutions over the years. While in graduate school, I benefitted from multiple fellowships from UCLA, and an Autry Museum of Western Heritage Summer Research Fellowship. Two fellowships from the Huntington Library, a Western History Association–Martin Ridge Fellowship, and an Andrew W. Mellon Foundation Fellowship, provided crucial support for transforming a dissertation into a book. Utah State University offered the generous support of a New Faculty Research Grant, as well as a research leave in 2007. A John Topham and Susan Redd Butler Faculty Fellowship from the Charles Redd Center for Western Studies at Brigham Young University facilitated a research trip to Phoenix. I am especially grateful to the Historical Society of Southern California, which offered me support in the form of Haynes Research Grants in 2001, 2004, 2005, 2006, and 2007. Such repeated generosity was exceptional, and for that I am exceedingly grateful to the HSSC, and all the other institutions listed here.

Since I began teaching in the Department of History at Utah State University, I have benefited tremendously from colleagues who offered their insights and advice. I particularly wish to thank David Rich Lewis, Colleen O'Neill, James Sanders, and Chris Conte. To all the other members of the department, as well as all the students who had portions of this book tested out on them as class lectures, I express my thanks as well.

In the journey through my educational and professional careers, I made other friends, all of whom contributed to this book in their own way. As an undergraduate, I was fortunate to be taught by professors Jesse and Shirley Jackson. As a master's student, I began my graduate study of history with professors, Carol O'Connor and Clyde A. Milner II. Other friends from college, graduate school, and various public history institutions who also deserve special mention include Laurie Eubanks, Michael Lansing, Jennifer and Steven Schimmelpfennig, Frances Clymer, Juti Winchester, Fiona and Charles Halloran, Michael Easterly, Barbara Bernstein, Peter Alagona, and Thomas Andrews.

My acknowledgements thus far have been preoccupied with traveling—with where I was going. There remains the place I came from. My family has always supported me, even when I was engaged in something as idiosyncratic as getting a PhD in history. To my mother, Rosemary Tenney, my father, Larry Culver, my sister, Marcella Culver, and my stepfather, Keith Tenney, I say, truly, thank you. My relationship with my family obviously long predates my interest in history as an academic course of study or professional career. Yet history lies at the heart of those familial relationships as well. My family has a longstanding interest in history, and also a long history with education, with multiple teachers and professors in the family tree. I will be able to share this book with some members of my family. For others, now gone, I can only wish that I could do the same. I dedicate this book to them all.

THE FRONTIER OF LEISURE

INTRODUCTION

The View from
Fantasyland to Main Street, U.S.A.

I N JULY of 1955, Walter Elias Disney unveiled his new amusement park in Anaheim, California. Opening day proved less than perfect; crowds jammed the park, rides malfunctioned, and women in high heels found their shoes sinking into the still-soft asphalt of Main Street, U.S.A. Even so, with rides and costumed characters drawn from its creator's successful animated films, and a national-television broadcast hosted in part by the Hollywood actor Ronald Reagan—broadcasting live from Frontierland—Disneyland soon proved an immense success. In the decades since its debut, the park has drawn praise and scorn. Disneyland has been portrayed as everything from a model of urban planning to a sinister mechanism for social control. Despite such divergent views, observers have generally agreed on one essential characteristic of Disneyland—that it was a place without precedent. Though borrowing from Hollywood, older amusement parks, and world fairs, Disneyland, they assert, was something fundamentally new under the Southern California sun.[1]

This book will demonstrate that Disneyland was not a point of origination, but rather one of culmination, the product of a longer regional and national history. When Walt Disney unveiled his new park, he invited tourists to enjoy its varied self-contained realms of leisure. There was Frontierland, with its iconic western landscapes; the exotic cultures and tropical atmosphere of Adventureland; the fairy-tale realm of Fantasyland; the small-town nostalgia of Main Street, U.S.A.; and alluring Tomorrowland, where visitors could ride the Carousel of Progress into a future of contentment and abundance. What was striking about these different realms of leisure was that at different times Southern California had been promoted as each of these places. It was presented as a pastoral agricultural frontier, an exotic destination for adventuresome tourists, the embodiment of traditional American values, a Hollywood fantasy where every dream came true, and a model of the American future, filled with immense promise. These successive promotions, beginning in the decade following the Civil War, and a quarter century after the U.S. annexation of more than half of Mexico, would transform Southern California. Yet they would also shape the future of the United States. In the process, this region would remake American attitudes toward leisure and nature, and alter the course of urban growth and architecture across the United States.

The geography of the park itself serves as an architectural manifestation of much larger cultural processes. At the heart of the park stood its central landmark, Cinderella's Castle, the portal to Fantasyland. If tourists standing before this gateway looked back toward the park entrance, they saw Main Street, U.S.A., with its recreated small-town storefronts and middle-American ambiance. This book is an attempt to explain how something seemingly fantastic and exotic became mundane and ordinary—how the tourist leisure and recreational culture of Southern California spread across America, and developed into a new suburban, middle class culture.[2]

To understand how Southern California, its leisure, and its promotion could prove so influential, one must travel generations earlier to the 1870s, when Southern California emerged as a contact point between diverse cultures and divergent nations. Like the rest of the Southwest, this was the uneasy meeting point of the Anglo-American West and the Mexican North, which had been claimed in the name of American Manifest Destiny. Local speculators, still giddy from the territorial gains of the U.S.-Mexican War, even clamored for the annexation of Baja California, as if all Mexico could be divided at Anglo-American will.[3]

This was also the place of transition from an older U.S. West to a newer one. In Southern California, the westward migration of Euro-Americans was transformed from what had been a frontier of labor to what would become a frontier of leisure. Americans had previously conceived of the West as a place where land, minerals, forests, and animals were transformed into wealth through work. This was the view of the "Great West," from the stockyards of Chicago to the grain silos of Omaha. Even the dreams of gold-rush wealth had been predicated on both labor and luck. Although Los Angeles, the main city of the "Great Southwest," would eventually become an industrial metropolis, it was perceived as a very different place, and leisure was what set it apart.

For white Americans in the nineteenth century, "the frontier" meant the West—and opportunity. This meaning is still invoked when twenty-first century Americans speak of the "frontiers" of space or technological advancement. Yet historical frontiers were also places of conflict, exploitation, and dispossession, where the ambitions and desires of Anglo-Americans collided with those of Mexicans, Asians, African Americans, and Native Americans.

In recent decades, historians have capably debunked the mythology of the rugged individualist pioneer as the sole settler of the West. Capitalism, technology, and federal power were no less responsible for its development. American individualism was in fact often trumped by American communalism, as western settlers banded together to found towns and territories, create schools, colleges, and churches, and write constitutions and elect legislatures.

Historian Frederick Jackson Turner encapsulated and enshrined the mythical frontier in 1893, when he declared it closed. Yet the mythology of the frontier survived. Many of the individuals discussed in this book were fervent believers in this myth—that their new frontier in the Southwest could regenerate them or even regenerate the nation. This book uses the term "frontier" in its full and complex meaning. The frontier of leisure it explores offered both opportunity and oppression, happiness and hardship. In the twentieth century, a people once obsessed with collective endeavors proved increasingly isolated and atomized, demanding gated communities and privatized security forces. Nowhere was this drive greater than in Southern California, which had a long and troubled history of white efforts to restrict and control public space, particularly recreational space. In Southern California, recreation and leisure became synonymous with privacy and with whiteness. Leisure was a restricted privilege, and labor was performed by others. Such unequal relations of class, race, and power would shape the culture, communities, and society of Southern California, and have implications far beyond the region itself.

By the late nineteenth century, other locales, such as the resort hotels of Colorado Springs and the tourist spectacles of Yellowstone and Yosemite, also offered an escape from work. Other cities would also subsequently utilize tourism as a means to spur development. Santa Fe and Las Vegas were two very different cities that prospered through tourism, and both were linked to the ascent of Southern California. Many cities in the region, such as San Diego, Santa Barbara, and Riverside, also attracted tourists, though they would not grow as large as Los Angeles. South Florida and New Orleans would both begin courting tourists in the early twentieth century, and other cities and regions would follow. The crucial difference was that in the nineteenth century—and well into the twentieth—those places still offered leisure as a temporary condition, as a vacation or respite from everyday living. Southern California would instead offer leisure as a permanent way of life.

Urban and regional promotion were popular activities in the American West and other regions of the U.S. in this era. These promotional efforts took many forms, and had diverse aims. Some were initiated by corporations, such as railroads hoping to sell land. Other promotional efforts were led by local governments or chambers of commerce. Some boosters were independent, selling one region or another to make money, and sometimes because they had also become fervent believers in the city or region they championed. In the post-Reconstruction South, the "New South" rhetoric of white southern boosters was intended to draw northern investors, restore the South's place in national politics, and gloss over its racial problems. In the interior West, such as the Great Plains, promotion was aimed primarily at farmers and prospective farmers, hoping to homestead on land of their own. Promotional materials varied as well, from pamphlets to travel guidebooks, and articles written by magazine or newspaper editors or by authors who distributed them to periodicals.

In the Southwest, promoters had to overcome longstanding Anglo-American biases against the region. It was mostly arid or semiarid, the settled population mostly Mexican, and nomadic Indians, especially the Apache, were still viewed as a threat. In the case of Southern California, a mild and less arid climate made the sale a bit easier, and Mexicans and Native Americans were recast in booster rhetoric as laborers. Hoping to attract new residents and investors, promoters perceived tourism as key to the region's success. Tourists spent money, but many of them would return as investors or new residents. Selling climate and leisure sold Southern California to tourists and future residents alike.[4]

The success of this campaign proved undeniable. Los Angeles County mushroomed from a population of thirty thousand in 1880 to more than two million in 1930, and would continue to grow throughout the twentieth century while still offering leisure alongside new economic activities, approaching ten million residents by 2000.[5] Faced with such imposing demographic growth, historians have struggled to explain the rise of Los Angeles. Since the 1990s, a remarkable flowering of historical writing about Los Angeles has appeared—cultural, environmental, labor, social, and urban histories that have greatly enlarged our understanding of the city. Even so, many national histories still treat the nation's second largest city and metropolitan region as an exotic outlier, somehow disconnected from "real" U.S. history. Popular histories of the City of Angels have generally espoused two opposing plots—one a romance, the other a tragedy, or, in local parlance, "sunshine" and "noir."

The sunshine view, popularized by historian Kevin Starr in his *Americans and the California Dream* series, asserts that Los Angeles was "dreamed" into existence, a metropolitan vision achieved by intellectuals, writers, and city leaders. The result, he claims, is a city that, despite smog, violence, natural disasters, and stucco sprawl, remains to some degree a citrus-scented land of sunshine. The "noir" view has been best encapsulated in Mike Davis's polemics, *City of Quartz* and *Ecology of Fear*. For Davis, Los Angeles represents the urban will to power, a super-city that appropriated water, built a port, and oppressed labor with ruthless and implacable force. Davis's metropolis was and is still led by a shadow elite that ignores ecological and social realities and concocts vast real estate schemes, manipulating the masses and transforming land and water into wealth and power.[6]

Both the sunshine and noir views, however, ascribe too much power to the city's leaders. Los Angeles did not grow solely because elites, sinister or not, manipulated the masses. The fact that so many individuals *wanted* to come to Los Angeles ultimately says something more complex about the city, and the nation, than any analysis of elites. The promotion of Southern California was a strange and often contradictory process, mixing profiteering and idealism, resource development and romance. Only a conceptualization of regional history that acknowledges both positive and negative elements, and the breadth and diversity of both a regional and national public, can hope to encompass the complexity of Los Angeles.

More than with other American cities, where urban histories have focused on topics such as economic growth, infrastructural development, or social change, interpreters have attempted to find the "meaning" of Los Angeles.[7] One of the consistent points of contention has been the city's much-advertised exceptionalism. Carey McWilliams, author of the seminal *Southern California: An Island on the Land*, felt certain that L.A. was destined to become "the most fantastic city in the world."[8] More recent historians, worried that claims of exceptionalism only advance booster promotional agendas, have been more likely to focus on the things that made Los Angeles the ultimate dystopia—the most perfect model of urbanism gone wrong. The city's exceptionalism, ironically, remained intact.

Another common question concerns the broader applicability of L.A.'s experience. Is the sprawling urbanism of Los Angeles a model, or merely a mess? This serves as a central question for the "L.A. School" of urban studies, which has attempted to explicate the urbanism, appearance, and social relations of Los Angeles, and the degree to which its evolution was a portent for future urban development. Some scholars positioned L.A. as the first postmodern metropolis, while others saw it as the only third-world megalopolis to appear in the first world.[9]

A third hallmark of studies of Los Angeles has been the coupling of the city's growth with the ascent of modernity, and the technological, economic, and social revolutions that remade America after the Civil War. Historian Elaine Tyler May, for example, asserted that Los Angeles was "born modern." Yet she acknowledged the traditionalist views of many of the middle-class whites who relocated to the city, hoping that in Los Angeles they could blend "Victorian familial values with the fruits of modern progress." Those who assert L.A.'s modernity often link the city with the birth of modern consumer culture, or cite its role as the home of the Hollywood film industry. Historians such as William

Leach and Jackson Lears pinpointed the late nineteenth century—the era of Los Angeles's first boom—as the moment a new consumer culture was born. Yet, as Richard Bushman demonstrated in his *The Refinement of America: Persons, Houses, Cities*, American consumerism did not suddenly appear in the late nineteenth century but had long played a prominent role in American society and culture. This book asserts that Los Angeles contributed to the history of consumption in one key respect: the new mail catalogues and department stores of the 1880s and 1890s, such as Marshall Field's in Chicago or Wanamaker's in Philadelphia, touted the consumption of material goods. Los Angeles would instead promote the consumption of a particular way of life—or, to use a term that came into common usage in the twentieth century—a lifestyle.[10]

Unlike consumption, Hollywood was definitely something new. Film created a major industry in Los Angeles, but one unlike any existing industry. It had no "establishment" of old elites or monopolists—indeed, this very openness was what drew many Jewish entrepreneurs to it, since they faced discrimination in other industries. This new industry paid huge salaries to a select few, but employed a vast number of workers—editors, accountants, set and costume designers, camera and sound technicians, writers, and directors. Film thus provided Los Angeles with a new elite, as well as a large professional and artisan class.

Film also gave the city, the region, and the resorts there a degree of national and global visibility that was unsurpassed. Urban boosterism was common in American cities in this era, but only Los Angeles possessed Hollywood. By the 1920s, 100 million Americans attended films at least once a week, and the films and newsreels they watched showcased the bungalow neighborhoods, the beaches and mountains, and the seemingly carefree resorts of Southern California.[11]

Hollywood spurred an influx of new residents—individuals less likely to conform to societal norms than Midwestern retirees, and more self-consciously "modern" in their behavior. They would shape local leisure culture as well, patronizing resorts that in time proved more tolerant of everything from racy swim attire to interracial mingling to gay and lesbian vacationers. Yet these bohemians were not entirely disconnected from their time and place. Many of the underlying issues in Hollywood history, such as its roots in vaudeville, issues of immigration and assimilation, ethnic and class divisions among film audiences, and the depiction of racist stereotypes in film, were intimately connected with larger—and often problematic—issues in U.S. history.[12]

This project does not take Los Angeles and Southern California as its focus in order to study "America in flight from herself," as British Unitarian minister and author L. P. Jacks described the region.[13] Instead, it sees the promotion of leisure in Southern California as a national phenomenon, as the region was first shaped by changes in national culture and society, and then, in turn, played a crucial role in reshaping the nation. Los Angeles and Southern California were indeed exceptional at times, but did not exist apart from a larger national and, indeed, international history. As such, they provide a model of development and urbanism that can be applied elsewhere. Similarly, Southern California's urban and tourist development was linked to the ascent of modernity, and Los Angeles was profoundly marked by modernism of many forms, but this modernity did not obliterate the region's connection to an older local history.

That history, whether real or imagined, was endlessly promoted to tourists and residents, influencing urban and regional development in profound ways. Anglo-American L.A. may have been "born modern," but the fact remains that the city was "born" in 1781, when it was settled by predominantly Native American and mixed-race citizens of New Spain on the site of a preexisting native Tongva community called Yangna. It became a regional center after Mexican independence in 1821, growing with the Californio cattle-ranching economy. After annexation in 1848, it remained a border city, profoundly affected by the U.S.-Mexico War and the Anglo-American political and economic annexation of California. Despite a large influx of white middle-class Americans in the late nineteenth and early twentieth centuries, the city and the diverse population of the region retained ties to this Native American, Spanish colonial, and Mexican past.[14]

Tourism and recreational perceptions of nature were hardly new either. As Eric Hobsbawm demonstrated in *The Age of Capital, 1848–1875*, the commercialized travel of a leisure class dates to the dual economic and political revolutions that transformed Europe, particularly Britain and France. The Industrial Revolution eventually allowed a broader swath of society to travel as well. It was no accident that the main thoroughfare in the French Mediterranean resort of Cannes was named the "Promenade des Anglais," for it had been the British who "opened this new frontier of moneyed leisure." Geographer Denis Cosgrove asserted that it was in Italy and Britain that landscapes were first divided into spaces of production and consumption—land that was used for agriculture or industry and land that served as scenic vistas for the wealthy. The landscapes of estates, once the site of villages and grazing livestock, were remade as arcadian panoramas testifying to the gentility of the landowners. The English ha-ha, a concealed ditch dug to keep wandering livestock—and local peasantry—from entering the arcadian precincts of great estates was blunt testimony to the division of land into places of production or consumption, labor or leisure, and the social costs of that division.[15]

If the history of Los Angeles has been dominated by a conflict between sunshine and noir, the history of tourism has seen no such divide. Scholarly studies of tourism have often been relentlessly grim. The general rule seems to be that if anyone is having a good time, someone else is being exploited—perhaps even the individuals who think they are enjoying themselves. Though tourism contains many deeply problematic elements, this viewpoint is overly simplistic. Many studies of tourist leisure still begin with the ideas of economist and sociologist Thorstein Veblen from his *Theory of the Leisure Class*. Veblen's formulations of "conspicuous consumption" and "conspicuous leisure" offered a simple explanation for tourist behavior and recreation, grounded in a critique of capitalist society. Recreational travel and all its accoutrements were merely markers of class status deployed consciously or unconsciously by those affluent enough to enjoy it. One traveled in order to be seen traveling.[16]

This book attempts to conceptualize leisure as a broader phenomenon. It considers the leisure not solely of the affluent, but the leisure enjoyed by all economic classes, including the leisure of people of color. That does not mean it will ignore leisure's negative effects. Leisure, when coupled with whiteness and wealth, was used to separate and segregate, to control and regulate, both people and places. It was often a mark of class, race, and power, separating the leisured from the laboring. While ever mindful of the negative effects of tourism and leisure, this book does not assume that tourism and leisure are inherently damaging. In fact, it argues that at times leisure in Southern California offered economic, social, and cultural opportunities, however circumscribed, to the working class and peoples of color.[17]

This book moves beyond an analysis of tourism alone to a broader study of promotion, tourism, and residential recreation. It will examine what the promotion of leisure meant to tourists and residents, and how it shaped the experiences of tourists and the places they visited. In this way, it aims to avoid presenting tourist destinations and resorts as stage sets for tourist fantasies. It will also eschew the tendency to perceive all tourists as undifferentiated agents of destruction, while remaining mindful of the ambivalent consequences of tourism. Yet residential recreation is also key to this project. In Southern California, some tourists would return as residents, and recreational leisure would evolve alongside tourist leisure, with each influencing the other. This book will demonstrate that leisure, initially used to promote Southern California, would directly shape the region's development, and ultimately influence the nation as a whole.

Located at the intersection of cultural, urban, and environmental history, this book takes the promotion of leisure in Los Angeles and Southern California from the 1870s forward, across the twentieth century, as its subject. It attempts to answer three essential questions: Why did the promotion of Southern California as a realm of leisure prove so popular? What effect did this promotion have on the region's diverse population, and its cultural, urban, and social development? Finally, in what ways did the leisure of Southern California shape national culture and urbanism?

This book asserts that Los Angeles and Southern California played a central role in the democratization of American leisure. The region first domesticated leisure, making it nonthreatening to an established social order, and then offered an ever-wider array of leisure activities to an ever-broader swath of the American public. This conceptualization of leisure first manifested itself at regional resorts, but gradually came to influence national society and culture, architecture, and urban development. In Southern California, and across the nation, social orders shifted as types of highly visible consumption and modes of leisure came to delineate class status in a way older markers of class once had. The aspirational aspect of class consciousness was nothing new—purchasing the correct china or clothing was already a preoccupation for rich colonials before the Revolution. Now, however, leisure became a much more explicit class marker, and one that the middle class, and even the working class, could aspire to. Over time, this opened a new leisure society to groups that had been excluded, ranging from Jewish tourists in Palm Springs in the 1920s to gay and lesbian tourists at the same resort in the 1970s.[18]

This newly democratized leisure did not come without costs. Leisure sparked racial and class conflict in Los Angeles at beaches, swimming pools, and parks. Leisure in the private sphere, such as that found at Catalina Island, owned entirely by the Banning and Wrigley families, was deemed safe and controlled. Leisure in the public sphere, particularly in the city of Los Angeles, was not. This perception led to exclusion and conflict, but also demonstrates how leisure and recreation created a new public sphere and new kinds of public space. While many are familiar with Manhattan's Central Park and its place in the history of nineteenth-century American urban recreation, this book illustrates how the beaches of Los Angeles and Southern California resorts were no less significant in shaping urban recreation—and struggles for civil rights—in twentieth-century America.[19]

Beyond issues of public and private leisure, a fundamental fact remains: Southern California was created as a place of white leisure dependent upon the labor of people of color. This would have profound and sometimes dire consequences for the region. Mexican Americans and Native Americans, in particular, were expected to play roles in a fictionalized and romanticized version of regional history. That was problematic enough, but for groups not included in this narrative, such as African Americans, exclusion could prove even worse. Yet, despite these problems, people of color sometimes found opportunities in this new realm of leisure and fought for the right to enjoy its benefits as well.[20]

Leisure in Southern California played a profound role in national perceptions of the region and national thinking about nature. Here, at the terminus of Anglo-America's western expansion, goaded on by the rhetoric of Manifest Destiny, white Americans believed that they could find rejuvenation by reconnecting with nature, community, and tradition. If the independent "island community" of the preindustrial era had been lost, perhaps it could be founded anew. If not, at least individuals and families could attain a degree of autonomy removed from an industrializing, urbanizing nation. The "shelter"—both literal and metaphorical—offered by bungalows, citrus plantations, Spanish Revival houses, and indeed all of Southern California— attested to a desire for autonomy, a fact that made an illusory vision of the Mexican rancho life of the earlier nineteenth century so compelling for many Anglo Americans. They would recast the Californio rancho families, the Pueblo Indian communities of New Mexico and Arizona, and other cultural groups as peoples with deep connections to the land and to each other, members of harmonious communities so unlike the large, anonymous, and chaotic industrial cities of the East.[21]

Yet the way to attain this autonomy and reconnect to nature and tradition was through leisure and consumption. Thus the nationalist racial redemption of the nineteenth century was traded for the consumerist ethos of the twentieth. The same transformation was visible in the role Southern California played in changing perceptions of nature. Certainly, nature in Southern California was transformed by development. An open landscape of grasses and California oaks—which had already been altered by heavy cattle grazing and the introduction of nonnative species—was successively replaced by agricultural fields and orchards, towns, and mass urbanism. In his study of the growth of Chicago, William Cronon utilized concepts from Karl Marx and Georg Wilhelm Friedrich Hegel to describe this process of development in which a "first" nature was subsumed by a "second," manmade nature. Yet in Southern California this material second nature was accompanied by a second nature of the mind. An idealized vision of an earlier pastoral nature, and the purportedly idyllic society that inhabited it, profoundly shaped how individuals in the region interacted with nature on both material and cultural levels. Ultimately, this region mediated a new relationship between Americans and nature, one based on recreation. At the same time, however, the recreational or historicist view of nature propagated by Anglos sometimes conflicted with Mexicans, Native Americans, Asian Americans, and others who had to make a living in nature, not just play in it.[22]

Nature had previously been utilized to buttress American nationalism, Christianity, or Transcendentalist thought. Now it entered the realm of popular and consumer culture, gaining new meaning as a source of health and a place of recreation. This book aims to reorient the common historical perception of the evolution of American environmental thought. Instead of focusing on environmental writers and thinkers, such as Thoreau, Muir, or

Leopold, it considers how ordinary people related to nature, and how their perceptions were manifested in how they remade their houses and yards, and made choices about how they lived and played. Indeed, recreation is central to any understanding of how modern Americans have interacted with nature, and the evolution of conservation and preservation. At the same time, however, the growing interest in nature, and in architectural and urban forms that allowed Americans to live close to nature, did not necessarily denote true ecological awareness, and it almost never led to environmentally sustainable development. Instead, it led to dependence upon automobiles and petroleum. It necessitated the hydraulic reengineering of western North America to carry water to large populations settled in arid regions. It also placed millions of Americans in places of dire ecological hazards, from earthquakes to wildfires.[23]

Inextricably connected to changing views of nature were evolving ideas about urbanism, and Southern California's conceptualizations of urbanism would decisively shape the future of the nation as a whole, as changing views of nature transformed the American landscape. The city of Los Angeles, which flourished as the core of a resort region in the late nineteenth century, evolved into one of the world's largest cities. It transcended its regional origins to become a modern metropolis in every sense, eschewing the quaint historicism of Santa Barbara or Santa Fe. Yet in fundamental ways it was permanently marked by an anti-urban vision that embraced the ideal of the single-family home, dependence on the automobile, and scant concern for parks or public space. Conceptualized as the perfect merging of city and country, the megalopolis marked the arrival of the twenty-first century while still grappling with planning choices made many decades before. Los Angeles has often been perceived as the city of the future, but it was no less a city of the past, shaped by its inescapable prior history.[24]

Yet Los Angeles and other communities and resorts in Southern California would play a profound role in the evolution of the urban and suburban United States. During the Progressive Era in the United States, and indeed in many cities around the world since the Industrial Revolution, nature has been perceived as the antidote to the excesses of urbanism and industry. By creating parks, playgrounds, and open space, nature could be brought into the city. Southern California, and the suburbs that emulated it, followed a very different model. Instead of bringing nature into the city, they brought the city out into nature, dispersing housing and allotting private yards rather than public parks. Suburbs had long been places of retreat for the wealthy few, but this new mass suburbia was a radical departure from traditional patterns of urbanism. American suburbia, especially in the post–World War II Sunbelt, was heavily influenced by ideas emanating from Southern California. Suburban developments that mimicked agricultural or wilderness areas, residential golf clubs, houses with backyard swimming pools, patios, and barbecues—all of these were popularized in Southern California. Sprawl brought nature to the masses, even as it destroyed nature in the process. Thus, this book also argues for a reorientation of the traditional historical understanding of the rise of suburbia. In so doing it does not ignore the role of British garden communities or early eastern U.S. suburbs. It does assert that Los Angeles and resorts such as Palm Springs were as important to the formation of modern American suburbia as the nineteenth-century precedents of the pattern homes of Andrew Jackson Downing or early suburbs of New York such as Westchester County. Levittown was constructed on Long Island, but what it and similar large suburban housing developments offered buyers by the 1950s, when the cramped Cape Cod homes first built in the 1940s had been replaced by larger California Ranch houses, was in many ways a transplanted vision of the Southern Californian suburban residential ideal. To understand how and why the United States became the world's first suburban nation, one must start by looking at Southern California.[25]

The history of suburbia is inextricably connected to issues of labor and leisure. Twenty-first century Americans, the majority of whom live in suburbs, have no sense of how radical a break with the past their neighborhoods represent. For almost all of settled human history, homes were sites of labor and production. Farmhouses were certainly places of labor, as were the homes of artisans. In cities, many merchants lived adjacent to or above the shops in which they worked. The move to suburbs represented a fundamental rupture in this relationship of residence and production, at least for men. (Wives and mothers certainly continued to labor, regardless of their husbands.) Increasingly, the home was reserved for leisure and family. This encouraged a sense of autonomy, of independence from a larger urban region or society, that, however illusory, proved immensely appealing. Labor occurred elsewhere—or was performed by others.

Think of how so many Americans experienced work by the second half of the twentieth century: fathers driving into the city to work in the 1950s, or working couples driving separately to different "edge cities" for work in the 1990s; African American maids arriving in suburban neighborhoods for work in the 1950s, or immigrant maids, nannies, and gardeners arriving for a day's work in suburbs across the nation in 2000. Laboring and leisured, suburban and urban, white and nonwhite, citizen and noncitizen—these divided identities are inextricably connected. To understand the complexities of these relationships, we must more fully understand the history of leisure and its place in the history of Southern California and the Southwest.[26]

To address these issues, this book examines leisure as a cultural product, as a resort phenomenon, and as a facet of urban and suburban life. It will not, however, examine leisure in every locality within Southern California.

Partisans of Santa Barbara and San Diego, for example, can rightfully claim that those cities, and others, get scant coverage in the pages to follow. Nor will it offer a complete history of suburbia or the Sunbelt. Instead of geographic comprehensiveness, it aims for a chronological perspective, focusing on key moments, places, and people—tracing how, over time, tourist leisure and residential recreation, promotional agendas and individual desires, evolved together to create a regionally distinct and nationally significant culture of leisure.

Chapter 1 explores the promotion of Southern California that began in the 1870s, epitomized by the career of Charles Fletcher Lummis. An author and editor, Lummis did more than simply promote Southern California as a tourist attraction. He promoted it as a way of life. What began as simply a regional manifestation of late Victorian leisure was supplanted by new forms of leisure that influenced the nation after first emerging in Southern California.

Chapter 2 examines leisure in Los Angeles, a city that was transformed from tourist boomtown to global metropolis. In the process, it incorporated a conceptualization of leisure that held highly ambivalent consequences for the city's subsequent development. It placed recreation at the heart of its civic identity, yet rarely planned for parks and recreational space, and repeatedly attempted to limit which groups could enjoy recreation in a region promoted as the frontier of leisure. At the same time, Los Angeles would become a model, however problematic, of subsequent urban development in the United States. Its promise of an idealized suburban metropolis, merging city and country, residence and recreation, in a fundamentally new kind of urban form, would have potent appeal in the city and across the nation.

The successful promotion that aided the growth of Los Angeles also led to resort development. The book then takes Santa Catalina Island and Palm Springs as its two central case studies. While Southern California contains many resort areas, these two provide an encapsulation of the history of resort development in the region, from the early emergence of regional resorts that drew upon local promotional methods, to the evolution of national resorts that served as recreational and residential models far beyond Southern California. Catalina and Palm Springs differed in many ways, yet both achieved regional and national influence as distinctly Southern Californian manifestations of leisure.

Chapters 3 and 4 concern Catalina, the first self-contained corporate resort in the United States, which pioneered a business model of resort and tourist development, converted regional booster rhetoric into material form, and offered a less formal and structured resort atmosphere than many eastern resorts. The island also engendered a new, nationally significant understanding of marine environmental resources centered on recreation and conservation. This resulted in the creation of one of the first sport fishing and marine conservation organizations in the United States, permanently linking modern leisure and environmentalism.

Chapters 5 and 6 take Palm Springs as their subject. Palm Springs popularized new resort attire, sunbathing, and sport. It created a new appreciation of American deserts, though this concern was grounded in consumerism and aesthetic sensibilities rather than true environmental understanding. Most importantly, Palm Springs pioneered new architectural and urban forms replicated not only at other resorts but in cities across the United States, making the nation more Southern Californian in the process. At both resorts, Anglo-American leisure depended upon—and often conflicted with—the labor of people of color. Both witnessed conflicts over the use of and access to natural resources, often pitting recreational use against older resource-extraction or subsistence uses.

As Los Angeles and Southern California increasingly became a model for urban development, the region's attributes and failings would be replicated in American cities and suburbs after World War II. The book's final chapter examines this process. Using Phoenix as a primary example, it demonstrates how the cultural, demographic, and political emergence of the Sunbelt facilitated the Californiazation of America. Many cities across this vaguely defined southern tier of U.S. states, though they varied widely in their prior history and environments, began to utilize the promotional tools, tourist and recreational development, and pro-business politics and policies that had marked the rise of Los Angeles and Southern California. Earlier than other Sunbelt cities, Phoenix combined the growth model of Los Angeles with federal initiatives, particularly housing programs, which spurred its growth to become the largest city in the interior Southwest.

Central to this process and the emergence of a distinct suburban culture in the Sunbelt was the popularization of Ranch House domestic architecture, as well as a new conservative political movement that drew on the rhetoric and ideas of generations of Southwest and Southern California boosters. In this sense, that political movement's first candidate for president, Arizona senator Barry Goldwater, the 1964 Republican nominee, was the product of a long regional history. The central role of that history in the larger history of national politics has been little understood. The ranch house, enthusiastically adopted by homebuyers and developers alike, was likewise a product of the histories of architecture, regional promotion, and resort leisure culture in Southern California, and became the most popular form of residential architecture in the nation by the 1950s. Not just an architectural form, but a cultural and ideological one as well, the ranch house symbolized the national spread and scope of Southern California's leisure culture. *The Frontier of Leisure* traces these intertwined histories, and in the process illuminates the inextricable connections between Southern California, American leisure, and the nation as a whole.

Chapter One

INVENTING THE FRONTIER
OF LEISURE

Charles Fletcher Lummis and the Creation
of the "Great Southwest"

CAJON PASS separates the San Bernardino and San Gabriel Mountains, which, along with the Tehachapi and San Jacinto Mountains, curve across the southernmost portion of California. The pass, and the mountain ranges it traverses, were all created by the ceaseless movement of the San Andreas Fault, the most fearsome of all the earthquake faults that undergird the region's landscape. To the east lie the Mojave and Colorado deserts. To the west and south lie a series of smaller ranges and valleys, and beyond them the coastal plain. This undulating landscape, protected from desert heat by the mountains and bathed in moist air from the Pacific, entered the nineteenth century as a sparsely populated region of Alta California, a far-flung province of New Spain. It would leave the century as Southern California, the most heavily advertised portion of the United States.

Two of the agents most responsible for the promotion of the region both entered Southern California through Cajon Pass, and did so in the same year. In 1885 the Atcheson, Topeka, and Santa Fe Railway completed a line through the pass, connecting Los Angeles to the East, and breaking the twelve-year monopoly of the Southern Pacific Railroad. The resulting fare war would produce the region's first boom. Earlier that year, Charles Fletcher Lummis had also traversed Cajon Pass. Leaving Ohio in 1884, Lummis had walked across the country, hoping to leave physical, financial, and marital problems behind. His destination was Los Angeles, where a job awaited him at the *Los Angeles Times*. As his trek neared its conclusion, Lummis walked down from the pass and through the foothills and looked out at the landscape beyond.

It proved an Edenic vision: "It was the last day of January. The ground was carpeted with myriad wildflowers, birds filled the air with song, and clouds of butterflies fluttered past me."[1]

For the rest of his career, Lummis would promote himself, the region he came to call the "Great Southwest," and the city he proclaimed to be its capital, Los Angeles. Countless others also promoted Southern California and the Southwest, and Lummis typified this entire booster class. Lummis, however, would have been appalled to be selected as the booster exemplar.

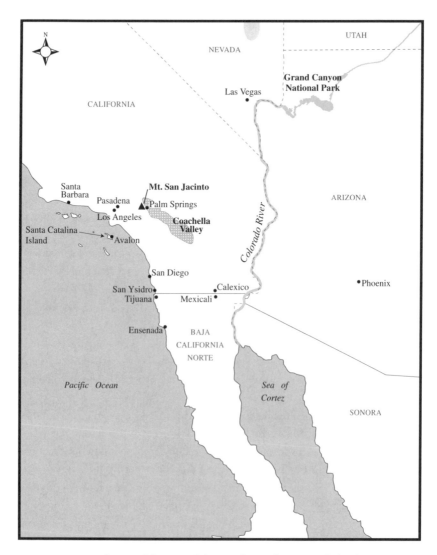

FIGURE 1.1 Southern California and the Pacific Southwest Borderlands. Map courtesy of Alexis McCrossen and the Clements Center for Southwest Studies, Southern Methodist University.

He always asserted that his interests in history, archaeology, and folk culture were the motivation for his writing, and that his "boosting" was the product of his deep identification with the region, and his hope that it could provide a model that would change the United States. Nevertheless, Lummis's career offers a particularly illuminating example of boosterism. His extensive correspondence with readers and the records of his magazine, *Land of Sunshine*, offer an opportunity to examine the reception of his agenda and the nature of his audience.

Lummis would promote a romantic vision of the landscapes, history, and cultures of the Southwest and Southern California. For him, the "Great Southwest" would be a place where Anglo-Americans could escape what he perceived as the maladies of modern life and adopt a life that was simpler and more connected to nature and tradition. Unlike earlier boosters, Lummis did not present this region as merely an interesting vacation destination or a promising locale for agriculture or land speculation. His "Great Southwest" offered leisure as a way of life. It democratized leisure, converting it from a privilege or even a vice of the rich into a middle-class right. Others, from philosopher John Ruskin to Henry David Thoreau, also advocated a return to nature, or the pursuit of the "simple life." In Southern California, however, this antimodernist vision would be used to promote the most successful tourist attraction in American history—Los Angeles. Lummis's southwestern pastoral was utilized to build a southwestern metropolis, creating irreconcilable tensions that damaged Lummis's career and his relationship with the city he promoted for decades. Proclaiming Southern California and the Southwest as a realm of Anglo-American leisure would also have ambivalent consequences for the diverse population already inhabiting the region. Lummis's Southwestern gospel of leisure would nevertheless leave a profound impression. He would irrevocably link Los Angeles and Southern California with the changing nature of American leisure.

The Early Promotion of Southern California

Before Lummis, and before the Santa Fe Railroad, national awareness of Southern California grew gradually. The first account for many eastern readers was Richard Henry Dana's description of coastal California in *Two Years Before the Mast*, published in 1840. His book, a memoir of life as a sailor in the 1830s on one of the many Yankee merchant vessels that traded Californio cattle hides and tallow for U.S. finished goods, offered readers a vision of a picturesque, exotic region. Like many other Anglos, his depiction of elite Californio life in Santa Barbara and other towns was essentially an endless

fiesta of dances, games, and leisure. The brutal racialized labor system of
the rancho economy, adopted from the mission labor system it replaced, was
anything but carefree, and bore more than a passing resemblance to the slave
labor system of the American South. Dana did note the plight of Indians in
Mexican California, perhaps foreshadowing the abolitionist views he would
later espouse. Most of his critique of Mexican Californians, however, concerned their purportedly lax morals and vices such as gambling, hardly surprising charges for a Protestant New Englander to level against Catholic,
mixed-race Californios.

It was the landscape of California that drew most of Dana's praise, as
well as readers' attention. With Texas already detached from Mexico as the
Lone Star Republic, and the U.S.-Mexico War soon to begin, many readers, like Dana himself, viewed California not merely as a remote and exotic
region, but as potential future U.S. real estate. He cataloged the forests and
fisheries, cattle and crops of California, and boasted of its climate that "there
can be no better in the world." In the most famous line in his book, Dana
praised California's landscape while simultaneously denigrating its residents:
"In the hands of an enterprising people, what a country this might be!" Yet
he worried that California would prove too comfortable to maintain Yankee
industry. According to Dana, the children of Anglo settlers "are brought up
Spaniards, in every respect, and if the 'California fever' (laziness) spares the
first generation, it always attacks the second." Dana fretted that the seemingly leisurely life of the Californios would infect Anglos—that in California
leisure was a dangerous contagion. Such impressions, however ungrounded
in fact, proved lasting.[2]

The Gold Rush brought a vast wave of migrants and immigrants to San
Francisco, Sacramento, and the Sierra Nevada goldfields. Statehood arrived
in 1850, and California was inundated by Anglos who brought dispossess-
sion to Californio landowners and disaster to countless Indians. In Southern
California, bypassed by the Gold Rush, Mexican California lingered. There
the rancho economy held on until a severe drought in the 1860s, mercenary
Anglo land speculators, and increasing property taxes gradually led to the
loss of most Californio holdings.

The interior Southwest attracted even less Anglo interest. After the
elation of conquest, Americans discovered that much of the new territory
they had conquered seemed a vast and desolate disappointment. Patches of
arable land lured agricultural settlers to places such as the Salt River Valley, where a small settlement emerged in the 1860s near the future site of
Phoenix, and later on copper drew mining interests to Apache-dominated
southern Arizona and New Mexico. Yet much of the rest of the region seemed
unfit for development. John Russell Bartlett, the first American head of the
postwar U.S.-Mexico Boundary Commission, was sacked after committing

two unpardonable crimes: compromising with his Mexican counterpart on the location of the boundary, and publicly stating that much of this new American territory appeared worthless. His replacement, William Emory, while more attuned to the territorial aspirations of the Southern slaveholding interests who had pushed for war, was nonetheless likewise hard-pressed to paint an overly positive picture of the region. His best hope was that technological development—railroads—and military suppression of the Apache would render the region more amenable to development, preferably through slave agriculture.[3]

If Anglos found the landscape of the Southwest daunting, they also proved quick to demean its inhabitants. In 1852, Secretary of War Charles Conrad suggested paying the entire Hispano population of New Mexico enough money to relocate to some more profitable region, free of Apache raiders. That Hispanos seemed less than entirely grateful for having been forcibly added to the American empire was bad enough. Their Catholicism and mixed racial heritage only worsened perceptions of them among Anglo Protestants. Moreover, their favored building method—adobe—warranted particular rebuke. In 1880, General William Tecumseh Sherman proclaimed that "I hope ten years hence there won't be an adobe house in the territory. I want to see you learn to make them of brick, with slanting roofs. Yankees don't like flat roofs, nor roofs of dirt." Sherman could hardly have imagined that a decade later regional promoters, Charles Lummis chief among them, would begin repackaging this same architecture not as primitive, but rather as picturesque, and that mission revival, Spanish revival, and what came to be called "Santa Fe style" would permanently mark the region, and even the nation.[4]

Until after the completion of the transcontinental railroad in 1869, most guidebooks and travel accounts aimed at the nascent western tourist market informed prospective travelers of three primary areas, each transformed by mining rushes: cosmopolitan San Francisco, the Colorado Rockies, acclaimed as "America's Switzerland," and the California Sierras, especially Yosemite Valley. These areas, in addition to being those most likely to be appreciated by Eastern urbanites and tourists steeped in the Romantic affinity for sublime mountain vistas, were also the places most accessible by train or boat. The Southwest, in contrast, warranted little attention. When Southern California appeared at all in such texts, it was as a remote and exotic realm, with a balmy "tropical" climate. One 1869 account referred to "Los Angelos," "far away in the South of California, where the tropical fruits grow so luxuriantly." George Crofutt's 1878 guidebook expounded upon the region south of the "Mojava" Desert, where Los Angeles, the "city of gardens and groves," lay surrounded by "magnificent plantations" containing "the wealth of the tropics."[5]

More substantial guides to Southern California offered more detail, but also touted the region's aura of tropical verdure. The first such book to discuss Southern California extensively was journalist Charles Nordhoff's *California: For Health, Pleasure, and Residence*, published in 1872. Nordhoff, a Prussian immigrant who spent his later childhood in Ohio, proved a devout believer in American democracy and capitalism, yet was troubled by the urbanization and monopolistic business practices of the Gilded Age. Most of all, this immigrant was appalled by what he saw as the inundation of East-ern cities by a "semi-barbarous foreign population" of southern and eastern European immigrants. Like some other regional boosters to come, Nordhoff seemed as intent on denigrating the East as in promoting the West.[6]

Nordhoff's book posited Southern California as a place where middling white farmers could live in a citrus-scented agricultural utopia—a veritable Jeffersonian Polynesia. It was the region's seemingly magical climate that made this new Eden possible. Here, in "the first tropical land our race has thoroughly mastered," white America could enjoy "the delights of the trop-ics, without their penalties." Enervated by the rush of modern life and threat-ened by "mongrel" immigrants, Americans could here be cured of illness and regain their vitality, without falling prey to the diseases of more humid tropi-cal climes. In an era when disease was common, and tuberculosis a constant danger, a climate that encouraged health would prove irresistible.[7]

In addition to its climate, moreover, Nordhoff asserted that Southern California possessed other resources of significant value. His writings made clear that this new land would prosper not from the labor of diligent white farmers, but instead through workers drawn from a preexisting resident non-white population. He asserted that the Chinese made excellent servants despite their vices, which included opium, gambling, and doing business on Sundays. As for Californio rancho families, Nordhoff pronounced them picturesque, and the "moderate" pace of their lives admirable. He proved especially impressed by the cordial—but never overly familiar—relationship between rancho dons and their dependent servants. Nevertheless, Nordhoff devoted the most time to discussing another group—Native Americans. The book even contained a chapter unambiguously entitled "The Indians as Laborers." In Southern California, Nordhoff asserted, "it was thought a great advantage for a man to 'have' Indians"—claiming that that they were docile, knew how to handle horses, and would work for little money. For Nordhoff, these Indi-ans, already subdued by the Mission padres, were "a useful people," totally unlike the "brutal Apache." In this view, Nordhoff echoed other writers who likewise perceived the Indians of Southern California differently than other Indians, not primarily as a threat, or a hindrance to development, but instead integral to it. An 1852 report by Benjamin Wilson, appointed the federal Indian Agent for Southern California, asserted that the region's Indians were "domesticated," despite their vices of drinking and gambling. Yet even this Indian agent, steeped in nineteenth-century Anglo racism and stereotypes, readily admitted how indispensible Indians were to Southern California: "let us remember, these same Indians built all the houses in the country, and planted all the fields and vineyards. There is hardly any sort of ordinary work for which they do not show a good-will."[8]

Here was a fundamental difference from other, earlier American "Wests." Elsewhere, Anglo-Americans had most often pushed Indians away, confined them to reservations, or—especially in much of the rest of California—simply exterminated them. In Southern California, however, they would provide essential labor, along with Mexicans and Asian immigrants. This was especially true at citrus farms—more like plantations—which Nordhoff predicted would bring wealth to wise investors. Nordhoff, who espoused hope for Southern California as a refuge for yeoman farmers, was instead using the region's climate and existing population to imagine a future that shared more with the Deep South, or subsequent American possessions such as Hawaii and Puerto Rico, than it did with the pioneer homesteads of the archetypal Anglo-American West.[9]

In its review of the book, the *Nation* pronounced Nordhoff "an excellent *raconteur*," with the tone "of a man who half expects his audience to put their tongues in their cheeks at what he is telling them." The magazine scoffed at his book's attempt to herald an agricultural utopia in an age of industry: "If he had any purpose more than another in writing it, we should say it was to recommend the climate to invalids, and not to preach the superiority of agriculture to mining as a means of comfortable living and even of affluence." The elite eastern press might dismiss the attributes of distant Southern California, but others would not. The book would sell three million copies by the end of the century. Anglo investors in Southern California were so impressed by the impact of Nordhoff's book that they employed him again in 1888 to pen a new book, *Peninsular California*, touting the potential of their land holdings in Baja California. His payment was the vast Rancho Ramajal, fifty thousand acres of coastal land south of Ensenada. Nordhoff and his sons operated the rancho for decades thereafter.[10]

Many more books by other authors would follow. The sheer output of Southern California booster literature, however, is in some ways less impressive than its striking consistency. The same attributes, the same advantages, would be heralded again and again, with little substantive difference between authors. Some alterations did inevitably occur. Later writers and promoters eschewed the term "tropical," for it proved less likely to instill visions of paradise in the minds of eastern readers than specters of pythons and malaria. Instead, they claimed that the climate was that of an idealized Mediterranean, as did Charles Dudley Warner in *Our Italy* (1891), and Peter Remondino in *The Mediterranean Shores of America* (1892). Remondino provided a wide amount of "scientific" climatic data to prove that Southern California possessed the healthiest climate on earth. Warner had coauthored, along with Mark Twain, the book that gave the Gilded Age its name. Like Nordhoff, he saw Southern California as the antidote to a growing gap between the very rich and the rest of society: "The picture I see is of a land of small farms and gardens.... It is the fairest field for the experiment of a contented community, without any poverty and without excessive wealth."[11]

The View from the Raymond and Mount Rubidoux: Early Tourism in Southern California

While guidebooks aimed at tourists and settlers sometimes found a ready market, travel to the region, and settlement within it, remained slow. New arrivals were generally limited to three categories: moderately prosperous settlers planning to "homestead" a citrus farm, the affluent, who could travel regardless of expense, and the desperate—sickly individuals who hoped that the fabled climate of Southern California could cure them, or at least stave off death for a time. Perhaps as much as a quarter of all those who migrated to Southern California before 1900 fell into this last group.[12]

A new regional center began to emerge, however, when the Southern Pacific Railroad constructed a route traversing the San Gabriel Mountains through Soledad Pass. After threatening to lay the tracks to San Bernardino, the Southern Pacific succeeded in extracting money and land from Los Angeles, and the rail line reached the city in 1879. Another Southern Pacific line followed, entering Southern California from Arizona. This track crossed the Colorado River and then traversed the Coachella Valley. Fares, however, remained prohibitively high. The most impressive infrastructure constructed during this time was a series of grand resort hotels, catering to tourists for whom money was not a major concern. Modeled upon earlier western resort hotels, such as the Del Monte in Monterey, or the hotels constructed in Colorado Springs, these hotels offered a luxurious, enclosed eastern world. The clientele was overwhelmingly eastern, and the cuisine, amenities, and recreational activities guests enjoyed all followed the models of eastern resort hotels such as those in Newport, Rhode Island, and Saratoga, New York.[13]

These large hotels, constructed like great houses on country estates, were usually removed from Southern California's "urban" areas. The Arlington Hotel opened in Santa Barbara in 1876, adjacent to the town's wharf and a hot spring. Other hotels opened after trains improved access to the region. The Hotel Del Coronado opened on Coronado Island, across the harbor from San Diego, in 1888. Yet the epicenter of this resort hotel construction was in Pasadena, suitably removed from Los Angeles, but accessible via both the Southern Pacific Railway and its new competitor, the Santa Fe. Here the Raymond Hotel would open in 1886, later joined by the Hotel Green and the Huntington Hotel.[14]

The Raymond, owned by the same company that owned the Del Monte in Monterey, perfected the art of entertaining wealthy eastern tourists. The hotel sat on a hill donated by the Santa Fe Railway, and was surrounded by gardens and orchards, kept green with free water provided by Pasadena. Virtually its entire staff was shipped in from the East each winter, with its managers drawn from prestigious eastern hotels. It drew guests from the East and even from Britain, but the majority were New Englanders, especially Bostonians, as were the partners in the firm of Raymond and Whitcomb, which owned the hotel and arranged "Raymond Excursions" to the Raymond and Del Monte each winter.[15]

Amy Bridges, a young woman who resided in Hopkinton, Massachusetts, traveled west with her parents on two Raymond excursions, one in the spring of 1882 and another in the winter of 1886 and 1887, with a long stay at the Raymond during its inaugural season. Her travel diaries offer an invaluable window into this world of transplanted eastern leisure. The first trip, a tour of the Colorado Rockies, the Southwest, and California, made Southern California just one attraction among many, and demonstrated the degree to which this easterner was not yet ready to appreciate many of the less familiar aspects of the West. Bridges found the Pueblo cliff dwellings of the Southwest, so soon to be romanticized by artists and writers, unfit for any human habitation. She was bewildered by the adobe architecture of Santa Fe. Though impressed by the Colorado Rockies, her view of the desert was decidedly less favorable.

Then, however, the Raymond excursion train passed through the mountains, heading towards the less arid lands to the west. The train entered the heart of Southern California, and for Bridges, who was astounded to see flowers, orchards, and streams after passing though the barren desert, it was love at first sight: "The whole country was completely changed.... The Sierra Madre Mts., not distant, were covered with a purple haze and the sky was a beautiful blue. The sun sank gloriously as we reached Los Angeles and this was our introduction to the Pueblo de la Reina de los Angeles as is its full Spanish name." While in Los Angeles, the Bridges family would visit orange groves, Mission San Gabriel, and Chinatown, and loll upon the beach. The Raymond party then headed north for a stay in San Francisco and a visit to Yosemite.[16]

When the Bridges family returned to Southern California in December of 1886 with a Raymond Excursion group of 120, they arrived in a region then in its first boom, and far more attuned to the tourist market. The most striking manifestation of this was the imposing Raymond Hotel itself. Within it and its freshly planted grounds, vacationers pursued a daily routine that would likely seem stultifying to tourists of later generations. The usual entertainments of affluent Victorian society—elaborate meals, dances, billiards, singing, lectures concerning art or nature, and gossiping about various romantic intrigues—kept guests occupied in the hotel. Other guests lounged on the hotel's three verandas, reading, talking, sewing, and enjoying the pastoral scenery and spectacular sunsets. After winter storms cleared, guests thrilled at the sight of snow-covered peaks looming above acres of orange groves.[17]

More "adventurous" guests took long strolls through the growing community of Pasadena, admiring its homes but complaining of its either muddy or dusty streets. Sometimes they visited other easterners who had rented homes in Pasadena, or who were buying homes for winter residences. Surreptitiously plucking the occasional orange or flower from orchards and yards, Bridges, like other tourists, marveled at the balmy climate: "When I am walking through the orange groves with the bright sun-shine and the soft wind I can hardly believe that it is only a few days to Christmas, but think I am at some summer resort."[18]

Though impressed by Pasadena, Bridges was no longer enchanted by Los Angeles. The growing community had already traded in pastoral picturesqueness for the messy bustle of a frontier boom town:

> I think Los Angeles is the dirtiest city I ever saw. The buildings are not very high and a great many seem to be only the cheap little buildings which were first put up when this place began to grow. Most of the stores are dirty little holes and even those which are very nice within would hardly have you suppose so from their outside. There are many land and real estate offices, and they manage to squeeze themselves into the smallest quarters possible.[19]

The Bridges would remain in Southern California until 11 March 1887. Most of that time was spent at the Raymond, with side trips to Riverside and San Diego, which Amy found a far more impressive city than Los Angeles. In Riverside the Bridges stayed at the Glenwood Inn. This small hostelry would later serve as a centerpiece of a new, distinctly Southern Californian tourist experience. It was transformed by its owner's son, Frank Miller, into the Mission Inn, a baroque mission-revival wedding cake of a hotel, with extravagant exterior façades and opulent interiors filled with Spanish antiques and Gustav Stickley's Craftsman furniture. The entire hotel became a stage set for elaborate racial mythologizing, a reimagined fantasy past that aimed to connect the Anglo-American, Protestant present with the "Spanish," Catholic past. Miller also commissioned John S. McGroarty to pen *The Mission Play*, a landmark in the mission revival movement, and oversaw it for its first several seasons. In the courtyard of the Inn Miller replanted what was purported to be the first navel orange tree in Southern California, the progenitor of the region's entire citrus industry. Oranges, like limes, lemons, olives, and vineyard grapes, were in fact an important legacy of the missions—Mediterranean crops, already in production, which Anglos found profitable in an initially exotic agricultural environment. No less a personage than President Theodore Roosevelt arrived to help plant the venerable tree. When told of its prodigious output and numerous progeny, Roosevelt replied that he was glad to see that the tree showed "no signs of race suicide."[20]

Yet if Miller helped create a new and regionally distinctive form of tourism, he also played a central role in developing a place that served as the setting for rituals that encapsulated and preserved the ideology of tourists in the late Victorian era of Amy Bridges. This was Mount Rubidoux, a rocky hill that rose immediately west of Riverside. Mission Inn guest Jacob Riis, the muckraking journalist whose writings and photographs had done so much to highlight the woes of eastern cities, suggested to Miller that the hill would be an excellent setting for an Easter sunrise service. With money from real-estate and commuter-train magnate Henry Huntington, and engineering assistance from Hiram Chittenden, a former superintendent of Yellowstone who had overseen the development of roads in the national park, Miller supervised the construction of a road to the top of the hill and the construction of large cross dedicated to Father Junipero Serra.

While the cross might have been dedicated to the founder of the California missions, it served entirely Anglo-American purposes. Each Easter morning, residents and tourists alike—sometimes totaling a crowd of more than ten thousand congregants—ascended to the summit. They enacted rituals that connected Riv-

FIGURE 1.2 The road to the summit of Mt. Rubidoux, and a view of the agricultural landscape of Southern California. Huntington Library, San Marino, California.

FIGURE 1.3 A sunrise Easter service atop it in 1910. Huntington Library, San Marino, California.

erside with Manifest Destiny, and claimed the natural environment of Southern California for themselves. Atop this promontory, their avid pursuit of health and happiness through recreation seemingly received divine approval. Among the regular features of the service was a reading of Henry Van Dyke's poem "God of the Open Air." Another component was a call and response, which included the following invocation, paraphrasing Exodus 6:4: "For I have established My Covenant with them, to give them the land of their pilgrimage wherein they were strangers." Here was the culmination of the heady mix of religion, racial ideology, and nationalism that had propelled white Americans westward across the continent in the nineteenth century. Whatever else Anglo-Americans might assert they had inherited from the padres, they certainly could not claim humility.[21]

———————————✺———————————

Resorts and hotels isolated travelers like Amy Bridges from the diverse population of the Southwest—indeed, racial exclusion would prove a hallmark of the recreational places and spaces created for the enjoyment of leisure. Yet privileged, leisured tourists such as the Bridges and those who followed them occasionally encountered others who were neither privileged, leisured, nor white. Often these interactions were fraught with all the racism endemic to nineteenth century America. Such was the case when the Bridges walked from the Glenwood Inn to an "Indian Town" about a mile from Riverside, along the steep banks of the Santa Ana River. Walking through the clearly destitute assemblage of about twenty thatched houses, Amy and her family intruded into Indian homes and lives that seemed alien. Amy rendered her judgment of these people after peering into one such home: "There was nothing in the hut. I saw a few rags…nothing at all to make life in the least comfortable, not even our necessities. I wonder how human beings can live so. I can not imagine how low in the scale of human life they could be—almost animals. They are digger Indians which is the lowest tribe living."[22]

Yet other interactions between tourists and residents could prove more ambivalent. Again and again in the world of white leisure, other people appeared. In Raton, New Mexico, there was the "Mexican" who sold pinyon nuts to Amy's mother. At the train station at Lamy, near Santa Fe, there were a large number of Pueblo women selling crafts. Bridges wrote that the women usually danced for tourists, "but this time their governor would not let them as he says they are lazy and will not work on their farms if they can get money so easily from the excursionists." According to her diary, the governor's decision so annoyed the women that they deposed him and chose a new governor on the spot. Though this young white woman obviously possessed no knowledge of Native American politics, her prose does suggest the incredible tensions and transformations that the new cash economy and nascent Southwestern tourist industry engendered for Native Americans.[23]

Even at the Raymond Hotel itself, that enclosed eastern world of white leisure, nonwhites could appear. One example was the Chinese man who occasionally walked up the hill to the hotel, carrying merchandise in buckets suspended from a yoke on his back. He utilized the Raymond's verandas to ply his wares. As Bridges related it, "He spread them out in tempting piles—dainty boxes—delicately carved woods—soft pale colors in crepe and silk and paper—and the ladies have lively times bargaining with him." This bargaining—this give-and-take—perhaps best expressed the most positive aspect of interaction between whites and nonwhites in the sphere of tourist leisure. This was a still a place of clear inequalities and prejudices, but this new world of tourists and leisure could sometimes offer opportunities to Native Americans, Mexicans, and Asians. Certainly, it also offered possibilities to Anglos looking for a fresh start.[24]

The Career of Charles Fletcher Lummis in the Land of Sunshine

After traversing Cajon Pass, Charles Lummis strode into San Gabriel late in the afternoon of 1 February 1885. He was twenty-five years old, lean and tanned, with one arm in a sling. Waiting to meet him, either at a hotel or in the twilight at Mission San Gabriel—depending upon which of Lummis's various versions of the story one believes—was Harrison Gray Otis, editor of the *Los Angeles Times*. The two then walked together the remaining ten miles to Los Angeles. Otis had paid Lummis to send letters ahead to the *Times*, and promised a job as city editor when he arrived in Los Angeles. The letters, revised and altered to make the most positive impression—and the best story—subsequently appeared in Lummis's 1892 book, *A Tramp across the Continent.*

Beyond the promise of a new job, other motives also drove Lummis to Southern California. He was born in Lynn, Massachusetts, in 1859, the son of a Methodist minister. He had attended Harvard, but devoted less time to his studies than to romantic pursuits and enjoying his summers hiking, mountain climbing, and writing poetry while employed at a relative's resort hotel in the White Mountains of New Hampshire. Lummis failed out of school, married Dorothea Rhodes, a medical student he had met while at Harvard, and fled New England. He likewise failed in a new occupation, as a newspaper editor in Chillicothe, Ohio, the home of his bride's family. His marriage to Dorothea soon faltered, and to make matters worse, Lummis contracted malaria. He decided that he needed a fresh start—a new life in a new climate. Lummis contacted Otis with the idea of his "tramp," and once arrangements were finalized, Dorothea went ahead by train to set up her medical practice in Los Angeles. Though Lummis recovered from the malaria, he broke his arm in northern Arizona Territory, yanking the bone back into place himself with a canteen strap. Lummis took great pride in his rugged approach to medical care, but such a cavalier attitude would haunt him. He suffered from a succession of health problems and periodic collapses. Lummis's life would be marred by struggles with—or flights from—monetary, physical, and emotional distress.[25]

In fact, Lummis would flee back into the interior Southwest three years after his arrival in Los Angeles. Chronic overwork, too little sleep, too much alcohol, and continuing marital problems resulted in a stroke that paralyzed his left side. Amado Chaves provided the means of escape, offering to let Lummis recuperate at his New Mexico rancho. Lummis had befriended Chaves, scion of a prominent New Mexico family and former speaker of the territorial legislature, during his continental "tramp." Lummis insisted on recuperating in his own rugged way. He limped about the rancho, and learned to ride, fish, and shoot with one arm. Later, he even broke wild horses. Such activities may have further endangered his health, but probably saved his sanity. Lummis, who valued an active outdoor life and masculine hardiness above all else, found himself barely twenty-nine years old, and quite possibly disabled for life.[26]

In September 1888, Lummis moved to Isleta Pueblo in New Mexico, where he would live for four years. He hoped that he could now experience Indian life as he had already experienced Hispanic. He arranged to rent a room and moved in. The Isletas, after failing to remove him, grew to tolerate his presence. By expressing great interest in Pueblo culture, and being generous with tobacco and candy—earning him the nickname Por Todos, "For Everyone"—Lummis attempted to ingratiate himself into Isleta society. Yet a Tiwa-language nickname for Lummis—translated as "The One Whom We Worry About"—probably better conveys the Indian view of the strange, ailing outsider in their midst. Lummis grew increasingly interested in Pueblo folklore and history, and tried to assist the Isletas in their struggles with government Indian policies, especially the forced removal of Pueblo children to Indian boarding schools.[27]

While living at Isleta, Lummis's paralysis lessened, and he met his future second wife, nineteen-year-old Eva "Eve" Douglas, a Catholic schoolteacher. Here he also wrote the books that brought him the most renown. In 1892 he published *Some Strange Corners of our Country* (republished as *Mesa, Cañon, and Pueblo* in 1925), and *The Land of Poco Tiempo* followed in 1893. He would also publish a series of books on Native American folklore, including *The Man who Married the Moon* (1894) and *The Enchanted Burro* (1897).

He first published a series of short stories in *St. Nicholas*, a magazine aimed at children. As such, many of these accounts were rollicking adventure yarns, with Lummis cast as the hero. Some of these would later reappear in *Some Strange Corners of our Country*, which offered readers a lively travelogue of Southwestern places and peoples. Over time, his prose became more polished, but certain underlying characteristics remained. A romantic tone and exuberant Victorian descriptiveness suffused Lummis's prose. The goal was to give educated eastern readers—Lummis's intended audience—the flavor of the land of "sun, silence, and adobe." In his books, Lummis strove to popularize the scenery and cultures of the region he called the "Great Southwest." These supposedly scholarly texts, however, often read more like travelogues—to the extent of providing directions for tourists. Despite his bravado, Lummis actually described a fairly limited part of the Southwest, mainly northern Arizona and New Mexico—or more specifically, an area within a forty-mile band north and south of the Santa Fe Railroad. He hailed as a happy accident the fact "that the Santa Fe route…skimmed the cream of the artist's interest in the Southwest." Yet he could not classify as accidental the fact that the Santa Fe Railroad appreciated the effect of his books enough to grant him a free travel pass on their lines. Lummis was always defensive on this point; he wished to be a scholar, not just another booster.[28]

Nevertheless, in an era of railroad tourism, Lummis's glorification of the Southwest aided both the company and the city of Los Angeles. By annexing the entire Southwest as a vast recreational hinterland, Los Angeles gained added allure—and a means of combating more cosmopolitan San Francisco. That city had long promoted Yosemite and the Sierras as additional attractions for tourists arriving by train. San Francisco–bound tourists also experienced another bonus—passage through the Colorado Rockies. The route to Southern California offered no comparable mountain vistas. Instead, the Southwest would offer an exotic world to tourists—all of it accessible from the Santa Fe Railway and the Fred Harvey Hotels along its route, which sold Indian crafts and exotic regional atmosphere along with meals and accommodations. Eastern tourists bound for San Francisco could have the Rockies and Sierras; those bound for Los Angeles would have the Grand Canyon. Though Southern California and the interior Southwest occupied different environments and were products of divergent histories, their superficial similarities were enough to unite then in the minds of railroad tourists, who saw these regions in only the most cursory way. Both were more arid than the East, both possessed a "Spanish" atmosphere, and both still retained Indian populations, providing exotic tourist appeal. Dismissed a few decades before as a barren waste, the interior Southwest would prove so attractive that even the Southern Pacific Railway began to funnel tourists to California on a longer—and more profitable—southerly route originating in New Orleans.[29]

This emphasis on the exotic would lead later scholars, analyzing texts produced by Lummis and other southwestern writers of his era, to detect the hallmarks of "orientalism," an exoticizing of Indians and Mexicans into an alien "other." This "orientalism" also took on a more literal form, as the desert Southwest became the American Egypt in the imagery of travel writers. Lummis certainly did see the inhabitants of the Southwest as different from, and usually subordinate to, Anglo-Americans, but contrary to the "orientalist" critique, he did not see them as alien or irrelevant.[30]

The Land of Poco Tiempo, Lummis's second book, demonstrated how Lummis intended to map a "new cultural geography" for the Southwest and its residents, and to posit it as not merely scenic, but instead as the salvation of Anglo America. The book would serve as an *ur*-text for the emerging Anglo-American fascination with the Southwest, and helped popularize everything from regional tourism to "Santa Fe Style" architecture and interior decor. In this book Lummis presented a Pueblo culture as complex as white society, yet far more balanced and contented. Again and again, though sometimes employing orientalist imagery, Lummis connected Native Americans to Euro-American culture. The peaceful Moqui (Hopi) were the "Quaker Indians." The pueblo towns were democratic republics before Columbus sailed. Cliff dwellings and the great structures at Chaco Canyon were the "first American skyscrapers." The masonry of the Anasazi made them "as Yankee as the Yankees," and the exquisite baskets and pottery produced by contemporary Southwestern Indians conferred upon their makers the title "Yankees of the Southwest." And, as Lummis noted acerbically, it was just this authentic American art that government Indian schools were attempting to obliterate.[31]

For some Euro-Americans threatened by urbanization, industrialization, and the excesses of the Gilded Age, the Indians and Hispanos of the "Great Southwest" seemed more authentically American than the rapidly changing society in which whites lived. The "romance" of the Southwest was often less the allure of the exotic than the nostalgia for an earlier American era. Indians' supposed closeness to nature, or the intimacy of community relationships in a Pueblo or Hispano village, epitomized values apparently lacking in the urban East. In Southern California, Helen Hunt Jackson's 1884 novel *Ramona*, a melodramatic romance intended as an indictment of the maltreatment of Native Americans, instead enshrined a myth of missions and ranchos that seemed a lost idyll. A nation that had denigrated Mexicans and conquered more than half of their territory was enchanted by Jackson's picturesque depiction of Californio life, and *Ramona* became one of the most popular novels of the nineteenth century. It also inspired film adaptations, a pageant still performed annually, and even a Southern California community named Ramona. The potent appeal of Lummis's and Jackson's romanticized Southwest lay in an idealized—and largely invented—past. Their idealizations hearkened back to an illusory past when there had existed a harmony between individuals and between humans and nature. The need for these illusions spoke to underlying anxieties about modern humanity's alienation from nature, and the subjugation of personal relationships to ones dictated by capital.[32]

To the degree that twenty-first century Americans posses any historical memory of the 1890s, they may hazily recall the "Gibson Girl," or the appellation the "Gay Nineties," vague remnants of a simpler era. Americans who lived during the 1890s, however, endured a series of alarming traumas. The stock market panic of 1893 triggered the deepest depression in U.S. history. The Pullman strike of 1894 was only one of many episodes of labor unrest and violence. The agrarian revolt of the Populists culminated in the 1896 Democratic presidential campaign of William Jennings Bryan, who won most of the South and West with his apocalyptic rhetoric, railing against the gold standard for currency, and vowing that "you shall not press down upon the brow of labor this crown of thorns, you shall not crucify mankind upon a cross of gold." Even as the incorporation and industrialization of America irrevocably transformed the nation, it seemed that the wheels were in danger of falling off the great capitalist machine.

On a more local level, the first real-estate boom in Los Angeles had been followed, inevitably, by the first real-estate bust. While Southern California promised a new sort of frontier, its cyclical economy proved all too typical of the boom-and-bust economy of much of the American West. In short, Lummis's books, like Jackson's, arrived at precisely the right moment. Readers across the nation desperately wanted to fall under the seductive spell of the romantic, harmonious Southwest, purportedly a relic of a simpler time. In Los Angeles and Southern California in general, land speculators desperately needed the nation to fall under the sway of the seductive Southwest as well. Cultural and economic imperatives met and merged, irrevocably shaping the future of Southern California, the Southwest, and the nation.

Thus, although Lummis presented Indians as people who could enrich American culture, and even as embodiments of republican virtue, he also depicted their communities and region as refuges from modern life. The escapist subtext that appeared in Lummis's descriptions of Indians proved the dominant motif in his descriptions of Hispanic culture. Late in life, Lummis recalled the profound imprint left by his first encounter with Hispanic New Mexico:

> Though my conscience was Puritan, my whole imagination and sympathy and feeling were Latin. That is, essentially Spanish. Apparently they always had been, for now that I had gotten away from the repressive influence of my birthplace I began to see that the generous and bubbling boyish impulses which had been considerably frosted in New England were, after all, my birthright.[33]

This reaction to "Spanish America" as a place that fostered a dual sense of belonging and release was strengthened by Lummis's stay with Amado Chaves, and cemented by his visits with the del Valle family. The del Valles were an old Californio clan who resided at their rancho, Camulos, in the Santa Clara River Valley north of Los Angeles. They had a long history of impressing Anglos, and tenaciously held on to their ranch through the droughts and depredations of the 1860s and 1870s. A map produced by the Wheeler Survey in the later 1870s, one of several federal surveys undertaken to map the new lands of the West and Southwest, depicted much of Los Angeles County, and listed a variety of landmarks, from Spanish missions to the "San Fernando Plains." It also carefully delineated the locations of agricultural landholdings. Of all of these, Rancho Camulos was the only Mexican-owned rancho included on the map. If federal surveyors had been impressed by Rancho Camulos, Lummis was enthralled by it. He came to call the valley the "Land of the Afternoon." Introduced to the del Valle daughters by the Chaveses, Lummis fell in love. Yet he also fell in love with their lifestyle, seemingly so different from the frenetic pace of Eastern, urban America. In a verse he composed about Rancho Camulos, Lummis rhapsodized: "Untaint by greed of riches,/ That is our modern shame;/ . . . Its heart the heart of mother Spain—/ Of Spain before the fall!"[34]

FIGURE 1.4 Portrait of Charles Lummis taken while he served as city editor for the *Los Angeles Times* from 1885 to 1887. Newly arrived in Los Angeles, Lummis had already adopted the green corduroy suit, beaded Native American belt, and wide-brimmed hat he wore for much of the rest of his career. His costume, like his books and articles, was intended to enhance his reputation as the self-appointed arbiter of all things Southwestern. Braun Library, Autry National Center, Los Angeles.

FIGURE 1.5 "Del Valle Girls." This photograph, taken by Lummis on the veranda at Rancho Camulos, documented his interest in the del Valle daughters. The frank gaze he received in return from at least one del Valle suggested that his interest and self-assurance was answered in kind. Braun Library, Autry National Center, Los Angeles.

Here was Lummis's true view of Californio culture—a precapitalist Eden. Lummis likely wished that he could have been one of the Yankee merchants who came to California before American annexation, married daughters of prominent families, converted to Catholicism, and became Californio dons. Lummis even attempted to follow this pattern, proposing to Susana del Valle while living in New Mexico. Charles Lummis could become Don Carlos—a moniker he did indeed later adopt. He initiated a divorce with Dorothea, but then found that Susana's father would not permit a marriage with a propertyless, divorced Protestant. Unbelievably, Dorothea took him back again.[35]

Even more than Pueblo life, Hispanic culture seemed to offer the ultimate succor for this ailing Yankee workaholic. Lummis later claimed that he recovered his speaking voice, slurred by the stroke, by singing Spanish folk songs. *The Land of Poco Tiempo* took its title from a Spanish phrase meaning "a short time," but which he translated as "pretty soon." In the title chapter of the book, Lummis asked: "Why hurry with the hurrying world? The 'Pretty Soon' of New Spain is better than the 'Now! Now!' of the haggard United States. The opiate sun soothes to rest, the adobe is made to lean against, the hush of the day-long noon would not be broken. Let us not hasten—*mañana* will do. Better still, *pasado mañana*."[36]

Though Lummis was perhaps unique in his adoration of all things South-western, he was not alone in urging Americans to rest. An increasing num-ber of his fellow citizens—particularly in the urban Northeast and Lummis's native New England—called on Americans to embrace a more leisurely life. Their arguments were buttressed by changing realities and perceptions in American society. As the nation grew more prosperous, both the middle and upper classes began to shed the old Puritan abhorrence of leisure. Some indi-viduals also fretted that their society was too mercenary, and that American culture could never be refined until its citizens renounced their unending pur-suit of the almighty dollar. At the other end of the socioeconomic spectrum, social reformers and some physicians charged that industrial workers were trapped in mindless, menial labor that threatened their physical and mental health. Like Lummis, these other proponents of leisure argued that rest could be curative—restoring vigor to a nation that had been rendered effete by Victorian manners and enervated by the closing of the frontier.[37]

❋

Lummis might have imagined a life of leisure, but in reality he had to work. After his divorce from Dorothea and marriage to Eva Douglas in 1891, and the birth of their daughter Turbesé a year later, Lummis relocated his fam-ily to Los Angeles, and then immediately left to accompany archaeologist Adolph Bandelier on an expedition to Latin America. The funding for the trip fell through, however, and Lummis returned to Los Angeles with a horde of Peruvian artifacts and photos—but no money.

Salvation came in the form of Charles Dwight Willard, the secretary of the Los Angeles chamber of commerce. Willard had arrived in Los Ange-les at age twenty-six in 1886, desperately ill from tuberculosis. He, like so many others, hoped that the climate of Southern California would cure him. It did not, but he remained in Southern California, becoming a booster like Lummis. Like some other boosters, his promotion was not all advertising flim-flam—he desperately needed to believe in Southern California's pur-ported curative qualities while suffering attacks of tuberculosis for twenty-eight years until his death in 1914.[38]

As for the chamber of commerce, founded in 1888 after the first local real-estate boom went bust, it pursued the promotion of Los Angeles with relentless ambition. One of the first actions the new organization undertook was to pass a resolution calling upon the federal government to annex the peninsula of Baja California from Mexico and create a new state, combining it with Southern California—with Los Angeles as its inevitable capital city. In the years that followed, it produced literally millions of promotional booklets and pamphlets, most directed at readers in the Midwest. In June 1894, Willard and two other Los Angeles businessmen, Frank A. Patee and Harry Brook, commenced publication of *Land of Sunshine*, a promotional magazine that showcased Southern California, especially Los Angeles. The three investors hoped that the Chamber of Commerce could be persuaded to purchase the magazine in bulk, distributing it in the East as yet another promotional tool. Willard convinced the organization to proceed, and the magazine also began to sell on its own, proving as popular with locals as with easterners.[39]

With increased readership, however, the magazine needed a real editor, someone who could produce the magazine competently and develop a national reputation for it as a periodical with a gloss of culture, rather than just another promotional pamphlet. Willard turned to Lummis, who was less than enthusiastic: "The matter had no appeal to me whatever, and I turned him off rather emphatically." Yet Willard proved convincing, promising complete editorial control, as well as $50 a month, another $25 a month in stock, and a third of the business. Lummis accepted, and his editorship began with the January 1895 issue.[40]

Lummis may have been ambivalent, but this new position offered him far more than a regular income. It gave him a platform for regional and even national visibility. Now he could be more than just an editor—he could present himself as the premiere authority on the Southwest and Southern California. He soon inaugurated a new column, "In the Lion's Den," from which he would hold forth for the duration of his tenure. In January 1901 Lummis changed the title of *Land of Sunshine* to *Out West*, bearing the motto: "The Nation Back of Us, The World in Front." The magazine would also serve as the cornerstone of two organizations he founded: the Landmarks Club, organized to restore the crumbling Spanish missions, and the Sequoya League, which aimed to improve the material conditions and political status of Indians in California and the Southwest.[41]

Despite Lummis's grand aspirations, his magazine's success proved more modest. Though financial and subscription records are sporadic, it appears that as many as eight thousand individuals subscribed to the magazine after its title changed to *Out West*, though subscriptions may have been highest in the late 1890s. These individuals were concentrated in California, the Midwest, and the Northeast, with a smaller number in the interior Southwest. Fifty public libraries also took it. Most important to the solvency of the magazine were the bulk orders for tens of thousands of copies that the chamber of commerce distributed in the Midwest.[42]

Yet less important than the number of readers was their identity. Lummis's magazine was read by a variety of highly influential people. Least surprising were the number of Los Angeles and Southern California boosters and businessmen who received the magazine. More surprising were influential eastern readers, from officials in the Bureau of Ethnography and the U.S. Geological Survey to New York publishers. Nationally known conservationists such as John Muir and George Bird Grinell also received it. Another regular reader was President Theodore Roosevelt, an acquaintance from Lummis's Harvard days. Several officials in the Mexican government and at the Museo Nacional in Mexico City also subscribed, perhaps pleased to see a U.S. publication with a positive—and therefore decidedly different—view of Mexico and Latin America. The same was true of a number of Catholic seminaries, monasteries, and missions, who likewise would have found Lummis's embrace of Catholic history, art, and architecture appealing.[43]

In Lummis's earlier books, regional promotion had been implicit. In *Land of Sunshine* and *Out West*, by contrast, boosterism was utterly explicit. Lummis endlessly promoted Los Angeles and the "Great Southwest." Yet he always claimed that his magazine was not a boosterist rag, and that as editor he maintained a "scrupulous segregation of the 'pure reading matter'" from everything of a "'boosting' nature," with any article written solely to promote real estate "shut severely back among the ads."[44]

While Lummis rarely wrote anything explicit as a real estate advertisement, the entire magazine was a monthly adulation of the Southwest, Southern California, and Los Angeles. He could promote Indian crafts, Hispanic music, and regional attire and cuisine. Lummis also urged the adoption of regional architecture, from the cooling properties of thick adobe walls to the social possibilities of a backyard patio. In this sense, *Land of Sunshine* functioned as one of many "shelter" magazines that appeared late in the nineteenth century. Periodicals such as *House Beautiful*, *House and Garden*, *Bungalow*, and Gustav Stickley's *Craftsman* offered readers a comforting vision of homes and modes of living, building, and decorating that would improve home life in a world that often seemed unpredictable or threatening. Southern California architecture would in fact subsequently influence the nation as a whole. Yet *Land of Sunshine* did not simply promote homes. It promoted all of Southern California and the Great Southwest as "shelter" from a rapidly changing world many Americans found troubling.[45]

Further, the magazine allowed Lummis to proclaim his gospel of leisure, using the Southwest, its climate, and its cultures to teach workaholic white Americans the value of rest and recuperation. Lummis asserted that the climate of the Southwest would work on Americans whether they wanted it or not: "The people of the United States know less about the art of recreation than any other people now extant. They haven't time to live. But the Southwest is appointed schoolmaster—and the lesson is going to be learned." The new residents of the region were "destined to show an astonished world the spectacle of Americans having a good time."[46]

As far as *Land of Sunshine/Out West* was concerned, no place on earth offered the same opportunities for recreation as the region surrounding Los Angeles. The city boasted beach resorts "strung along the sea-board like pearls on a silver wire," as well as Santa Catalina Island, "a wandering mountain range, stranded offshore." Then there were the mountain resorts, nestled "in the deep cañons of the Sierras." In the deserts to the east there were a multitude of attractions, especially the oasis of Palm Springs, with its healing waters, palm canyons, and stark vistas. All of these places, collectively comprising Los Angeles's recreational hinterland, offered residents and tourists alike unparalleled opportunities to enjoy a seemingly endless variety of escapes, whether for a day or a lifetime.[47]

Nevertheless, Lummis did not espouse leisure and the enjoyment of life because he envisioned a future republic of slackers. Escape from the tyranny of the time clock was instead intended to restore mental and physical vitality to white Americans, making them ready to achieve ever greater things. California, according to Lummis, "has the population most exclusively of *converts*," of whom even "the most habituated never forget to be grateful, every day, that they are not somewhere else." Thus the urbanization of Los Angeles was fundamentally different

FIGURE 1.6 This photograph, identified as "Charles Lummis in Pasadena, 1906," apparently showing an entry in the Tournament of Roses Parade, has not been conclusively linked to Lummis. It nevertheless attests to his and other boosters' indefatigable promotion of Southern California, its climate, and, at least in this case, its flora and fauna. Huntington Library, San Marino.

from the growth of eastern cities: "Eastern cities are swelling with Americans who move in to make Money; California is filling (country and city) with Americans who move in to make a Life. In a word, it is the Chosen Country."[48]

Lummis, however, made clear that the growth of Los Angeles differed from that of San Francisco, which boomed into existence as a result of the Gold Rush: "The unprecedented rush of '49–'51 was not so much a population as an infestment. Its best were adventurers; its worst something less." He asserted that the two rushes to California after its annexation were profoundly different, more dissimilar even than "the first European settlements of Mexico and New England." If the first was "Sheer Adventure," the second was "Reasoned Migration," with treasure hunters replaced by home seekers. The new population of Los Angeles resulted from "the least heroic migration in history but the most judicious; the least impulsive but the most reasonable." According to Lummis, the "Second Invasion of California" was without precedent—individuals and families rejecting urban woes, unpleasant winters, and hectic schedules. And it was these migrants—with education, a degree of affluence, and a respect for leisure—who would ensure that Southern California and the Southwest would be "the theater in which for the first time an English-speaking race has the opportunity to repeat the glories of classic days—the art, the music, the literature and the life of ancient Greece and Palestine and Italy."[49]

✳

Lummis hoped he could help Anglo-America learn to relax, but the lessons derived from his writings could prove less benign for other Americans. There was a thin line between relaxation and laziness. Euro-Americans had long used supposed indolence—signified by a lack of cities or permanent agricultural areas—as justification for dispossessing Native Americans. Even though Pueblos and Mexicans clearly had these social structures, their purported lack of industriousness could still be seen as a mark of inferiority, even if Lummis did not intend such a judgment. His romanticization of a pastoral Hispanic past contributed to the mission and Spanish Revival movements, which popularized modern attempts at mission and Spanish architecture, and propagated a variety of fiestas and pageants. The movement also glorified the "Spanish" residents of California's past, while ignoring the "Mexicans" of California's present. Although Lummis recognized historical inaccuracies within mission revivalism, he nevertheless played a central role in the process that transformed the Spanish-speaking residents of California from the "subjects" to the "objects" of regional history—from those who acted, to those who were acted upon. No less significantly, his obsession with the "Spanish" elements of Mexican history enhanced the longstanding elite Californio agenda of claiming a "white" European identity, even though almost all Californios were of mixed ancestry. Elite Californios and Anglos clashed over issues of land and politics, but the old Castilian obsession with *limpieza de sangre*—purity of blood—meshed perfectly with the rabid Anglo-Saxonism of late nineteenth-century America.[50]

On a fundamental level, Lummis did not understand the cultures and individuals he claimed to know so well. He and his Anglo-American audience were oblivious to the remarkable dynamism of the region he was describing, and the agendas pursued by those deemed "passive" and "timeless." In both New Mexico and California, the apparently oblivious Lummis befriended Mexicans who hoped that his writings would bring modern economic growth to the region, not encase it in a timeless idyll. He presented his friend Amado Chaves and his elite New Mexico family as heirs to a romantic Spanish past, even as the Chaveses allied themselves with the new U.S. political and business elite, and aggressively—sometimes coercively—acquired the communal village lands of poor Hispanos. Amado Chaves was elected mayor of Santa Fe in 1891, and later served on the New Mexico State school board.[51]

For their part, the del Valle family hardly dozed in "the land of the afternoon." Helen Hunt Jackson visited Rancho Camulos while working on her novel *Ramona*, and it became the basis of the adobe rancho home depicted in her book. In the case of both Jackson and Lummis, the real family, as well as the fictional one, was depicted as self-sufficient and independent, with close-knit bonds to each other and to the land, yet also refined, living in a home decorated to demonstrate their gentility.[52]

Ramona was one of the most popular novels of the late nineteenth century, and the tourism it spawned guaranteed a regular influx of visitors at Rancho Camulos, as well as any other spot claiming some connection, however tenuous, to the novel. The impact this had on architecture, particularly the ascendant popularity of mission and Spanish revival, has been overlooked. For the first time, Anglos, equipped with copies of the novel and guidebooks written for *Ramona* tourists, were taught to respect and admire Mexican architecture and arts and crafts. Seeing Rancho Camulos as a comfortable and functional home, rather than something primitive to be disdained, must have made Anglo-Americans more amenable to Hispanic regional architecture, and aided the exploding popularity of those styles from the late nineteenth century well into the twentieth. Rancho Camulos would even reappear later in the twentieth century as a key model for new suburban home style, the ranch house.[53]

The del Valles shrewdly built on the attention Lummis and Jackson drew to Rancho Camulos. They remade their greatly diminished cattle ranch into a successful corporate citrus ranch, and marketed produce under the "Home of Ramona" label. They also publicized Rancho Camulos as the "Home of Ramona" to garner tourist revenue, and even convinced the Southern Pacific to place a train station near the rancho to facilitate visitation. The family initially offered visitors food and lodging, hosting them as guests had been welcomed at Californio ranchos half a century before. This familial hospitality ended as the flow of travelers became a torrent, snatching anything from oranges to cutlery as souvenirs. Even with the crowds, however, the illusion was complete. Tourists bound for Rancho Camulos believed they were journeying into the past, while the family inhabiting the rancho was moving confidently into the future.[54]

The del Valles encouraged flattering representations of regional history elsewhere as well. Lucretia del Valle starred in John S. McGroarty's hugely popular *Mission Play*. She played the role of Josepha Yorba, a California matriarch "of the Blood of Castille." Del Valle appeared at the end of the play to lament the ruins of Mission San Juan Capistrano in 1847, and to express hope that American newcomers to California would remember the heroic, pious Spanish past. She did so while costumed in dresses and jewelry billed as del Valle family heirlooms. Del Valle also took a leading role in fundraising for the Landmarks Club founded by Lummis in an effort to preserve the crumbling Spanish missions, which, though newly popular as tourist attractions, had long been neglected. Skillfully utilizing the nostalgia of Anglo-Americans, the del Valle daughters married well, and the sons rose to such positions as the president of the board of the Los Angeles Department of Water and Power.[55]

At Isleta, Lummis wrote of the timeless world of the Pueblo Indians. Yet the community he wrote about was the only pueblo located next to a major railroad line, and was consequently inundated with tourists on a regular basis. Far from living in a supposed premodern harmony, traditionalist and Americanizing factions bitterly fought for political control of Isleta. Other pueblos, such as Taos and Zuni, seized upon the romantic image Lummis and other Anglos crafted to further their tribal land claims. In each case, his agenda was used to pursue goals that differed markedly from his own.[56]

⁂

For that matter, Lummis often had testy relations with his fellow Anglos. Just as he proclaimed Los Angeles the capital of the Great Southwest, he positioned himself as arbiter of all things Southwestern in his adopted home. He also embraced the reformist tendencies of the Progressive Era, supporting conservation and bemoaning the loss of city-owned public pueblo lands, remnants of the Spanish and Mexican past of Los Angeles, which could have been used for parks and government buildings, but were instead sold for development. While many such reformist efforts were beneficial, there were also certain unfortunate similarities between the Progressive reformist urge to remake cities and people and Lummis's urge to be the region's premier booster and tour guide, and to insist that everyone play the parts he had assigned to them. Progressive efforts to enforce the use of English or to discourage traditional cuisine chafed many immigrants subjected to such "benevolence." With Lummis and other boosters, there always seemed to be an obsessive effort to steer and control tourists' experiences—to see the Grand Canyon from the correct overlook, to appropriately appreciate the aesthetics of a Spanish mission. This controlling tendency often veered into outright bossiness that was at times comedic. Fulminating against Midwesterners mangling the Spanish pronunciation of Los Angeles, he tried to convince the city council to install a corrective sticker in every taxi in the city: "The lady will remind you please, her name is not Lost Angie Lees." The city council demurred.

Lummis's relationship to Los Angeles politics and civic leaders was complex. The city benefited from his promotion, but he did not seem to acknowledge that all his preaching about the redemptive power of the Southwest was used by them for purely material ends. Harrison Gray Otis and other city leaders were relentlessly opposed to unions and anything else that threatened the basis of the region's growth formula: cheap land and cheap labor. The city continually suppressed even the slightest hint of labor unrest, particularly rallies or speakers in public recreational spaces such as parks. Lummis was often silent about labor issues, and was usually a reliable cheerleader for whatever Otis and local politicians wanted, such as the city's hijacking and rerouting of the Owens River from the eastern flanks of the Sierras to the San Fernando Valley. Lummis might have thought of himself as a scholar and public intellectual, but as far as Otis, Henry Huntington, and other local magnates were concerned, he was first and foremost an advertising man. If he veered away from that role, his utility dwindled.

Lummis also misgauged his own magazine's readership. His insistent refrains proclaiming the Southwest and Southern California as the cradle of the coming American millennium raised the hackles of readers for a variety of reasons. Some easterners, unsurprisingly, tired of the continual denigration of their region and the implication that they were collectively imbecilic for not yet having relocated to the nation's paradise. Sometimes, however, Lummis received criticism from individuals with more immediate reasons to feel aggrieved. One embittered reader criticized Lummis's endless sunny boosterism: "Either you have taken to write up the state, only seeing superficially or else [you were] *bought*—would that such as you had to carry out an existence as a rancher, and saw tons of fine fruit rotting—no market." The rhetoric of *Land of Sunshine* did not necessarily intersect with the realities of California agriculture and economics.[57]

By far the most letters—and outright hostility—were incurred by Lummis's unconventional views on race, particularly his admiration for Indians and Mexicans, and his loathing of American foreign policy. In the heady imperialist climate of turn-of-the-century America, Lummis stood out as a vociferous opponent of overseas expansion and the cant of the "white man's burden." This stance elicited angry protests, such as one written by Carl C. Marshall, a recipient of a sample copy of *Land of Sunshine*. He had enjoyed "this piquant nosegay from the far southwest corner of Uncle Sam's garden" until he reached "The Lion's Den," and was appalled by its attacks on the U.S. occupation of the Philippines:

> Do you people of California ever stop to think what the conditions of your own beautiful state would be today, had not the expansion policy of 1845 rescued her from Spanish dry rot, and opened her up to American civilization? ... Do you rage in righteous indignation because President Polk did not "recognize the rights and liberties" of the hoard of unwashed greasers and half breeds, who populated your state in those days, and turn the country over to their control?"[58]

Lummis's outspoken views cost *Land of Sunshine* and *Out West* readers. By 1902, despite promises of editorial freedom, the Los Angeles Chamber of Commerce would also terminate orders for issues to distribute in the East. Only a substantial "loan"—actually the first of several donations—from Phoebe Apperson Hearst, widow of mining magnate George Hearst, mother of William Randolph Hearst, and a friend of Eve Lummis, kept the magazine afloat. "The Lion" may have seen his magazine as a suitable vessel for his views on foreign policy, but the majority of readers were uninterested. Most read the magazine because they were considering travel to the West, relocation to the region, or, like many subscribers to later travel magazines, simply enjoyed escapist literature about an interesting place they might, or might not, visit. Such was the case with one reader, who had been solicited for a renewed subscription and queried if he felt the magazine was, among other things, "fine, strong, and beautiful." His reply was succinct: "Do not flatter yourselves too highly. Your magazine may be 'fine' and 'beautiful' and some of the vaporings of the conceited ass who styles himself 'the Lion' are 'strong,' but if it were not for the local interests of Southern California so well illustrated upon your pages, I would have none of it."[59]

Yet Lummis's tumultuous personal life proved even more damaging to his career than his outspoken views. His embrace of the Southwest included regionally correct attire and diet, and the construction of an arts-and-crafts-influenced Spanish Revival stone house, El Alisal, in the Arroyo Seco neighborhood northeast of downtown Los Angeles. Here he would display his vast collection of artifacts, hold raucous parties, and assemble a regional salon of writers and artists including author Mary Austin and painter Maynard Dixon. Here also the Lummises would have three more children.

FIGURE 1.7 Exterior of El Alisal under construction. Lummis Collection, Braun Research Library, Autry National Center, Los Angeles.

FIGURE 1.8 El Alisal interior, with Lummis's collection of Southwestern artifacts and photographs prominently displayed in the "Museo," a large room on the first floor. His collections served as the initial core collection of the Southwest Museum, founded by Lummis in 1907. Lummis Collection, Braun Research Library, Autry National Center, Los Angeles.

From a distance, Lummis's flamboyant lifestyle possessed a certain charm, and many who were invited to parties—called "Noises"—had fond memories of El Alisal. Up close, however, his personal life proved catastrophic. Perhaps as a result of the death of his second child, Amado, at age six, and the growing financial tensions at *Out West*, Lummis had begun to drink more

FIGURE 1.9 View from the Museo into the Arroyo Seco. Here Lummis literally framed his view of the Southwest, surrounding the windows with glass plate photographs from his travels in the Southwest, Mexico, and Latin America. Huntington Library, San Marino.

heavily, resulting in rages that terrified Eve. Despite an additional job as chief librarian of the Los Angeles Public Library, their precarious finances—for Lummis could never live within his means—caused more tension, as did the various colorful characters Lummis invited to stay at El Alisal.

Most of all, there was the endless string of women. Lummis's chronic philandering grew more blatant as the years passed, even including his live-in secretaries. He had long rebelled against Victorian sexual prudery, just one manifestation of his bohemian tendencies that his wives apparently tolerated. Nonetheless, his ego and philandering grew with his fame. Eve, who possessed a better grasp of Spanish and Pueblo Indian languages than her husband, was increasingly relegated to the role of a household manager of Lummis's social events, and often treated as such by his friends and lovers.[60]

In 1909, Eve left Lummis, taking the children and retreating to the San Francisco home of Phoebe Hearst. Lummis's divorce from Dorothea had been relatively discreet, but this separation was different. Each spouse promised the other a bruising court battle, with Lummis making wild accusations about Eve, and Eve promising to use Lummis's own journals to document his infidelities. Lummis even threatened to sue Phoebe Hearst for kidnapping his children. By 1912, the lurid charges convinced both parties to settle for a quieter separation, with Eve divorcing Lummis for failure to provide.[61]

The disintegration of Lummis's family coincided with the collapse of his professional life. There would be no more Hearst donations to *Out West*. His increasingly controversial editorializing—to say nothing of his personal life—soured relations with the chamber of commerce. Lummis resigned as editor in November of 1909. He would contribute a few more pieces, but the magazine eventually halted publication. In March of 1910, he resigned his position as city librarian, claiming that he intended to devote more time to writing books. In reality, rumors about his divorce and complaints about his continual absenteeism due to his preoccupation with other matters led to his resignation. His Landmarks Club and Sequoya League were eclipsed by newer organizations and withered without the visibility they had received from *Out West*. For the rest of his life he would never be far from poverty.[62]

In Los Angeles, the city that was outgrowing his regional vision, Lummis turned away from boosterism and toward institution building. He had long urged the creation of a Southwest Museum in the city to showcase historical relics and Indian artifacts—as well as his vision of the "Great Southwest." In 1904 he founded the Southwest Society, a subsidiary of the Archaeological Institute of America. In 1907, the Southwest Society incorporated the Southwest Museum Foundation, and announced a museum fund and a proposed site. The building site, on a high hill, intentionally isolated from the bustle of the city, offered a panoramic view of the Arroyo Seco. Not coincidentally, the site also lay close to El Alisal.[63]

Lummis had initially considered consolidating his efforts with those of a number of Progressive Los Angeles club women—including his former wife Dorothea Moore—who hoped to construct a more conventional municipal museum of European and American art in the city. Lummis, however, had an entirely different sort of museum in mind. In a 1907 article in *Out West*, Lummis adopted a conciliatory tone, but his real opinions shone through:

> The Southwest Museum has no antagonism to any other move-
> ment, or plan, or dream, of art galleries. The city is large enough
> and active enough to maintain as many art galleries as it cares to pay
> for; but in the long run the Great art gallery of the Southwest will
> be part of the Southwest Museum—in a location without rival, up
> to standards not local but international; and in its regulations not
> provincial but eternal.[64]

The Southwest Museum opened to great accolades in 1914, but institutional tensions and personal conflicts soon fractured the new museum. Lummis viewed the institution as a personal possession; the fact that others had paid for it was immaterial. Repeatedly outvoted by the museum board, he resigned in 1915. Nevertheless, the museum continued to provide Lummis with a monthly stipend as "director emeritus." The money, however, reflected not so much a sense of gratitude as a concern over the negative publicity that might result from the discovery that the museum's founder was living in penury at the foot of the home he had secured for it.[65]

The Southwest Museum continued to grow in the decades that followed, accumulating a globally significant collection of Native American art and artifacts, archival collections pertaining to regional history and ethnography, and sponsoring archaeological projects of scholarly significance. Yet as the city surrounding it gradually lost its southwestern identity, becoming a global city rather than a regional one, the museum increasingly seemed like a memorial to an older version of Los Angeles. Local schoolchildren were still taken to it by the busload in fourth grade, when they studied California state history and invariably constructed model Spanish missions out of sugar cubes, but fewer and fewer of them ever went back. The museum, which might have been the crown jewel of Albuquerque or Tucson, as the Heard Museum was in Phoenix, suffered as its community visibility, visitation, and revenue declined. One caustic commentator later referred to it as the "Southwest Mausoleum," where the Southwestern heritage of Los Angeles lay embalmed and forgotten.[66]

———————— ✳ ————————

Long before falling out with "his" museum, or even before he resigned his editorship at *Out West*, Lummis's writings already hinted that he was growing disaffected with the city he had championed for so long. Increasingly urbanized and congested, it seemed ever more remote from the pastoral world he idolized. In the May 1905 issue of *Out West*, Lummis eulogized Señora Doña Ysabel Varela del Valle, matriarch of Rancho Camulos and the del Valle clan. For Lummis, she had been the last of the "California that Was." Here he invoked the independence that he thought had been at the core of rancho life:

> An hacienda of those old days was a kingdom by itself. If all the rest of the world had been suddenly amputated from round about it, life would have gone on unchanged. . . . The little patriarchy was self-centered and self-sufficing. . . . You were not a slave to our modern conveniences. There was no "servant" problem. No bills, no meetings, no wire from your ear to your enemy's mouth, "no nothing" of the multitude of "facilities" which today oppress us.[67]

Lummis was not merely lamenting the passing of a California matriarch. He was connecting to a deep and longstanding longing in American culture, for freedom without restraint. This longing preceded the technologies he bemoaned, and would far outlast his lifetime. It was inextricably connected to the mythology of the frontier and the West in popular culture, and even to the drive to begin a new life by moving elsewhere, whether to Los Angeles in 1910 or Levittown in 1950. The potency of this fantasy of autonomy and independence was not lessened by its being utterly untrue, occluding the actual history of California and the Southwest.

This vision of a hacienda pastoral willfully ignored the elaborate trade patterns that Californio life depended upon, and the vicissitudes of a cattle economy. Lummis's desire to live as a patriarch betrayed his ostensibly progressive attitudes toward women, particularly regional writers such as Mary Austin whose careers he had aided by publishing them in his magazine. More fundamentally, his vision ignored the very "servant problem" Lummis claimed had not existed. The ranchos, like the missions before them, operated on the back of coerced Indian labor. Though Lummis was an activist for Indian welfare, he overlooked past abuses of Indians when committed by the "noble Spaniard," whether the Spaniard (or Mexican) in question was a rancho don or a missionary such as Junipero Serra. He likewise overlooked the sometimes brutal efforts of local political and business leaders to suppress labor unions in contemporary Los Angeles. The leisured life of the ranchos, with its gentility and conspicuous consumption of luxuries, shared fundamental characteristics with the slave plantations of the antebellum South. Though Lummis professed racial views different from those of Charles Nordhoff decades before, their underlying visions for the region were nevertheless similar. The image of modern California as a place of orchards, gardens, gracious homes, and resorts likewise ignored all the labor performed by people of color to maintain the fiction of an Anglo-American world of leisure.

In the years that followed, Lummis, who had once been a nationally known figure, increasingly faded from the public stage. Age, health problems, and constant financial worries took their toll. In the autumn of 1927, Lummis visited his doctor and was diagnosed with advanced brain cancer. Instead of fostering despair, the terminal illness energized him. He rushed to gather a final collection of poems, *A Bronco Pegasus*, and one last book of essays on the legacy of Spanish America, *Flowers of our Lost Romance*.

If Lummis reflected on the achievements and failures of his life, he may have known that *Flowers of our Lost Romance* bore a personal title, for the book relived *his* lost romance. For Southern California, the romance was not so much lost as forgotten, a pastoral dream discarded on the region's way to a vast urban future that transcended even the wildest predictions of its boosters. On 28 November 1928, Charles Fletcher Lummis died at the age of sixty-eight. He was buried in Pueblo fashion, carried out of El Alisal on the redwood burial board he had selected himself, wrapped in his favorite Indian blanket. His ashes were interred with those of his son Amado in a vault in the wall of his home.[68]

Don Carlos was gone, and some would argue that his dream of an Anglo-America that embraced the nature and cultures of the Southwest had died with him. The cult of the Southwest, however, drawing newer acolytes such as Mabel Dodge Luhan and Georgia O'Keefe, simply decamped for

Taos and Santa Fe. There writer Mary Austin, author of *The Land of Little Rain* (1903) and the most gifted literary talent Lummis's magazine had sponsored, would inaugurate a new Southwest salon.[69]

Still, Lummis's legacy was not entirely erased. Southern California would indeed develop its own distinctive regional culture. Aspects of that culture—outdoor living, casual dress, an obsession with physical fitness—echoed Lummis's florid example. Local resorts, many of which already affected a Spanish or Mediterranean atmosphere, would also increasingly offer more active and athletic forms of recreation, connected to the landscapes or seascapes they occupied. While Los Angeles outgrew the regionalism of Lummis's "Great Southwest," the city and region wholly embraced the leisure that lay at the heart of the appeal of his regional formulation.[70]

The boosting of Los Angeles and Southern California would, of course, continue long after Lummis faded. By the 1910s, however, Los Angeles boosterism was aided by an entirely new form of media and community—Hollywood. The motion-picture industry precipitated another boom and wrought changes in the city that Lummis proved unprepared for. He could have seen film as a medium through which to share his view of regional history and cultures with a larger audience than his books or magazines could ever reach. Film, however, was a fundamentally collaborative medium, something the highly individualistic Lummis could never tolerate. Filmmakers also had little use for Lummis's insistence upon historical "accuracy." When he agreed to serve as an historical advisor for a film version of *Ramona*, he was infuriated when his suggestions were ignored, claiming that "Movie People are on average the most conscienceless pirates I have ever met."[71]

The irony of this was that whatever else film taught the masses, it inculcated within them two fundamental lessons Lummis had tried to impart. Seeking backdrops for the action, films showcased the mountains, coasts, and deserts of Southern California, as well as the streetscapes of Los Angeles, lined with palm and orange trees and filled with pleasant bungalows. Motion pictures told the world—as no single booster ever could—that Southern California might be a wonderful place for recreation—or for residence. Early film studio productions, often society melodramas, were replete with depictions of the rich and glamorous. They showed filmgoers a way of living—a world of material wealth and, above all, a world of leisure. Celebrities, whether acting in films or appearing in later newsreels frolicking at Catalina, Palm Springs, or other area resorts, served as models of, and ambassadors for, leisure.

The fact that the nation's growing middle class accepted and emulated this life of consumerism and leisure would have profound implications for Southern California and the nation as a whole. By the 1910s and 1920s, the hordes of tourists and residents crowding the beaches of Los Angeles, taking steamers to Catalina Island, or driving into the mountains or the Mojave to picnic or hike attested to profound cultural and socioeconomic shifts in the region and the nation since the heyday of the exclusive, somnolent resort hotel culture that had dominated the region a generation before. Lummis may not have convinced white Americans to adopt the customs of Californios or Pueblo Indians, but his contribution to the promotion of Southern California as the frontier of leisure proved an immense success.[72]

When Lummis died at El Alisal, workers in nearby downtown Los Angeles were constructing a new city hall. The building, though structurally a modern skyscraper, also reflected the influence of Mediterranean architecture in Southern California. On its walls were mottoes intended to inculcate good citizenship in city residents, and good behavior in the officials they elected. On the topmost floor of the tower stood a chamber that offered sweeping views of the city and the mountains and coast beyond, visible through the clear air then still prevalent in Southern California. To the south, in the azure Pacific, visitors could see the rocky promontories of Santa Catalina Island. To the east, they could see the western slopes of Mount San Jacinto, which towered above Palm Springs. In this room, which provided a panoramic overview of the greater Los Angeles resort region, there were words, paraphrased from Aristotle, emblazoned along the ceiling in gold: "The city came into being to preserve life—it exists for the good life." Intended as a philosophical statement about the role of cities in history, this quotation instead could stand as a motto for Los Angeles, the city that had emerged in the 1870s as a refuge for the ailing, but which by the 1920s drew hundreds of thousands of tourists and home seekers, and sold leisure to the world. Selling leisure, however, proved far simpler than controlling it in the city it had helped create.[73]

Chapter Two

THE CITY OF LEISURE

The Contested History of Public Recreation
in Los Angeles

T HE GROWTH of Los Angeles was inextricably connected to its promotion as a place of recreation. During the late nineteenth century, L.A. and Southern California pioneered the use of tourism as a strategy to foment regional development, a model other cities and regions would later emulate. Regional promotion aided the growth of resorts and the city itself. Tourist leisure served an important economic function, but as tourists became resident recreationalists, leisure took on profound social and cultural meaning.

The city's new civic monuments reflected this mindset. In addition to the city hall completed in 1931, offering views of the recreational areas of the city and region and mottoes extolling the good life, there were also the history murals by Albert Herter in Bertram Goodhue's Los Angeles Public Library, completed in 1926. On one wall, a "rancho fandango," apparently borrowed from the Ramona Pageant or a Santa Fe Railroad pamphlet, depicted señoritas, whiter than the palest Castilian, dancing languidly while California Mission Indians, garbed in Plains headdresses and Navajo blankets, lounged picturesquely. On another wall was a depiction of Juan Cabrillo's California expedition of 1542. His jaunty galleon was shown sailing into the Bay of Moons, instantly recognizable to hundreds of thousands of tourists as Avalon Bay, gateway to the resort of Santa Catalina Island. Recreation was ingrained into the public life and civic identity of Los Angeles.

In this multiethnic and multiracial borderlands city, Charles Fletcher Lummis and other boosters promoted recreation relentlessly, but as something available only to middle-class and rich Anglo-Americans. In this cultural and social formulation, all the other residents of the city and region were perceived as merely laborers in a land of leisure. This racial and socioeconomic division of leisure and labor would have profound consequences for the city, Southern California, and the suburban places across the nation that would emulate Southern California after 1945. While the first chapter of this book focused on the promotion, idealization, and allure of leisure in Southern California, this chapter instead explores its far more complicated reality. It examines the history of public leisure in Los Angeles as this regional culture developed and Los Angeles was transformed from a regional community to a national metropolis— the era between the late nineteenth century and the mid-twentieth century, when Los Angeles and Southern California became national models for urban development.

While subsequent chapters will explore leisure at the resorts of Santa Catalina and Palm Springs, Los Angeles offers a crucial opportunity to examine public leisure in an urban setting and the leisure of resident recreationalists alongside that of tourists. Forms of recreation in cities and at resorts are usually considered separately, as distinctly different forms of recreation. Yet underlying issues of race and class, power and privilege, connected leisure in these different places. Examining them together permits a deeper understanding of the place of leisure in Los Angeles and in modern America. It also helps explain how leisure came to be so explicitly—and so problematically—linked with whiteness.

In resorts, leisure was often contained within a private realm. In Los Angeles, leisure often occupied public space. In a city notorious for privileging private over public, recreation was one of the few things Angelenos did publicly and collectively. Leisure created a public space, sometimes shared, and sometimes contested. Here issues of race, class, and gender were never far from the surface, and sometimes provoked social conflict. Poor and nonwhite Angelenos demanded access to leisure and recreational spaces, and in the process would create a distinctive and often overlooked chapter in the history of U.S. civil rights. At resorts local residents sometimes clashed with owners and developers over the use of public space, or efforts to control various kinds of labor or leisure. The same dynamic proved true on a much larger scale in Los Angeles. Promoters such as Charles Lummis could project their imagined frontier of leisure on Southern California, but the society evolving there was far too diverse and complex to reduce to such a simplistic stereotype. Many members of that society, particularly the growing African American population of the city, would fight back against efforts to restrict access to leisure and create recreational spaces of their own. Anglos, in short, were not the only people imagining a distinct future for Southern California, and their own place within it.

Playing at Home: The Bungalow as House, Symbol, and Myth in Los Angeles

The late nineteenth century and the Progressive Era of the early twentieth century witnessed a variety of efforts in many cities to create recreational amenities and to alleviate the crowding and pollution of cities with parks and open space. It might seem likely that a city promoted as the playground of the world and as a pastoral retreat from eastern urban woes would likewise preserve open space and create urban parks. Instead, L.A. set aside less parkland than any other major U.S. city. Yet it created one of the nation's first municipal playground departments, made outdoor recreation and nature appreciation part of the city's school curriculum, and purchased beaches and mountain camps to ensure public access. In contrast to its reputation as a morass of unplanned sprawl, Los Angeles actually inaugurated one of the first citywide zoning systems in the nation, even if its enforcement was sometimes lax. Yet city leaders ignored the fact that accelerating growth would greatly diminish the pastoral beauty of surrounding countryside and restrict urban access to nature. Critics of Los Angels have ascribed this to simple greed. The profit motive was certainly not inconsequential in Los Angeles, but it does not solely explain the city's course of development. Instead, one must understand how the recreational promotion of Los Angeles, and the idealization of the single family home, hindered, rather than helped, the development of recreational space in the city.

In the nineteenth century, recreational policy in American cities was primarily an issue of the acquisition and development of parkland. Green spaces offered a chance to enjoy the aesthetic contemplation of bucolic scenery without leaving the city. In the United States, this conceptualization of parks as places of repose motivated the development of parks as part of the City Beautiful movement in the late nineteenth century. This era witnessed the creation of parks, parkways, and green spaces in a variety of cities, such as Boston and Chicago. Many of these borrowed from the design of the nation's premier urban oasis, the naturalistic Central Park in Manhattan.[1]

The architects of Central Park, Frederick Law Olmsted and Calbert Vaux, hoped that their park plan, unveiled in 1857, would serve as the basis for a democratic meeting place for all the residents of New York. Olmsted had been a supporter of abolition who envisioned Central Park as a democratic commons where all the diverse residents of the city could gather.

In Olmsted's conceptualization, parks were a civil right, essential for the functioning of cities and the nation. This vision was not achieved in the nineteenth century, as the park instead became a place primarily for the affluent to see and be seen.[2]

As cities in the American West grew, they gradually developed park systems similar to those of eastern cities. Some, such as San Francisco, were heavily influenced by the City Beautiful movement. Yet western cities differed in important ways from those of the East. They often grew far more rapidly than older eastern cities, had less-established elites and a smaller philanthropic class, and, most importantly, often possessed a far more racially diverse population. Some western cities also initiated a new form of "park," envisioning a new relationship between nature and urbanism. Rather than purchasing tracts within a preexisting urban area, they instead secured scenic land removed from the cities themselves. Politicians and promoters realized that residents and tourists might be as enamored of surrounding scenery as of green spaces in cities, particularly as the automobile made surrounding areas accessible as recreational hinterlands. One example was Denver, which began buying tracts of land in the Rocky Mountains in the 1910s, creating a system of "Denver Mountain Parks." In San Diego the development of an urban park system was accompanied by the purchase of vast tracts of desert and mountain landscapes in the 1920s and 1930s. These ultimately became Anza-Borrego Desert State Park.[3]

Los Angeles did not adopt a City Beautiful plan, nor did it buy undeveloped landscapes for recreational purposes. Rapid growth, facilitated by cheap land, a balmy climate, and a massive regional publicity campaign, was one reason why the city did not plan more extensively for parkland. A local political culture that unfailingly catered to the wishes of developers, allowing profits to take precedence over the public good, was another. Yet these were not the only reasons why Los Angeles lagged in park development. Local promoters and outside observers alike asserted that Los Angeles was a new sort of city, unlike those of the East or even other western cities. Some of them believed that this new city would not need an extensive park system, for it had transcended the traditional urban ills that made parks necessary. Los Angeles seemed to offer a radically new relationship between city and country. Instead of bringing nature into the city in the form of parks or playgrounds, in L.A., and in the sprawling, suburbanized U.S. cities that developed along similar lines after World War II, the solution was to take the city itself out into the country—to provide private backyards instead of public parks.

Beyond climate and land, Los Angeles and Southern California sold a lifestyle—one that proved irresistible in a nation of growing affluence and longevity. This was to be a place where retirees—an entirely new demographic class—could enjoy an old age of leisure, rather than labor on some marginal farm. Middle class families, rather than living in rural isolation or in cramped city quarters, could instead have a bungalow, complete with a garden and citrus and palm trees. The protosuburban, semifictionalized lifestyle Los Angeles sold to the nation would prove irresistible. Los Angeles was, according to historian Robert Fishman, the first truly suburban metropolis, in which the suburbs became the city and suburban life was made available to a much greater portion of the city's residents. Spiraling growth would make this suburban metropolis increasingly gridlocked and unmanageable, but in the early twentieth century it must have seemed to many Anglos that Los Angeles *was* a truly new kind of city, a suburban utopia of homes, pastoral landscapes, and endless recreation. This vision, however flawed, haunts the city still.[4]

The bungalow was the perfect residential architecture for this Anglo-American imagined region. The bungalow originated with the *baṅgalo*, a typical peasant hut in seventeenth-century India. It was adapted by the British, who found it an acceptable residence for the warm Indian climate, offering ventilation and overhanging rooflines that offered protection from the elements. The British constructed similar structures in other tropical regions of their empire, from Africa to Australia. Over time, however, the bungalow emerged as a form of inexpensive housing ideal for beachfront resort towns and vacation homes. It was in this incarnation, as a house offering leisure and a return to the "simple life," that the bungalow proved most appealing to Americans, a place of shelter and remove, where life could turn inward and focus on the individual family, rather than a broader community or city at large.[5]

In the United States this housing form served as the apotheosis of a new, middle-class suburban ideal—a home separated from other residences, intended for a single family, with its own plot of land for lawn and garden. The bungalow, however, did not begin as housing for the masses. The Arts and Crafts movement, originating in Britain and popularized by William Morris (1834–96), argued for a return to the "simple life," with houses built for living rather than show, and filled with handmade furniture and crafts. "Simple," however, did not equal inexpensive, as all the labor required to produce all those handmade furniture pieces and architectural elements did not come cheap.

The American proponent of a more democratic Arts and Crafts residential architecture was Gustav Stickley (1848–1942). Stickley's magazine, the *Craftsman*, which began publication in 1901, contained innumerable illustrations of furniture, houses, and house plans, all intended to offer a simple, refined mode of living, where furniture and home merged into a *gesamtkunstwerk*, a "total work of art." Similar motives drove Frank Lloyd Wright to develop his Prairie School style in the same era, and his innovative designs owe something to the bungalow. Unlike Morris, and unlike most of Wright's houses, Stickley made his designs more affordable by incorporating machine manufacturing methods. Bungalows as built—as opposed to how there were idealized—were also vessels for revolutionary new residential technologies—plumbing and electricity. The exterior might recall a pastoral past, but the tiled bathrooms and kitchen stoves and refrigerators promised the latest in consumer technological comfort.[6]

Though a national architectural phenomenon, the bungalow achieved its greatest popularity in California and on the West Coast. It became the archetypal home for middle-class white families, bourgeois communities united by Protestant and largely conservative social values. Yet while timber frame and shingle houses might seem sensible in Seattle or Portland, with vast forests and lumber industries nearby, they were not the most logical housing type for a city built in a semiarid region with limited timber. Bungalows were, however, inexpensive to build, and therefore appealing to homebuilders and homebuyers alike. The balmy climate of the region also made the bungalow advantageous.[7]

The fact that new housing tracts, cities, and the region as a whole were hyped by a massive promotional effort certainly helped as well. In boosterist rhetoric and imagery, Los Angeles and the rest of southern California was presented as an Arcadian ideal, a pastoral escape from the urban, industrial East. The bungalow, with its connotations of leisure and openness to the outdoors, was the perfect residential architecture for this Anglo-American imagined region. Indeed, the garden was an integral element of the bungalow ideal, and residents exploited the floral possibilities of Southern California's climate with exotic flowers and trees. The backyard became another social and leisure space for the house, relegating the living room to a retreat for times of inclement weather. These houses, with their casual, outdoorsy informality, proved immensely popular with new arrivals from the East and Midwest, who happily abandoned frigid winters and humid summers. Not for nothing is one neighborhood in Pasadena known as Bungalow Heaven. This desire for houses that suited local climate and landscape and facilitated a leisure-oriented family life indoors and out would outlive the bungalow, and appear in subsequent architectural styles, most notably Spanish revival and the postwar ranch house, as well as a smaller but architecturally significant number of modernist residences.

By the 1910s, historicist styles that echoed or elaborated on Mexican and Spanish architecture led to increased construction of homes in mission or Spanish-revival style. Bungalow construction nevertheless continued, and a stucco exterior and red-tile roof granted even a bungalow a gloss of "Spanish" style. For that matter, Charles Lummis's home, El Alisal, was a mixture of Arts and Crafts and mission revival architectural elements. Spanish-revival verandas,

patios, and courtyards also continued to facilitate outdoor leisure and socializing, just as the backyards of bungalow homes did. Spanish revival marked
tourist locales as well. Just as tourists had flocked to rancho homes associated
with the fictional Ramona in the late nineteenth century, by early twentieth
century they came to see the spectacular Panama California Exposition in San
Diego, constructed in a particularly florid version of Spanish revival. They
could also take a drive on "El Camino Real," a modern highway that retraced
a route connecting the state's Spanish Missions. The mythology of missions
and ranchos propagated by Lummis, Helen Hunt Jackson, and others had been
made manifest as architectural and urban fact, and as daily lived experience for
residents and tourists alike. Its appeal would endure as well.[8]

More affluent agriculturalists could relocate to a Southern California citrus plantation and live in haciendas more grand than anything the Californios
could have imagined. Romanticized by imagery on countless citrus crate labels,

FIGURE 2.1 Harry Vroman and friends on the front porch of his bungalow on
Ezra Street in Los Angeles, c. 1915. A photographer, Vroman documented the
growing city. Residents paid for pictures of their new bungalow homes which could
be made into postcards and mailed to friends and relatives elsewhere—a tourist
pastime turned into a residential activity. Vroman's bungalow, like many others,
was surrounded with a lawn and lush plantings that survived only with water
increasingly imported from elsewhere. Such houses, which offered access to the
outdoors and recreation, proved a potent symbol of the life Southern California
could offer. Braun Library, Autry National Center, Los Angeles.

such plantations permitted owners to enjoy all of life's luxuries—including inexpensive labor provided by Mexican immigrants and Mexican Americans, Native Americans, and Asian Americans and Asian immigrants. Dispersed communities were connected by Henry Huntington's Pacific Electric interurban train system, which allowed the development of a sprawling, suburbanized landscape, neither city nor country, which seemed to combine the best qualities of both. Trains also provided access to beaches, resorts, and other attractions in the growing communities within Los Angeles County.[9] Surrounded by recreational amenities, Los Angeles seemed not to need to plan for parks or public space. It was instead the southwestern pastoral that would serve as the antidote to industrialization, "un-American" immigration, and all the other urban woes of the East.[10]

If homeownership was central to the Southern California good life and presented as something available to all, it was also perceived as the guarantor of the continuation of the conservative politics and anti-union sentiments of Southern California business and political elites. Sprawling development allowed homes to "spread out over the land," and the result was that "every resident, no matter how humble, could, if he so desired, have his own little house, surrounded by a lawn and garden and trees," and every citizen also had the right "to play part of the time."[11] This purportedly made ordinary residents upstanding citizens, not members of a restive underclass or potential union agitators. Instead, homeownership made them booster capitalists: "Everybody in Los Angeles had a lot or a house to sell at a profit" and this "produced an interesting psychological effect in the city; even the workers were boomers and boosters." The result was "contented and efficient labor."[12]

Abundant recreational amenities, from beaches to national forests and parks, provided inexpensive recreation, and as a result, a family in Southern California "learned to play and had more real fun than was its share elsewhere." Recreation at home and tourist recreation away were merged into a continuous way of life. Local residents were "undoubtedly the greatest apostles of life in the sunshine and the breezes, under the stars, among the trees, on the sands of sea or the desert." Once their houses are built in some bucolic and scenic spot, "the owners spend much of their time on the road, seeing how their neighbors live, or seeking the solitude of open country."[13]

The advent of the automobile only accelerated residential access to recreation and suburban growth. Residents of Los Angeles founded the Automobile Club of Southern California in 1900, and by 1910 had the highest per capita rate of car ownership in the world. Automobiles allowed development to sprawl ever further outward, beyond the reach of Huntington's trains. It also allowed residents to escape the city, venturing up into the mountains or out into the desert for recreation. The car, like the bungalow, was an essential part of the projected Los Angeles lifestyle. Harry Carr, a journalist and author, asserted that autos were ubiquitous and essential to living the

Southern California good life: "Nearly every family in Los Angeles spends a large part of its time out-of-doors—and outside the city. It is unusual for any family on a pay-roll not to have a motor car." Even his maid and gardener, he claimed, both had their own cars, and he asserted that used cars could be had inexpensively if owners were willing to tinker to keep them running.[14]

Many Angelenos, of course, did not have picturesque homes or automobiles. Many renters could not afford to buy their own homes, or were barred from doing so by racial housing covenants. Many more would be discouraged or actively banned from recreational areas because of their race or ethnicity. The myths wrapped up in the idealization of homeownership and a leisurely lifestyle fused the nineteenth-century southwestern frontier of leisure imagined by Lummis and others with the ruthlessly segregated twentieth-century city of Los Angeles. Tourist leisure became a way of life, but so did the segregation of leisured and laboring, white and nonwhite. Working-class white neighborhoods certainly could not access the same levels of leisure as affluent neighborhoods. Yet, through homeowners associations, the collusion of realtors, and the actions of local police, they could definitely still achieve the same degree of monochromatic whiteness. That same effort would attempt to claim recreation spaces in the city and metropolitan region for whiteness as well. It would also lead to conflicts on a smaller scale over power and public space in resorts such as Santa Catalina and Palm Springs, and in future sunbelt suburbs. In Los Angeles, recreation became synonymous with whiteness, and by the middle of the twentieth century, American suburbia would as well.[15]

Planning a City and Planning Play in L.A.

In thrall to its own myths of suburban perfection, the white political class of Los Angeles only haltingly accumulated a system of urban parks, most coming in the form of donations, or created from preexisting city properties. The first public space in Los Angeles was the Plaza, created when the pueblo was founded in 1781. Subsequent to the annexation of California and the rest of northern Mexico into the new Southwest of the United States, the Plaza was officially designated a city park in 1856. Several other city parks, either in whole or in part, were also created from unsold communal pueblo lands. These included Pershing Square, Westlake (later MacArthur) Park, and Elysian Park, which was created from several hundred acres of hilly terrain north of downtown. This tract, which the city had been unable to sell, constituted the bulk of Los Angeles parkland until the mid-1890s.

The Charter of 1889, created to help the city cope with rapid growth, included provisions for a park commission. This commission, like those of eastern cities, conceptualized parks as places of genteel recreation for more affluent residents and tourists. As such, it largely concerned itself with plantings, pathways, and concession operations, such as rowboats at Westlake Park. By the 1910s and 1920s, it also made arrangements for motion-picture companies to use city parks for filming, and operated a series of municipal auto camps for tourists.[16]

Aside from remaining pueblo lands, most early parks came through donation. These included Echo Park, donated in 1891, and Lafayette Park, given in 1899. By far the most significant donation came in 1896, when local magnate Griffith J. Griffith gave the land for Griffith Park to the city in perpetuity. Griffith called the 3,500-acre park his "Christmas gift" to the City of the Angels. While the donation of the largest urban park in the United States might have seemed a boon, the response of local political leaders was underwhelming. The park languished for years, suffering from illegal squatters and timber harvesters. Film production companies appropriated parkland for sets and film shoots. Griffith was bitterly disappointed by the city's reaction to his gift.[17]

City leaders had ample reason for their lack of enthusiasm. The park initially lay outside the city limits and away from streetcar lines, a tract of scrubby hillside near a city still surrounded by large expanses of undeveloped land. Griffith himself, moreover, was hardly a paragon of philanthropic decorum. Already a controversial figure when he presented his gift to the city, Griffith shot his wife in a drunken rage in 1903, convinced that she intended to use his fortune to fund Catholic conspiracies for global domination. Griffith's wife lived, but the city continued to disdain the park until his death in 1919. At that point it finally accepted the $700,000 Griffith had set aside for the park's improvement. Most of this money was used for the construction of the Greek Theater and Griffith Observatory.[18]

Though Los Angeles city leaders neglected parkland acquisition, others advocated an expanded Los Angeles parks system. An early example was Charles Fletcher Lummis. In *Land of Sunshine, Out West,* and other publications, he criticized the city's sale of remaining pueblo land, which could have been utilized for parks and civic monuments. Instead, the city had "impoverished its future," and sold the land for a pittance: "We would have the finest parks in the world, and the finest public buildings—and all endowed beyond the dreams of avarice. As it is, nothing was left the city but the Plaza and some riverbed when we began to take notice."[19]

Local governments, institutions, and individuals did, however, produce reports, surveys, and studies that amply demonstrated the general paucity of parkland in the region, and the limited recreational opportunities for many of its residents. Perhaps the most comprehensive—and certainly the most elegant—of these was the 1930 study by the Olmstead-Bartholomew firm, "Parks, Playgrounds and Beaches for the Los Angeles Region." Its authors called for the creation of vast urban parks, parkways, beach recreation areas, scenic drives, and a variety of other amenities which, if enacted, would have created a very different city and region from the one that actually came to be. Yet this plan did not propose the construction of some fanciful arcadia. It planned for a vast urban area, complete with a large network of traffic arteries that foreshadowed later freeways. The report gave primary consideration to lower-income residents, who, as the authors pointed out, made up a majority of the city's population, and had less leisure time and available recreational space than the more affluent.

The Olmstead-Bartholomew report skillfully merged the aesthetic concerns of the City Beautiful movement with the social concerns of the playground movement. It also portended the increasing attention paid to environmental concerns by city planners, as well as the large scale of urban planning in the twentieth century. Nevertheless, fears about taxes, the cost of implementation, and worries about the Depression prevented the plan's adoption. The report was shelved without even being released to the public.[20]

The Los Angeles County park system developed much later, and more slowly, than the city system. In fact, its initial development shared more with the preservation of open spaces pursued by some other western cities than it did the history of urban parks in the East. The first county "parks" were not parks at all, but wilderness camps. The first, Big Pines Park, a mountain camp leased from the U.S. Forest Service, opened to the public in 1922. Another camp, Crystal Lake, followed. In 1929 the County Commission created the Department of Recreation Camps and Playgrounds. In July of 1929, two public beaches managed by the county were also placed under the new department's jurisdiction. Still, the county park system remained small. Only seventeen areas were designated as parks between 1922 and 1939.

Local governments more clearly foresaw the need to preserve public beach access. Besides being favorite destinations for locals, beaches were one of the most important tourist attractions in the county, and therefore an important part of the region's economy. Unlike parks, playgrounds, or community recreation centers, which were usually under the sole authority of either the city or county, public beaches were administered in a variety of ways. Some were operated by the beachfront cities, including Long Beach, Los Angeles, and Santa Monica. Others were operated by the county. Later, beaches would also be acquired by the state of California to be operated by the state parks system. Since beaches were used by residents across the region as well as tourists, municipalities and the county gradually set up a system that spread the cost of purchasing and maintaining beach properties among local governments. For example, Los Angeles County paid Santa Monica and other beach cities to help defray the cost of lifeguards at municipal beaches, which were frequented by many nonresidents.[21]

✳

In contrast to their lax attitudes toward the development of parks, city leaders carefully planned the growth of their metropolis in many other respects. While critics of Los Angeles have condemned it as the epitome of unplanned sprawl, it was in fact often intricately planned. The city was placed under a comprehensive zoning ordinance in 1908, one of the first in the nation; New York City would not pass a similar ordinance for another eight years. Even though enforcement of the 1908 ordinance, and others that followed, proved sporadic, they delineated the city into different areas. Industry was separated from recreation, and whites from nonwhites. The Westside was classified as "higher class" residential only, with some allowances for commercial establishments. A linear swath of south Los Angeles, adjacent to the Los Angeles River, was classified as industrial. "Residential only," in reality, meant white only, and even "ethnic" whites, such as Jews, were sometimes unwelcome. In areas such as Bel Air, high land prices effectively prevented nonwhites from buying property, since so few could afford to do so. In middle-class and working-class white neighborhoods, meanwhile, realtors and white homeowners' associations maintained this color line.[22]

In the same era that Los Angeles was subjected to a rigorous planning regimen, the city pursued a new avenue in recreational policy. In 1904 the city was one of the first in the nation to create a Department of Playgrounds and Recreation—a landmark in the national playground movement. The playground movement asserted that parks could serve as places of physical recreation and interaction rather than just settings for aesthetic contemplation. This new movement, part of larger Progressive Era efforts to improve American life, did not completely abandon the elitist attitudes of earlier park proponents. The masses would now be encouraged to visit parks, but parks—and especially new playgrounds—were strictly controlled to ensure that everyone enjoyed recreation "properly." Far from just offering a place for play or relaxation, parks were charged with an essential mission; they were intended to keep the public physically and mentally active, ensuring their participation as productive members of society. Additional recreation programs, aimed not only at children but adult workers, were designed to teach immigrants to socialize with the larger population. The goal, through proper instruction, was to "Americanize" immigrants by teaching them to play, dress, work, and live as middle-class whites did. At the same time, however, playgrounds allowed children from very different backgrounds to play together, and permitted a remarkable degree of multiethnic and multiracial interaction among children in the city, "Americanizing" them in ways recreational planners and parents might never have intended.[23]

This agenda also influenced the public school curriculum in Los Angeles. Students were taken on field trips to the La Brea Tar Pits, and on hikes to collect insects in the foothills and marine life in tidal pools. In the classroom they were taught about conservation, and about hunting that was "proper," rather than wasteful. The goal of this instruction was to help each student "better know himself as part of nature." Exposure to the outdoors was also intended

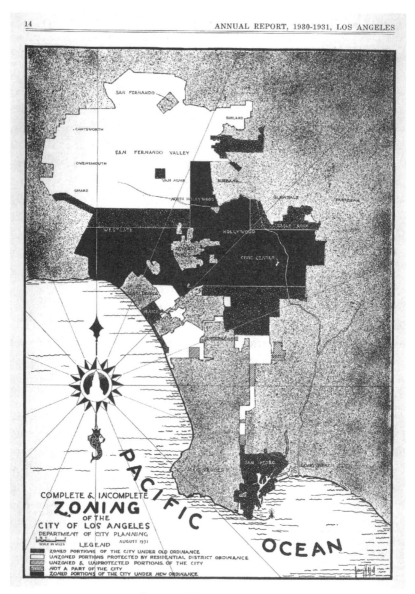

FIGURE 2.2 Zoning Map of Los Angeles, 1931. This map reflects the expansion of zoning that occurred as the city continued to grow after 1908. "Annual Report, Board of City Planning Commissioners, July 1930—July 1931," 14. Archival Research Center, Doheny Library, University of Southern California.

to promote health. To that end, the city's school system experimented with outdoor "teaching porches," akin to the "sleeping porches" attached to many houses of the era, and provided instruction in physical activity and hygiene.[24]

Like city planners who divided prosperous residential and recreational areas from poorer or industrial ones, and codified racial restrictions in housing, the Playground Department took as its mission the separation of spaces for safe, productive play, removed from the dangers of urban life. For the employees of the new department, children's play was serious business. On a series of annual reports, the Playground Department emblazoned the motto "The test of whether a civilization will live or die is the way it spends its leisure."[25]

The Playground Department asserted that "from all sections of Los Angeles come clamors for local playgrounds, grounds within walking distance." Instead of paying for reform schools, the department urged taxpayers to fund playgrounds, for "a well-supervised playground will direct the

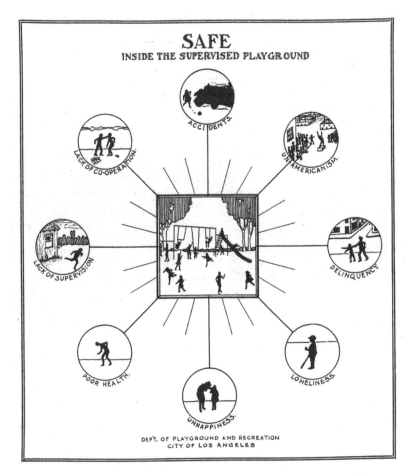

FIGURE 2.3 The Los Angeles city playground as a haven from society's dangers, 1930. Los Angeles Department of Parks and Recreation, "Annual Report of the Department of Playground and Recreation, City of Los Angeles, 1930," 33. Special Collections, Young Research Library, University of California, Los Angeles.

misused energy of dozens of boys into channels more distinctly helpful to themselves and to the community." The language was revealing; though the city eventually added programs for girls, most playground activities, like subsequent recreation programs at parks and pools, were intended for men and boys rather than women and girls.[26]

The societal function that playgrounds could purportedly serve was illustrated in a drawing printed in a 1930 Playground Department annual report, entitled "The Playground—A Haven of Protection form Childhood's Dangers." Within a square border was a depiction of a safe playground. Outside the playground was a series of circles, each containing a scene of peril. These included lack of cooperation, lack of supervision, poor health, unhappiness, loneliness, delinquency, accidents, and "un-Americanism," which was depicted by an image of a crowd listening to a man talking on a soapbox in the street.[27]

The Segregation of Recreational Space in the City and County of Los Angeles

California did not enshrine Jim Crow laws in its constitution, as did states in the South. Nevertheless, racism could sometimes be as pervasive in greater Los Angeles as in cities in the South. A complex web of laws regulating housing, land ownership, labor, and marriage targeted people of color, and immigration laws added another layer of coercion to the lives of Mexican and Asian Americans. Los Angeles, however, differed from southern cities, and indeed from almost all eastern cities, because of its diversity. In the East, racial issues were almost always portrayed as a matter of black versus white, and systematized white racism in L.A., when manifested in recreational space, was most consistently targeted at African Americans. With the aid of national organizations such as the NAACP, African Americans combated the restriction of recreational space in a more systematic way than other nonwhites. Yet in Los Angeles, whites and blacks were only two groups within a racial and ethnic mix that included Mexicans, Japanese, Chinese, and Filipinos, as well as California Indians and Native Americans from other regions. Boosters might try to sell Los Angeles and Southern California as a balmy version of the Midwest, but even they could not entirely ignore its remarkable diversity.[28]

The ordinances that governed Los Angeles city parks, playgrounds, and other recreational areas in the first decades of the 20th century made no reference to race. Indeed, it appears that parks and pools were initially integrated, though that did not necessarily mean that they were always welcoming to nonwhites. The first publication of the Playground Department, an "annual report" from shortly after the founding of the department, depicts black and white children playing together. Later reports would occasionally show children who appear to be Mexican American, but black children would virtually disappear from Playground Department reports for decades. The reasons for this remain not entirely clear, but it seems likely that whites in Los Angeles were influenced by both national and local trends that were manifested in recreational policy.[29]

In the 1910s and 1920s, a series of events profoundly affected race relations in the United States; these included memorials commemorating the fiftieth anniversary of the Civil War, the nationalism roused by World War I, the popularity of filmmaker D. W. Griffith's *Birth of a Nation*, the national resurgence of the Ku Klux Klan, and the election of Woodrow Wilson, the first southern president since Reconstruction. Systemic segregation spread out of the South and appeared in various forms in other parts of the county.

The 1910s and 1920s witnessed the beginnings of a great out-migration from the American South. While "Okies" are associated with the Dust Bowl of the 1930s, significant numbers of poor whites from the South, the southern Great Plains, and Texas began migrating to California and Los Angeles by the early 1920s, bringing their racial views with them. By 1924, the editors of the *California Eagle,* the first African American newspaper in the city, fretted that "part of Texas seemed to have been transplanted in and near Los Angeles." Simultaneously, large numbers of African Americans began the "Great Migration" out of the South in search of employment in the North, and to a lesser degree the West. Though still small compared to the African American population of major eastern cities, Los Angeles's black community expanded. The African American population of the city grew from 15,579 in 1920 to 38,894 in 1930, and would grow to 63,774 by 1940, the largest black population of any city in the West outside of Texas.

Among these new residents were a significant number of incipient middle-class African Americans, who were drawn to the region for many of the same reasons as middle-class whites. Despite restrictions, they could buy homes and cars, vote, and live lives that seemed filled with opportunity, especially compared to the prospects of poor blacks in the Jim Crow South. Further, they were not subject to the harsh immigration laws that affected Mexican and Asian immigrants, or restrictions on "alien" land ownership. These African American migrants, therefore, possessed the resources to enjoy life and leisure in Southern California, and the fact that they could lay a claim to the recreation and recreational space that stood at the core of the city's civic life and identity made them seem more of a threat to white dominance than poorer migrants or immigrants.[30]

Blacks also posed a problematic "theme" element for white boosters. Asians and Mexicans could be passed off as quaint relics of regional history and culture. Thus tourists flocked to Chinatown, to the Spanish-revival market at Olvera Street, and to resorts themed in Spanish or Mexican style. They also bought houses designed in Spanish-revival style, though that made them no more sensitive to the Mexican Californians surrounding them. African Americans, however, did not fit into this convenient booster formula. They were not reminders of the romantic past. They were instead reminders of contemporary national racial tensions—something Los Angeles had purportedly transcended. Thus, the disappearance of blacks from printed representations of Los Angeles parks and playgrounds reflected a national trend, but likely also represented a changing white population and local white anxieties concerning the appearance of a growing African American presence by the 1920s.[31]

Swimming along the Divide: Segregating Pools and Beaches in Los Angeles

In Los Angeles, segregation and recreation collided in the issue of swimming at public pools and beaches. Until the 1920s, swimming in most public pools in the United States had been strictly divided by gender. Now, however, men and women began swimming together in large numbers for the first time. For segregationists, public bathing was a potentially explosive issue, mixing issues of race, gender, and the body in disturbing ways. For them, the prospect of males and females of different races swimming together in revealing swimming attire was unacceptable. Even among bathers of the same sex, the sharing of public locker rooms and showers forced a degree of physical intimacy that a significant number of whites found troubling. In 1920, the Playground Commission set aside Vignes Pool as the "Negro pool." The commission scheduled hearings on "the racial question," but then cancelled them. By 1923, all city pools were segregated. In 1927, a group of African Americans asked that the Los Angeles city council appoint an African American to the City Parks Commission, no doubt hoping to end racist policies. Their request was denied. When the NAACP became involved, Los Angeles built Central Pool exclusively for blacks, hoping to preclude court action.[32]

The city and the NAACP were engaged in a strange legal dance, in which each side's desire to win was tempered by the prospect of its opponent's victory. Stakes were high. If Los Angeles lost, it would have to repeal the laws that white citizens had demanded enacted, and, in a fundamental way, lose control of recreational space. For the NAACP, a ruling in favor of the city could mean the spread of Jim Crow nationwide.

Swimming-pool segregation limited nonwhite access to one of the most popular forms of recreation in the city. One survey found swimming to be the single most popular mode of recreation for men under the age of forty-five and women under the age of thirty-five. Neither backyard pools nor air conditioning would be common among middle-class residences until the 1950s and 1960s. Pools, like the array of weekend, afternoon, and evening recreational programs offered by city and county parks, drew legions of residents in the decades before television competed for the attention of Americans in their free time. As a result, public pools were crowded oases during the heat of summer, and were popular for much of the rest of the year.[33]

The swimming pools at Exposition Park, adjacent to both white and black neighborhoods, served as a focal point for African American efforts to combat segregation. In 1926, a Mrs. King filed suit against the city because she and her child were not allowed to swim at Exposition Park. Her husband, however, was a veteran of World War I, and the city, in a surge of postwar patriotism, had proclaimed that all veterans were granted the right to swim in all city pools at any hour they were open to the public. Confronted by a conundrum of its own making, the city eventually allowed the Kings to use the pool.[34]

In 1931 the city faced another challenge to its pool policy. Ethel Prioleau, an African American mother of two children, sued the Los Angeles Board of Playground and Recreation Commissioners, likely after receiving encouragement from the NAACP. Her children were barred from swimming in the public pools at Exposition Park even though they lived in the neighborhood and their property was assessed local taxes to pay for park improvements. The city contended that Prioleau's children were required to swim at either Central Pool, which was black-only, or Evergreen Pool, which was black-only on Mondays. Neither of these pools were as near Prioleau's residence as those at Exposition Park.

The Los Angeles County Superior Court sided with Prioleau. The court ruled that the city code did not give the Playground Department the power to make regulations based on race. If the city wished to segregate, the California state constitution would have to be rewritten to reflect the "separate but equal" language found in state constitutions in the South. The Playground Department countered that the ruling undercut its power to regulate its own facilities, and that the race issue was a secondary concern. The department repeatedly asked the city council to appeal the ruling. Nevertheless, after a debate and an eight-to-six vote, the council decided not to appeal. Officially, all city pools were integrated from this point forward. If "custom" or hostility expressed by individual whites or mobilized homeowners' groups still kept some pools white-only, that was not the official policy of city recreation facilities.[35]

The segregation of swimming pools was not just an issue in Los Angeles. Pasadena's Brookside Plunge, a public pool in the canyon of the Arroyo Seco, near the Rose Bowl, opened 4 July 1914. It was available to people of color only in the afternoon and evening on Wednesdays. When a group of African Americans challenged this rule, the city of Pasadena classified the pool as white only. This continued until 1929, when it was opened to nonwhite swimmers on Tuesdays, between two and five in the afternoon. At the close of each euphemistically named "International Day," the pool was drained and cleaned to be ready for six days of white bathers. The NAACP challenged this policy and won a court case in 1942. Rather than comply, the city simply closed the pool. The NAACP responded with a court injunction, and Pasadena grudgingly reopened the pool as a desegregated facility on 4 July 1947.[36]

Yet pools were just one place where people of different races might swim together. A far larger area of contention was the seventy-five-mile coastline of Los Angeles County. This expanse of sand and surf was the premier recreational amenity for the entire region—an unofficial "park" that served as public and recreational space. Indeed, the image of the beach became a central component of the projected Southern California good life, and would continue to serve that function throughout the century, from 1965's *Beach Blanket Bingo* and other youth-oriented films to television's *Baywatch* in the 1990s.[37]

During the 1920s, the Department of Playground and Recreation estimated that on a summer weekend or holiday half a million people converged at local beaches—a number representing a quarter or more of the total population of Los Angeles County at the time. Beaches were also a primary tourist destination. Various cities in Los Angeles County had already taken steps to police beaches and maintain sanitation. By the 1920s, the city and county of Los Angeles began purchasing and managing beaches to ensure public access, and urging voters to support more beachfront purchases. Political leaders, however, also had another agenda. White politicians feared that private ownership could mean nonwhite ownership, and this was a possibility they could not countenance for the region's most important recreational and tourist asset.[38]

The money for such purchases, as well as for the maintenance of public beaches, initially came from taxpayers in individual beach municipalities. Yet the realization that beaches were a regional resource led to new methods of assessment that spread the cost of the public beach system more equitably. Ultimately, all taxpayers in Los Angeles County paid for the beaches they enjoyed through either municipal or county taxes, and sometimes both. Yet at least one group of taxpayers was prohibited from the recreational resource they helped pay for. African Americans were banned from almost all beaches in Los Angeles County. Worse yet, they were forced to pay taxes to buy up even more beach land that would expressly prohibit them.[39]

This segregation appears to have happened at most beaches relatively early, whether through explicit ordinance or by "custom." Blacks who arrived at local beaches did not necessarily need to see signs or encounter police to know to leave. As was the case with white homeowners, white beachgoers did not hesitate to confront African Americans—and others—who dared to enter a "public" beach. For example, on one occasion in the 1920s, three black men went fishing at Redondo Beach pier. A white man approached them and handed one of the men a pamphlet, "Ideals of the Ku Klux Klan." On it he had scrawled, "Colored folks beach three miles north." Such confrontations could turn violent. When Arthur Valentine arrived at Santa Monica Beach on Memorial Day in 1920, he was accosted by local police. When he refused to leave, he was brutally beaten and then shot. Valentine survived and took the police to court. His case was dismissed, but remains significant as possibly the first court case involving police brutality in California legal history.[40]

At one time, the *only* beach in Los Angeles County that African Americans could visit was Bruce's Beach. George Peck, the developer of Manhattan Beach, set aside two blocks along the waterfront for use by nonwhites when the city was incorporated in 1912. A black couple, Charles and Willa Bruce, bought the first two lots and began development of the resort known as Bruce's Beach. Peck assisted them in developing the beach area. Yet as the region's African American population grew and the resort drew more and more black recreationalists, local whites became increasingly hostile. Members of the Ku Klux Klan tried to terrorize the Bruces by making threatening phone calls and attempting to set their house on fire. Blacks arriving for a day at the beach could face harassment, vandalism to their cars, and bogus signs proclaiming a ten-minute parking limit in the area. In spite of this, the resort endured.

In 1924 exasperated city officials, who lacked Peck's enlightened views, condemned the beach, claiming that it had been selected as the site of a park. The Bruces and others sued. While the court ruled that they were guaranteed the right to buy other land in Manhattan Beach with the compensation they received for eviction, they were not allowed to buy beachfront property. Nevertheless, African Americans continued to frequent the beach, despite "no trespassing" signs posted by city officials. In 1927, after the arrest of several beachgoers, the NAACP forced the city to remove the no-trespassing signs when city officials admitted that the signs were aimed only at African Americans. Soon thereafter, however, the city tore down all the structures on the beach. The Bruces took their financial settlement and left the city, and their former beachfront development remained vacant for decades.[41]

Another African American beach, called the "Inkwell," was located in Santa Monica. It lay at the terminus of Pico Boulevard—the site of a sewer outlet—and ran only the width of the street. The beach became a black beach in 1924, probably in response to the impending closure of Bruce's Beach. Unlike Bruce's, the Inkwell remained in operation for years as the only major beach area left open to African Americans. Even so, blacks who went to this beach could still face harassment from local whites and police, and the city of Santa Monica shut down clubs that catered to blacks within walking distance of the Inkwell.[42]

As with swimming pools, African Americans fought back against the restriction of beaches. The NAACP even organized a "swim in." As with the public pools, this resulted in the abandonment of an explicit policy of segregation at beaches in the city of Los Angeles during the early 1930s. Just as the official integration of public pools did not necessarily make integration a reality, the end of segregation on city beaches by law did not mean the end of segregation of beaches in fact. For that matter, some other communities still maintained official segregation.

In the 1940s, Mexican American high school students reported that some "public" beaches remained closed to them. Some such beaches may have been kept all-white by aggressive local police or homeowners' associations. Others apparently tolerated Asian, Mexican, and African American visitors—but only as long as their attire and haircuts were "clean-cut" and their numbers remained small. Venice Beach, for example, had an African American lifeguard as early as the 1930s, and was one of the most racially tolerant beaches. Lifeguards at Cabrillo Beach were predominantly Mexican American, and beachgoers there often were as well. A discrimination complaint made decades later by employees at a county-operated public beach in Manhattan Beach in 1967 stated that white and black beach employees were segregated, with whites working on the northern portion of the beach and blacks at the southern end. Though an investigation by the county determined that this segregation did indeed exist, it concluded that the segregation was not "deliberate." Whatever the county may have determined, the presence of employee segregation strongly suggests that de facto public-beach segregation continued through the 1960s in some areas. The decline of mass transit, particularly of the Red Car lines that once brought thousands to the beach, also made beaches less accessible to the poor and people of color. For that matter, some affluent homeowners in coastal communities such as Malibu would continue to prohibit all beach visitation, even though all beaches in California had become public under state law.[43]

This "informal" segregation suggests the type of discrimination that was likely most common at city and county pools, parks, and playgrounds. While county or city policies might not have explicitly banned nonwhites,

FIGURE 2.4 "Group of Young People at the Beach." ca. 1925. Shades of L.A. Archives, Los Angeles Public Library. Though the city and county of Los Angeles actively discouraged African Americans from bathing at local beaches, and segregation was widespread at beaches and public pools in the 1920s and 1930s, black Angelenos did in fact frequent the few beaches that welcomed them, as this group of young people enjoying a day at the beach illustrates.

local police, homeowners' groups, and average citizens could take on the role of self-appointed enforcers of white sentiment. This continued well after the U.S. Supreme Court struck down racially restrictive housing covenants in decisions in 1948 and 1953. It seems highly unlikely that the LAPD, whether in the 1920s or the 1950s, would actively discourage these white arbiters of racial space. For that matter, an African American family—or any non-Anglos—who arrived at a park, playground, or other recreational area and received a chilly reception would likely leave before law enforcement arrived.

From Covert Picnics to the "Black Palm Springs": Nonwhite Recreation in Los Angeles

While African Americans and other people of color fought back against white attempts to control recreational space, they also created their own places of leisure. Despite pollution and the dangers of sudden floods, Mexican children swam in the Los Angeles River and other watercourses. Another favorite swimming spot was an abandoned water-filled quarry called Sleepy Lagoon. This swimming hole became popular as a place where young Mexican Americans could enjoy swimming and socializing without the hostility they might encounter at Anglo-dominated public swimming pools. It is now best-remembered for its association with the Sleepy Lagoon trial of 1942, in which seventeen Mexican American youths were convicted of the murder of another youth at Sleepy Lagoon in 1942. The convictions were later overturned, but the trial remains a landmark in the history of Anglo-American fears about "Mexican" violent crime. Mexican American families also picnicked in local cemeteries, combining a practice common in some eastern and European cities with their own cultural traditions, such as the Day of the Dead. On some occasions, Mexican Americans turned a picnic into a thinly-veiled statement about the paucity of parkland and recreational space in their neighborhoods; they would drive or take streetcars to west Los Angeles and hold makeshift picnics in the front yard of some Westside estate. Sometimes this was sanctioned by the residents, who knew the picnickers through employment as maids, nannies, or gardeners. On other occasions it was not sanctioned, but such unauthorized picnics sometimes, surprisingly, went undisturbed by Anglo residents.

The recreational habits of Asian Americans varied widely by generation. Conservative views brought from the homeland about the mingling of men and women, or the public visibility of married women and unmarried daughters, limited the recreational activity of some Asian Americans. Many younger, American-born Japanese and Chinese Americans, however, frequented beaches and parks as regularly as Anglos did. Individuals of all races participated in the team-sports leagues organized by the Department of Playground and Recreation, from basketball to baseball and soccer. These teams were often organized by race and ethnicity. They therefore functioned as a form of socialization within individual racial and ethnic groups, but could also facilitate socialization between different groups when they met on the court or playing field.[44]

Perhaps the single most remarkable example of a place of recreation and leisure created as an escape from white-dominated social space was a resort created by African Americans. Though little-remembered later, Val Verde was known for decades as the "Black Palm Springs." The resort was founded in 1924, perhaps in response to the closure of Bruce's Beach. A group of black community leaders, including Charlotta Bass, editor of the *California Eagle,* real-estate agent Sidney P. Dones, Norman O. Huston, founder of Golden State Life Insurance, and community leader Hattie S. Baldwin, agreed to work toward the creation of a resort where African Americans could experience "outdoor sports and social life in the most beautiful surroundings without discrimination."[45]

The group first tried to purchase property in Palos Verdes, but Los Angeles County condemned the land to prevent black infiltration of this locale, which was being developed as an exclusive white residential area. Laura Janes, a white woman who supported the project, served as the official buyer of a thirty-acre tract in San Martinez Canyon, near the later city of Santa Clarita. It also lay near the old del Valle Rancho Camulos, which had entranced Charles Lummis and attracted earlier tourists as the "birthplace" of Ramona. The founders initially called their resort "Eureka." The resort grew in popularity, ultimately drawing thousands of visitors on weekends and holidays who stayed for the day or rented accommodations in hotels and cabins. Middle-class and affluent African Americans, including Hollywood actors, built vacation homes. As many as 750 families lived at the resort much of the year. During the 1930s outsiders also helped the community. White businessman Harry Waterman donated fifty-three acres for a park, and Los Angeles County used WPA workers to build a pool and bathhouse.[46]

In its heyday, Val Verde served as a communal getaway for African Americans in the Los Angeles region. The African American–aimed *Los Angeles Sentinel* announced the beginning of its summer season, with updates on available activities and news of celebrities vacationing there. Church picnics, pageants, performances by famous musicians, sports, and socializing fostered a cohesive sense of community among African Americans from a range of socioeconomic backgrounds and different parts of Southern California.

The resort endured into the 1960s. Efforts to join the Los Angeles County water system engendered hostility among white ranchers and residents of the nearby community of Santa Clarita, who feared the potential growth of a substantial black population center. At least one house was burned down. Yet the true death blow for Val Verde came from racial progress. The integration of recreational areas, hotels, and resorts undercut the purpose of the African American resort. The small community endured, but had transcended its original purpose.[47]

Making Recreational Space White: Fiscal Discrimination and Physical Transformation from the Plaza to Pershing Square

The segregation of recreational areas, or the outright banning from them of some groups, is certainly the most obvious instance of racial bias in the development of the Los Angeles city and county park and recreation systems. Yet more subtle forms of discrimination were far more pervasive, and just as damaging. The funding—or more accurately the lack of funding—for recreational spaces and amenities in nonwhite areas of the city and county functioned as a pernicious form of fiscal discrimination. If fiscal discrimination was not enough, the city could pursue more radical policies as well.

Since neighborhood parks and playgrounds in the city were normally funded by neighborhood assessment, affluent neighborhoods could more easily pay for parks—as well as contribute more to the city's tax revenues. Other neighborhoods were less lucky. One of the worst off was Watts. Since almost all other neighborhoods had restrictive racial housing covenants, Watts was one of the few places black migrants could find housing. As the population in Watts expanded, the scarcity of parkland grew increasingly dire. Yet Watts residents found little support at City Hall. In 1937, when local residents asked that the city council acquire more land for parks and playgrounds, as well as construct another public swimming pool, their request was forwarded to the Playground and Recreation Commission. The commission replied that it already operated two playgrounds in the area at cost of $7,455. If a pool were added at the 109th Street Playground, the cost would run about $10,000 annually. Yet the Playground and Recreation Department tax of six cents per $100 of assessed valuation yielded the department a total of $2,164 per year from Watts. The Playground and Recreation Department asserted that if the pool were built, it would cost $110,000 for land and improvements. The cost of maintaining the existing playgrounds and a new park would be approximately $20,000, "or a sum nearly ten times as great as the amount contributed for the support of the department by the district known as Watts."[48] A swimming pool was ultimately constructed at the 109th Street Playground, but only after the Works Progress Administration paid $40,000 of the

$61,000 total cost, which was significantly lower than the amount that the Play-ground and Recreation Department originally claimed.[49]

Watts residents continued to petition the city council for improved park facil-ities, but they were largely ignored. Yet even the records of the Department of Playground and Recreation indicate that park and playground facilities in Watts were minimal. Many city parks operated concessions, such as food and bever-age stands, and charged fees for equipment rental, reserving a playing field, and reserving a recreation-center auditorium for a meeting. Private concessionaires operating in city parks also had to pay licensing fees. All such concession fees nor-mally went toward the operation of the park, pool, or playground at which they were located. In some parks, income from concessions became an important sup-plement to other funding sources. Large concession revenues also indicated that a park or recreational facility had a variety of amenities that drew people to use it. In 1936, prior to the construction of the new pool, the Department of Playground and Recreation's annual financial report listed Watts Playground as one of only two in the entire city with no concessions income. In 1937 it was the only one. The only park to share this dubious distinction in subsequent years would appear a decade later in the Sawtelle neighborhood—an area that became home to many Japanese American families returning from World War II internment camps. The fact that Sawtelle Park would suffer the same lack of concessions income in the late 1940s can hardly be coincidental. This fiscal discrimination, the unwilling-ness of a white-controlled government to expend funds for nonwhite parks and recreation, was accompanied by the consistent devaluing of nonwhite desires and concerns in the area of parks policy. It would resurface again in 1978, when white homeowners voted for Proposition 13, which gutted recreational funding for less affluent—and often nonwhite—Californians.[50]

Perhaps the most striking examples of the privileging of the concerns of the white, affluent, and "respectable" over those of anyone else were the entwined fates of the Los Angeles Plaza and Pershing Square. City officials first remade the Los Angeles Plaza, then shifted funding to a new park, Per-shing Square, and ultimately remade Pershing Square into a less pleasant but more policeable form. The Plaza, created in the heart of the city when it was founded in 1781, originally served as the city's focal public space. Moreover, until the late nineteenth century it continued to function as a Spanish and Mexican plaza, a multiuse public space for markets, religious observances, festivals, and political events. During the 1880s the new Anglo-dominated city government remade the Plaza into an ornamental park—a place liter-ally restricted by a new fence and plantings to claim it as Anglo recreational space.[51]

By 1900, however, remaking the Plaza, which was located in a Mexican and Mexican American neighborhood, was no longer enough. By then gov-ernment attention—and money—had shifted westward to a square called the

FIGURE 2.5 Pershing Square, before: A view of shade trees and foliage in the park during the 1930s. The landmark Biltmore Hotel overlooks the park to the right. Historic Photograph Collection, Richard J. Riordan Central Library. Los Angeles.

"South Plaza," or "Central Park," which lay in the heart of the new down-town, surrounded by office buildings and hotels. This park was subsequently renamed Pershing Square, after General John Joseph "Black Jack" Pershing, who, perhaps not coincidentally, had led the U.S. "punitive expedition" into Mexico to try to capture Pancho Villa during the Mexican Revolution of the 1910s. The Plaza was retained as a part of the historicist makeover of Olvera Street, as the city attempted to transform what had been a center of the city's Mexican American community into a shopping and tourist attraction. Pershing Square's fountain and lush landscaping made it a favorite lunchtime gathering place for white-collar workers.

As downtown declined, however, Pershing Square also lost its luster. The park became a focus of LAPD surveillance owing to its popularity as a place for drug dealing, for activists to make speeches and stage protests, and as a covert meeting place for gay men. The city passed ordinances banning alcohol and vagrants, and ultimately gouged out the park in the 1950s, leaving only a sparse garnish of greenery atop a subterranean parking structure. The parking was intended for white professionals, and the removal of trees and foliage made it easier to police the park. It also made Pershing Square

FIGURE 2.6 Pershing Square, after: A view of the park in the late 1950s, shortly after completion of the underground parking structure. Historic Photograph Collection, Richard J. Riordan Central Library. Los Angeles.

a far less pleasant place to linger. The Department of Recreation and Parks described the new park design as a "see-through, walk-through park."[52]

———————※———————

Though Los Angeles would experience significant changes in the decades to come, particularly in the visibility and public power of its nonwhite citizens, the sad fate of Pershing Square is perhaps a fitting coda to the story of public recreational space in Los Angeles. World War II brought transformative changes to the city. The city's industrial base expanded as wartime munitions and aircraft factories opened. Wartime Los Angeles witnessed a huge influx of industrial workers and military personnel. The city had to accommodate these new arrivals as well as plan for the future. Yet World War II did not simply increase the population of the Los Angeles region—it also accelerated the area's growing diversity and demographic changes in various neighborhoods. The number of black Angelenos, for example, jumped from 64,000 in 1940 to more than 171,000 in 1950.

Diverse Boyle Heights, located east of downtown, had been the center of the city's Jewish population. After the war, however, Jews moved in large numbers to the Westside, where new synagogues and Jewish

Community Centers offered opportunities for recreation and a sense of community in a formerly Protestant bastion, and as religious restrictions on housing faded. Boyle Heights, meanwhile, was gradually transformed into a predominantly Mexican American neighborhood. These demographic changes affected recreational policy, and some political leaders saw recreation as a means for the city to successfully navigate its complex transformation.[53]

Change, however, did not come without conflict. The Zoot Suit Riots of 1943 and the Sleepy Lagoon murder trial were only the most infamous examples. Prescient politicians and urban planners worried that these violent events portended a dire future for civic life in Los Angeles. Some political leaders began to see parks as a way to ameliorate racial conflicts. An example of this new concern was the Echo Park Study of 1950, undertaken after four youths in the neighborhood were convicted of murder. The study concluded that owing to a concentration of poverty, displacement caused by freeway construction, and the assimilation pressures facing Mexican American youth, the neighborhood would see more violence. The report urged the creation of more recreational areas in the neighborhood, and ended on a foreboding note: "Though the Echo Park Area has attracted attention because of past events, there are other similar districts in the Los Angeles metropolitan area which, though dormant, are potential tension spots... These areas should be studied before rather than after the tension has exploded and assumed violent forms."[54]

By the 1940s and 1950s, the governments of the city and especially the county included racial progressives who worked to improve conditions for nonwhites and saw access to recreation and recreational amenities as crucial to this effort. With the election of County Supervisors John Anson Ford and later Kenneth Hahn, nonwhite neighborhoods gained two powerful advocates for recreational development. Ford represented East Los Angeles and assorted eastern suburbs from 1934 to 1958; Hahn, who was elected to the board of supervisors in 1952, represented south Los Angeles and the industrial suburbs adjacent to it. Both advocated park construction in their districts. Previously, the county had largely limited its parks-related efforts to beach acquisition and other regional park needs. Ford and Hahn both secured county funds for local parks and community centers. The sheer number of new facilities in the 1950s and 1960s, particularly in Hahn's district, and the huge attendance at new public swimming pools in the area, demonstrated how great the need was, and how it had been needed for so long.[55]

These much-appreciated improvements, however, were too little and too late. Park acquisition simply could not keep up with population growth and the spread of residential and commercial development across the landscape. Moreover, most of the new parks were placed in suburban neighborhoods, rather than in the crowded nonwhite areas of the city and county that needed them most. By this point, actually fulfilling all the recreational needs of the city and county of Los Angeles was probably unattainable. The only hope was to try to keep pace and prevent shortages from becoming more severe.

Besides, for African American Angelenos, the lack of recreational space was just one of a growing number of problems. In the early twentieth century, Los Angeles had seemed to them a place of wondrous possibility. Such was no longer the case by 1950. As Jews, Italians, and incipiently middle-class Mexican families moved to new suburban housing developments, blacks, who had once lived in diverse communities, quite unlike eastern cities, now found themselves trapped in increasingly monolithic black slums that would have been all too familiar to the residents of Atlanta or Detroit. Blacks had long competed for low-wage jobs with Mexican Angelenos. The postwar economy, increasingly linked to Cold War aerospace and other industries, offered employment to highly trained and educated workers—but few prospects to black workers with restricted access to education. African Americans would continue to gain political clout in Los Angeles—culminating in the election of Tom Bradley, the city's first black mayor. More would also become middle class, but when they did, many moved away to better schools and housing in suburbs, from nearby Pasadena to the distant Antelope Valley. The socioeconomic decline of black L.A. was well underway.[56]

In Los Angeles, public recreation had consistently lost out to private recreation, and an idealization of family recreation centered on the home and yard rather than recreation in public spaces. Indeed, for the rest of the century, Los Angeles would remain profoundly shaped by the visions of its nineteenth-century boosters, who promoted Southern California as a pastoral frontier of leisure for middle-class Anglo-Americans. They conceived of Los Angeles as the city of leisure, a place designed for recreation. Throughout the twentieth century, public recreation did provide a crucial, if contested, public space for Angelenos. Parks, pools, and beaches, no matter how restricted by racism or neglected by developers' greed or politicians' indifference, were public spaces where residents of the city met, sometimes quarreled, and sometimes mingled. Recreation would remain inextricably connected with how outsiders viewed Los Angeles, and how residents perceived it. Yet this vision of carefree leisure could not accommodate massive population growth, nor did it provide for all those who were excluded or lacked the resources to enjoy recreation intended for white middle-class homeowners with automobiles. It also linked leisure with racial and class privilege.

It was this very vision that would guide recreational policy and urban planning in much of the postwar suburban Sunbelt, designed around the automobile and the family home. Los Angeles, originally an escape from urban America, would instead become an urban model that reshaped the twentieth-century American landscape. In much of American suburbia, parks and recreational space would be scarce indeed, and suburbanization meant that funding for inner-city parks and recreation would decline as well. If, as writer and urban historian Lewis Mumford observed, suburbs represented a contradiction—the collective effort to live a private life—then those suburbs would inherit the contradictions of Los Angeles. Los Angeles had indeed been designed as a city of leisure. It had not, however, been designed as a city for all.

Public leisure in Southern California proved problematic, both for the Anglos who attempted to restrict it, and for the African Americans, Mexican Americans, and others who demanded access to it. Yet another form of leisure, wholly private, was also taking shape elsewhere in Southern California. To examine this new form of leisure, one that proved highly influential in the region, as well as far beyond it, one must leave the city and venture forth into the larger resort region beyond it, where various resort areas served as recreational suburbs for the larger suburban metropolis. Tracing the evolution of this tourist leisure in resort communities across time from the late nineteenth century to the late twentieth requires exploring an island and also an oasis of leisure—Santa Catalina and Palm Springs.

Chapter Three

THE ISLAND OF LEISURE

Tourism and the Transformation of Santa Catalina Island, 1887–1919

O FF THE coast of Southern California rises a rocky archipelago called the Channel Islands. All are semiarid, some with rugged mountains rising two thousand feet above the Pacific. In marked contrast to the mainland, the Channel Islands are largely undeveloped, with most controlled by the National Park Service or the U.S. military. Only one of the largest islands, Santa Catalina, possesses a permanent population. More than twenty miles long, Catalina consists of two large areas of land connected by a narrow isthmus, with a coastline composed of numerous small coves and bays, most with sheer mountain walls rising abruptly from the ocean's surface. The interior is rough mountain and canyon terrain, with seasonal streams and few permanent sources of water. Lying twenty-six miles southwest of the port of Los Angeles, Catalina is privately owned, promoted since the late nineteenth century as a tourist attraction and resort.[1]

Charles Lummis and other boosters hailed Southern California as the playground of the world, a place where Americans would finally learn to embrace leisure. As the first of a series of booms began in the 1880s, Los Angeles and Southern California witnessed an influx not just of visiting tourists, but of new residents. These new inhabitants may have lived in a place sold as the playground of the world, but they too still wanted an occasional vacation. Where once there had only been a few exclusive hotels for eastern tourists, now the coastal communities of Los Angeles County saw the spread of beach boardwalks, inexpensive hotels and boarding houses, and every conceivable type of amusement. Instead of a single Coney Island, greater

Los Angeles witnessed the creation of multiple beachfront recreational areas, from Santa Monica to Long Beach. Connected to Los Angeles and other communities by train or trolley, beaches and the new beachfront attractions drew large numbers of local day-trippers and visiting tourists, and, as the previous chapter examines, also precipitated racial and ethnic conflict.

Santa Catalina Island evolved as a different sort of oceanfront resort. Isolation and inaccessibility would turn out to be its greatest asset. Though it would become a national tourist destination, Catalina initially evolved as the first resort in Southern California to cater to Southern Californians. While most eastern tourists came to the region in winter, Catalina's tourist season was in summer. Its primary clientele was the new middle and upper economic classes of the region, people who wished to venture further than the beach, away from the masses, and had the money and time to achieve this objective. In this era, Catalina essentially functioned as a summertime recreational suburb for the mainland. The exclusive nature of Catalina ensured that the tensions of race and class, so evident in the booster literature of this era, also manifested themselves in the society of leisure created at Catalina. Legal and political conflicts between island owners and island residents would also occur. Catalina also produced distinctive gender roles and relations for vacationers and workers, and among vacationers themselves. The gender roles and relationships among the leisured revealed that Catalina evidenced broader cultural shifts, reflecting the Gilded Age mores prevalent when its development began, yet also serving as a premonitory example of gender roles in mid-twentieth-century suburbia.

Island proprietors, most notably the Banning family, which owned Catalina from 1892 to 1919, improved transportation and accommodations to bring more visitors and increase the volume of ship passenger fees that were their primary source of island revenue. In this regard, Catalina provides a case study of the broader development of tourist locales in the American West. As at Yosemite, Yellowstone, or the Grand Canyon, developers harnessed capital and transportation technologies to create a tourist economy. Yet at Catalina, the Bannings and their Santa Catalina Island Company created the first corporate resort in the West, and arguably in the nation. In their efforts to restrict access to the "right" tourists and to "theme" Catalina—to make it conform to tourist preconceptions of Southern California, the Southwest, or the Mediterranean—the Bannings created a model that would be followed later at ski resorts, and even at Disneyland.

The island's history also shares similarities with eastern resorts and recreational areas, from Newport and Cape May to Saratoga and the Adirondacks, places developed earlier in the nineteenth century. The major seaside resorts of France and Britain, such as Nice and other resorts of the Côte d'Azur, Brighton, and Bournemouth, evolved in the same era. All of these resorts, whether in Europe or the eastern United States, evolved to cater to existing urban populations in New York, Philadelphia, and other cities. Yet unlike those eastern resorts, as Catalina grew in popularity, it did more than attract vacationers from nearby urban areas; it also attracted potential residents. In this sense, Catalina increasingly functioned as part of a larger resort region centered on the most successful tourist attraction in American history—Los Angeles.[2]

The saga of boosterism and development that played out on a regional scale also appeared at Catalina, which encapsulated better than any other single place the booster mythology of Southern California. Here the imagined leisure of the boosters was transformed into material fact—a complete and enclosed world. As on the mainland, Catalina promoters advertised a salubrious climate and a romanticized image of local history, cultures, and landscapes. Even more than on the mainland, however, Catalina's boosters focused upon the island's environment—its landscapes, seascapes, and abundant marine life. Foremost among these boosters was scientist and author Charles Frederick Holder, who shared more than a few similarities with Charles Lummis. Like Lummis, Holder saw Southern California as a stage upon which he could act out a highly theatrical, hypermasculine athletic ruggedness. He perceived Catalina as a new sort of resort, one that embraced the possibilities of marine recreation and made it a crucible of Progressive Era marine conservation. Boosters and the Bannings fostered an island atmosphere that, though exclusive, was at once more socially relaxed and more athletically vigorous than most resorts of its age—Catalina might have some similarities with eastern resorts, but it was also recognizably Southern Californian.

All these developments drew tourists, but they also had troubling consequences for the island's small resident population, which coped with wrenching changes as an economy based on fishing and agriculture was supplanted by the tourist industry. The Bannings and other island owners were not immune to larger forces as well; they aspired to run Catalina as their private fiefdom, but sometimes found themselves beset by disgruntled residents, government regulators, economic downturns, and, most trying of all, the fickle tastes of an American public increasingly in search of recreation and leisure. Future owners would face similar challenges. Though Catalina may lay off the coast of Los Angeles, its unique corporate history, its issues of environment, gender, race, and class, and its special role in Southern California's tourist development and booster mythology place it at the heart of the history of American leisure.

Santa Catalina's Early History

The island's early history hardly suggested such a future. Some of its flora and fauna were unique, making it a sort of Southern California Galapagos, home to species evolved from animals stranded when ocean levels rose at the end of the last ice age, severing Catalina from the mainland. The place Europeans would call Santa Catalina was inhabited by humans for millennia before their arrival. Tongva Indians, who also inhabited the mainland, lived in dozens of small settlements located at sheltered bays and inlets on the coast of the island, which they called "Pimug-na" or "Pimu." Residents subsisted on abundant fish and shellfish, and occasionally on seal or sea otter; they gathered acorns and nuts in the island's interior. Canoes, some as much as thirty feet in length, were used for fishing as well as travel to the mainland, where the Catalina Indians traded the soft, easily carved steatite, or soapstone, found in abundance on their island for mainland goods. At the time of contact, what may have been the largest settlement was at a place translated as the "Bay of Seven Moons"—a site occupied centuries later by Catalina's only town, Avalon.[3]

Early contacts with Europeans were brief. Juan Rodriguez Cabrillo landed in 1542, and Francis Drake sailed through the area in 1579. Yet it was the arrival in 1602 of Sebastian Vizcaino that would have more lasting consequences. Vizcaino bestowed upon the island its modern name of Santa Catalina, as he arrived on the feast day of Saint Catherine of Alexandria. He also provided ample reason for island inhabitants to distrust Europeans. Traveling inland with friars and soldiers, Vizcaino came upon a religious shrine composed of a circle of stones around a statue. The Spaniards scratched a cross upon the face of the deity and shot two large ravens—a species held sacred by the islanders. The natives were horrified.

For nearly two centuries after this trauma, islanders remained largely unmolested. By 1800, however, this had changed. The Franciscans considered the construction of a mission on Catalina, but decided that it lacked sufficient fresh water. More ominously, in 1805 and 1806 a measles epidemic swept the Channel Islands and decimated the Indian population. Soon after, Russian and Aleut sailors, hunting sea otters, began preying upon Santa Catalina's animal and human residents. In the 1820s the remaining population of Santa Catalina and the other Channel Islands was forcibly relocated to Mission San Gabriel. Baptismal records show that many islanders, even less resistant to European disease than mainland Indians, died within a year or two of relocation. The few that remained were swept up in the chaos of the secularization of missions—a policy of "liberating" mission Indians and transferring valuable mission labor and land to civilian control. The result was a dispersion of mission neophytes, who often became rancho laborers. The Mission Indians of San Gabriel, later called Gabrieleños, remained, but the native population of Catalina was lost as a distinct cultural group.[4]

The Mexican era in California brought little change to Santa Catalina. Now depopulated, the island sat vacant aside from occasional visiting sailors. It was sometimes also visited by those looking for potential rancho land. One such person was Thomas Robbins, an Anglo-American who had married into Californio society. As early as the 1830s, he began petitioning to gain access to the island, an effort finally rewarded in 1846, when Pío Pico, the last Mexican governor of Alta California, signed a deed granting Santa Catalina to Robbins.

Despite any initial ardor, Robbins kept Catalina for only four years and sold the island for $10,000. In the first decades of American rule, Catalina changed hands repeatedly. Owners leased grazing rights for cattle and sheep operations, and by the mid-1860s there may have been as many as six hundred head of cattle and twenty-two thousand sheep grazing on the island. The consequences for native flora and fauna were severe. Prospectors found gold, silver, and lead in limited quantities in the early 1860s, and a small mineral rush began. Hopeful miners and merchants mapped out a town called Queen City at the island's isthmus, only to see this potential Leadville-by-the-Sea wither when the rush ended.[5]

In January 1864 the United States Army built a small outpost on the isthmus. The outpost was ostensibly meant to defend the coast from Confederate ships; in reality, the army was surveying Catalina as a potential reservation for Indians from the northern half of the state. This no doubt would have antagonized Anglos in the south, already fulminating about the large number of Californios and Indians living in the region. The Department of the Interior vetoed the plan, which was never made public, and the army outpost was abandoned. Officials may have deemed Catalina still economically viable, or found the local Anglo-American population, rife with Confederate sympathizers, too volatile. Or perhaps surveys of the rugged, arid island deemed it too agriculturally marginal—even for Indians.[6]

Indeed, Catalina proved to be of limited economic value. Grazing operations, which initially seemed productive, foundered due to the island's limited and irregular rainfall. Any enterprise, however, ultimately confronted an even more fundamental problem—isolation. Everything had to be shipped to the island, and anything produced at Catalina had to be transported back to the mainland. That transportation cost ate into the profits of any potential enterprise. The same problem limited the small ranching operations started on some of the other Channel Islands. Fishing certainly continued around Catalina and the other islands, though fishermen returned to the mainland with their catch. Ultimately, like some other parts of the American West, Catalina was too remote, and its lands too marginal, to succeed through typical economic means.[7]

George Shatto and the Arrival of Tourism at Catalina

In this isolation lay Catalina's economic destiny. As the population of Los Angeles and Southern California began growing rapidly in the 1880s, isolation suddenly had a value. Catalina had not succeeded as a typical agricultural or commercial center. As an urban getaway and tourist destination, however, its prospects seemed decidedly brighter. In fact, Catalina already drew small numbers of visitors to its shores, though they had to brave occasionally choppy seas and a total absence of tourist facilities. Those who came to the island hiked into the rugged interior, enjoying spectacular vistas from mountaintops, or set up tents and rustic cabins near the ocean.[8] The trustees of the estate of James Lick, who had bought the island in 1864, offered Catalina for sale in 1885. A booklet printed for potential buyers extolled its salubrious climate, fisheries, mineral wealth, and agricultural potential, from citrus orchards to cattle graz-ing. Despite this apparent material wealth and natural fecundity, readers were also assured that few settlers lived on the island, and those who did so remained only due to leases that could be terminated as any future island owner saw fit. Further, any "owner or company would here have an advantage of independent control scarcely to be over estimated; property and laborers being free from the serious annoyances of baneful influences" of the mainland.

Indeed, Catalina was offered not as just another potential property, but as a principality unto itself, which owners could operate as they wished. Though touting various economic opportunities, the Lick estate advertised Catalina first and foremost as a potential travel destination and health refuge:

> Of greatest importance to an owner is the sustainability of this island as a health resort, and the consequent influx of population and set-tlers. A sanitarium located at any of the proper sites, would never cease to attract those desiring out-door life in continual sunshine, and equable temperature with gentle but exhilarating sea breezes, freedom from the vexations of more crowded resorts, and escape from the ravages of consumption, rheumatism and malaria.[9]

The first person to exploit this opportunity was George Shatto, a Michi-gan entrepreneur recently relocated to Los Angeles. In 1887 he and a group of partners purchased the island for $200,000. At the time, the only village was Timm's Landing, which sat alongside the Bay of Moons and consisted of a few cabins and shacks used by fishermen, who were mostly immigrants from Mexico, Japan, and Italy. The only substantial house was a wood-frame home occupied by two sheepherders, one of several structures scattered about the island for this purpose. At one end of the beach was the only business—the "Hardware Store," which sold necessities, including a major source of rev-enue, alcohol.

The following year Shatto constructed the three-story Hotel Metropole in Timm's Landing. Digging for the foundation of the hotel, workmen stumbled upon a vast collection of Indian artifacts—bowls, pipes, beads, and arrow points, many made of the soapstone that had once served as a valuable trading item for Indian inhabitants of Catalina. Before any could be collected for a museum, or at least a tourist exhibit, scavengers took virtually everything. Shatto rechristened the village "Shatto City," and directed the surveyor to leave a space of ten feet between the beach and Crescent Avenue, which ran along it. This strip was not intended for sale. With it, Shatto hoped to control the beachfront, blocking any unauthorized boat landings and attempts to sell liquor to bathers.[10]

Soon, however, his wife's sister-in-law, Etta Whittney, suggested a more alluring name that alluded to the island's climate and the region's purported healthfulness. She recalled the conclusion of Alfred, Lord Tennyson's recently published epic, *Idylls of the King*. As Arthur lies mortally wounded, he tells his grieving knights that he is bound for "the island valley of Avilion: Where falls not hail, or rain, or any snow,/ Nor ever wind blows loudly... [there] I will heal me of my grievous wound." Willingly surrendering posterity to profitability, Shatto gave the town the name it has borne ever since— Avalon—albeit changing Tennyson's spelling.[11]

Initially, Shatto's venture seemed to prosper. On 13 October 1887, he chartered an excursion train from Los Angeles, which proceeded to the harbor, where passengers who had each paid three dollars for passage and a lunch in Avalon boarded the steamer *Los Angeles*. The trip was a grand success, and lots in Avalon went on sale the next day. Prices ranged from $150 for a small house lot to $2,000 for prime commercial locations fronting the beach on Crescent Avenue. In all, perhaps two hundred lots were sold. All lots were dry; if any buyers sold alcohol on their property, the lot reverted to Shatto. Shatto also succeeded in closing down the "Hardware Store" in 1888, though the business continued for a time by simply relocating to a barge in the harbor. By that year the tiny settlement had perhaps twenty-five residents and many more seasonal visitors. Accommodations could be had in the Metropole Hotel's one hundred rooms, and in approximately two-hundred multiperson tents.[12]

The year 1888 also witnessed the opening of Avalon's first souvenir shop, the Avalon Shell Store, located in a tent and run by Englishwoman Jane Elms and her three children, Jimmy, Harry, and Laura. Her husband, Henry Elms, a doctor, owned a drugstore on the mainland. Two years later, at the age of seventeen, Jimmy opened a fish and bait shop in Avalon, partnering with two former fishermen, one Italian, the other Turkish. Harry Elms would later become the community's first postmaster. The family souvenir store sold polished sea shells and other marine curiosities, as well as Indian relics the family found on the island. Alongside the Elms' tent, George Ramsey, Avalon's first African American permanent resident, offered his services as a barber.[13]

Shatto also worked to increase publicity for his island. Naturalist and noted game fisherman Charles Frederick Holder was invited to the island to spend the summer, and "incidentally do some writing, with fishing thrown in." Holder's fish tales drew tourists, as did accounts of swimming, hunting, and other recreational activities. Shatto's publicity effort even included spreading a rumor of sightings of a Catalina "wild man," "clad only in fish skins and rabbit fur," who had purportedly been sighted in the mountainous interior, but who had screamed and fled whenever other humans approached him. No matter how fanciful, each story brought more tourists to the island, and, as Shatto knew, "each new proselyte did some advertising on his own account."[14]

Shatto and his associates also began the island's first newspaper, the *Catalina Jew Fish* [named for a species later called the giant sea bass]. The four-sheet paper, which sold for ten cents, included a fictitious list of "editors," which seemed to include most residents of Avalon. Shatto's paper printed as many names as it could of the people who came to the island, in the knowledge that their mention in some amusing story would probably result in a request for more copies. Though whimsical, the newspaper served its purpose, and was even quoted in a Paris newspaper. The Parisian editor was baffled as to what exactly a "jewfish" might be, but admitted that "California is certainly a great country, and wonders will never cease."[15]

By the summer season of 1889, Catalina had developed its own dress code and ethos. Bathers gathered in front of the newly constructed bathhouse in the mornings. Men and women wore bathing clothes throughout the day, with men sporting "gypsy" bandannas and women using long sleeves and hats festooned with flowers or dried seaweed to ward off the sun. Such attire was hardly risqué, compared to the bathing fashions of later decades, but in the 1880s and 1890s, wearing it all day was considered a surprising departure from strict Victorian mores. While some bathers wore this attire at eastern resorts, the warm, generally less-humid weather at Catalina was more conducive to bathing costume, whether wet or dry. As the author of one guidebook, actually a bit scandalized, observed: "campers...don their bathing suits in their tents, and walk down to the beach in this garb, no matter the distance be two blocks or ten." Wearing such attire all day was shocking indeed. As one writer at the time noted, "The secret of success in Avalon was freedom from restraint."[16]

That summer, the *Catalina Jew Fish* instructed vacationers in the proper way to enjoy Catalina in an article straightforwardly entitled "What to Do and How to Do It": "Avalon is essentially a resting place...the finest place for tired people in the world. You can sleep more, and have more time to do it, than any place in America...Within three hours of Los Angeles, a city of 80,000 inhabitants, you have a succession of cloudless days, a balmy delicious atmosphere—sleep-promoting, soothing to the nerves, a liberal haven of rest." If readers worried that so much sloth might leave them bored, the *Catalina Jew Fish* assured them that Catalina also offered vigorous recreation: "The amusements are boating in smooth water, perfectly safe for ladies and children; fishing, wild goat or cattle hunting, quail shooting, horseback riding over steep trails, trips to the Indian graveyards, to the sea-lion rookery; to the

FIGURE 3.1 Avalon Harbor in the 1890s. The Metropole Hotel is the large wooden structure to the right of the pier. Catalina Island Museum Archives. Avalon, California.

isthmus, the haunts of the abalone, and many more." Nevertheless, rest was presented as the island's most potent lure: "Don't go fishing every day. Take things easy and only go when you want to go very badly. Don't talk religion, politics, or business. Do just as your fancy dictates.... Do just as little as you want to do and you will go back to the mainland a new man, or woman, primed for another year of work."[17]

Tourists might enjoy balmy languor or exciting sport, but either way, the role of Catalina was clear—a temporary escape from the workaday world, from which tourists would return rejuvenated and energized. This attitude reflected a national middle-class conceptualization of leisure as something that ultimately had to be productive, not simply as an end in itself. The idle rich might wallow in sloth, but the aspirant middle class and the newly prosperous would not permit the virtue of occasional leisure to become an addictive vice. In this respect, Catalina reflected the attitudes expressed at many American resorts, where leisure was seen as a necessary respite, but something that posed a danger if enjoyed for too long.[18]

Though similar in many ways to eastern resorts, Catalina was not identical to them. The emphasis on outdoor activities clearly linked the island to Southern California's claim as a place of health and rejuvenation and its embrace of outdoor living. A later brochure would claim that "Santa Catalina is a natural sanitarium, combining all that is best in the Madeira Islands and the famous Riviera, without any of the objectionable features." Yet this was a vigorous sort of sanitarium, and the "strenuous life," soon to be so heavily promoted in the Progressive Era, was already much in evidence at Catalina. In this respect, Catalina presaged both the emerging regional culture of Southern California and the new, increasingly more rugged forms of leisure Americans would embrace in the century to come. It also portended the more relaxed and open vacation culture of the twentieth century, less constricted by social mores.[19]

Whatever its societal or cultural role, Catalina certainly drew tourists. Still, transportation costs from and to the mainland increased Shatto's expenses, and maintaining a fresh water supply proved difficult. By 1891 he was struggling to make mortgage payments. In January 1892 the island reverted to its former owners, the trustees of the James Lick estate. Later that month, three brothers—William, Hancock, and Joseph Banning—bought the island for $280,000. Two years later, they formed the Santa Catalina Island Company (SCIC), a subsidiary of the Banning Company, which controlled a variety of family enterprises. For Catalina, a new era had begun.[20]

The Banning Family and the Creation of a Regional Tourist Destination at Catalina

The father of the three brothers, Phineas Banning, had made a fortune in transportation and shipping, ultimately controlling rail, wagon, and ocean freight lines across California and the West, and becoming in the process one of the wealthiest men in Southern California. Like Harrison Gray Otis and Henry Huntington, Banning would also be remembered as one of the "founders" of modern Los Angeles, though he died in 1884 at age fifty-five as the result of a wagon accident, just before the region's first boom. Nevertheless, he left his young widow and his three sons, all in their twenties at the time of his death, a vast fortune and a shipping empire. They took over operations of those enterprises and applied these resources to the development of Catalina. They certainly intended to use the island for their own recreation, and had frequented the island under Shatto's tenure. The Bannings, however, planned for much more than just their own enjoyment: they could control shipping to the island—the very thing that had stifled all other economic enterprises. In fact, boats owned by the Wilmington Transportation Company, another Banning Company subsidiary, had provided much of the tourist access to

Catalina during Shatto's era. Hancock Banning Jr. remembered that this was key: "Catalina...hardly ever paid for itself. It was the transportation where we made our money." Now, with a fleet of ships owned by the Wilmington Transportation Company, and Shatto's Hotel Metropole, the tourist promotion and development of Catalina could begin in earnest.[21]

During their twenty-seven year tenure, the Banning brothers systematized tourism operations at Catalina. This obviously had local consequences, but there were also broader implications. The SCIC set out to create a resort—just as the Union Pacific Railroad would create Sun Valley, Idaho in the 1930s, or, a generation after that, the Janss Development Company of Los Angeles would remake Sun Valley and also create Snowmass, Colorado. Like the Union Pacific, the Banning Company would also control all access to their resort playground. The Union Pacific would be forced to search in the Rocky Mountains far from any major city to find the perfect secluded spot, where isolation could screen out any undesirables—people not of a certain quality, income, or race. Even though their tourist resort lay only twenty-six miles from Los Angeles, the Bannings could achieve the same ends with the ocean and a monopoly on all passenger ships that crossed it. This power brought with it a prickly relationship with Catalina's growing resident population, a relationship that remained strained for most of the Bannings' tenure.[22]

The demographic characteristics of Avalon and Catalina in the late nineteenth and early twentieth are difficult to ascertain. According to the census of 1920—the first one in which figures for a "Catalina Township" appear, the island's population was fairly stable. It listed 634 residents for 1920, and also included numbers from prior censuses—487 residents for 1900, and 670 for 1910. These figures, however, appear to conflict with the enumeration rolls from each census, as well as with the memory of the enumerators who compiled them. John D. MacLean, the enumerator in 1900, stated that he counted 865 residents. In 1910, he found only 510. The enumerator for 1920, John Windle, stated that his count stood at 1643.[23]

Whatever the figures, successive censuses did not effectively document the characteristics of the community. "Catalina Township" was usually enumerated in the early spring, and this figure would not include seasonal workers who lived on the island in summer, nor some island residents who often spent spring on the mainland procuring goods and supplies for the coming season. It also did not include seasonal homeowners in Avalon, even though some such homeowners stayed on the island for long periods. The summer population of Avalon might have been three thousand summer residents by 1900, and ten thousand summer inhabitants by 1910.[24]

Moreover, these figures did not include all the tourists staying in hotels, cabins, and tents, as well as day-trippers, a figure that could reach well into the thousands. The Bannings' largest steamer, the Cabrillo—just one of the ships ferrying tourists to the island—could carry nearly a thousand people. By 1910, the SCIC claimed that its hotels and vast tent-cabin villages could accommodate as many as ten thousand people overnight. Though Avalon's exact population might be difficult to verify, its most obvious characteristic— extreme seasonal variability—is obvious.[25]

Another notable characteristic of the island's population was its racial and ethnic diversity. Traditional commercial fishing faded as a major component of the local economy, but the diversity it spawned continued. The new tourist-service economy employed many people of color. The most numerous were likely Mexicans and Mexican Americans, hired for basic labor on ships, in hotels, and for construction projects. The restaurant staff of the Metropole Hotel was African American, as were the porters on the SCIC steam ships. The hotel's bellhops were Japanese. Many other people of color found employment at other hotels and restaurants, or as domestic employees in vacation residences. By the 1910s Avalon also possessed a sizeable population of Eastern Europeans, mostly Slovaks, who found employment in a variety of tourist-service-industry jobs. Though "white," they were still viewed as a "foreign" element by many Anglos. Unfortunately, Avalon exhibited some of the same racial discrimination found in much of the United States in this period. A small section of Avalon became known as "Sonoratown." Like similar areas on the mainland, this predominantly Mexican district also housed other people of color who were not welcome in white areas. Some day workers may have also commuted to the island by ferry during the tourist season, spending nights with families on the mainland.[26]

The Banning brothers may have employed many people of color, but this did not mean that "their" island was necessarily welcoming to nonwhites, or to anyone who did not pay for tickets on Banning ships. Their consistent priority was the maintenance of the Banning monopoly over transportation to and from Catalina, their primary source of island revenue. Preserving this monopoly required methods that were rarely genteel. Visitors who arrived by private boat were allowed onshore—as long as they paid a "disembarkation fee." Those who refused and insisted on their right to land–asserting that Avalon was a public community, with a post office and other public facilities— were allowed to occupy only the narrow space between low and high tide at Avalon beach. Anyone who made a run for the town was accosted. Eventually, the Santa Catalina Island Company constructed sea walls and barbed wire fences, and used fire hoses to fend off mainland "illegals" attempting to disembark from "tramp boats." This occasionally resulted in brawls on Avalon's pier, with ticketless visitors shoved back onto their boats or dunked in the harbor. Some such "illegals" were no doubt attempting to shirk the Bannings' transport fares, but some were likely visitors accustomed to an earlier era, when some mainlanders regularly came to the island to fish, hike, or visit friends and relatives in Avalon. At the San Pedro ferry terminal, plain-clothes detectives hired by the Bannings also turned away "undesirables." Efforts to screen passengers were not without precedent; Santa Monica had been incorporated in part to combat crime on its oceanfront, and the *Los Angeles Times* decried robberies and gambling at area beaches.[27] This policy of screening passengers officially commenced after a rash of pickpocketing, but also concealed something more unpleasant—the same segregation preva-lent at so many beaches and swimming pools on the mainland. The Santa Catalina Island Company had no explicitly segregationist policy, but leisure at Catalina remained largely white-only in the Banning era.

Avalon was only a little community, but its battles over access and con-trol reflected on a small scale many of the concerns and conflicts playing out in Los Angeles over access to recreation and recreational space, and the regu-lation of recreation itself. Indeed, as a small and isolated resort town, such issues assumed immense political and economic importance, and variations of its local squabbles could likely be found in many resort communities. Its marine isolation, however, was largely unique.

While the Banning transportation monopoly excluded some potential tourists, it was an even more pressing issue for island residents and busi-ness owners. High cargo costs could make their businesses unprofitable, and exorbitant passenger rates would keep tourists away. Other companies, unsurprisingly, envied this monopoly on an increasingly popular resort. By 1897, 38,000 people paid Wilmington Transportation Company fares to go to Avalon, and company ships carried 150,000 tons of freight. That year, a law-suit brought by the Meteor Boat Company forced the Bannings to open the island to other ships, but it did not prohibit them from charging disembarka-tion fees or limiting access to the island interior to those who had not paid for passage on a Banning boat.[28]

Despite complaints and lawsuits, some Avalon business owners found the Bannings' dominance of Catalina shipping acceptable. Perhaps they approved of the restricted transportation that kept "undesirables" to a minimum. In 1909, the Avalon Freeholder's Association, a pro-Banning, pro-Santa Catalina Island Company group, was granted title to Avalon's streets by Los Angeles County. The freeholders agreed to give the SCIC an exclusive franchise for all passengers bound for hotels, businesses, and residences owned by the Association, which constituted much of Avalon. In exchange, the SCIC gave the freeholders control of the Avalon pleasure pier and promised to continue subsidizing roads, utilities, and tourist promotion. In essence, the Banning monopoly had been restored in most of the commu-nity. In fact, this plan had been agreed to before the Freeholder's Association approached Los Angeles County about gaining title to Avalon's streets. As part of a covert agreement laid out beforehand, the SCIC agreed to a series of demands to pay for local projects. The Freeholder's Association would have control of the glass-bottomed boats, fishing boats, and pleasure boats, and revenue collected from these sources would be used for the entertainment of tourists. The Bannings also agreed to advertise Wilmington Company ships and SCIC hotels and attractions separately, so that independent concessionaires had a better chance to do business.[29]

Not everyone approved of this cozy new arrangement. This eventually prompted another lawsuit, one that went all the way to the Supreme Court. The suit, brought by J. H. Miller and E. Donaldson, two Avalon merchants, asserted that the SCIC and Wilmington Transportation Company charged exorbitant rates, which hurt business and reduced travel to Catalina. The Wilmington Transportation Company retorted that "the rates charged produce but a fair return," and that without these revenues the efforts to maintain and promote the island would end. While these claims seem plausible, the Bannings also asserted that the California Railroad Commission had no right to regulate Catalina traffic, as the Wilmington Transportation Company and SCIC were engaged in foreign commerce in international waters, and were therefore beyond state jurisdiction. The fact that the island and town of Avalon were part of Los Angeles County was immaterial. The Supreme Court, however, was not amused. It sided with the Railroad Commission in 1915, and the Bannings had to submit to state regulation of their shipping business.[30]

Another pressing issue was the availability of alcohol. Unlike Shatto, the Bannings were not teetotalers, and they secured a liquor license for the Metropole Hotel soon after taking possession of it. Still, they tried to limit the availability of liquor in Avalon—no doubt in part to boost profits at the Metropole. The community was split on the issue; many permanent residents, who depended on the tourist trade, knew that liquor could provide lucrative profits. Many of the houses in Avalon, however, were owned by affluent mainlanders who maintained the residences as vacation homes, though some had transferred their residency there. These seasonal residents bitterly resisted the availability of liquor, and their sentiments would ultimately result in the prohibition of liquor in all unincorporated areas of Los Angeles County in 1913—an act that spurred the incorporation of Avalon later that year.[31]

Immediately after incorporation, town council meetings were often devoted to debating the number and costs of liquor licenses to be granted. Some permanent residents asserted that only they, rather than seasonal "residents," should be allowed to vote on the subject. Significantly, the Santa Catalina Island Company was not involved in these deliberations, since it had been granted a liquor license the first day the new council met. Indeed, while some residents may have resented the Bannings, the town relied on the SCIC for water, trash collection, and street cleaning and spraying. Residents complained about the company's inability to secure a stable supply of fresh water and unfulfilled promises to pave streets. They wanted more Banning involvement in these island affairs, not less.

The town's increasing tourist revenue was indivisible from the company's efforts to promote the island and transport tourists to its shores. The Bannings, in turn, ultimately realized that heavy-handed policies could create bad press, and that it was in their interest for locals to become allies of the SCIC, rather than adversaries. As Joseph Banning stated in an internal memorandum, "If we secure and retain the good will and cooperation of [Avalon's] citizens, we induce a state of harmony and mutual protection greatly to be desired, if not absolutely necessary to our business success." The residents of Avalon—most of whom were now employed in some capacity in the tourist industry—depended on the Bannings for transportation, basic services and utilities, and the continuation of the tourist trade upon which they depended. Like communities in the rural West surrounded by federal land or dependent upon national park visitation, Avalon might chafe at outside control, but was destined to remain in a state of uneasy dependency with the Santa Catalina Island Company.[32]

Life, Leisure, and Labor at Avalon

Beyond controlling access to Avalon, the Bannings worked to improve the town's aesthetic appearance. Roads were graded, and the litter and kelp that collected in the Bay of Seven Moons was vigilantly removed. Since many small house lots had been sold during Shatto's ownership, the Santa Catalina Island Company could not demolish Avalon and start over. Company representatives tried to buy back all the lots they could, and forced out renters and leaseholders who did not sign new lease agreements with them. When it came to civic beautification, however, the SCIC could only try to convince locals to adopt a more aesthetically pleasing appearance for the town.[33]

Most of the Bannings' efforts were devoted to improving tourist facilities and amenities at Catalina and publicizing the resort, resulting in substantial expenditures for the family. Santa Catalina Island Company advertisements, booklets, pamphlets, and flyers were seemingly produced by the ton, all emblazoned with the SCIC motto for Catalina: "In all the World, No Trip Like This!" The Hotel Metropole was expanded and remodeled, and construction began on a vast tent-cabin village, billed as "the largest one-story hotel on earth." Passengers sailing into Avalon's harbor were greeted with such an expanse of tent canvass that locals began referring to the town as "Rag City." The brothers built restaurants and a golf course, and hired hunting, fishing, and tour guides. Visitors willing to brave winding, narrow roads skirting precipitous cliffs could take Banning coaches into the interior. Tourists could also ride in Banning-owned glass-bottomed boats to peer at the "Marine Gardens," or take night tours to see flying fish.

These marine voyages proved to be among the most popular attractions on the island, and perhaps the best-known beyond Southern California. Excursionists arriving at Avalon were greeted by a cacophony of sales pitches from glass-bottomed boat operators, each claiming to offer the best view of Catalina's "Marine Gardens." Some of these men had previously been fishermen or sheepherders on the island. Such was the case with Joseph Adargo, who had once worked for the Frank Whitley Sheep Company at Catalina, but moved his family to Avalon to take advantage of the new tourist trade in 1892. He was subsequently hired by the SCIC to operate its fleet of glass-bottomed boats. His son Everett, born in 1891, was one of many local youths hired as divers to accompany the glass-bottom tours. The divers would retrieve (and keep) coins passengers tossed into the water, and bring up abalone shells or other marine animals or artifacts to thrill the tourists.[34]

Charles Frederick Holder claimed that these craft were first constructed after some locals saw him using a box with a glass bottom to observe marine life in Avalon harbor. He was, however, not their actual inspiration. In 1890 an abalone fisherman devised a glass bottom for his rowboat, making abalone easier to locate. Other fishermen modified their boats as well, igniting a tourist craze.[35]

First used for tourism in 1895, these were the first glass-bottomed tourist boats anywhere. Previously, they had been utilized primarily by scientists, fishermen, and naturalists. Catalina visitors saw kelp forests, various types of fish, sea urchins, jellyfish, sea anemones, starfish, and octopus. Guides pointed out algae-covered rock formations, each named to suggest their size and impressiveness, such as the "Great Divide," the "Yosemite," and the "Grand Cañon of the Sea." For landlocked Midwesterners—and former Midwesterners—these were thrilling sights indeed. Other resorts had beaches or balmy weather, and might have possessed similar undersea scenery; yet it was at Catalina that these marine attractions were first exploited. Locals' knowledge of nature and fishing, labor, and Banning money combined to create a new recreational experience, and Catalina, at least for a time, had a unique attraction.[36]

The Bannings offered a range of accommodations and activities, priced for tourists of various means. Of course, the poor could not afford to come to Catalina at all, and while a day trip was not exorbitant for middle-class excursionists, a vacation of a week—let alone a month—was limited to the affluent, and to retirees or professionals with money and flexible schedules. Diversions owned by the Island Company were usually free. Tourists paid a flat rate for passage and could enjoy all island amenities. Package tours included lodging and meals. Rates were generally reasonable, with a range of prices available. Round-trip ferry tickets—the primary source of income for the Santa Catalina Island Company—cost $2.50, and visitors bringing their own tents could camp for free. Company tent accommodations ranged from spartan singles to tent "houses," with a living room and four bedrooms. The most inexpensive tents, eight by ten feet and without a floor, could be rented for $1.50 a week, or $4.50 per month. Guests could rent a furnished single tent for six dollars a week or a double for ten. All tent spaces had "water closets," garbage removal, and available maid service. Those who arrived by private boat, however, received no camping privileges, and were denied excursion permits into the interior. For big spenders, summer rates for rooms in the Hotel Metropole, the resort hotel for the "Bar Harbor of Southern California," ranged from $17.50 to $21 a week.[37]

Tent cabins, with plank floors and canvas walls stretched over wooden frames, provided shelter for many vacationers, whether they built their own on lots they bought or leased, or rented tents in the SCIC's tent-cabin village. Some such "cabins" could be relatively elaborate. One tourist, writing in August 1898, bragged that her abode was "one of the most picturesque here," with a view of "the whole bay, the town, and the mountains." The potential for people watching was just as good: "We can recognize people at the bathhouse, and often hear what they say." This tourist, Mary Elise Groff, described her tent cabin, still under construction, to her husband Gregory, offering a view of what these structures were like:

> The little house is 10 × 12, shake roof, matched floor, rustic and can-vas sides, door with upper part glass, so that we can look out on the water in stormy weather.... The dining room juts beyond the tent, still nearer town, so that it, too has an ocean front, as well as over-looks all Crescent Ave. It will be 12 × 12, with gable roof, covered with cloth—cloth and mosquito netting sides. The little kitchen comes behind, farther up the hill, but on the same level.[38]

Just as this architectural arrangement was common, so was this social arrangement. In the summers of the 1890s, Avalon was often a place domi-nated by mothers and children. Husbands remained on the mainland to work, but spent weekends in the cooler, relaxed atmosphere of Catalina. In this regard, Catalina portended the stereotypical suburban family of the 1950s, with fathers traveling to work elsewhere and mothers remaining at home with their children. This arrangement divided spouses but offered a remark-able degree of autonomy to adolescents and young adults who accompanied parents or friends to the island.

FIGURE 3.2 The tent cabins of Avalon, constructed by individual vacationers or the Santa Catalina Island Company, soon became a popular form of accommodation on the island. By 1910, SCIC tent villages could house thousands of guests, and the vast expanse of canvas visible to arriving tourists earned Avalon the nickname "Rag City." Catalina Island Museum, Avalon, California.

Since tourists expected the Santa Catalina Island company to prevent "undesirables" from reaching the island, they viewed the resort as a safe place for their children. Reserved mainly for affluent whites, the island offered a place where some of the formalities and mores of broader society could be relaxed, and sometime flouted entirely. As a result, adolescents and young adults of both sexes took hikes into the interior, ranging all over the island. At night they engaged in dancing and singing on the veranda of the Metropole long after other guests had gone to bed and were trying to sleep, much to the annoyance of the hotel's manager. This boisterous crowd had in fact often included William Banning, Hancock Banning, and Hancock's future wife, Annie Smith. Young adults and adolescents likewise enjoyed midnight swims and moonlit sailboat rides after most parents had gone to bed. With all sorts of secluded nooks nearby—such as Lover's Cove, a short walk from Avalon—it seems likely that some of these young people engaged in more than nature appreciation during these rare chances to escape societal mores and parental authority. Walking around in bathing attire was one thing; this was something else altogether. The tacit acceptance of such behavior—or at least the willful ignorance of it—suggests that Catalina was already adopting the far more relaxed social mores of later eras, and perhaps even of the beach-centered California youth culture that emerged in the twentieth century.[39]

The Santa Catalina Island Company, whether in the Banning era or later, had to handle this issue carefully. A sense of release, of escape from normal mores and standards of behavior, was a draw for Catalina, just as it would later be for Palm Springs, Tijuana, and Las Vegas. Discretion, however, was key. Catalina was the "Isle of Romance," after all, and not the Island of Vice. Affluent and middle-class tourists would not publicly frequent a place known as a sink of iniquity.

While Catalina offered release to affluent whites, its working-class and especially nonwhite workers were strictly controlled, subject to the most stringent Victorian mores. Perhaps in part to limit opportunities for illicit behavior—particularly relationships that transgressed class or ethnic boundaries—the female employees of the SCIC, most of whom worked at the Metropole, were carefully monitored. At night the women slept in a group of cabins near the hotel, surrounded by a high fence. The gate was locked nightly at eleven o'clock, and men were not allowed inside the compound that local wags dubbed the "Ostrich Farm." With this system, female employees were policed much like the New England textile-mill-town women of the early nineteenth century, who were housed in employer-owned dormitories.[40]

Sport Fishermen and Fish Gaffers: Promoting Sport, Marine Conservation, and Conflict at Catalina

Despite all of the Bannings' projects and expenditures, promoting Catalina required more than the simple expansion of tourist infrastructure. People had to be convinced to go there. Catalina had to undergo a transformation from a rocky, arid island into a renowned tourist destination, with scenery, adventure, and culture. This transformation did occur, but this was only partially because of the Bannings, who produced innumerable pamphlets, guidebooks, and promotional photos. As the island grew in popularity, boosting took on a life of its own, attracting individuals who promoted the island more for their own goals than those of the Santa Catalina Island Company.

In the 1880s and 1890s, a substantial population of affluent Midwesterners and New Englanders settled in Pasadena. During the hot Pasadena summers, it sometimes seemed as if the entire town had relocated to the Pacific, with Catalina serving as "Newport, Miami and Narragansett Pier all rolled into one." The summertime phalanx of recreating Pasadenans included individuals who would further Catalina's national prominence.[41]

Foremost among these boosters was Charles Frederick Holder, who had first been invited to the island by George Shatto. Born in 1851 in Lynn, Massachusetts—also the birthplace of Charles Lummis—Holder attended the

U.S. Naval Academy but left before graduating. He served for several years as the assistant curator of zoology at the American Museum of Natural History in New York, and authored a number of books, including biographies of Charles Darwin and Louis Agassiz. In 1885 Holder came to Southern California to recuperate from a lung infection aggravated by overwork, much as Lummis had arrived in Southern California an ailing workaholic. Holder had been offered a position at Sierra Madre College, but found upon his arrival that the infant college, strapped for cash, had already closed. Enamored with the region, Holder decided to stay. He supported himself with writing and lecturing at Pasadena's Hotel Raymond, perhaps presenting one of the evening entertainments Amy Bridges recorded in her journal. In 1891 Holder secured a permanent position when he became professor and chair of the Department of Zoology at the newly established Throop University, later renamed the California Institute of Technology. Holder became a prominent member of Pasadena society, helping found the tony Valley Hunt Club, which organized equestrian fox and coyote hunts. He was also credited as the originator of the Pasadena Rose Tournament Parade in 1890.[42]

Catalina Island, with its claims to healthfulness and distinctive flora and fauna, was an encapsulation of everything Holder loved about Southern California. In books such as *Santa Catalina: An Isle of Summer* (1895), he rhapsodized about his subject, calling it "a bit of Southern California anchored offshore," and "nearer the perfect insular resort than any I know of." Catalina again featured prominently in his *Life in the Open: Sport with Rod, Gun, Horse, and Hound in Southern California* (1906) and *The Channel Islands of California: A Book for the Angler, Sportsman, and Tourist* (1910). These books contained a substantial amount of natural history and observations of flora and fauna, but also copious Southern California boosterism and tourist information, particularly on deep-sea fishing, Holder's favorite of all "true manly sports." In Southern California, Holder could be the rugged outdoorsman and vigorous Anglo-Saxon, in the same public-scholar/spokesman/sportsman mode as Theodore Roosevelt. For Holder, as with so many of the Progressive Era, "true" manhood was connected to vigorous exertion in the outdoors, a bit of essential exposure to the tests of the frontier for an otherwise modern American male.[43]

While amazed at the abundance of marine life at Catalina, Holder was appalled by what he saw as the wanton destruction of the island's fish. Indeed, such destruction also raised the ire of some on the mainland. Lummis, for example, authored editorials in his magazine, *Land of Sunshine*, in which he railed against tourist "fish hogs" who committed "fish massacres" by catching hundreds of fish, only to be photographed with them and then have the entire catch dumped at sea to avoid befouling Catalina's beaches. Unfortunately, many other conservation-minded critics would turn a blind eye to the offenses of white tourists.[44]

Most often, criticism was leveled at commercial fishing operations, particularly larger boats with nets that swept up everything before them. Author Henry Van Dyke, infuriated by fishermen's complaints that conservation rules harmed their business, described the effect of such boats at Catalina. He first painted a scene of Edenic natural beauty, where people played and a variety of fish swarmed in an abundance of marine life. Then, however, came the "Spoilers of the Sea": "Three snub-nosed, thick-set vessels, piled high with nets, owned by firms of fish dealers, manned by foreigners, came butting down the coast...sweeping in everything that came in their way." According to Van Dyke, the once abundant fish of Catalina were gone, and the consequences were dire:

> Those were the fish that would have spawned around the kelp-beds and gravel-banks of Catalina...Those were the fish that would have given good sport to thousands of Californians seeking their recreation on this ideal island. Those were the fish upon whose continuance and propagation the living of the Catalina boatmen—three times as many as the foreign net-haulers—must depend.

Van Dyke urged a ban of commercial net fishing within three miles of the shores of California and its islands. Despite his histrionics, Van Dyke's prognosis was not unfounded. The fisheries of the California Central Coast would experience a catastrophic collapse in the mid-twentieth century. Monterey's Cannery Row, made into a picturesque tourist attraction, serves as a monument to a dead industry, and its renowned Monterey Bay Aquarium contains an abundance of marine life that vanished in the bay for which it is named.[45]

In 1898 Holder founded the Catalina Island Tuna Club, which combined conservationist policies with a glorification of rugged outdoor living and masculine sport. Initially, "active" membership, open solely to men, could be attained only by reeling in a tuna of at least one hundred pounds, or a swordfish of two hundred pounds, with rod and reel and without assistance. Less accomplished anglers could become associate members. The club cost $100 to join, plus $10 a year for California residents. Members who caught record-breaking tuna became club president, and trophies were awarded in various categories. The club's membership, which included "honorary" members, contained a variety of local and national notables, such as all three Banning brothers, Henry Huntington, George S. Patton, Walter Raymond of the Raymond Hotel, David Starr Jordan, president of Stanford University, and polar explorer Admiral Robert E. Peary.

Membership also came to include many prominent conservationists of the Progressive Era, including forester Gifford Pinchot and President Theodore

Roosevelt. The Tuna Club's constitution stated that the organization aimed to achieve "the protection of the game fishes of the state of California, and to encourage and foster the catching of all fishes, and especially tuna, yellowtail, sea bass, etc., with the lightest rod and reel tackle," and to discourage "unsportsmanlike" commercial fishing.

Only sport fishermen, not those who fished for a living, were eligible for membership. The club drew class distinctions between "sportsmanlike" and "unsportsmanlike" fishing that bore close parallels to the class-based distinction conservationists often perceived in hunting: those with the money

FIGURE 3.3 Charles Frederick Holder with fish gaffer Joe Presciado and trophy tuna, 1898. Catalina Island Museum Archives. Avalon, California.

to hunt for leisure were sportsmen, while those who hunted for subsistence were "poachers." In another parallel with conservation on land, fish were divided into "game" species, to be treated with care, and "nongame" species to be hunted at will. Thus members took great pains to catch trophy tuna in a "manly" manner but enjoyed the "sport" of shooting at the island's iridescent flying fish with buckshot.[46]

This class-based conceptualization of conservation also contained an unpleasant racial element. Most commercial fishermen were Asians, Mexicans, or "ethnic" whites such as Italians. Even travel writers unconcerned with conservation issues noted the ethnicity of fishermen, such as the author of an 1894 article in the *Los Angeles Times*, which asserted that most fishermen who frequented Avalon were Italian. Often, however, mentions of nonwhite fishermen were disapproving or angry. In 1909, for example, the *Times* noted that a group of Japanese fishermen harvesting abalone had not been arrested, as the island game warden was not present. The same article noted that whites considered the abalone inedible, as they were taken from near the outlet of Avalon's sewer. Californians often complained about "foreign" fishermen, making no distinction between those who sailed into California waters, and those who were California residents. One critic of state fishing regulations epitomized this view: "We have at San Pedro on Terminal Island a little Japan, across the bay, a little Italy, and many other foreign fishing nations represented. More than 72% of the people engaged in commercial net fishing are not even citizens of the United States, yet we permit them to directly or indirectly to [*sic*] dictate the laws governing the taking of our fish and our national food supply."[47]

This fixation upon commercial and non-Anglo fishermen pointedly overlooked the excesses of tourist fishermen—and women. Despite Holder's sportsman machismo, sport fishing proved to be hugely popular with women as well. They, like their male counterparts, often caught huge numbers of fish only to be photographed with their haul and then have the entire catch dumped back into the ocean. Some working-class fishermen also saw through the "sporting" ethos of more affluent tourist fishermen. One sport fisherman, for example, remembered an unusually frank exchange with a fishing guide, who complained about the excesses of sport fishermen, and their negative views of commercial fishermen:

> Most o' these here sports wanta pile 'em up like corkwood. I come across from here with fish that durn near stunk me off 'n th' boat, they was so rotten. An' what for? Jus' so some bird could have his picture taken 'long side a string o' marlin. Didn't make no difference if it took him two weeks to catch 'em! I'm tellin' ya, I heard a lot 'bout these here sportsmen, but I ain't seen many. They squawk

an' holler 'bout market fishin.' That's all right when market fishin' wipes th' fish out. I'm agin these big nets all th' time. Jus' th' same them sportsmen fergits that th' market fisherman eats, or don't eat, accordin' to whether he gits fish, or don't git 'em."[48]

No matter how troublesome their views, the efforts of Holder and other members of the Tuna Club ultimately resulted in conservation legislation. Catalina had once possessed one of the richest fisheries along the Pacific coast, but by 1912 the annual catch was only a quarter of that of 1885. The island's famous big tuna were nearly gone—thanks in part to the Tuna Club's trophy hunters—as were its once abundant abalone. All the Channel Islands were designated a sea-lion preserve in 1909, a decade after courts had ruled on behalf of fishing interests to reduce the sea lion population, a campaign waged only too effectively. In 1913 Holder succeeded in getting the island's waters, up to a three-mile radius from shore, classified as a fish preserve where only recreational hook-and-line fishing would be permitted. Commercial net fishing was banned. Catalina would remain off limits to fishermen, whether from the mainland or from the island's own contingent of commercial fishermen. After 1913, local fishermen either had to relocate, find new employment, or make the transition from fisherman to recreational fishing guide.[49]

One fisherman who made the transition was "Mexican Joe" Presciado. Born in Sonora, Pesciado originally came to Catalina as a child in the 1850s. He worked as an employee of the Whitley family, who maintained a large sheep herd on the island. Presciado worked as a hunter and fisherman. When the island developed as a tourist center, Presciado partnered with another fisherman, George Michaelis, to operate a charter fishing boat in Avalon. "Mexican Joe" became a fixture in Avalon and the community's best-known "gaffer"—someone who helped anglers haul in their catch. He appeared in countless photos of tourists posing with their numerous—and sometimes gargantuan—prizes. As on the mainland, local non-Anglos served both as laborers and as part of the "themed" identity of Southern California—quaint and helpful rather than threatening. His wife, Felipa Redona de Presciado, gained notoriety as a swimmer, and accompanied her husband on expeditions around the Channel Islands to collect Indian artifacts.[50]

Other fishermen also adapted to the new tourist economy. In fact, many used their knowledge of local nature—knowledge gained through labor, rather than leisure—to find new ways to survive and even prosper in a changing economy. One was the development of a new bait-fishing industry. Tourists had long complained about a lack of bait—whether preserved or, preferably, alive. As early as the 1880s, tourists bemoaned its scarcity. Avalon's newspaper recorded that "The Italians haul it in every morning, but sometimes bait is not to be had onshore, for love or money." The same paper contained an irate letter from a hotel manager who responded to complaints by defending his hotel staff's efforts: "I have five Italians, boss fishermen, engaged to catch fish for guests to eat, and fish for other fish to eat. The go out at 12 o'clock every night, and do their best to return by daylight. . . . When a large catch is made most of it goes to waste, as herrings and smelt will not keep alive in captivity when in any quantity, and when dead keep only a few hours."[51]

He concluded his retort by advising tourists to fish for bait on the wharf at Avalon or "engage in the bait selling business themselves."[52] Commercial fishermen, rather than tourists, would in fact undertake exactly this enterprise. Commercial nets, designed to catch large fish such as tuna, were useless for catching small bait fish. In 1910 a group of Japanese tuna fishermen devised a new type of net. This "blanket" net was lowered into the water, chum was used as bait to attract fish, and then the net was raised using poles attached to both sides, trapping the fish in the closed net. In 1912, they began using a round-haul net, which was trolled behind the boat, and when reeled in could entrap a school of small fish. These quickly became popular with other commercial fishermen, as boatmen caught live bait in the early morning, stored the small fish in tanks or floating boxes, and then hosted sport fishers the remainder of the day. Some eventually became solely bait fishermen to supply increasing demand. Faced with the curtailment of regular commercial fishing, these fishermen, rather than leaving Catalina's waters, had instead created a new market in which their commercial fishing could continue. Many gaffers also maintained commercial fishing licenses in order to sell the excess catch of sportsmen to Catalina hotels and restaurants, as well as buyers on the mainland.[53] Though they lacked the political power of Holder and his allies, these fishermen and fish gaffers, like those who remade fishing vessels into glass bottomed boats, demonstrated that it was not only Anglo tourists or the Bannings who would play a role in the future of Catalina.

At the same time, the fishing ban and SCIC policies certainly reduced traditional fishing at Catalina. The Santa Catalina Island Company required any fishermen who landed on the island to pay for a permit. Such permits prohibited commercial fishing boats from carrying passengers or freight to the island, and stated that holders of these permits could not hunt birds or animals, collect firewood, or travel into the interior of the island without SCIC consent. In 1909 an article extolling Catalina as a resort noted that fishing boats were an inescapable part of the scenery in Avalon. Many of these, however, were no longer seaworthy, just listing hulks dotting the shoreline. In Avalon, old fishing boats had been "adapted to ornamental garden purposes" by being towed ashore, "filled with earth and planted with flowers." These strange marooned garden planters, as much as anything else, testified to the socioeconomic change underway on the island.[54]

Promoting Santa Catalina to America

While no other Catalina booster left a legacy of legislation such as Holder produced before his death in 1915, other Anglo Californians produced guidebooks, novels, and poems that furthered the island's fame and augmented the Santa Catalina Island Company's impressive publication output. Tourists sometimes succumbed to the muse, usually producing dreadful treacle that was occasionally printed in regional and national publications. Such poetry did little to elevate the American poetical canon. It did, however, publicize the island to a national audience. These Catalina Ciceros and Sapphos, however, soon took a backseat to the professionals.[55]

Boosters and travel writers found in Catalina inspiration for vast amounts of purple prose. In 1904 George Wharton James, one of the most prolific regional promoters, authored the *Traveler's Handbook to Southern California*, in which—borrowing liberally from the prose of other writers—he hailed Catalina as "a park in the Pacific, a mountain range at sea; a bit of the world by itself, which . . . comes as near perfection as one can find." Unlike James, whose prose was written in the unrelenting tone of a continuous swoon, Charles A. Keeler also discussed a decidedly unromantic condition that often afflicted Catalina-bound tourists in his guidebook, *Southern California* (1902)—seasickness.[56]

Much of the Catalina literature, whether produced by boosters or by the Santa Catalina Island Company, echoed the same themes used to promote the mainland—a balmy, healthy climate, scenic vistas, and a relaxed pace that contrasted with the urban East. In some other respects, however, Catalina was unique. The eras of Spanish and Mexican rule had left no architectural imprint on the island, no picturesque mission or adobe for mission revivalists to enshrine. This, however, did not prevent Catalina from borrowing the "fiestas" and Hispanicized Easter services—though Protestant, of course—popular on the mainland. Still, with a jumble of privately owned timber-frame houses and hotels comprising the architecture of Avalon, a Mission Revival makeover was impossible. When the Bannings built a lodge at the village of Two Harbors at Catalina's isthmus, they hired architect Irving Gill, a modernist who was the most skilled designer of modern structures cognizant of the region's architectural history. Still, Gill's design for the lodge was Craftsman, not a reinterpreted Spanish style. Perhaps the Bannings, who, like other Southern Californians, saw Spanish and mission-revival architecture multiply on the mainland, enjoyed escaping *Ramona* mania on occasion. Nevertheless, the Bannings avidly pursued Mexican, Spanish, or "Mediterranean" themes—and any other themes—if they seemed lucrative. Travelers arriving at Avalon could be serenaded by a mariachi band and also receive leis and cries of "aloha" as their ship left the harbor.[57]

Gradually, however, Catalina developed themes of its own. Drawing upon the island's Native American history, ancient mythology, and a largely concocted "maritime" history, a variety of Catalina aficionados and boosters provided it with a cohesive image and a sellable past. This collective image first coalesced around Native American prehistory. As in the Southwest, archaeology proved a source of great fascination, but actual archaeological finds rarely interfered with crafting a good story. The retelling of the native history of Catalina had far less to do with the Indian past than with the American present. Holder certainly betrayed this tendency. In 1902 he published *The Adventures of Torqua*, a fable focusing upon the island adventures of three teenaged boys—one the son of an Indian chief, the other two noble Spaniards banished as part of some palace intrigue. The story was utterly implausible, but managed to mention nearly every scenic spot in Southern California.[58]

Though Holder would hardly have considered himself a booster, his novel highlighted the function Catalina served for Los Angeles area boosters. The island served as one of a series of attractions in the greater Los Angeles region, and promoters of Los Angeles eagerly incorporated the new resort into their collective sales pitch. Tourism promoters hoped to create a new summer tourist season, and real-estate speculators knew that a tourist was a prospective resident. Charles Lummis's *Land of Sunshine* regularly featured Catalina as one of many Southern California attractions. The island was always presented as an integral recreational amenity for Angelenos, a centerpiece in the larger resort region marketed to tourists and prospective residents alike.[59]

In 1894, Los Angeles inaugurated "La Fiesta de Los Angeles," a parade and pageant intended to compete with Pasadena's Tournament of Roses, as well as to distract attention from a looming Pullman strike. The Fiesta also served as an elaborate narrative of racial "progression" and Anglo-American superiority. Lummis choreographed the spectacle, which included floats representing a heavily mythologized history of California, the Southwest, Native Americans, and "Spanish America." By the second season, the official program for the Fiesta included photos of "the Great Resort, Catalina Island." Catalina also took the starring role in a bizarre mythology cooked up to serve as a mythical basis for the Fiesta. According to an epic poem penned for the occasion, Catalina had been the home of a noble Grecian race discovered by the gentle padres. These classical Catalinans, however, retreated beneath the waves when California was swamped by coarse gringos, gold rush migrants, and other assorted riff raff—in other words, the central characters in the historic heritage of Anglo-American San Francisco. Then, however, people of "quality" discovered the sunny land of health and citrus in Southern California, and a new bourgeois, Anglo-American civilization evolved, finally capable of appreciating and developing the art, culture, and environment of its region. Once this enlightened new society had emerged, the golden race of Catalina rose again above the waves to join La Fiesta and parade through the streets of the glorious fulfillment of Californian civilization, Los Angeles.[60]

The End of the Banning Era at Catalina

While the boosters, writers, and poets penned their romantic odes to Catalina, tourism prospered. Yet by 1919 the island would change hands again. This transition had various causes. The first was that this "Isle of Summer" was hindered by being too literally an "Isle of Summer," for tourists came from June to September and stayed on the mainland the rest of the year. Winter and spring were cool and windy, with occasional dense fog and heavy rains. The island's tourist season largely missed the larger Southern California tourist influx, which was almost entirely a winter phenomenon. In contrast, winter sometimes found the Bannings securing loans or asking creditors for patience. When Catalina prospered in the Banning era, it did so primarily as an urban resort for Los Angeles—not as a national destination.[61]

A no less important factor was that Banning-family operations on the mainland, particularly in the burgeoning port of Los Angeles, produced far more revenue, and required most of the brothers' attention. While Catalina did not need to be a gold mine, the Bannings could not afford for it to drain their collective finances. Yet it is clear that the island increasingly did just that. According to an audit conducted by the California Railroad Commission in 1915, the Catalina Island Company made a profit of $37,647.70 in 1903. It would never again make as much money for the Bannings. Profits varied from year to year, but crept inexorably downward as the decade progressed. By 1910 profits had disappeared; the SCIC operated at a loss of $22,425.81. In 1911 matters were even worse, as the Island Company lost more than $28,500. Aside from a lone year of surplus in 1913, the SCIC continued to operate in the red. The Banning brothers began to bicker about the fate of their island and who should be blamed for its problems. Joseph Banning urged the SCIC to "return to and carry out the original policy for which the island was purchased, i.e. *The Island for the Transportation—the building up of a dependable trade to and from the island*." Conversely, Hancock Banning felt that the policy of charging a flat rate for ferry service while keeping most amenities and attractions free had proven disastrous.[62]

As early as 1909, the Bannings considered offers to sell some or all of Catalina. In 1916, a year after they lost their case against the state railroad commission in the U.S. Supreme Court and had to surrender their unregulated near-monopoly on all island shipping, the brothers offered to sell all of the island east of the isthmus. This would have meant selling the two-thirds of the island that was developed, including Avalon, as well as the steamers *Cabrillo* and *Hermosa*, for $2.5 million. They also considered creating a trust to prevent the total loss of Catalina.[63]

This desire to sell was greatly heightened by a calamity that had occurred the previous year. On 29 November 1915, much of Avalon—a town of wooden buildings and canvas tents—burned to the ground in a fire that may have begun as arson. The Bannings did not seek an exit immediately. They rebuilt the tent village and used the fire-insurance settlement from the Metropole to build a new hotel, the St. Catherine, in 1918. They could not, however, rebuild the entire town. Just rebuilding basic facilities meant that the Catalina Island Company had to shoulder $1.25 million in bond debt as a result of the fire. More ominously, as the decade drew toward a close, visitation began to drop significantly. Automobile ownership had become possible for a growing number of Southern Californians. By 1920 Los Angeles County had the highest per capita rate of car ownership in the world. The car opened up new worlds for Angelenos looking for a vacation. Catalina was no longer their primary place of escape. The island faced tough competition from new resorts and attractions in the region, most easily accessible by private automobile.

The Bannings had made Catalina a successful tourist attraction and publicized it to the nation. Their hotel and tent village housed thousands, and their ferries carried thousands more. In many respects, their tenure had been a success, even if the changes it wrought posed many challenges for island residents. What Catalina now needed was someone with deep pockets—someone for whom seasonal fluctuations would not be a cause for dire concern, emergency loans, or unpaid bills. The Banning brothers began courting potential buyers, both for the island and the Santa Catalina Island Company, along with its concessions, and the Wilmington Transportation Company's fleet of ferries.[64]

They found one in William Wrigley, the chewing gum magnate and owner of the Chicago Cubs. Wrigley, however, was no stranger to Southern California, for he and his family already wintered at their mansion in Pasadena. Just as the Bannings had brought resources and systemization to George Shatto's tourism efforts, Wrigley would now bring his vast wealth and successful business acumen to the island. A new era for Catalina—its golden age as a resort—was about to begin. Wrigley would democratize Catalina, opening it to a wider swath of the public than the Bannings ever had.

He would transform Catalina from a regional to a national resort. Wrigley and his son, Philip, would make their island famous worldwide as a tourist destination, synonymous with Los Angeles, Hollywood, and American leisure. Despite all their resources and skills, however, the Wrigleys, like the Bannings, would find themselves subject to Americans' changing appetites for leisure.[65]

Chapter Four

"IN ALL THE WORLD NO TRIP LIKE THIS"

Santa Catalina in the Wrigley Era

T HE TRANSFER of Catalina Island from the Banning family to William Wrigley initially seemed more a transition than a transformation. The change in island proprietorship was made public on 13 February 1919, after Wrigley paid three million dollars for Catalina, as well as majority shares in the Santa Catalina Island Company and Wilmington Transportation Company. The Wilmington Transportation Company became an SCIC subsidiary the following year. The transaction appears to have been amicable, and William Banning would remain on the SCIC board until 1929.[1]

In some respects, Wrigley's tenure was a continuation of the Banning years. The Banning family had already made Catalina a well-known resort and maintained passenger and cargo lines to facilitate tourist development. Many of the recreational activities the island offered to visitors and promoted in its advertising continued as they had before. Yet Catalina would change in fundamental ways under the ownership of William Wrigley and his heirs. The Wrigleys would transform Catalina from a regional attraction, a recreational suburb for Los Angeles, into a national resort, and also transition from regional boosterism to modern advertizing. Catalina would evolve from a retreat for the affluent to a middle-class getaway. What had been the nation's first corporate resort would become its first fully themed resort, encapsulating and refining even more effectively the regional booster mythology of Southern California.

Wrigley differed from the Bannings in one crucial respect: for Wrigley, it did not really matter whether the island turned a profit. William Banning recalled that Wrigley had told him the island was a pleasant diversion: "He'd been a good boy all through the war and paid his taxes. Now he was going to play with Catalina." Economic independence, born of great wealth, meant that Wrigley could develop Catalina in ways he found aesthetically pleasing or morally proper, not just in ways most likely to turn a profit.[2]

Perhaps the single greatest irony of the Wrigley era was that it took a multimillionaire to welcome the masses to Catalina. The Bannings had limited access to "their" island for two reasons. Their longtime monopoly on all passenger traffic served as the primary source of revenue from their Catalina operations. Limited access to Catalina also gave it an air of desirable exclusivity that beachfront hotels and attractions on the mainland lacked. Catalina under the Bannings was no Venice Boardwalk or Santa Monica Pier. Instead, it was a place for Southern California's affluent to summer, to see and be seen.

William Wrigley, in contrast, wanted everyone to come to Catalina and did not care how they arrived. All boats would be welcome. The active "screening" of passengers to prohibit nonwhites was also curtailed, though the number of non-Anglos who could afford a trip to Catalina remained small. Middle class whites, both Southern California locals and visiting tourists, would constitute the majority of island visitation under the Wrigleys.

Yet this more open and democratic Catalina was in some other respects more restrictive. The old Catalina, limited to the affluent and off-limits to "undesirables," had been a place where the select few could temporarily escape the stringent mores of late Victorian America. This had been most striking for the young, who found liberties unavailable on the mainland. With the island now open to a broader swath of the public, firmer social control would set in. The Wrigleys carefully monitored guest behavior, and many middle class tourists, less secure in their class status than the rich, needed reassurance that they, and the places they frequented, were respectable.

While Wrigley's personal wealth was the most obvious asset he brought to Catalina, there were other, less obvious, aspects of his personality that augured changes for the future. Wrigley was a salesman par excellence, who had made a little-known novelty—chewing gum—into a commercial empire. Unlike the Californian Bannings, who had developed Catalina as part of a regional shipping network, and who still viewed Catalina primarily as a regional attraction, Wrigley brought a more national perspective.

Under William Wrigley and his son, Philip K. Wrigley, Catalina, which had been the first corporate resort in the nation, emerged as the first successfully "themed" resort in the United States, and in the process was transformed into a national destination. In this effort the Wrigleys would be aided by the rise of a new industry and community—Hollywood. Film, as well as radio, would greatly aid their promotion of Catalina. They would further benefit from the creation of the All-Year Club of Southern California, which was founded by Los Angeles's business elite, and which intended to build a summer tourist season by eschewing the erratic output of boosters in favor of a more organized effort at regional promotion.

The Wrigleys would also face new challenges, however. If Catalina under the Bannings had been emblematic of regional processes, encapsulating the interplay of leisure-focused boosterism and development in Southern California, then Catalina in the Wrigley era is most instructive as an exception, providing a means of measuring the vast social, economic, and cultural changes that occurred on the mainland but not at Catalina. As greater Los Angeles burgeoned into one of the nation's largest metropolitan regions, its increasingly diverse population demanded a wider array of recreational experiences than Catalina could offer. The perfect encapsulation of circa-1895 booster mythology would turn out to be a hard sell later in the twentieth century. As the region grew ever more dynamic, Catalina seemed increasingly staid, no longer offering a sense of escape from social restrictions. While technologies such as film and radio could aid promotion of the island, the increased availability of other technologies—car and air travel—would diminish its prospects. Even the island's natural environment, which for earlier boosters had been the setting for energetic outdoor adventures such as sport fishing, became instead a nostalgic escape, a place to contemplate a vanished pastoral Southern California. The Wrigleys, with all their wealth and business acumen, would still prove vulnerable to regional change and the fickle tastes of the American public and their appetite for leisure.[3]

From Regional Resort to National Destination: William Wrigley and the Remaking of Catalina

Born in Philadelphia in 1861, and a longtime resident of Chicago, William Wrigley had been profoundly influenced by the lavish window displays and exuberant interior decor of the massive new department stores of the 1880s, such as Wanamaker's and Marshall Field's. Like many other Americans, he had been awed by the "White City" of the Chicago Columbian Exposition of 1893. Though he skillfully utilized the regional booster mythos already attached to Catalina, these eastern visions of spectacle, of the potential of a society created by consumer capitalism, would influence Wrigley as he altered Catalina by refining its advertised identity, changing its architectural image, and improving its tourist infrastructure.

When Wrigley made his purchase public, he announced grand plans for the future of Catalina, and professed that the island had utterly seduced him. Such pronouncements might have been expected from a man who took as his personal motto "Nothing great was ever achieved without enthusiasm." His first public statements concerning Catalina were uttered in a breathless tone worthy of the best boosters; Wrigley pronounced the island a place without parallel: "I have seen the temples of the world, and have been on almost every ocean, but they are not to be compared with Catalina and the Pacific. The marine gardens, the glass bottomed boats, the fishing, bathing. . . . I am almost sure that Eve gave Adam that fatal apple on Catalina Island!" According to Wrigley, it was "unthinkable to mar the beauty of such a spot with roller coasters and the like." This was a place "with hills to climb and flowers to pluck." It was not intended for intensive resort development, let alone the bathhouses, swimming plunges, amusement parks, and sideshows found on mainland beaches.[4]

On a boat tour to the island's isthmus shortly after making his purchase, Wrigley claimed to be overcome by the mountains and ocean vistas before him. He could only recall the nationally publicized postcard written by a young woman who had traveled to Chicago in 1893: "My Darling Mother: I have just been to the World's Fair. Oh! Oh oh! oh! oh! oh! oh! oh! oh!" In light of his prior life experience, retelling this particular anecdote was likely not coincidental.[5]

Wrigley quickly switched to less extravagant, more businesslike appraisals of Catalina and the future he planned for it. Unlike the Bannings, who had derived most of their income from their monopoly on shipping passengers and freight, Wrigley had no interest in limiting passenger traffic: "Many restrictions have been placed on the landing of passengers at Catalina, and undoubtedly this has kept a lot of people away. These restrictions will be removed—the island will be thrown wide open to the public." Wrigley also envisioned an island resort that offered different amenities to various sectors of the public. Avalon would continue to draw Southern Californians and middle-class tourists visiting the region. A new resort community he planned to build at the island's isthmus, however, would be far more exclusive. Wrigley asserted that "there is plenty of room on Catalina, which has some 50,000 acres, for the building of a playground [for people] of moderate means, and also for a resort which will meet the desires of wealthy Easterners." With this two-tiered resort plan, Wrigley felt assured that he would make Catalina "the crowning jewel of Southern California," and that it would become "one of the greatest assets to this wonderful country, which is attracting people from all over the United States and even abroad. Wrigley would have great success at Catalina, but not all of his ambitious plans would be realized.[6]

New tourism-related projects did not begin immediately. Wrigley first set about finding a suitable location for a spring-training facility for his baseball franchise, the Chicago Cubs. Atop a hill adjacent to the town, renamed Mount Ada as a gesture to his wife, Wrigley built a large mansion in Georgian style, which would not have looked out of place at Newport or another eastern resort. The house boasted spectacular views of his new possession. This was the family's second home in Southern California—their first was a mansion on Orange Grove Avenue in Pasadena, which later became the headquarters for the Tournament of Roses Parade.

Wrigley also experimented with new enterprises that might supplement tourist revenue. The most successful of these was the manufacture of Catalina tiles and porcelains, which were available not only in island gift shops and used in local construction, but were also sold in department stores nationwide, including Marshall Field's. He also expanded the local infrastructure, building a new municipal waterworks for Avalon that included a series of reservoirs and pumping stations to end dependence on shipped water. This project in particular garnered glowing coverage in the community's newspaper, the *Catalina Islander*, as well as a resolution of commendation from the Avalon Town Council. The lack of a reliable water supply had hindered development, and sometimes caused shortages in late summer—the height of the tourist season. It had also been a source of friction between residents of Avalon and the Bannings. Wrigley, however, could easily afford the $500,000 price tag for the project. Yet even Wrigley could not change the basic environmental fact about Catalina—it was a semiarid island. His efforts improved the water situation, but droughts could still induce shortages.[7]

Beyond commendations for combating Avalon's water woes, Wrigley appears to have enjoyed a generally amicable relationship with local residents. His delving into his deep pockets to support improvements to infrastructure and maintenance in Avalon was partially responsible for this. The same was true of his eagerness to surrender the monopoly on travel to and from Catalina, a monopoly that had certainly proven a repeated source of contention with the Bannings. Wrigley also seemed gifted with a lighter touch and a more diplomatic sensibility than the Bannings, particularly in their early years as island owners.

The most basic difference, however, lay not with Wrigley or the Banning brothers, but instead with the community of Avalon itself. The Bannings had tangled with island residents who had no interest in the tourist trade, and expected to be able to come and go, conduct their business without interference, and generally do as they wished. That population of commercial fishermen, sheepherders, and others unconnected to the tourist trade was now largely gone. Catalina was wholly a tourist island, and Wrigley did not have to contend with residents who thought otherwise.

Avalon's population tripled from 1920 to 1930, then remained stable through the 1930s. This increase was likely because of the improved water supply and the growing tourist industry at Catalina. After growing from a tiny settlement in the 1880s, Catalina's population, which was seasonal and marked by mobility between the island and the mainland, was officially enumerated at 634 in 1920. In 1930, however, Catalina's population was counted at 1,986 persons, of whom 1,897 resided in Avalon. Only 21 black residents were counted, but 246 were foreign-born, and another 322 had foreign or mixed parentage. This undoubtedly included European immigrants, but strongly suggests that the island was home to a sizeable Mexican population. In 1940, island population stood at 1,933, with 1,637 residing in Avalon. Of these, 1667 were white, 238 were foreign-born whites—which again likely indicates a sizable Mexican population—nineteen were African American, and nine classified as "other." By 1950, population had crept up to 2,037, with an estimated summer population of 25,000.[8]

Thus, though the population was small, Avalon remained fairly diverse. A significant number of Mexicans and Mexican Americans lived in Avalon, though, as on the mainland, they were usually relegated to positions as day laborers. Though fewer in number, African Americans found wider opportunities for employment. They comprised a sizable segment of hotel staff and passenger-ship personnel, including the chef and restaurant manager of the Hotel St. Catherine, the hotel built by the Bannings after the fire of 1915 and expanded by Wrigley. One African American, Nat Laws, became the managing airplane mechanic at Catalina's airport during the 1930s. When he returned to the mainland during World War II, he found that skilled jobs such as his were closed to black workers. Unlike in the Banning era, African Americans could travel to Catalina on SCIC boats. In the *Los Angeles Sentinel*, the city's preeminent black newspaper, notices appeared for newlyweds honeymooning at Catalina, as well as others taking vacations there. Whether or not they could stay in SCIC hotels is unclear. Some stayed in private residences, which may suggest that the hotels remained either all-white or segregated, or at the very least not entirely welcoming. It seems certain, however, that residential housing remained segregated. African American employees of the St. Catherine and the SCIC lived in company housing alongside Mexican workers—but both were separate from Anglos.[9]

———————✺———————

Now that Avalon was decidedly a tourist town, Wrigley's efforts to facilitate tourist development were generally met with acclaim. He sold off some former tent-cottage lots, and unlike the Bannings, who often leased such lots instead of selling them, he urged buyers to construct permanent homes. Wrigley rebuilt most of the Bannings' "Island Villa," and added "Villa Park," resulting in a complex of 1,250 wood frame 'bungalettes," which were sturdier structures than the tent cabins they replaced. While the Bannings had been concerned with controlling all transportation to the island, Wrigley satisfied himself with providing the *best* transportation. He purchased a 1,600-passenger Great Lakes steamer and rechristened it the *Avalon*. He then commissioned the construction of a new passenger ship, the *Catalina*. This, however, was no mere ferry.

The *Catalina* was 285 feet long, and carried 2,200 passengers in grand style. In fact, it often carried many more, resulting in fines for Wrigley. This ship, the "Great White Steamer," would be beloved by generations of island tourists.[10]

Unlike the Bannings, Wrigley had the resources to remake Avalon and the island to fit the idealized imagery of its boosters. Besides his own vast wealth, which he used to buy up house and business lots from property owners, Wrigley's other advantage was the disastrous Avalon fire of 1915. As a result, Avalon could look however Wrigley wanted it to look because so little of the old town remained. The rhetoric of Catalina boosters would now take architectural form, as Wrigley began transforming Avalon into a more aesthetically unified community. Lots were purchased, owners of houses and businesses in prime locations were bought out, and leases were not renewed. With these properties in his possession, Wrigley could now pursue larger projects.

Above all, Avalon and Catalina would be tasteful and refined. There would be no more ticky-tacky shacks and ramshackle beachfront stands. Wrigley may not have had a master plan in mind, but he clearly knew that he wanted Catalina to be "not a Coney Island." The same vision would later guide Walt Disney in the creation of his own magic kingdom. Beachfront merchants and food vendors were strictly controlled. The longstanding tradition of local boys diving into the harbor for coins tossed by tourists arriving or departing by ship was prohibited. Wrigley worried that the youth of Avalon spent too much time "loafing" and knew that tourists who threw in small change were likely to be the subjects of obscene tirades.[11]

Next, with a few exceptions for local residents, businesses, and tour operators, cars were banned from Catalina. Never enamored with automobiles, and an avid equestrian, Wrigley enjoyed riding around Avalon on horseback, inspecting construction projects or watching his baseball team's practice sessions. Now no cars would frighten his horses, and a glut of autos, roadside cabins, gas stations, and parking lots would never mar the scenery and relaxed pace of Catalina. With the car officially banished, Catalina would become a remnant of the pre-urbanized mainland. Wrigley even bought stagecoaches, modeled on the ones once used in Yellowstone National Park, to take tourists on journeys through the island's rugged interior. Tourists might still choose to go to Palm Springs or mountain resorts, but Wrigley's reenvisioned Catalina—without cars and with strict zoning, comprehensive architectural plans, regulation of tourist access, and firm control of tourist behavior—now offered the most complete and refined escape from Los Angeles.

———————— ✦ ————————

The Bannings and the boosters had already created the image of Catalina as a healthful place of active recreation, colored by romantic evocations of Indian or mythological pasts. If anything, booster output increased in the 1920s and was accompanied by a substantial rise in Santa Catalina Island Company publications. In the Banning era, Catalina boosterism, which was strongly influenced by zoologist and sport fisherman Charles Frederick Holder, had often stressed the marine attractions and undersea wildlife the island offered. Those themes persisted, even though the trophy tuna and swordfish that had enthralled Holder were largely gone. Though Catalina's waters offered protection to these game fish, the small marine sanctuary around the island could do nothing to prevent the overfishing of sardines off the Southern California coast. The sardine population had dwindled by the 1910s, dooming the larger fish that depended on them for food.[12]

With local opportunities for sport fishing diminished, interest grew in the "history" of the island—or, more accurately, an invented Anglo-American imagining of the Indian past. This proved a hallmark of Catalina boosterism in the 1920s. William Wrigley actively fanned public interest in the subject by entering into an agreement with the Field Museum of Natural History in Chicago, which granted the museum the exclusive right to excavate Indian artifacts on Catalina. This arrangement was also intended to reduce the large number of artifacts scavenged by tourists and souvenir-shop owners.[13]

A series of fanciful short stories and novels concerning the island's Indian history were also published in this decade, and some made Charles Frederick Holder's earlier attempt at Catalina fiction (*The Adventures of Torqua*, 1902) seem a model of scholarly ethnography. One such work was *Their Mariposa Legend: A Romance of Catalina*, written by Charlotte Bronte Herr. This saga focused upon Wildenai, princess of the "Mariposa" tribe, the supposed inhabitants of Catalina. In the course of the novel, she learns that she is not an Indian, but actually a Spanish princess, banished as an infant in a palace intrigue (Holder had used the same plot device in his novel). Though smitten with a young member of Francis Drake's expedition, she ultimately marries Juan Cabrillo, and the sixteenth-century portion of the story ends. The narrative resumes on Catalina in the early twentieth century, when two tourists, descendants of the earlier characters, find true love, historical reconciliation, and priceless artifacts from Wildenai's wedding in a sea cave near Avalon.[14]

"Factual" accounts of Catalina's prehistory proved only marginally more accurate, and were far more explicit in their boosterist intentions. After the exhumation of one unusually tall skeleton, Catalina literature repeatedly claimed that the island's inhabitants had been larger and healthier than mainland Indians, and the same was asserted of Catalina's terrestrial and marine fauna. Such claims only confirmed the island's reputation for healthfulness. Also, despite exhumations of skeletons that suggested that some native Catalinans had met violent ends, ancient Catalina was portrayed as a place of peace and recreation. For example, one tourist book published by the Santa Catalina Island Company asserted that it "would seem that Catalina, even in prehistoric times, had the same soothing, gentle influence on its inhabitants as now—a study doubtless of interest to psychologists." The same book, discussing the likelihood that mainland Indians journeyed to the island in summer to fish, deduced that "Catalina was the summer playground of the mainland 'Indians' in prehistoric times, just as it is the white-man's playground today." Thus the subsistence patterns of Indians in prehistory became the leisure of white Americans in the modern era.[15]

Those enamored with Catalina would occasionally forego the Spanish or Indian past, rhapsodizing instead on possible links to far older history. Avalon, after all, had been renamed to allude to Tennyson's imagined island retreat for King Arthur. If Los Angeles and Southern California stood at the terminus of Anglo-America's westering history, perhaps Catalina was linked to ancient European legends of islands far to the west, such as the Isles of the Hesperides, or, as writer Mary Austin ruminated, perhaps even the biblical Eden.[16]

The apogee—or nadir—of this mythologizing was arguably *Catalina: A Poem*, penned by Nellie Dashiell in 1924. In it, Dashiell combined Greek and Arthurian legend, a variation of the Atlantis myth, and Anglo-Saxon racial theories to produce an epic poem concerning two young lovers, residents of an ancient Catalina inhabited by whites under constant threat from dark-skinned mainland Indians. The story was a vehicle for Dashiell's racial theorizing, taking readers back to an epoch when Catalina, "this sea-girt jewel," was "a newly-arisen uplift of the great Lemurian Continent, the Land of the Third Root Race of Humanity." These ancient Catalinans, however, were degraded and destroyed by interbreeding and "race decay." Such incoherent ramblings echoed the dark underside of regional boosterism, which asserted that the urban East was lost to immigrant "mongrel" races, and positioned Southern California as the birthplace of a hoped-for "Anglo-Saxon" civilization in the Southwest.[17]

Eager tourists nevertheless lapped up this romantic rhetoric, and repeated it almost verbatim in their diaries, albums, and scrapbooks. One example is a photograph album documenting the 1922 travels of two Ohio couples, the Humms and the Hassenfluhs. After visiting elderly relatives who had retired to Los Angeles, the couples boarded a steamer to Avalon. According to the handwritten comments of Mrs. Humm, Avalon had once been a "prosperous Indian village," home to natives who were "attractive and refined, the whole population being superior to the Indians of the mainland." The album also contained reminiscences of their ride in Catalina's trademark marine attraction, a glass-bottom boat. Mrs. Humm, however, sounded a note of caution on this subject: "Don't take this trip after a big dinner. I did!"[18]

From Regional Boosterism to Professional Promotion: Catalina and the Changing Nature of Tourism

Upon buying Catalina, Wrigley had told the Banning brothers, "If I can make people chew my gum, I can make 'em go to Catalina in the wintertime." That optimism proved unwarranted, but it did not dim his enthusiasm for remaking Catalina and marketing it to a national audience. Wrigley even orchestrated motorboat races and a 1927 cross-channel swim marathon, which resulted in extensive national media coverage—even if the race resulted in more near drownings than successful crossings. Indeed, his efforts on the island led him to become more involved in the tourist industry, for in 1929 he and a group of other investors opened a new resort hotel, the Arizona Biltmore, in Phoenix. Wrigley became the sole owner of the resort the following year.[19]

In addition to his own considerable efforts, Wrigley enjoyed the benefits of a new regional promotional program and the advent of a new industry. Catalina's increase in visitation during the 1920s was primarily the result of substantial growth in summer attendance, summer having always been its primary season. By the 1920s, Los Angeles was moving from a seasonal winter destination to a year-round attraction, and this meant more tourists for Catalina, particularly ones not from California. This had less to do with Wrigley's efforts than with the marketing program begun by the All-Year Club of Southern California, founded in 1921 by *Los Angeles Times* owner Harry Chandler and other business leaders. The All-Year Club undertook a more systematic program of promotion than those of individual resorts or boosters, marketing the region as a whole. It also conducted sophisticated surveys and studies to determine how to increase tourism, and to discern the value of the tourist industry to the local economy.

According to its own figures, the impact the All-Year Club had on Southern California tourism was remarkable. By 1931, the Club reported that greater Los Angeles welcomed a million tourists each year. These visitors spent an average of eight million dollars a week, and one in ten—a hundred thousand—would return as new residents. In 1920, the region garnered $62 million in revenue from tourists, compared to $152 million from agriculture. By 1928, agricultural output had climbed to $255 million. Yet tourism's impact on the local economy had climbed to $317 million. In 1929, 53 percent of tourists came in summer, a marked increase from earlier decades. Whereas winter tourists spent an average of 52.6 days in the region, summer visitors averaged only 16.2, and spent less than half as much money. Yet these middle- or upper-middle-class summer travelers would provide the bulk of the increased tourist traffic at Catalina. The All-Year Club continued its operations for decades, and would ultimately evolve into the Los Angeles County Convention and

Visitors Bureau, serving a key role in the transition from romantic regional boosterism to modern urban tourist and convention promotion.[20]

While statistics provided by the All-Year Club demonstrated the growth of tourism during the 1920s, they also highlighted other economic changes in the region. By the end of the decade, manufacturing output had nearly quadrupled, from $158 million to $613 million. Los Angeles had emerged as a major industrial center, and even though it might be acclaimed as "Nature's Workshop," it could no longer promote itself as a pastoral, nostalgic retreat. Newer promotional materials, while still employing older rhetoric, now sold the region as a place of activity and urbanism, even if leisure was still the key component of its continuing allure for tourists.[21]

A Los Angeles County Junior Chamber of Commerce publication, for example, presented Southern California as "the world's ideal playground," a place nature had "dedicated...to the happiness of mankind." While this overwrought language was hardly new, the recreation it emphasized was. Attractions included playgrounds, golf courses, beaches "now under proper supervision"—perhaps a veiled reference to the beach segregation imposed in the early 1920s—and "gay fiesta cities which compete each week for the favor of your attention." No longer a place of somnolent repose, Southern California offered modern recreation in an expanding urban setting. Santa Catalina, as well as its newer rival, Palm Springs, still offered a more relaxed tourist experience, but each now existed as a recreational suburb of an expanding metropolis, rather than as a small part of a larger, pastoral Southern California.[22]

Wrigley also benefited from a new regional industry—filmmaking. Individuals who worked in the film industry, from minor technicians to major stars, all frequented the island. As Catalina became popular as a filming location, Hollywood began to serve a function similar to earlier boosters, creating an image for the island and attractions for tourists. Early film productions at Catalina included several "prehistoric" dramas, including *Man's Genesis*, a 1913 Biograph picture, as well as *Cavemen's War* and *Primitive Man*, both filmed in 1914. Historical and biblical epics, such as *The Vanishing American* and *King of Kings*, both made in 1925, were another staple. Unsurprisingly, a number of marine film productions also took advantage of Catalina's scenery, including *Moby Dick* (1930), *Sea Wolf* (1930), *Mutiny on the Bounty* (1935), and *Captains Courageous* (1937). Far more useful to the Bannings and Wrigleys, however, were the increasing number of films and shorts that depicted leisure and recreation at Catalina. These included *Day at Catalina* (1914), *Swordfishing with Rod and Reel at Catalina* (1918), *Catalina, Here I Come* (1927), and *Seeing Catalina* (1927). Such films did more than any booster to highlight the attractions of the island, as flickering images of Catalina appeared in theaters all over the world.[23]

Newsreels of celebrities frolicking in the Catalina surf or "aquaplaning" (water skiing) only drew more tourists. Visitors could even rent rooms in former film sets. According to author Harry Carr, who had summered on the island in his youth during the 1890s, Catalina tourist accommodations in former film sets were eclectic, to say the least: "For a price you can have lodging for the night in what was once an officer's club in Samoa; the grass hut of the heroine in *Bird of Paradise*, . . . a guard room in a Norman Castle, or the water-front saloons of Singapore."[24]

Film also provided the most famous animal imports to Catalina, lending the island an incongruous "Wild West" image to accompany the more refined atmosphere Wrigley orchestrated. Famed western author Zane Grey, who had summered at Catalina since the late 1910s, relocated permanently in 1924, building a massive house "of Hopi Indian design" and continuing to turn out novels set in the West of legend. An emblem of that legend also came to the island in 1924, for thirteen bison bulls were shipped in for the shooting of a western film, appropriately enough Grey's Indian saga *The Vanishing American*. After filming, the bulls proved difficult to recapture, so Wrigley had thirteen bison cows shipped to the island, forming the basis for a herd that still remained in the twenty-first century.[25]

❋

The centerpiece of Wrigley's "new" Avalon was the Catalina Casino. Designed by architect Sumner Spaulding in a style described as "Adriatic," the Casino was a colossal round structure, jutting out onto a point at the far end of Avalon's harbor. Here, in May of 1929, it seemed that Avalon and Catalina had finally arrived, manifested as the Monaco of the Pacific. The upper level contained a spectacular round ballroom, complete with an inlaid wood floor. Regardless of the building's name and allusions to European pleasure spots, Wrigley permitted no continental-style debauchery. Clothing regulations—coats and ties for gentlemen, no slacks or short skirts for ladies—were strictly enforced, as were rules prohibiting dancers with wandering hands or those aspiring to more intimate contact off of the dance floor. Even after Prohibition, alcohol was banned, though this did not stop tourists from smuggling in flasks, or Avalon residents from covertly selling homemade brews to visitors. The ban on liquor would not change until after World War II, and clothing regulations were not relaxed until 1950, in marked contrast to a very different style of nightlife emerging in places like Palm Springs and Las Vegas. Catalina only grew more famous as the Casino's ballroom became a showcase venue during the 1930s and 1940s big-band era of Glenn Miller and Perry Como. By 1940, radio listeners nationwide knew Avalon as the setting for a wide variety of musical broadcasts.[26]

The lower level of the Catalina Casino, insulated from the sound of pounding feet by an elaborately layered wood-and-cork flooring system, featured a large theater, complete with murals by Hollywood studio artist Gabriel Beckman, who would later serve as the art or set director for a variety of films such as *The Maltese Falcon* and *Casablanca*. The Art Deco wall murals depicted Indians, padres, and animals. On the proscenium curtain was an image of two Indian figures—one looking ahead, the other behind with bow drawn—who appeared to be surfing the crest of a large wave as a tuna, perhaps borrowed from the dolphin murals of the Minoan palace at Knossos in Crete, leapt in front of them.

FIGURE 4.1 "Catalina, the Magic Isle." Santa Catalina Island Company pamphlet advertising the new Avalon Casino, 1929. Images such as these promoted recreational amenities, but also hinted at romantic opportunities for men—and possibly, also women—at Catalina in the 1920s. Catalina Island Museum Archives. Avalon, California.

FIGURE 4.2 View of Avalon Harbor with Wrigley steamers and Catalina Casino, ca. 1929. Catalina Island Museum Archives. Avalon, California.

FIGURE 4.3 Ballroom of Avalon Casino in "Big Band" era, 1938. Catalina Island Museum Archives. Avalon, California.

In the background, on a field of gold, was a giant map of Catalina Island. The image was entitled "Flight of Fancy Westward," though it might as well have borne a name derived from the mantra of expansionist, westering nineteenth-century America: "Westward the Course of Leisure Takes Its Way."[27]

For indeed the American empire of leisure had come to Catalina. By the late 1920s annual visitation surpassed 400,000, making Catalina one of the largest attractions in the American West. Yellowstone National Park, by comparison, drew half that number in the same years. In 1930 visitation reached 700,000, and it remained strong during the Great Depression, even as many other travel destinations languished. By the 1930s, the island had become such an integral recreational amenity for Los Angeles residents, and such a potent draw for tourists, that author Harry Carr stated that any attempt to describe Los Angeles and its environs without discussing Santa Catalina would be akin to "telling of New York without mentioning Central Park."[28]

No less important were the types of visitors coming to Catalina. While affluent Pasadenans and other members of the older regional elite still frequented the island, the newer social community of Hollywood now claimed Catalina as its summer retreat. By the 1920s film stars were vacationing on the island and buying homes in Avalon. Tom Mix built a home, while Stan Laurel, Oliver Hardy, Charlie Chaplin, and later John Wayne were regular visitors. Errol Flynn, Clark Gable, director Howard Hawks, and Mississippi novelist William Faulkner, sojourning during the 1930s and 1940s in Southern California as a Hollywood screenwriter, hunted foxes, boars, goats, and other animals in the island's mountainous interior.[29]

A comparison of the membership rolls of the Tuna Club and the Catalina Island Yacht Club, a social club that was formed later than the conservation organization, reveals the transformation. At the turn of the century, Tuna Club members had included the Pasadena elite, as well as some of the brightest stars in the Progressive firmament, from locally known Charles Frederick Holder to Gifford Pinchot and Theodore Roosevelt. In the 1920s and 1930s, the membership of the Yacht Club included Johnny Weissmuller, James Cagney, and Rudolf Valentino. The "Isle of Summer," or "Isle of Romance," had been transformed into the "Island of Glamour."[30]

Philip Wrigley and the Continuing Promotion of Catalina

William Wrigley died on 26 January 1932 at the age of sixty-one. He was placed in an imposing family mausoleum located on a hillside in Avalon's botanical gardens. The Avalon city council passed a resolution eulogizing him as a "kindly friend and neighbor who used his large means with great generosity, and devotion to our welfare, to bestow many blessings upon this community." His death, however, did not mean the end of the Wrigley era. His son, Philip K. Wrigley, born in 1894, succeeded him. He became president of the Catalina Island Company at his father's death, and would remain president until 1977.

Far from resting on his father's laurels, Philip Wrigley redoubled efforts to draw more tourists and to remake Avalon architecturally. Along Crescent Avenue, Avalon's beachfront street, palm trees were planted, and walls and fountains decorated in Catalina tile were built to form a pedestrian promenade. Buildings constructed of wood were covered in stucco. Electric and neon signs advertising restaurants, hotels, and stores were banned, and replaced with new signs created by an SCIC artist. Even employee uniforms and SCIC stationery were altered to fit an "early California" theme.

Though perhaps not as colorful a character as his father, Philip Wrigley still possessed his father's formidable skills in business and salesmanship. In addition, he exhibited a remarkable focus and discipline. Even more than his father, Philip Wrigley demonstrated a special talent for "theming" Catalina—selecting an image for the island, promoting it through carefully calibrated advertising, and staying "on message" at all times. In addition, while the father had been enamored of the island's natural beauty, the son worked in a far more systematic way to protect its natural resources. If William Wrigley had overseen the transition of Catalina from a regional to a national resort, Philip Wrigley would perfect it.[31]

For the younger Wrigley, everything was part of a larger plan. He carefully oversaw advertising campaigns, and even tried to rein in the postcard industry, which produced countless unauthorized images of Catalina. In pamphlets from the 1930s, Avalon was depicted as a Spanish-revival remnant of "Old California," the island's rugged interior as a Wild West, complete with bison and cowboys, and the isthmus as a Polynesian paradise. Wrigley also ensured that Catalina was represented in the California Exhibition Building at the 1933 Chicago Century of Progress Exhibition by a wide array of artifacts—similar to items that had been sold or displayed on the island for decades. Mounted fish, coral, shells, and kelp reminded viewers of the island's marine attractions, just as a mounted goat, raven, and quail represented terrestrial fauna. A range of "Indian relics" served to document Catalina's ancient past. Meanwhile, a display of Catalina tile and pottery vases, plates, and other items demonstrated the vitality of Catalina crafts in the present and served to remind viewers that such items were likely on sale in their local department store.[32]

Even the house Wrigley built in the 1930s in the hills above Avalon for himself and his wife fit into a promotional agenda. The Santa Catalina Island

Company touted the fact that the tile roof, wrought-iron fixtures, and wall pigments were all island products. Constructed in a "Cabrillo-Spanish" architectural style, with exterior walls "painted in natural pigments blending into the colorings of the surrounding hills," the home was an architectural advertisement for the invented history and natural beauty of Catalina. If there was ever a private residence themed to promote tourism, this was it.

This historicist theming, applied so consistently at Catalina, was not always followed in advertising on the mainland. A new SCIC ticket office built in the late 1930s in downtown Los Angeles abandoned historicist architecture for sleek modernism, as designed by Richard Neutra. The building featured a metal and glass façade, highlighted by the neon signage that was banned in Avalon. A scale model of Catalina stood in the large front window, beckoning passersby to venture inside. Perhaps Wrigley, despite his fondness for an "early California" theme, already sensed that Catalina needed an updated image to stay relevant in ever-changing Los Angeles.[33]

Promoting Catalina in a Changing Nation and Tourist Region

When the United States entered World War II, Catalina tourist operations ceased. With Southern California gripped by fears of a malevolent Japanese navy plotting an attack, the prospect of a boat trip twenty-six miles out into the Pacific was unpopular indeed. The Coast Guard ordered an end to regular passenger service on 23 December 1941. The United States Maritime Service leased several hotels in Avalon, and the coast guard leased SCIC facilities at the isthmus. The SCIC ships *Cabrillo* and *Catalina* were chartered by the government to ferry troops in the San Francisco Bay area. While military personnel and their families rented living space in Avalon, and community residents continued to make a living catering to these visitors, the island's tourist industry essentially went into hibernation for the duration of the war.[34]

This long period of inactivity may have prompted the Wrigley family's decision to remove William Wrigley's remains to a Pasadena cemetery. Thus the Wrigley Mausoleum became the "Wrigley Monument." Though the reasons appear to have been personal—including the aging Ada Wrigley's desire not to have to voyage across the Channel anymore to visit her husband's grave—some island residents interpreted this move as part of the Wrigley family's increasing disengagement from Catalina. In fact, there is some evidence that the Wrigleys were considering divesting themselves of the island, if not selling it outright. In the late 1940s, Los Angeles County Supervisor

John Anson Ford was apprised of rumors that the Wrigleys were concerned about the inheritance-tax liability Catalina posed, and were receptive to offers that might include the purchase of the island by a public entity. Regardless of these rumors, such plans were not acted upon in the 1940s.[35]

Santa Catalina Island Company operations resumed after the war. Following the gas rations and limited travel opportunities of the war years, Philip Wrigley expected a new tourist boom. Commercial air travel now linked the nation together, and Wrigley, who had served as a navy pilot during World War I, understood the tourist potential of air travel. Since 1940, small aircraft had in fact been servicing Catalina's "Airport in the Sky," an airstrip graded on a mountaintop in the island's interior. Hydroplanes had brought tourists to Catalina as early as the 1920s. Tourists could fly to Catalina for less than fourteen dollars, or about three times the basic ferry rate. Wrigley knew that increased prosperity would bring more car tourists to Southern California as well. By 1950, three and a half million tourists visited Southern California each year.[36]

Though his father's plan for an upscale resort community at the isthmus had not come to fruition, Philip Wrigley would now promote the isthmus as a secluded retreat that offered an exotic escape. He instructed Alma Overholt, publicist for the SCIC, to inform travelers that the isthmus would not have all the activities offered at Avalon: "The feature of the isthmus is its remoteness and the fact that it offers simply a pleasant place to relax and do nothing." Wrigley also oversaw the development of advertising slogans for the isthmus: "As secluded as you want to be…as lazy as you can be." A "Polynesian" atmosphere was crafted for the new resort area and promoted aggressively. According to the SCIC, the isthmus was "informal as a grass skirt," a place where tourists could indulge in the "poetry of pure indolence," and the "luxury of laziness." Here was the perfect refuge for overworked white urbanites—with an emphasis on white: "This is the place to be yourself— your chance to 'go native' for awhile. Trade your city clothes for a coat of tan. Forget the white man's burden."[37]

Wrigley's emphasis on organization and careful attention to theme had already proven a Wrigley hallmark, but now it was accompanied by a sense of urgency. With a new tourist era dawning after the war years, Wrigley was intent that Catalina remain a national destination, rather than revert to the regional attraction it had once been. To do this, he stressed the exotic nature of Catalina's indigenous flora and fauna, as well as the botanical gardens and aviary constructed by his father. The island itself needed to appear more exotic and sophisticated to a traveling public that was more savvy, more affluent, and had more access to long-distance travel than any population that preceded it. The tent villages were demolished, in part because they were a fire hazard, but also because the accommodations they offered were no longer suitable for tourists accustomed to chain hotels and motels across the nation. The big bands and radio broadcasts had focused national attention on Catalina prior to the war, and Wrigley himself had negotiated the contract to have concerts broadcast nationwide on CBS Radio. Now, however, the popularity of big band music was in decline. Wrigley reduced the size of the dance floor in the Catalina Casino, adding a restaurant to the ballroom. He thought that band concerts were too seasonal and aimed at too narrow an audience. There was also the problem of the inability to connect the big bands to the island's image. According to Wrigley, "there was absolutely no travel theme in a name band at the Casino."[38]

Wrigley's correspondence sometimes betrayed a bit of exasperation with how Southern Californians continued to view the island he was attempting to remake: "If we are ever to get away from the local idea that Catalina is the West Coast Coney Island, and including local zoological and botanical gardens the same as are maintained in New York's Central Park, Chicago's Lincoln Park, and so forth, and if we want people to think of Catalina in terms of travel we must associate it with travel and preferably world travel." Henceforth, the "Submarine Gardens" visible from Catalina's glass-bottom boats would be compared to Australia's Great Barrier Reef, rather than romantic fairylands or echoes of American landmarks, as they had been in decades past.[39]

———————— ✳ ————————

Like his father, Wrigley also tried to maintain moral standards on his island. In the 1890s and 1900s, Catalina had offered exciting possibilities for young people to escape parental authority and the usual mores of society. That sense of possibility was now more muted, for the opportunities for intimate relations were now contained within the heterosexual courtship rituals of a somewhat more liberated society. Though excessive intimacy was discouraged on the dance floor of the Casino, strangers were encouraged to dance together, and the SCIC had no control over the actions of dance partners once they left the Casino. While Catalina could not sell sex in the way that Las Vegas later would, it certainly did sell "romance." The decision of actors Mary Pickford and Douglas Fairbanks to honeymoon on Catalina only heightened its renown. The fact that Catalina-brand swimwear was marketed nationally and featured styles far more revealing than those that had once raised eyebrows in Avalon certainly did not hurt the island's image either.

Decades after tourists of the 1890s had produced poetic reveries of Catalina, generations of songwriters penned their own odes to the island. These included songs such as "Avalon" (1920), in which Al Jolson sang about supposedly finding and leaving a lover on the island; "Catalina, My Isle of Love" (1932); Catalina Island, Isle of Romance" (1946), in which songwriter Harold Spina's lyrics stated that Catalina had "haunted, taunted me to take a chance," and "Catalina Honeymoon" (1950). The most famous song the island inspired, however, was probably "Twenty-Six Miles" (1957), by the Four Preps. Here Catalina was seduction made emblematic, the "island of romance, romance, romance, romance." This was a heterosexual male tourist fantasy come true, a "tropical heaven out in the ocean covered with trees and girls."[40]

Philip Wrigley's determination to showcase Catalina as an exotic destination was not merely a response to demographic changes in the tourist market. American tourists had become more geographically venturesome. In addition, a substantial number now had tastes that would have left the late Victorian patrons of Avalon aghast. While Wrigley consistently claimed he wanted Catalina to be an exotic and alluring national tourist destination, he was clearly concerned about another "exotic" travel destination that was uncomfortably close—Mexico. Southern Californians had long exhibited an intense—and not entirely friendly—interest in northern Mexico, particularly Baja California. Avalon, for that matter, had been remade in an "early California" architectural style, complete with Mexicans hired to perform as dancers, musicians, and singers. The Auto Club of Southern California published a travel narrative and guide to Baja California in 1930, but well before that, Los Angeles investors and corporations—including the *Los Angeles Times*—produced publications aimed at increasing travel and investment in Mexico. As early as the 1880s, Tijuana had been promoted as a tourist destination, with hot springs equal to those at the famed Arkansas resort. Such publications evidenced Anglo-American interest in Mexico's economic and tourist potential that was not entirely benign. Harrison Gray Otis, the publisher of the *Times*, had once been one of the loudest voices in a throng of Southern Californians who had urged the United States to purchase—or simply annex—Baja California so that it could become an extension of Southern California.[41]

In the 1920s and 1930s, Mexico drew two very different sorts of tourists. Some were simply more adventurous members of the tourist throngs that already flocked to Southern California, as well as those who had made a home there. These travelers went to Mexico to see the charm of "old California," visiting missions, quaint villages, and enjoying picturesque scenery unmarred by the rampant development north of the border. Catalina undoubtedly lost some tourists to these attractions, particularly after the development of short cruises along the coast of Baja California, as well as the development of Ensenada as a tourist port. The fact that Mexican waters also offered an escape from U.S. fishing conservation laws undoubtedly drew away some sport fishermen who had once frequented Catalina. The Coronado Islands, in fact, which lay only twenty miles from San Diego, made this a theme in promotional materials aimed at the American market.[42]

Most materials created to draw American tourists, however, sounded much like the rhetoric used decades earlier to draw Midwestern tourists to Southern California. Whether produced by American or Mexican entrepreneurs, American corporations, or even the Mexican government, promotional materials all deployed the rhetoric of romance, urging Anglos to travel along the "Roads of Romance Land." As tourism in Mexico became a larger industry, however, resorts in Mexico began to promote themselves as places of glamour, sophistication, and excitement. The Agua Caliente resort in Tijuana, for example, boasted a spa, casino, golf course, dog track, and dinners with a floor show. It claimed to be the "Playground of the Stars," a place where locals might speak a "strange language," but everyone spoke in "in a tongue understood by all . . . happiness."[43]

The post-Revolution government of Mexico perceived tourism as an ideal industry, attracting capital and aiding infrastructural development. It could also be used to highlight and publicize the ancient cultural and architectural heritage of indigenous Mexico, as well as the urban cosmopolitanism of Mexico City. In this view, playing host to Americans—citizens of the same nation that had forcibly taken half of Mexican territory in 1848—could bolster the economy and stature of Mexico. Further, government leaders hoped to emulate Southern California's great success, and Los Angeles, San Diego, and regional resorts were seen as key models by government and business leaders in Mexico City and border communities.[44]

Resorts such as Agua Caliente made no secret of the fact that the Mexican government permitted regulated gambling, and, unlike the United States, did not prohibit alcohol during the 1920s and early 1930s. While casinos and liquor drew a crowd that enjoyed "sophisticated" vices, Mexico also drew tourists with markedly different tastes—people in search of drugs and prostitution. The border towns of Tijuana and Mexicali drew large numbers of Americans seeking escape from the social restrictions of their own society. The social costs these communities faced as a result of being used as a moral escape valve for Americans were dire. Concerned Mexican citizens even coined the term "tijuanización" to describe the spread of vice along the border. In 1934, Lázaro Cárdenas was elected president of Mexico, and he terminated the government's toleration of vice.[45]

Such government action, however, could not curb the appetites of American tourists. After a lull, Tijuana boomed anew during World War II, when it witnessed a vast influx of American soldiers and sailors. Gambling and prostitution soon found refuge within the United States as well. After 1934, Las Vegas began its career as Sin City. In Santa Monica Bay, a series of ships anchored just outside the three-mile limit of government jurisdiction served as floating casinos, and lured Angelenos from the late 1920s until World War II. When the federal government banned gambling in American waters, the most successful casino-boat operator, Antonio Cornero Stralla, better known as Tony Cornero, simply relocated to Las Vegas, where he planned the construction of the Stardust hotel and casino. The boosters of Los Angeles had once hoped that the growth of the region would rejuvenate white Americans and in turn transform the nation. This sort of transformation, however, was not necessarily the kind they had envisioned. A new and decidedly different frontier of leisure was now spreading outward from Southern California, as Las Vegas became an adult playground for Los Angeles.[46]

Catalina's Decline as a Resort Destination

Despite all of Wrigley's disciplined efforts, Catalina visitation declined in the 1950s. Some of this decline resulted from the postwar resurgence of auto tourism and family trips to places such as national parks. Mexico and Nevada also drew former Catalina visitors. A major reason for waning attendance, however, was the 1955 opening of Walt Disney's new theme park in Orange County. Southern California families now had a metaphorical island retreat from urban life conveniently located on the auto-dominated mainland. Just as William Wrigley had been deeply imprinted by the Chicago Columbian Exposition of 1893, so had Walt Disney. His father, Elias Disney, a carpenter, had helped construct the "White City" at the Columbian Exposition that had so dazzled Wrigley, and he now aimed to create a permanent version of that fair. Disneyland, like Catalina, was a place "themed" to evoke historical and mythological pasts. As at Catalina, the tourist experience was firmly steered by a corporation that deemed what activities—and which visitors—were acceptable. While commentators at the time, as well as subsequent historians, presented the creation of Disneyland as an original, even unparalleled, event, it should clearly be understood instead as the culmination of longstanding regional trends.[47]

In addition to the advent of Disneyland, regional society had changed markedly. While in the 1890s Catalina had provided a marked contrast to the culture of Victorian resorts, by the 1950s and early 1960s it seemed staid in comparison to Southern California's emergent beach youth culture, centered on surfing and rock and roll. In the late nineteenth century, Catalina had offered young people an escape from prevailing mores and parental authority. By the 1960s, many teenagers or young adults would likely have viewed Catalina as a place dominated by the tastes of their parents'—or grandparents'—generation.

This more conservative image drew a more conservative crowd. According to a series of surveys of California-bound tourists conducted by the All-Year Club of Southern California in the later 1940s and 1950s, visitors to

Catalina were slightly less affluent and markedly more rural than tourists traveling to Southern California as a whole. They were significantly more likely to be staying with relatives rather than in a hotel, and spent less than the average tourist. Most came from smaller cities and towns in the Midwest, and they were more likely than other tourists to live on a farm. In the middle twentieth century, the average Catalina tourist represented precisely the same demographic that had been targeted in the late nineteenth century by the *Los Angeles Times*, *Land of Sunshine*, and Sunkist crate labels.[48]

William Wrigley might have been pleased that his island, once the preserve of the affluent, had undeniably become a middle-class attraction. He, however, would not have been pleased with the changing results of tourist surveys that inquired about the tourists' level of interest in various California attractions. In 1937, when it was at its apogee, Catalina had been ranked highest of any single attraction in the state, listed behind only such generalities as climate or varied scenery. A 1942 survey of tourists over the age of fifty ranked Catalina highly as well.[49]

Things had changed markedly by the fall of 1956, when the All-Year Club queried more than a thousand tourists bound for Disneyland. This group, which was likely dominated by families with young children, ranked Catalina last of all Southern California attractions that interested them. Perhaps not surprisingly, Catalina lost out to newer attractions such as Disneyland and Knott's Berry Farm. It even ranked behind Forest Lawn Cemetery and the Los Angeles Farmers Market.[50]

Tourists had changed, and the tourist industry had changed as well. With airlines expanding service and airfares dropping, a journey to a truly exotic island archipelago—Hawaii—became possible for a growing number of travelers, particularly those on the West Coast. In the 1960s, Catalina's slackening tourist visitation was further compounded by tax and labor problems, and by accusations that the Wrigley family was running the island as a private fiefdom.[51]

The aging Philip Wrigley, once so focused and disciplined, did not attempt to address these issues aggressively. Instead, his attention shifted from tourist operations and promotion to island environmental issues. He took the much-beloved steamer *Catalina* out of commission. For the first time since 1892, when the Bannings took possession of Catalina, the owners of the island no longer operated ships to bring tourists to its shores. Private ferry companies, with smaller, faster boats, more flexible schedules, and more trips per day, took over Catalina's passenger traffic. The SCIC leased its hotels, as well as the Avalon golf course and Country Club, to concessionaires. The SCIC-owned island utilities, which provided Avalon with water and power, were sold to the Southern California Edison Company.[52]

In 1953 the SCIC began a rigorous rangeland restoration project, including the prohibition of all cattle grazing on the island. At the isthmus, Wrigley commissioned a contour map of all the trees in the area to ensure that none were cut down, and oversaw the installation of a sewer plant to end the dumping of sewage in the ocean. He hired William Pereira and Associates to create a master plan for Catalina, which was unveiled in 1962. Its ambitious plans for development, including a rail line connecting Avalon with Two Harbors, the small settlement at the isthmus, were never enacted.[53]

By the early 1970s, Wrigley, no longer overseeing SCIC operations, took steps to end his family's direct oversight of Catalina, a relationship that had lasted more than five decades. In January of 1974, the Santa Catalina Island Company and the Wrigley family approached Los Angeles County with an offer to place 41,500 acres—85 percent of the island—under a conservation easement. The SCIC would agree to keep all the land covered by this easement undeveloped for twenty-five years. Avalon, Two Harbors, and two other bays would remain under SCIC control. In exchange, Los Angeles County property taxes, which cost the Wrigleys $300,000 per year at the time, would be reduced by 90 percent. The county presented a counteroffer, which extended the open-space easement to fifty years, required the SCIC to allow some island activities to be free to the public, and gave the county the right to veto any future SCIC development plans. The Wrigleys agreed, and subsequently donated 86 percent of the island to the Catalina Island Conservancy, a land trust that would preserve its holdings in an undeveloped state. The family retained control of 13 percent of the island. Only 1 percent, almost all of which was in Avalon, remained in other private hands. On 28 February 1974, the Los Angeles County Board of Supervisors approved the open-space easement.[54]

Politicians and environmentalists hailed the agreement as a landmark in the preservation of open space. Claims that the easement effectively doubled the amount of public parkland in Los Angeles County, however, were less credible. This "public" park lay twenty-six miles off the coast, and was only accessible by private boats. Nevertheless, the county department of parks and recreation drew up plans to increase public utilization of Catalina, where visitation had once approached a million people a year, but was now viewed as "publicly underused." Here was an isolated, rural antipode to an urban area of seven million people. The language used in Los Angeles County reports and planning documents reflected the imagery and prose of the Bannings, the Wrigleys, and generations of boosters: "Catalina Island is a destination point for the weekend, and perhaps even a vacation...It is ocean, archaeological remains, mountains, Catalina ironwood, lakes, wild goats and buffalo. It is a significant opportunity to escape urbanization—to undertake those recreational activities essential in understanding and thereby enjoying this splendid natural resource."[55]

The leisure Angelenos hoped to find at Catalina in the 1970s was far different from the leisure earlier generations had sought there. Decades before, the island had been touted as the best place to enjoy Southern California's scenery and active life in the outdoors. Catalina, Charles Frederick Holder and other boosters claimed, was the place that would restore the vitality of turn-of-the-century Americans by putting them back in contact with authentic, unspoiled nature. By the standards of the time, it also had offered release from societal constraints, a chance to let natural impulses take their course, though only for affluent Anglos. Now it was a place to escape the urban grid Southern California had become. Although residents of Los Angeles might still seek leisure that offered excitement, they no longer looked to Catalina. Though the county made extensive plans to develop public use of the island during the 1970s, these plans came to a halt in 1978, when the passage of the tax-cutting Proposition 13 gutted funding for parks and public recreation in Los Angeles and the rest of California. The plans were never revived.[56]

Catalina had grown popular by offering a more active vacation than most resorts of the nineteenth century, portending the outdoor athletic recreation of the twentieth century. Southern California initially rose to prominence as a place of lazy sunshine and magnificent vistas. Yet as metropolitan Los Angeles changed from a southwestern pastoral to a southwestern metropolis, the older, idyllic image grew strained. Los Angeles continued to prosper, however, drawing tourists and new residents not with promises of pastoral languor, but with the glamour of Hollywood and the excitement of new attractions such as Disneyland. During the same decades, Catalina still drew millions of tourists, including many attracted by the allure of celebrity culture.

Gradually, however, the island began to draw fewer visitors, and those who came did so for different reasons. No matter how much money they spent or how effectively the Wrigleys packaged it, the fact remained that Catalina was indelibly imprinted by an earlier era, one increasingly distant from society on the mainland. Catalina had once been the nation's first corporate resort and the first to be fully themed to embody physically the booster mythology of Southern California. The Wrigleys' island would still draw tourists looking for quaint architecture, marine recreation, or spectacular mountain and ocean vistas, but its time as a national destination and trendsetter for resort culture was largely over.

No longer primarily associated with vigorous outdoor recreation, or even with Hollywood, Catalina offered a nostalgic retreat to the past—a past based upon the boosterist visions of Catalina's earlier promoters. The island, more than ever, provided escape from the increasingly frenetic mainland and its rule of "autos über alles." Boosters of an earlier era had sold Los Angeles itself as a suburban paradise that transcended traditional urban problems and offered outdoor recreation to all. That myth was long gone by the late twentieth century. In the 1890s Charles Frederick Holder, Catalina's greatest booster, had called Santa Catalina "a bit of Southern California anchored offshore." By the 1990s, a guidebook would describe it as "Southern California without the freeways." Catalina had become a lingering outpost of an older Southern California and of the region's enduring image of itself.[57]

The same could be said of the island in the early twenty first century—it remains an achingly beautiful reminder of what Southern California once looked like in its pre-urbanized state. For some Southern Californians, however, it is a reminder of a far earlier past—the precontact Native American world of the Tongva and Chumash. The Tongva, who inhabited much of Los Angeles County and all of Catalina, continue to fight for federal tribal recognition and greater visibility in Los Angeles. They are also a more visible presence at Catalina in the early twenty-first century than at any time since their forced removal by the Spanish in the 1820s. An archaeological field school, representing a collaboration of the Cotsen Institute of Archaeology at UCLA, the Santa Catalina Island Conservancy, and Tongva tribal members, is currently cataloging Tongva sites on Catalina as part of the Catalina (Pimu) Island Field Archaeological Project to identify and protect Tongva sites on the island. In 1995, the *Moomat Ahiko* (Breath of the Sea), the first full-scale traditional Tongva plank-and-tar canoe built in generations, made its maiden voyage at Catalina. It was the first time such a vessel had appeared in the Bay of Seven Moons since the early nineteenth century.[58]

For the broader public, Catalina last received widespread media attention when wildfires threatened Avalon in 2007, a reminder of the terrible fire of 1915, as well as the frightening vulnerability of so many parts of urbanized Southern California to fire. Thankfully, the fire was beaten back, and Avalon still has its quaint homes and striking Mediterranean Catalina Casino. The sea is as azure as ever, and the flying fish still shoot out of the ocean and glide above the waves, to the delight of tourists. The fires may even have aided native plants in reclaiming more of the island's rugged backcountry. While Catalina remained subject to both historical and environmental change, it was no longer a national tourist destination, or a pace-setting resort. Perhaps a battle royal will erupt in 2024 when the open-space easement created in 1974 ends. The heirs of William Wrigley could conceivably return, with development plans more audacious that even those of their ancestors. Federal recognition of the Tongva could also lead to a change in legal status, or even the creation of a tribal reservation on the island, as was briefly considered in the 1860s. Barring such remarkable developments, however, Catalina seems to have arrived at a point of stasis. To find the dynamism and innovation that had characterized Catalina in its heyday, and a resort that proved more attuned to a more modern and urban Southern California—though one that would also possess a significant, and permanent, Native American population—one must abandon the ocean for the desert, and the island of Catalina for the oasis of Palm Springs.

Chapter Five

THE OASIS OF LEISURE

Palm Springs before 1941

DURING THE 1880s and 1890s, while Los Angeles boomed and Santa Catalina first emerged as a regional resort, most tourists to the region promoted as "Southern California" avoided the Mojave and Colorado deserts that lay to the east and north. One hundred miles east of Los Angeles, beyond San Gorgonio Pass, lay the Coachella Valley, part of the Colorado Desert that stretched south to the Mexican border. On the western edge of the valley stood Mount San Jacinto, one of the tallest peaks in Southern California. Along its eastern flank ran a series of canyons, lined with *Washingtonia filifera* palms. These palms, found in the Southwest and northern Mexico, are the only species of palm tree indigenous to the western United States. Near the mouth of one of these canyons, Tahquitz Canyon, stood a grove of palms. In their midst a hot spring issued from the sandy earth, creating a large pool.

This small oasis would serve as the nucleus for Palm Springs, one of Southern California's signature resorts. Initially a failed agricultural venture in the 1890s, and a tiny tuberculosis sanatorium in the 1910s, this community emerged as one of the most famous resorts in the United States between 1920 and the eve of World War II. It would serve as a destination for Hollywood, and for a national elite. It would influence national tourist, resort, and recreational culture, popularizing the suntan, sports, more casual (and minimal) dress, and relaxed social mores. Palm Springs would also influence resort and residential architecture, from modernist masterpieces to early versions of the later ubiquitous ranch-style house. It would even ignite a regional and national desert craze among tourists and environmentalists, and create new perceptions of desert landscapes, flora, and fauna attuned to the urban, consumerist society of the twentieth-century United States. As at Catalina, however, tourism would also lead to conflict between white tourists and nonwhite residents and workers, most notably the Agua Caliente Band of Cahuilla Indians, who had lived at the oasis for centuries. The Agua Calientes had been granted a reservation, and the lands of the reservation and privately owned tracts both underlay the resort town. This meant that the Agua Calientes, unlike the unfortunate Tongva residents of Catalina, could not be forcibly removed. They were a permanent fixture of the community, and in the longer term they would be far more than that, playing an important and ultimately unprecedented role in the history of Native Americans and tourism.

In some respects, Palm Springs resembled Santa Catalina Island. Its tourist economy developed after other economic enterprises had failed. Its boosters likewise promoted outdoor recreation and a healthful climate. Palm Springs would sometimes curry a historicist or fantastical themed atmosphere, drawing on regional history or allusions to exotic places elsewhere. Like Catalina, the resort first drew the affluent, but gradually attracted a more diverse clientele.[1]

Yet Palm Springs differed in fundamental ways from Catalina. It was developed by a small number of entrepreneurs, rather than a corporation. Its independently owned resorts and hotels would pursue varying architectural styles and development models, and would also draw varying clienteles. It would have its share of promoters and boosters, as had Catalina, but it would also have—virtually from the resort's beginning—Hollywood, which would grant it increased visibility; celebrities, furthermore, were fixtures not only as visitors but as semipermanent residents and political and economic players in the community. In Catalina, the mixture of resentments and dependency locals felt toward the Santa Catalina Island Company led to a bipolar, limited local political scene of the company versus locals. The SCIC, especially in the Banning era, was the guarantor of racial and class exclusion at Catalina. The more diverse community of Palm Springs would have a more complicated political history. There, as in Los Angeles, affluent Anglos tried to use government power to achieve the racial and socioeconomic exclusion they desired.

The older island resort, themed and controlled by the SCIC, had been affected by the same Gilded Age social and cultural currents that lured Anglo-Americans to Southern California in the first place. Their flight from eastern winters and humid summers, their fretting about "un-American" immigration, urbanization, and the growing power of corporations and industries that were remaking American society—all these attitudes shaped

Catalina's development. Its geographic status as an island was fortuitous, for Catalina, in both the Banning and Wrigley eras, was fundamentally insular. It was an escape from urbanism. The automobile was prohibited from its shores. To journey to Catalina was to step back in time to an older Southern California, preserved on the island like extinct creatures encased in amber. In this sheltered setting, Anglo-Americans could make leisure safely domestic and unthreatening. Abandoning the old view of leisure as a vice or a danger, Catalina offered healthful recreation and a respite from the working world, to which tourists would return refreshed and productive.

If Palm Springs likewise began as a retreat from urbanism, over time it would become a more urban place, and would even come to influence national urban development. The boosters and tourists who began venturing to Palm Springs after 1900, and especially after World War I, belonged to a different era. Some of them were also in flight from urban woes. Now, however, they were fleeing not the East but the burgeoning urbanism of Southern California. Unlike the first generation of Southern California boosters, for whom the region's appeal had been agrarian and pastoral—as typified by its citrus plantations—this generation sought wilderness and "pristine" nature. Unlike Charles Lummis or Charles Frederick Holder, who were motivated by purported end-of-the-frontier anxieties and a hypermasculine compulsion to prove oneself against nature, many of the early boosters of Palm Springs and the desert came in search of aesthetic contemplation, and were as refined as Lummis had tried to be rugged. Lummis had set out to test himself against the harshness of the desert, and Holder against the trophy tuna, for both men were eager to ensure the vitality of Anglo-America. Most new recreationalists, in contrast, would trade the overheated rhetoric of racial redemption, so prevalent in Southern California's early boom years, for giddy consumerism.

These new recreationalists were more cosmopolitan and more acclimated to modern life. No longer fretting as Lummis and his ilk had about the dangers of capitalism, most of these desert pilgrims came ready to consume. Consumption would be a primary way through which they would come to know the desert. These new desert aficionados, instead of trekking off into the wilderness, would create desert gardens in their backyards. Finally, these new recreationalists, and those who would follow, were increasingly unencumbered by fears about the potential dangers of leisure. They had already embraced it. Instead, they wanted to explore ever-newer diversions and possibilities, perceiving seemingly endless frontiers of leisure. The history of Palm Springs from its origins to World War II and beyond proved that they would take leisure—and it would take them—very far indeed.

The Agua Calientes and Anglo Settlers in Palm Springs before the Tourists

In the late nineteenth century, before Palm Springs had acquired its tourist name, the only residents of the desert oasis were the Agua Calientes, one band of the larger Cahuilla Indian cultural group, which occupied a vast swath of arid terrain in southeastern California. This band had never been directly subjected to the Spanish mission system, but became known to Anglo-Americans through the Spanish name for their warm spring, literally "hot water." The Cahuilla first encountered Europeans in the form of the Spanish De Anza expedition in the 1770s, on its way north from Sonora to the San Francisco Bay. The next Europeans the Cahuilla likely encountered were not humans but animals—stray cattle from Mission San Gabriel that wandered through San Gorgonio Pass. By 1809 baptisms of Cahuillas were recorded at the mission. They had adopted the Spanish language and acculturated to some Mexican lifeways, but still hunted and gathered in the surrounding desert and mountain terrain. They also raised livestock, agave, melons, and other fruit crops. After U.S. annexation in 1848, leaders of various Cahuilla bands signed the treaty of Temecula in 1851 with the Americans, and a reservation system was created in the 1870s. Some members of the band found

FIGURE 5.1 The landscape of Palm Springs. Cacti dot the desert floor of the Coachella Valley, while the snow-capped peak of Mount San Jacinto rises in the distance. The Agua Calientes' oasis, and the resort community it helped create, both lie at the base of the San Jacinto Mountains. Palm Springs Historical Society, Palm Springs, California.

agricultural wage labor in Anglo farming communities to the west, such as Riverside. Others helped build the Southern Pacific Railroad as it traversed the Coachella Valley. For these reasons the Agua Calientes' experience differed greatly from that of the natives of Catalina, decimated by disease, who had been forcibly relocated to the mainland during the mission era, where many had died.[2]

The Agua Calientes had also avoided the genocide and chaos that swept away so much of the native population of California's Sierras and Central Valley in the decades following the Gold Rush. Like some other Cahuilla groups, they were largely settled agrarians. As such, they were accorded a status akin to that of the Pueblo Indians—village dwellers who were deemed by whites to possess some manifestations of civilization and were therefore seen as less likely to pose a threat than purportedly violent nomadic tribal groups. As with the Pueblos, their crafts—in this case, basketry and pottery—were accorded high esteem. Anglos such as Stephen Bowers, the president of the Ventura Society of Natural History, argued in the 1880s that the Agua Calientes deserved better treatment than natives such as the Apache: "The Cahuilla Indians have received very little assistance from the government. While it has fed a class of murderous and thieving marauders, too lazy to work, and too vicious to make any advance in civilization, these peaceful Indians have been almost totally neglected." Of course, in some respects this neglect worked to their benefit.[3]

Nevertheless, the Agua Calientes had faced dire hardships as well. A smallpox epidemic in 1863, along with the cumulative tolls of other European diseases, meant that the total Cahuilla population had dropped from a precontact population of perhaps five thousand to a population of only one thousand by the 1880s. A severe drought that also began in the 1860s made game and edible vegetation scarce. Earthquakes posed dangers as well; both the San Andreas and San Jacinto faults snaked under the desert sands of the Coachella. Yet these faults also forced groundwater to the surface, creating springs that sustained the Cahuilla. Francisco Patencio, the last traditional tribal leader of the Agua Calientes, recalled stories of titanic earthquakes that struck during his early childhood in the 1850s. These likely included the last recorded rupture of the southern San Andreas, the Fort Tejon quake of 1857, as well as strong quakes that hit near San Bernardino in 1858. Streams and springs dried up, apparently never to return. Whites later noted that after any tremor the Agua Calientes always anxiously inspected the hot springs, afraid that movements in the earth might cut off the flow to the oasis that had been their lifeblood. No less traumatic than changes in available water was that these large earthquakes, according to Patencio, changed the land itself: "There came such earthquakes as had not been known to any of the people. Whole mountains split—some rose up where there had been none before. Other peaks went down, and never came up again. It was a terrible time. The mountains that the people knew well were strange places that they had never seen before."[4]

This language, vividly conveying the sense of dislocation they felt, was well-suited to the situation of the Agua Calientes as the nineteenth century drew to a close. Their valley, the landscape they knew better than any other, had unalterably changed. Yet this was not simply a matter of topography. The way they secured food, the way they made a living, their interactions with non-Indians—all had changed. And yet despite this, though affected by disease and the new cash economy, the Agua Calientes still occupied their traditional lands and held title to them. Claims to water were more complex, with the private water laws of the United States conflicting with communal Spanish and Mexican water laws and Cahuilla tradition. Still, the Agua Calientes would prove adept at navigating the treacherous currents of western water law as well. Whites often tried to override their interests but would find that the Cahuillas were an unavoidable part of Palm Springs. At first they would simply endure, a triumph in itself. Haltingly, however, the Agua Calientes would play an ever-larger role in Palm Springs. In the process, they created a new role for Native Americans in the history of tourism.

The Agua Calientes had maintained control of their land only through a tortured and circuitous process. The Southern Pacific Railroad constructed a line traversing the Coachella Valley, reaching Indio in 1867 and Yuma on the Colorado River in 1877, connecting Southern California and Arizona. As with other rail lines, the federal government rewarded the railroad with alternating mile-square sections of land on each side of the route. Only later, however, did the government realize that the Agua Calientes were entitled to reservation land in the same area. The railroad was allowed the keep its odd-numbered sections, which it gradually sold. Many alternate even-numbered sections were given to the Agua Calientes, as well as additional Cahuilla bands and other tribes in the region. The result was a grid-like patchwork of private and reservation land stretching across the valley floor. Later Anglo inhabitants, profiting from the rising real estate of a resort town, would call this the "golden checkerboard." This pattern was formalized in the Mission Indian Act of 1891. The act also granted Section 14—the 640 acres that included the oasis itself and would later lie at the heart of downtown Palm Springs—to the Agua Calientes. This pattern of land ownership would fundamentally shape the future development of the resort community.[5]

The first white homesteaders to buy land near the Agua Calientes were the McCallums, a family that had relocated from San Francisco in 1884. John Guthrie McCallum, born in 1826 in Vevay, Indiana, went to California in 1854, looking for two brothers who had struck out for the Gold Rush. He arrived in San Francisco to find that both had died in an epidemic. He nevertheless stayed in California, met his future wife, Emily Freeman, and moved to Oakland, where they had several children. The family survived an 1881 typhoid epidemic, but one son, Johnny, was diagnosed with tuberculosis. Doctors told his parents that their best hope was to move to a warmer, drier climate.[6]

McCallum took a position as an Indian agent in San Bernardino County. There, a Cahuilla Indian assistant, Will Pablo, told him of the oasis on the west side of the Coachella Valley. McCallum believed that the Coachella Valley's warm winter weather meant that fruit could be grown earlier here than anywhere else in California, arriving on the market a full month or more ahead of citrus crops from other parts of the state. He also hoped that the desert air would cure his son. The Southern Pacific Railroad had already built several small cabins at a station near Indio, southeast of the oasis, when consumptives could rent accommodations. The McCallums came to the desert, like so many had come to Southern California, hoping for health and wealth. They would find only disaster.[7]

McCallum was appointed Indian agent for the Agua Calientes, but, like many other Indian agents, he seemed far more concerned with his own interests than those of the Indians. He hired Indians to build an adobe ranch house near a stream emanating from Tahquitz Canyon, and then constructed a ditch that diverted the Whitewater River across the Coachella Valley to irrigate his land. He did this even though the Agua Calientes were guaranteed water from Tahquitz and other streams as part of their treaty with the federal government. McCallum hoped to use this water to irrigate and sell land in a new development he called Palm Valley, centered on 320 acres he had purchased. McCallum's Palm Valley Land and Water Company made $50,000 from the sale of 137 parcels in 1887. This acreage would later constitute the heart of non–tribally owned downtown Palm Springs.

Palm Valley did not prove a success. The Whitewater canal kept silting up, and some buyers began defaulting. Summer heat was so intense that some buyers simply left, leaving their crops to wilt in the sun. Severe floods hit in 1893, followed by a decade of drought. Personal tragedies compounded these hardships. Johnny McCallum died in 1891. His tuberculosis was aggravated by a cold he caught after falling asleep and accidentally drenching himself with cold water while tending his family's irrigation ditch. Another son, Wallace, died of a heart condition aggravated by alcoholism in 1896.[8]

A new Indian agent, Frances Estudillo, informed the Bureau of Indian Affairs of McCallum's unauthorized acquisition of the Agua Calientes' water. In 1897 the federal government ruled that the water did indeed belong to the Cahuillas. This sounded the death knell for the McCallums' settlement. John McCallum died that same year. His remaining son, Harry, took over control of his father's land company, but died during a business trip to Chicago in 1901, also a victim of tuberculosis. One of his two daughters, May, died a few years later of a heart attack. His widow, Emily, and lone surviving child, Pearl, were forced to sell fruit and firewood to survive, and eventually sold their shares in the Palm Valley Land and Water Company. Pearl left the Coachella Valley for Los Angeles, where she married Pasadena real-estate salesman Harold McManus in 1914. Her mother died the same year. Pearl managed to keep title to some of her father's land, and reclaimed some that had been sold. Over time, with her husband's assets, she was able to buy back more land. Most importantly, she was able to maintain title to the strip that would later be the frontage of Palm Canyon Drive, one of the most expensive stretches of real estate in the country. Her tenacity and frugality—not to mention her prickly personality—would not always earn friends, but she was a survivor. Her family's efforts in the desert had met with tragedy, but Pearl McCallum McManus would be back.[9]

———————— ✳ ————————

In marked contrast to the McCallums, subsequent Anglo-Americans to frequent the Coachella Valley were often far more affluent. A generation after the citrus industry had remade less arid portions of Southern California, agricultural entrepreneurs came to the desert, intent on creating a date industry. Investors canvassed the Middle East for date varieties, finally settling upon the "Deglet Noor." Orchards were planted around the new settlement of Indio, and the appropriately named community of Mecca. Even at the end of the twentieth century, this pattern of development remained prevalent. The northern Coachella Valley would become a resort region, while the southern Coachella, like the Imperial Valley to the southeast, would be dominated by agriculture and little visited by tourists. Health guru and cereal magnate W. K. Kellogg supported the effort, believing that fresh dates were more healthful than those packed and shipped from overseas, and that the sugar derived from dates was superior to that made from processed cane. Hoping to foster another domestic cash crop and lessen imports, the Department of Agriculture weighed in as well, asserting that "it is doubtful if there can be found a sounder, stronger race, with better digestion and finer, whiter teeth than the date-eating Arabs." Of course, such praise could not come without a derogatory element: "Investigations [as to the healthfulness of dates] will never be made in that part of the old world where the dates are grown, but must be undertaken by some country like America which is interested in increasing the number of its food products."[10]

Date cultivation soon proved successful. In many respects, it echoed the earlier development of the region's citrus industry. The capital outlay involved limited large-scale production to investors with aspirations of being gentlemen farmers or members of a plantation aristocracy. It depended upon a racialized system of labor, with local Indians and Mexicans, as well as Asians, tending, harvesting, and processing the crop. It also permitted allusions to "exotic" regions, cultures, and foodstuffs, now safe and healthful. Whereas the citrus industry had promoted the image of a domesticated tropical paradise, date agriculture permitted allusions to the Middle East and the "Holy Land." The date industry therefore provided a useful thematic element for the promotion of tourism in the Coachella Valley.[11]

Guests at California's Biskra who arrived on Camel-back.

FIGURE 5.2 The Coachella Valley's arabesque fantasy at its most florid. The "Arabs" are most likely local Cahuillas. This image appeared in a promotional brochure for a resort near Palm Springs that was never built. "Walled Oasis of Biskra: An Interpretation of the American Desert in the Algerian Manner." 1924. Special Collections, Young Research Library, University of California, Los Angeles.

Accordingly, the racial posturing already utilized to posit Anglo-Americans as the heirs of the Spanish padres was now used to link them and the Southern California landscapes they inhabited to a far more ancient past: "From earliest days, humanity has hovered on the desert's edge. The most ancient of known civilizations were built upon its sands. Egypt, Babylon, Chaldea, all cradles of the race, were desert lands. . . . The first civilization knew the desert and loved it. We of the present are also succumbing to its lure." John McCallum, in fact, had already utilized the Arab trope, hiring local Cahuilla Willie Marcus to dress as a Bedouin and loiter exotically at the Garnet railroad station, telling passengers about nearby Palm Valley, his agrarian settlement. Later developers even toyed with the idea of having teams of Cahuillas or Mexicans bedecked in Arabian Nights garb greet tourists at the train station, and then lead them by camel across the desert to their resorts, the caravansaries of Arabian fantasy. If any tourists did in fact brave a camel ride, few likely submitted to it again. Motion sickness—not to mention camels' propensities for biting and spitting—were likely hazards. Wagons, trains, and then cars, soon replaced the camel caravan as the best means of transit to Palm Springs.[12]

The agricultural industry that touted its connection to the ancient world of the Bible was nevertheless dependent upon modern technology. In 1905, investors diverted water from the Colorado River, planning to irrigate the Imperial Valley. The river flooded and broke through the irrigation channel, however, washing away the Southern Pacific's rail line and flowing instead into a basin in the southern Coachella Valley. This created an (initially) freshwater lake, which was named the Salton Sea. Thus an irrigation fiasco provided the first national media coverage of events in the Coachella Valley.

The Colorado and even the ocean had, in fact, inundated the Coachella before. Its name, though garbled by the U.S. Postal Service, had originally been Conchella (little seashell), alluding to the innumerable tiny fossilized seashells found in its sands. The Colorado's new course seemed immovable, destroying property in the valley and wreaking environmental havoc in the once lush Colorado River delta at the Sea of Cortez, doomed to desertification as the United States swallowed up all the water the Colorado could offer before it crossed the Mexico border. Eventually, the river's flow was restored to its original channel, though agricultural runoff ensured the survival of the increasingly saline and polluted Salton Sea into the twenty-first century.

An Aesthete and the Ailing Arrive in Palm Springs

Shortly prior to the creation of the Salton Sea, the Coachella would witness the arrival of its first booster. John C. Van Dyke was no mere chamber-of-commerce publicist. He was the art critic for *Century Magazine* and one of the best-known and widely read public intellectuals in the nation. He frequented Charles Lummis's salon at El Alisal, but remained firmly entrenched on the East Coast, where he was librarian at New Brunswick Theological Seminary, and the first professor of art history at Rutgers University. While Lummis was merely acquainted with politicians and social figures in the East, Van Dyke was entirely of their class. His bitter public feuding with novelist Edith Wharton resulted from the fact that she had the temerity to write novels exposing the flaws and hypocrisy of the elite society to which they both belonged.

Why, then, would such an august figure travel through a region as little known as the Coachella Valley? Americans had long gloried in the sublimity of Yosemite and the Rockies and had come to appreciate non-Alpine, authentically "American" sights such as the Grand Canyon. The Mojave and Colorado deserts, by contrast, seemed barren and monotonous, without vivid colors or titanic geologic features. This, as far as Van Dyke was concerned, was ideal. The deserts of California, to his eyes, contained the most delicate palette of colors imaginable. In Van Dyke's desert, subtlety was the ultimate sublimity. Understated refinement, rather than the theatricality of paintings by Albert Bierstadt or Thomas Moran, was the ideal. As John Ruskin had used the Alps to lecture Victorians on the proper ways to appreciate and artistically represent nature, so too would Van Dyke utilize the desert. Here, perhaps, Americans could be transformed into true aesthetes of nature.[13]

Van Dyke narrated his book *The Desert: Further Studies in Natural Appearances* (1901) as a solitary traveler, walking and riding through an uninhabited landscape. Even more than Charles Lummis, who neglected to mention that most of his rugged Southwestern adventures took place within a convenient distance of the Santa Fe Railway, Van Dyke concealed his actual travel habits. Moving from posh hotels to elegant rented accommodations, he never allowed his desert reveries to get in the way of the good life. Van Dyke, however, never claimed to be testing himself against the hardships of nature. Though Lummis raved about *The Desert* in his magazine, calling it a "poem and prophecy all in one," Van Dyke lacked Lummis's enthusiasm for the Southwest as a haven for middle-class whites, scorning the masses even as he hawked his book to them. Neither did he offer the close observation of desert flora and fauna that would characterize Mary Austin's *Land of Little Rain* (1902), a book written after the author's long, lean years as a struggling homesteader in the arid Owens Valley. Van Dyke's refined aesthetic contemplation of the desert was presented as a rebuke to the excesses of urbanism, industry, and capitalism—the too-muchness of modern America.[14]

Few readers knew, however, how closely Van Dyke was connected to the forces he claimed to disdain. His book bore a dedication to "A. M. C." Almost no readers would ever know that the initials were actually those of Van Dyke's close friend Andrew Carnegie, the steel baron who had done as much as anyone to ensure the passing of an older, natural landscape and its replacement with one of industry and urbanism. Seen in this light, *The Desert*, hailed by preservationists and literary critics for its environmental sensitivity, should instead be seen as either an elaborate joke or as a monument to the cognitive dissonance modern Americans could tolerate when thinking about nature.[15]

The first "tourists" to the Coachella Valley, however, were not motivated by aesthetic impulses. They, like Johnny McCallum, were suffering from various ailments, most commonly tuberculosis. Similar afflictions led large numbers of people to Southern California, perhaps as much as one quarter of the total influx prior to 1900. The Southern Pacific constructed a number of cottages for "consumptives" at Indio to take advantage of this travel market. The first permanent accommodation in the vicinity of the oasis was the Palm Springs Hotel, built by the self-described "Dr." Welwood Murray in 1888. Murray's small hotel lay just outside the boundary of tribal land, near the oasis, and also near the McCallum adobe. This hotel, as well as the nearby Green Gables Health Resort—a small collection of tents and cabins owned by Lavinia Crocker—catered wholly to the sick.[16]

After the courts granted them official title to the major surface water supplies in the area, the Agua Calientes seemed secure. Charles Lummis's Sequoya League, for example, which had been founded to advocate for the rights of Southern California Indians, asserted that the Agua Calientes "now have all the land and the water, practically, and further troubles are unlikely." That assertion proved overly optimistic. Tourist development, even on a small scale, soon precipitated new conflicts between Indians and whites. The Agua Calientes had constructed a small wooden bathhouse in the hot spring in the 1870s and charged admission to visitors who wished to use it. The Murrays, over the objections of the tribe, were granted a lease on the spring. They agreed to build a new bathhouse and pool, and to share part of their revenue with the Indians. This lease was renewed for ten years in 1892. The Agua Calientes, however, complained that the Murrays kept them out of their hot spring to reserve it for tourists and did not make promised improvements. Further, the money they had been promised never seemed to materialize. The Murrays, for their part, complained that the Indians insisted on using the spring, even though the lease agreement—which had been imposed without the Indians' consent—delineated the hours of the day that were set aside as Indian-only. The lease was not renewed in 1902.[17]

New conflicts soon emerged among the Agua Calientes themselves, however. As with other native groups in the West and Southwest, the Agua Calientes found themselves ever more enmeshed in a cash economy—one based increasingly on tourism. As with the community of Isleta Pueblo, which had fractured over the presence of Charles Lummis and train-traveling tourists, the Agua Calientes split into camps in favor of modernization and traditionalism, with the traditionalists often led by Francisco Patencio. Agua

Calientes who had intermarried with non-Indians, interracial tribal members, and those who had spent long periods away from the reservation as wage laborers were more likely to side with "modernization." Besides these two factions, the tribe also split over the very modern issue of the division and use of tribal money—in this case, the revenue from admission to the hot springs. Some tribal members thought that the money should be reinvested in an improved bathhouse and bathing facilities, which would draw more tourist revenue. Others felt that the hot-spring revenue should be used for other collective needs, such as a fence around the tribal graveyard. Still others believed that the money should be divided equally and disbursed individually to all tribal members, who could then use it as they saw fit. An exasperated Bureau of Indian Affairs would eventually take charge of the spring, deeming the Indians too contentious to decide the issue among themselves. Tribal members fought bitterly over various matters, none more problematic than the allocation of tribal land and the division of revenues from land leases. These issues would not be resolved for another half century.[18]

From Desert Sanatorium to the Desert Inn: The Tourists and Nellie Coffman Arrive in Palm Springs

Though the oasis at Palm Springs primarily drew the ailing, it also attracted a small number of tourists. John Muir visited the community, though he also hoped that his daughter's health would improve in the dry desert air. In 1904 Gustav Stickley, editor of the *Craftsman* magazine and purveyor of arts-and-crafts furniture and bungalow houses, visited Palm Springs with his wife, Eda, and their daughters Barbara and Mildred. Inveterate Southern California booster George Wharton James accompanied them; he would soon become associate editor of the *Craftsman*. Stickley's magazine carried an increasing number of articles about and advertisements for California, reinforcing the linkage between the promotion of Southern California and the search by some Anglo-Americans for "shelter" in either architectural or geographic forms. After his visit, Stickley even considered Palm Springs as a prospective site for a new community constructed around the precepts of the "simple life."

James and Stickley dived into the hot spring, an experience Stickley remembered as the highlight of his entire trip across the West. James described the oasis to prospective tourists in his 1906 guidebook, *Wonders of the Colorado Desert*, though he warned them that the sandy floor of the warm pool concealed the gurgling mouth of the spring itself. Sinking unawares into it "makes the heart leap," and could even cause "genuine terror" in bathers until the force of the water welling up from below inexorably forces them back out of the shaft.[19]

In December of 1908, another guest arrived at Murray's hotel. This was Nellie Coffman, the individual most responsible for the tourist transformation of Palm Springs. Coffman had been born Nellie Orr in Patoka, Indiana, in 1867. Her family moved to Abilene, Texas, and Nellie spent the rest of her childhood in that state. In 1887 she married contractor George Ball Roberson, who died in a fire while Nellie was pregnant with their first child, George Ball Roberson, Jr. The young widow moved to Los Angeles, where her parents had resettled, in 1889. There she met Harry Coffman, whom she married in 1891, and with whom she would have a son in 1892, Owen Earl Coffman. Harry Coffman would attend the University of Southern California, and then attain a medical degree in Philadelphia in 1901, returning to Southern California to open a medical practice in Santa Monica.[20]

Unfortunately, Nellie Coffman developed respiratory problems and a persistent cough. In 1897 she traveled to Idyllwild, a small resort community high on the forested western slopes of the San Jacinto Mountains, where the air was cool and clear. Coffman stayed in a small boarding house there, and the owner told her of an oasis on the eastern desert flank of the mountains, where she spent her winters with her family in a tent. Coffman, however, recuperated in Idyllwild, and returned to Los Angeles, though her respiratory ailments would periodically return. Later she read an article in *Sunset* magazine written by a Scottish immigrant who claimed to have been cured of Bright's Disease by a two-year regimen of taking the waters and sunbathing in Palm Springs. In December of 1908, after another severe cold, Coffman decided to attempt a desert cure. She and her eldest son, George, took a train to Garnet Station, several miles north of Palm Springs, and then traveled by wagon southward. Caught in a fierce sandstorm, both feared that that they would be blown off course and perish in the desert sands. Eventually they found their way to the small settlement and took up accommodations in Murray's Palm Springs Hotel, which Nellie Coffman found wretched.

The next day, however, the storm cleared, and Coffman was entranced by the sparkling air and desert vistas. Here was a place she might finally be rid of her health problems. She decided that she would build a hotel here as well, offering services and accommodations far superior to those of the lackluster Dr. Murray. She returned in 1909, paying $5,000 for 1¾ acres in the center of the small settlement, and established her new Desert Inn, which contained three bedrooms in the main house, four more in converted stables, and a number of tent cabins, not unlike those then ubiquitous at Catalina.

Coffman might have lacked the colorful personality of some other Southern California boosters, but she did have a flair for publicity. The first guests were two reporters from the *Los Angeles Times*, on their way to cover a story in the Imperial Valley. According to Coffman, the two "went away singing the praises of the little inn they had discovered in the desert." She also possessed business skills many boosters lacked: Coffman managed to have her hotel classified as a mercantile enterprise rather than a hostelry, meaning she could get wholesale prices on food and enjoyed greater leeway on bill repayment. Her husband and two sons relocated to Palm Springs as well, swelling the permanent non-Indian population to a total of thirteen. At the end of the hotel's first season, Coffman had $65 in the bank—and $50 of that went to the mortgage. For the first few years she spent her summers working at the boardinghouse in Idyllwild where she had once stayed to make extra money. From these modest beginnings the Desert Inn would grow to be the most famous resort in Palm Springs for more than half a century.[21]

In local lore, the Coffman saga took on the iconic, mythic status of a pioneer narrative. The Coffmans were the Donner Party and the 49ers combined, people who had survived hardships, and who, with foresight and determination, created a fortune for themselves and the settlement's posterity. World War II military reporter Ernie Pyle summarized Nellie Coffman's career in grandiose style: "She started what was to become the whole vast vogue of desert vacationing. All the great resorts—Tucson and Phoenix and Death Valley—the fancy hotels and the Southwest dude ranches and the thousands in trailers who have discovered the uncanny lure of the desert, it all began with Mother Coffman. The whole thing was built on one woman's spiritual love of the desert." Coffman was more prosaic. Her rationale at the time was that someday Palm Springs would be "Hollywood's sandbox to play in."[22]

In reality, Coffman's small hotel had not been designed for play at all, since it initially catered to consumptives. The guests rented the rooms and sat under shaded ramadas constructed out of palm fronds, which Coffman had copied from those she saw on the Agua Caliente reservation. Scattered around the hotel grounds were signs reminding guests to refrain from spitting and to use instead the handkerchiefs the hotel provided. These were intended to eliminate the unsightly splotches of bloody phlegm scattered over the hotel's grounds.[23]

The days of the tubercular sanatorium were numbered. Southern California promoters had worried for some time that the region had become too associated with the ailing, and those fears were heightened by growing medical knowledge of disease, including tuberculosis. The growing evidence that tuberculosis was caused by microbes, rather than "unhealthy" air, and that the disease was communicable, meant that resort communities began to ban or quarantine tuberculosis sufferers.[24] Coffman, aware of these developments, thought that her hotel would prosper with tourists rather than invalids. In 1915 the Desert Inn opened for its winter season welcoming regular tourists only, while tuberculosis patients were no longer permitted. This decision did not come without a cost. The Coffmans divorced in 1914, apparently in part because Harry Coffman had expected the Desert Inn to be a sanatorium, where his medical skills would have been in demand. Nellie Coffman would continue to operate the hotel with her two sons, George Roberson and Owen Earl Coffman.

By 1920, the Desert Inn could host one hundred guests, and had thirty-five bungalows and tent cabins, some with as many as ten rooms. Rates ran from $7.50 to $15.00 per day per person, less than Avalon's Metropole Hotel had charged twenty years earlier. Coffman also moved adroitly among the social set of the California tourist industry. She became a close friend of Frank Miller of the Mission Inn, and also of David and Jennie Foster Curry, operators of Camp Curry in Yosemite. During the summers, Coffman, her sons, and her regular employees operated the Village Inn, Arrowhead Lodge, and North Shore Tavern at Lake Arrowhead in the San Bernardino Mountains. As at Catalina, where many hotel workers found other jobs in winter, Desert Inn employees often took other positions for the summer. Some hotel workers, such as Frank Bogert, who would work at various local hotels and later become mayor of Palm Springs, moved between Palm Springs and Catalina on a biannual basis.[25]

Even more than Catalina, Palm Springs drew a diverse range of service-industry employees. That Agua Calientes should take jobs in the growing resort was no surprise, nor was it surprising that Mexicans and Mexican Americans would as well. By 1920 Cahuilla women were serving as maids and laundresses in the Desert Inn and other hotels, and Cahuilla men worked as gardeners and gathered firewood. Mexican men also found employment as gardeners. The Desert Inn had two cooks—one Chinese, the other African American. Many other Asians also took jobs in Palm Springs, such as Filipino Segundo Rigonan, who worked at the Desert Inn and was also employed at Nellie Coffman's summer home in Banning. When at the Desert Inn, he lived in a bungalow called the "Manila Cottage," which served as a residence for other Filipino employees as well. Employee housing at the Desert Inn may have been segregated, but Coffman's employees could at least count on housing. White workers could usually find adequate nearby housing, but other workers often could not. Most other hotels and restaurants offered no housing assistance to nonwhite employees, and many lived in tents, shacks, and lean-tos on the Indian reservation.[26]

Hollywood, the Oasis Hotel, El Mirador, and Palm Springs as an Emerging Resort in the 1920s

Coffman's decision to pursue the tourist trade coincided with a series of events—local, national, and international—that altered the future of the small settlement of Palm Springs. The growing popularity and affordability of the automobile meant that more Southern Californians were venturing into local deserts. Palm Springs still lay miles from the nearest railroad station at Garnet, but a new road to Banning—albeit composed only of oiled sand—now connected the small community with the larger world. A more permanent road to Banning was completed in 1924, a year after electricity became available. The beginning of American involvement in World War I also meant that Europe was off-limits to wealthy American tourists, and citizens were instead urged to "See America first!"—a slogan that preceded the war, but now gained added potency. This boosted tourism at various attractions in the United States, but it was especially significant for Palm Springs. With Baden Baden and other continental spas out of reach, rich Americans were forced to resort to American spas and health retreats, and visitation at Palm Springs rose markedly. Real estate began to sell as well. By the early 1920s, Palm Springs' permanent population had grown to approximately a hundred whites and fifty Agua Calientes, with other tribal members residing elsewhere in the Coachella Valley.[27]

Another development with great portent for Palm Springs was the arrival of Hollywood. Film production began in Southern California in 1907 and rapidly grew to become an important component of the economy of Los Angeles and its surrounding region. Inexpensive land, labor, facilities, and electricity made the region appealing, as did its proximity to the Mexican border, which proved useful in the early years when Pinkerton detectives, attempting to enforce Thomas Edison's motion-picture patents, pursued illegal film productions. The other great appeal of Southern California, however, was its widely varied scenery—thick evergreen forests atop the local mountains, beaches, rolling countryside, orchards and agricultural land, urban and residential cityscapes, and deserts, such as the Coachella Valley. The Coachella would stand in for the deserts of North Africa and the Middle East in countless films, as well as serve as a perfect Southwestern setting for westerns.

Film influenced the future of Palm Springs in three ways. Most obviously, it filled hotels and restaurants when actors and production crews arrived. As the resort grew, however, Hollywood established a more permanent presence in Palm Springs as actors, producers, and others in the film industry purchased vacation homes. Over time, some came to live in Palm Springs and other desert communities on a semipermanent basis, becoming part of local society and even retiring there. In this sense, these Hollywood vacationers-turned-residents portended the future of a resort that gradually became as dependent on retirees as tourists.

Film served a third crucial function for Palm Springs. Prior to World War II, Palm Springs remained a relatively small regional resort. Even though it attracted a wealthy clientele, it drew a limited total number of vacationers.

Yet film gave this resort community greatly heightened visibility, far exceeding its actual size and stature. Even more than Catalina, which was likewise publicized by radio and film, Palm Springs became a nationally known resort through the medium of film, and developments and innovations begun there thus had far greater influence.

With visitation growing, the Desert Inn expanded to meet demand. A swimming pool, the first in Palm Springs, was completed in 1925. That year, Coffman also hired a social director. Several new buildings opened the next year. The new lobby featured a mural depicting De Anza's trek through the Coachella in 1774. The expansive grounds could now host two hundred guests, and boasted stores, a coffee shop, a restaurant, and an E. F. Hutton brokerage for guests who needed to stay apprised of their investment portfolios.[28]

Other hotels opened in Palm Springs following the war. The two most significant were the Oasis Hotel, which opened in 1925, and El Mirador, which opened in 1928. The Oasis was built by Pearl McCallum McManus, the lone survivor of the failed McCallum clan. She placed her new hotel across the street from the Desert Inn, which was no coincidence. It was not merely that she intended to compete for the Desert Inn's clientele. The development company she founded with her husband, Pioneer Properties—of which she was president—played a major role in Palm Springs' development. She still—and indeed, always would—see herself and her family as the true founders of Palm Springs. In her mind, it was quite literally "their" town. The fact that Nellie Coffman had opened a hotel in it, and that she was seen as the originator of Palm Springs tourism, was irrelevant. For the rest of her life, Pearl McManus maintained a rivalry with Coffman and anyone else she perceived as a threat to her status in Palm Springs. This rivalry, however, was primarily a one-way affair. The Desert Inn remained the larger, more famous, and more profitable hotel.

The Oasis, nevertheless, was significant for more than its owner's envy. McManus wanted the hotel to make a bold statement, rather than simply echoing the more traditional Spanish-themed architecture of the Desert Inn. As a result, her hotel became one of the first modernist resort hotels in the United States. It was also one of the first major commissions of Frank Lloyd Wright Jr. Wright met McManus while courting his future wife, Helen Taggart. Taggart had been married to actor Reginald Pole, and the couple owned a house in Palm Springs. Wright's plan created a series of courtyards, accommodating cars and a swimming pool. The plan also integrated the new hotel with the existing McCallum adobe ranch house, which was subsequently relocated to permit the hotel's expansion. The interior courtyard, with areas for swimming and sunbathing where guests could loll or mingle while remaining secluded from the broader public, became a hallmark of Palm Springs hotels and residential construction. Wright's plan aimed to merge architecture and nature, to the point of leaving large cottonwood trees in place, with their trunks sprouting through the roof of the hotel's dining room like rough-hewn columns. McManus, who fondly remembered the trees from her years of living on her family's ranch, approved of this design as well. The Oasis, constructed out of concrete, included decorative "textile" blocks that recalled both the designs of Wright's father, as well as the son's later art deco styles. A tower in the center offered views of the desert beyond and also served as a distinctive signature landmark for the hotel. Filigree wooden screens on the tower and elsewhere on the building, like the textile blocks, created a modernist expressionist style, one that fused more formal modernism with an opulent tone complimented by tropical plantings and potted plants placed along the roof. The result was the perfect mix for a desert resort hotel that offered exoticism and the latest modern conveniences. This lush resort Modernism would become a hallmark of Palm Springs in decades to come.[29]

The other major hotel constructed in 1920s Palm Springs, El Mirador, did not break any new architectural ground. Constructed by Colorado cattle baron Prescott Stevens, the hotel was Spanish and Moorish revival at its most opulent, complete with a tower topped by a conical roof covered with a shimmering array of multicolored tile. Lush grounds, far larger than those at the Oasis, included a swimming pool, tennis courts, and areas for sunbathing. It also contained an I. Magnin clothing store, as well as other upscale retailers. Management, concerned about the transitory nature and occasionally spotty work of seasonal employees, made arrangements with large concession companies that ran hotels at Yellowstone and Yosemite. Long-term workers were offered winter positions at El Mirador, summer employment at Old Faithful Inn, Yosemite's Ahwahnee, or another park lodge, and a month off each spring and fall. Like the Desert Inn, El Mirador housed most of its workers, and likewise employed a racially diverse workforce. It also lay well north of the center of town, where the hot spring was located, and where the Desert Inn and Oasis had been built. This ensured a seclusion the other hotels lacked, and the hotel promised that guests here could "expect to find the kind of friendship you will treasure; distinguished, discriminating personalities who blend perfectly into the quiet, unruffled tempo of desert living."[30]

The significance of El Mirador was not its architecture, but rather its clientele. It was the first hotel in Palm Springs to cater expressly to Hollywood, becoming a favorite haunt of numerous celebrities. Many hotel guests later bought homes in the area around El Mirador, earning the nascent neighborhood the name "The Movie Colony." Eager to draw all of Hollywood, the hotel welcomed Jewish guests, which the Desert Inn and Oasis, aimed at Protestant clienteles, did not. El Mirador hired Frank Bogert to oversee

FIGURE 5.3 A 1920s postcard of the Oasis Hotel, designed by Lloyd Wright and built on the site of the McCallum homestead by Pearl McCallum McManus. The hotel's ornate tower proved a local landmark, and its luxurious, resort-style Modernism would inspire other resorts and residential developments in Palm Springs. Palm Springs Historical Society, Palm Springs, California.

FIGURE 5.4 The lush landscaping of the Oasis Hotel, like other area resorts, appealed to tourists despite the fact that such verdure was utterly alien to the Coachella Valley's desert landscape. Palm Springs Historical Society, Palm Springs, California.

publicity, and to ensure that every visiting star developed a mutually beneficial relationship with the hotel. Bogert photographed any visitor of note, and
the photos were then sent to the society editor of the *Los Angeles Times* and
the guest's hometown newspaper. In the process, their visit received flattering
local and national media coverage, and El Mirador enhanced its reputation as
the playground of the stars. This iconic status would draw less affluent auto
tourists and autograph hounds from Los Angeles and began Palm Springs'
appeal to a national tourist market.[31]

Sunbathing, Sport, and a Distinctive Resort Culture

With Hollywood firmly ensconced in Palm Springs, a distinct resort culture
began to emerge. In some respects it was a local manifestation of a region-
wide resort culture. The emphasis on outdoor recreation was hardly new,
such an emphasis having appeared decades earlier at Catalina. Yet if tourists
at Catalina had enjoyed frolicking in the surf, or hiking or hunting in the
island's interior, tourist activities at Palm Springs more often seemed to combine outdoor recreation with organized socializing. Sports such as tennis and
golf were primary examples of this trend.

This development did not escape Pearl McCallum McManus, and she
opened the Palm Springs Tennis Club in 1937 to offer both athletic and
social amenities. It quickly became the premier social club in Palm Springs.
Designed in stunning modernist style by Los Angeles architect Paul Williams,
the club featured a restaurant built on a rocky ledge on the side of Mount San
Jacinto. A broad, flat eave shaded the structure, while large sweeping windows offered desert and mountain vistas. Below was a trademark oval swimming pool, surrounded with palm trees, which offered more views of rugged
desert hillsides. This combination of wilderness and civilization, barrenness
and luxury, proved so compelling that the pool was utilized as the logo of the
California Chamber of Commerce.[32]

The emphasis on sunbathing so evident at local hotels and at the Tennis
Club, especially sunbathing for the express purpose of acquiring a tan, was
decidedly new. A generation earlier, women had prized pale skin, and a man
with tanned skin suggested the low social status of a day laborer. A tan also
required the exposure of human skin and the abandonment of the conceal-
ing—and cumbersome—bathing attire of earlier decades. At 1890s Catalina,
the spectacle of tourists walking several blocks to the beach in bulky Victorian
bathing attire had elicited surprise. In 1920s Palm Springs, men and women
often spent their entire day in far more revealing attire, dressing more formally only for dinner. Some Palm Springs partisans even claimed that shorts

for adults were invented—or at least popularized—at the resort. Celebrities, in particular, were photographed or filmed in bathing gear that might have elicited the ire of the censorious "Hays Office" if they had appeared in the same garb in a feature film. For celebrities of both sexes—particularly those of an age or attractiveness allowing them to aspire to be a sex symbol—the display of the body proved a hallmark of Palm Springs publicity photos. More specifically, the bodies on display at Palm Springs demonstrated the positive effects of good diet, exercise, and assorted beauty regimens.

Above all, however, they advertised the money and leisured time necessary to cultivate such bodily perfection. Once a refuge for the ailing, Palm Springs had become a retreat for the rich and robustly healthy. It was, as travel writer Ted Salmon noted in 1930, a place "to work at play rather than to play at work." He asserted, "I have never seen so many people taking their pleasures so seriously as at this resort and I believe that they could not fail to cure any disease, from housemaids' knee to elephantiasis, with such strenuosity."[33]

If Palm Springs sold heath and leisure, it now also sold other commodities. Catalina had traded in "romance"; Palm Springs was more frank in what it offered. Catalina, particularly in its earlier decades, offered an escape from usual mores. Late at night, tourists slipped away from hotels and tents in Avalon to rendezvous at Lover's Cove and other such romantic spots. At Palm Springs, the possibilities of romantic or sexual contact were far more open and apparent. The bohemian sexual and marital mores already apparent in Hollywood intersected with the resort atmosphere of Palm Springs, and this new, more open sexuality would gradually appear elsewhere in national tourist culture.

Hotels offered rooms with secluded balconies, as well as tanning "machines," which were actually only wheeled frameworks of translucent cloth enclosing a chaise longue or reclining area. Attendants could move these as the sun moved, and the machines, like the balconies, allowed guests to sunbathe sans swimsuit. Nudism, already a health fad in Europe, now arrived in Palm Springs, as it would in other parts of Southern California. Some modernist architects in Los Angeles also had clients who partook in this heath fad, and constructed private sunbathing courtyards or balconies for this purpose. In fact, the first modernist structure in the Coachella Valley had been a small cottage with screened, private porches built for Betty and Paul Popenoe in 1922 by Rudolph Schindler. Perhaps the most famous such house, however, was Richard Neutra's Lovell House, or "Health House," constructed in 1929 in the Hollywood Hills. Many Palm Springs homes included patios and balconies designed for residents to soak up the sun. Even at the beginning of the twenty-first century, despite all the well-publicized dangers of premature aging and skin cancer, Palm Springs still contained a number of nudist resorts and camps.[34]

Desert Vistas and Department Stores: Commodifying Nature in a Tourist Town

Just as Palm Springs drew vacationers intent on refining the body, it also drew travelers who aimed to heighten their aesthetic refinement, just as the desert had lured John C. Van Dyke decades earlier. The desert landscape, which had for so long simply been something to endure, became an attraction in itself. Some tourists and new residents hoped to escape modern life by retreating into the desert. Others instead attempted to incorporate the desert into modern life. Those in flight from modernity often pronounced themselves unimpressed with the bustling resort town of Palm Springs. British travel writer Ernest Young, for example, dismissed the town, with its lush plantings, brightly colored buildings, and festive atmosphere, as the artificial set for "a comic opera that does not know it is comic." Tourists divided their time between eating and shopping, and went about in scant clothing that was "a close approach to nakedness and much more indecent." While Young noted that some tourists did drive out into the desert for short sightseeing jaunts, they had "no intention of wasting their time trying to capture the lure of overwhelming silence, the utter crushing loneliness of the uninvaded wilderness." That lure called only to the select: "A few, but only a few, are called by the floor of the desert, the canyons, or the gaunt, splintered peaks of the mountain barrier lifting their purple heads above the pale grave face of the plain." Young, intent or narrating solitary encounters with the arid wilderness, railed against tourists and the transportation infrastructure that made his travels possible, much as Van Dyke had studiously ignored the same infrastructure.[35]

The single most prominent proponent of this antimodernist, anti-urban approach to the desert scenery of Palm Springs and the Coachella Valley was J. Smeaton Chase, author of *Our Araby: Palm Springs and the Garden of the Sun* (1920). Chase, an English writer who had settled in Southern California, consciously borrowed his book's title from Charles Dudley Warner's California booster tract of 1891, *Our Italy*. He was less dismissive of Palm Springs, perhaps in part because it remained so small when his book was written, with as few as three hundred permanent residents in winter, and only twenty-five in summer. The elitism, though more implicit, still remained abundantly clear in the goals Chase set for his desert guidebook: "This little book is designed to serve three ends: to invite people of the right kind—not too many—to a region that is meant for the discerning few; to help them while here to enjoy it to the full; and to please them, when they have departed, with recollections of things thought and felt, seen and done, in a tract of country wholly out of the ordinary." Chase did, at least, make some gestures to more "ordinary" travelers, giving hints on desert driving and admitting that watching desert film shoots and seeing celebrities could be enjoyable diversions as well.[36]

Chase claimed—no doubt much to the amusement of readers of later decades—that Palm Springs did not usually attract the rich, or the "hooligan element," which Chase asserted was endemic to beach resorts. Instead, Palm Springs drew scientists, writers, painters, musicians—"people who love quiet, thoughtful things." Palm Springs in its early years did indeed draw some such individuals, such as the desert naturalist Edmund Jaeger and the German-born artist Carl Eytel, who illustrated George Wharton James's *Wonders of the Colorado Desert*. Yet Chase was unknowingly delineating the same progression that had occurred at a number of other tourist destinations in the West, from Carmel and Big Sur to Santa Fe and Aspen. Intellectuals and artists often served as the vanguard of an onslaught of outsiders that culminated in the arrival of the highly affluent.[37]

Another precursor of large-scale tourist development was the setting aside of scenic areas as national monuments and parks. From Yellowstone to the Grand Canyon, federal recognition of natural beauty assured that boosters and tourists would soon follow. In the early 1920s, it seemed likely that the same would occur in Palm Springs. Palm Canyon, with its extensive groves of *Washingtonia* palms, was considered for national monument designation. Ultimately, Murray, and Palm Canyons were both considered for monument designation, as was a large swath of the valley floor, stretching all the way northeastward across the Mojave to encompass some portion of what would become Joshua Tree National Monument in 1937. If this plan had been followed, the Coachella Valley would have become a very different sort of resort region. Instead of a sprawling strip of resort communities along the base of the San Jacinto Mountains, with golf courses and condominiums stretching far into the desert to the east, the Coachella Valley might instead look like Jackson Hole, Wyoming, with a small resort community located in a large valley, bounded on all sides by federal land. There was, however, one glaring problem with this scheme. Much of the land in question was not federal land, but Indian land. The Agua Calientes were offered only a pittance to turn over their prized canyons to the Park Service. Not surprisingly, they refused. In his guidebook, Chase presented the new Palm Canyon National Monument as a *fait accompli*. In reality, it and the other canyons would remain under permanent Indian control.[38]

With federal recognition no longer an option, the desert aesthetes tried to colonize the canyons through other means. The most visible manifestation of this began in 1921, when *Fire*, a pageant penned by Mary Austin, was performed at the mouth of Tahquitz Canyon. The play melded classical and Native American mythology, and utilized a cast of local Anglos and

Indians. The idea for a play was no doubt inspired by *The Ramona Outdoor Play* and *The Mission Play*, both major successes. By this time, Austin had abandoned booming Los Angeles. She asserted that Southern California had been "overrun by what is probably the most impotent—culturally and spiritually impotent—society that has yet got itself together in any quarter of the United States." She ensconced herself in Santa Fe, a new capital of the Southwestern cult. In books such as *The Land of Journey's Ending* (1924), she now laid claim to be the chief writer, intellectual, and chauvinist of the Southwest, supplanting Charles Lummis, her onetime mentor. In place of his interpretation of the Southwest as a frontier of leisure that could rejuvenate harried Americans, Austin adopted a more mystical approach, in which Southwestern landscapes and cultures would be absorbed by Anglos, transforming their society. If Lummis had wanted Anglos to play, Austin now wanted them to go native. Other pageants, elaborating on Austin's themes, followed, most notably the "desert play" *Tahquitz*, which drew upon the malevolent figure from Agua Caliente legend for which the canyon was named.[39]

If some advocates of desert appreciation urged the select few to venture out into its vast silence, others aimed to draw the desert closer in order to domesticate it. Far from fleeing urbanism and modern consumer culture, these aficionados approached the desert precisely as consumers. One record of this mindset was *Desert Magazine*, which began publication in Pasadena in May of 1929. In some respects, the magazine looked like other conservation-minded publications. Editorials urged passage of laws protecting desert flora and fauna, the use of desert plants in civic plantings and parks, and nature education in schools. Other articles offered desert driving tips or information on particular attractions in California's arid lands. Another detailed Mary Austin's play at Tahquitz Canyon. Still others discussed the creation of the International Desert Conservation League, founded in Los Angeles. This organization, composed of Americans and white inhabitants of British imperial colonies, most notably South Africa, urged "the protection of desert life and the conservation of desert beauty spots in the form of park areas containing rare desert flora and fauna." Southern California "officers" included Emma Marian Chandler, daughter of Harrison Gray Otis and wife of Harry Chandler of the *Los Angeles Times* dynasty; Ellen Scripps of La Jolla and the San Diego–based newspaper chain; and Nellie Coffman. Coffman, regardless of her actual affection for the desert, no doubt saw the growing tourist fascination as a boon. The league additionally included among its ranks Gifford Pinchot, also a member of the Catalina Island Tuna Club. In Palm Springs, as at Catalina, tourism spawned conservation. Yet if the Tuna Club was centered on competitive sport, the Desert League was based on consumption—upon the commodification of the desert.[40]

Other articles in *Desert Magazine* demonstrated this very different approach to "desert appreciation." For example, "Bringing the Desert to Town" discussed staged exhibits of California desert plants, complete with rocks and painted backgrounds. Crammed with succulents, all harvested while in bloom or induced to bloom simultaneously, these displays offered a fictional landscape far more lush than any actual desert. Nevertheless, these dioramas were so popular that they won awards from the Garden Club of America, the New York City International Flower Show, and even London flower shows. The magazine offered tips on how readers could redesign their backyards into permanent versions of these desert fantasias. The desert had indeed been brought to the city. The profound difference between this type of desert appreciation and the earlier desert wanderers, who claimed to be in search of silence, solitude, and an escape from the crush of modern life, can hardly be exaggerated.[41]

Another striking manifestation of this was a desert promotion campaign begun by Bullock's Department Store in the later 1920s. Its flagship location in downtown L.A.—before it moved to a new suburban location on Wilshire Boulevard—even included a "desert resort bureau." Presaging a retail boom in the desert during the 1930s, when a number of department stores and expensive shops opened branches at the Desert Inn or along Palm Canyon Drive, Bullock's promoted the desert resort through a series of public presentations. T. H. Rosenberger, president of the Coachella Valley Camber of Commerce, spoke on "The Legend of the Deglet Noor, and The Winter Playground of America." Charles Francis Saunders, of the Nature Club of Southern California, spoke for the "Conservation of our Deserts." Laura Cooley, of the Los Angeles Public Library, offered an address on the "Literature of the Desert." A landscape architect gave a presentation on "Preserving Wildflowers in their Native Ground," and another speaker offered her insights on "The Desert Applied to Art." Here was the ultimate commodification of the desert. Patrons gained aesthetic refinement through nature appreciation, and Bullock's could expect their continued patronage as customers.[42]

Resort Residences: From Smoke Tree Ranch to the Ranch House

Instead of appreciating the desert on a vacation weekend or at a department-store lecture, the rich began to build vacation homes in Palm Springs. Such homes permitted a genteel life in the desert, one even purportedly in tune with its environment. One developer's florid promotional literature made this explicit:

Those who quest and seek for beauty have built here habitations of their own, some so lovely as to seem real bits of Paradise. These houses dot the landscape like jewels. Built largely of native material, they blend with their surroundings admirably, and their tiled roofs, pools, patios, balconies, gardens of desert growth, [and] splashing fountains, add their own charms to the establishment of Nature herself.

Such home-building "seekers of beauty" included razor magnate King Gillette and cereal mogul W. K. Kellogg. In case some homebuyers were less discriminating—or not effectively discriminated against—the developer also assured buyers that "carefully drawn restrictions protect the home owner and permanently maintain the high standards of the property, and while homes need not be pretentious, they must conform to an attractive style of architecture, and plans must be approved by an Art Jury." If this language were not clear enough, another developer, trying to draw a slightly less wealthy, but still affluent clientele, stated that "careful discrimination in the matter of lot buyers is also being made, as to race, desirability, etc., thus ensuring a high order of neighbors." Discrimination existed in commercial real estate as well, for prospective Jewish store owners and merchants, while not banned outright by law, were effectively prevented from buying property or businesses.[43]

Even in such a discriminating—and discriminatory—environment, residential construction in Palm Springs consistently valued private comfort over public appearance. One article tellingly summed up Palm Springs architecture:

One of the leading characteristics of Palm Springs architecture is its accommodation for outdoor living, combined with seclusion. Many of the larger haciendas of the Mexican type are built around a large inner court, where the center of attraction is apt to be a sapphire swimming pool or tennis court. Living rooms open onto a patio, thus insuring privacy both inside and out. While this type permits a somewhat bleak exterior to the street, it is a most pleasant arrangement for those who live in the house.

This inward orientation, away from the street and toward private interiors and backyards, would be a hallmark of future suburban housing as well.[44]

Thus, by the 1930s, the affluent had truly arrived in Palm Springs. This influx—as well as a growing tide of auto tourists—helped the resort town weather the Depression in relative comfort. Earl Coffman bragged that "we never heard of any Depression" in Palm Springs. One issue of a promotional magazine produced in the resort town during the 1930s included Hollywood

figures such as Walt Disney, Shirley Temple—who was such a regular feature that one of the cottages at the Desert Inn had been named in her honor—
Delores Del Rio, Martha Raye, Andy Rooney, Jack Benny, Leslie Howard,
and Cary Grant, as well as business tycoons such as Benjamin Fairless, the
CEO of U.S. Steel, and Water P. Chrysler.[45]

While the affluent had been building and buying vacation homes in Palm
Springs for some time, by the 1930s this real estate phenomenon had become
a veritable land rush. One of the most exclusive new resort housing developments appeared in the late 1930s. This was Smoke Tree Ranch, created
from a former dude ranch. Smoke Tree Ranch carefully maintained a rustic
atmosphere, and houses were required to be one story and constructed in
"rustic" architectural style. Homes sat wide apart on large lots, which were
required to be maintained as desert, with no lawns or nonnative shade trees.
Roads were narrow and initially unpaved. The gated community also provided hotel-like amenities, including meals in a clubhouse restaurant, a pool,
tennis courts, and maid service—in short, the "care of property by a capable all-year organization, and innumerable services the lack of which often
makes the ownership of resort property a burden." A half century before city
officials and city planners would begin to fret about the social and civic costs
of affluent "absentee owners" in resort communities such as Aspen or Jackson Hole, Smoke Tree Ranch already offered the amenities needed to create
an entire community of absentee homeowners. It also created an enclosed
world, where wealth and whiteness were assured, and the casual homes and
social relations it encouraged came about precisely because so many people
were excluded, as had been the case at Catalina decades before. Walt Disney, King Gillette, and the Weyerhaeuser family, among many others, would
build homes here. Disney would keep his Smoke Tree Ranch home until the
1950s, when he sold it to raise funds for his newly proposed theme park, Disneyland.

Yet while Smoke Tree Ranch offered a new model for resort design,
it also served as a model for residential home construction. Low-slung and
rambling, fusing rustic wood and stone with some modernist elements, the
houses in Smoke Tree Ranch looked unlike much of the architecture in
Palm Springs, particularly those structures of a Spanish- or Moorish-revival
design. From the perspective of a decade or two later, however, these homes
were instantly recognizable. They were clear early examples of the ranch
house—the domestic architectural style that would carpet the floor of the
San Fernando Valley after World War II and appear in virtually every community in the United States in the 1950s and 1960s. The houses in Smoke
Tree Ranch were highlighted in national architectural and popular culture
magazines. Dropped improbably among cacti, ocotillos, and the wispy, aptly
named smoke trees, these houses offered a simple façade to the street but

FIGURE 5.5 Dick Richards Home, Smoke Tree Ranch, Palm Springs, California, 1930s. This structure, with its low, horizontal orientation and outdoor patio, is a clear early example of the ranch house style, and exhibits other architectural lineages which contributed to the archetypal residence of postwar suburbia. The roof beams extending beyond the exterior walls recall the *vigas* of traditional adobe architecture, and were a common feature in older Mission and Spanish Revival designs. The large corner window on the right, however, where two windows meet at a right angle with no wall or pillar separating them, was a hallmark of many Modernist architects, such as Richard Neutra, who would later design several iconic homes in the Palm Springs area. Many Smoke Tree homes were built by Modernist architect Albert Frey, who found that he could introduce Modernist innovations into houses built in "traditional" styles. Courtesy of the Palm Springs Historical Society, Palm Springs, California.

seclusion and amenities to their inhabitants. They would serve as models of a resort-style architecture, leavened by a rustic simplicity and purported harmony with the landscape, that proved a dominant domestic architectural idiom of the United States in the twentieth century.[46]

Just as the Oasis Hotel presented a modernist rebuttal to historicist resort architecture, a few Palm Springs residences rejected both revivalist historicism and ranch rusticity, embracing instead International-style modernism. The most significant such house prior to World War II was Richard Neutra's Miller House of 1937. Grace Lewis Miller, a St. Louis socialite, commissioned Neutra to design a house suited to the practice and promotion of her movement and health regimen, the "Mensendieck System of Functional Exercise." Though fully acclimated to Southern California and its cult of the body, Miller did retain one lifelong interest betraying her Missouri roots—an obsession with collecting any historic trivia pertaining to the career of the explorer Meriwether Lewis.

Neutra found the idiosyncratic Miller a congenial client, and was intrigued by the possibilities of the desert landscape. He designed a small, single-story structure, rectangular and incised on one side. Wide overhangs helped keep the house cool, with the roof extended out over a reflecting pool at one corner, and a screened porch behind. The interior was simple and open, with a large room serving as living, dining, and studio space, and separate kitchen, bedroom, and bathroom opening off of it. The design was perfectly suited to the life of a single mother who required living and exercise space.

The exterior, composed of cement with aluminum trim, was designed to make the house fade into the desert landscape. A rock walk separated a swath of lawn from plantings of cacti and other desert plants, all artfully landscaped by Neutra. The style of the house was unabashedly new, even if it offered some of the same practicalities and appealing "simple life" characteristics of older bungalows. Though an anomaly in 1930s Palm Springs, the Miller House portended much for the architectural future of the resort community.[47]

A Decade and an Era End

As the 1930s drew to a close, Palm Springs was booming. What had been a failed agricultural venture in the 1890s and a tiny settlement of consumptives in the 1910s had now emerged as one of the most famous resorts in the United States. As far as whites were concerned, the resort town had truly arrived, and the time had come to mark that fact. At Avalon, incorporation had occurred in part so that locals could present a more united front to the monopoly-minded Bannings and their Santa Catalina Island Company. In Palm Springs, by contrast, locals voted for incorporation so that they could impose more control over the community themselves, particularly its burgeoning development. Palm Springs was incorporated on 20 April 1938, in an election in which drew seven hundred voters. A new city council took office that year. Voters also chose as the town's official name its already familiar title, which combined its palms with the spring at its heart. The town had in fact already renamed its streets, discarding Anglo-American and agricultural titles in favor of new ones, drawn from Agua Caliente family names and local landmarks, such as Amado, Andreas, Arenas, Baristo, Ramon, Cahuilla, Lugo, Patencio, Palm Canyon, and Tahquitz.[48]

For the Agua Calientes 1938 was also a milestone year, but for very different reasons. While they had maintained title to their land and water, the tribe, the Bureau of Indian Affairs, and prospective developers had never agreed on an equitable system for the distribution or leasing of their lands, or revenue sharing from profit-making operations on reservation land. The tribal rolls had continued to dwindle as old age, low birth rates, and disease took their toll. A smallpox epidemic at the end of World War I had been especially devastating. Then, in the same year whites voted to incorporate Palm Springs, Francisco Patencio died. He had been the last tribal chief, and a tireless defender of traditional ways. His daughter, Flora Silva, argued that there was now no one left who could serve as tribal head according to the old traditions. The Agua Calientes burned their round house, which had been the center of their traditional ceremonial life. They invited Nellie Coffman, the matriarch of the Anglo resort town, to attend Patencio's funeral. The old tribal leadership and traditions were gone. Now they would have to find a new means to make their way in a very different world.[49]

The following year, another calamity occurred. A fire, started by a careless tourist's cigarette, burned all the *Washingtonia* palms in Palm Canyon. Tourist promoters and Agua Calientes alike were distraught, albeit for different reasons. The verdant canyon was a popular draw for tourists, but it had also been a refuge for the Agua Calientes for centuries. Despite Indian and Anglo fears, the trees proved hardy. Most soon sprouted new fronds, and the canyon gradually returned to its verdant former appearance. Delicate as the desert ecosystem was, it was resilient. The Agua Calientes, despite all their ordeals, were resilient as well.[50]

At the decade's end, whites looked to the future with confidence born of success. Indians perhaps also looked to the future with confidence, the result of hard-won struggle. Since their arrival in the late nineteenth century, whites had often tried to ignore the Indians or pass them off as a tourist attraction. The Agua Calientes rarely had the luxury to do more than simply try to hold on to what they had and survive. Their conflicts would continue, and disputes over land would remain unresolved for another two decades. As World War II loomed, presaging the transformation of the United States and the world, neither group could be aware of just how wrenching—or unexpected—the changes of the future would be.[51]

Chapter Six

MAKING THE DESERT MODERN

Palm Springs after World War II

PEARL HARBOR and the advent of American involvement in World War II brought pronounced change to Palm Springs. The war would transform California from the Golden State into "Fortress California," and Palm Springs reflected some of those changes as well. The original boosters of Palm Springs had conceived of it as an oasis, a place of health, relaxation, and exotic scenery isolated from the broader world. World War II, and the events that followed, would draw Palm Springs ever closer to that outside world. Santa Catalina, which went into effective hibernation for the duration of the war, lay twenty-six miles off the California coast and was insulated from burgeoning postwar growth on the mainland. Palm Springs lay more than a hundred miles from downtown Los Angeles, but after 1941 it would be drawn ever closer to the megalopolis, becoming a more urban place in the process.

Before the war, Palm Springs had promulgated new forms of outdoor recreation and new attitudes towards desert scenery. While it would remain a tourist getaway, postwar Palm Springs increasingly played a role in the evolution of urban America. It had already served as a model for how houses, both architecturally renowned and mass-produced, might look in postwar America. Now it would offer a new resort architecture that promised the successful merging of technology, consumerism, and nature into a harmonious whole. New types of recreation, particularly golf, would transform the landscape of the Coachella Valley. In turn, Palm Springs would pioneer new urban forms, such as residential golf developments, that decisively shaped the appearance not only of other resorts, but much of American suburbia.

At the same time, however, the resort began to experience urban problems of its own, spawned by the unresolved status of the Agua Calientes and their land, and by the racial conflicts of a white resort town dependent upon the labor of people of color. As a result, the city of Palm Springs would acquire a reputation as perhaps the most ruthlessly exclusionist municipal government in Southern California in its efforts to preserve the affluence, atmosphere, and whiteness of its community, regardless of reservation law. The Coachella Valley would also witness the arrival of urban sprawl as other communities grew in the desert, some of which would become competitors with Palm Springs. The construction of condominiums and an influx of retirees would also change the community and, likewise, help Palm Springs serve as a regional and national model for retirement. Even so, some would interpret that retiree influx as proof that its era as a trend-setting resort was over.

Racial Conflict and Reservation Law in Section Fourteen

With the onset of World War II, the U.S. military arrived in the Coachella Valley. The U.S. Army found its desert terrain perfect for training troops headed for North Africa. General George S. Patton trained his tank corps in the Coachella. Over the course of the war, more than a million solders would train in the Coachella Valley and Mojave Desert. El Mirador, the resort hotel that had once been Hollywood's retreat in the desert, was purchased for $425,000 and converted into a military facility, Tourney General Hospital. Other major hotels, such as the Desert Inn, continued to draw guests, although gasoline rations reduced the number of auto tourists, and military personnel often supplanted vacationers. The military influx also forced Palm Springs to moderate its racial exclusivity, at least temporarily. Nellie Coffman invited soldiers to use the pool at the Desert Inn, and when Earl Coffman tried to stop African American solders from swimming, he received a sharp rebuke from his mother.[1]

Nellie Coffman's racial toleration, however, was not typical of propertied whites in Palm Springs in this era. The war had seen a significant influx of African Americans into Southern California, and Palm Springs was no exception, with blacks taking jobs in the tourist service industry, and as military workers. The large resort hotels prior to the war had provided housing for their nonwhite workers, much as the Catalina Island Company had for the workers of the Metropole Hotel decades earlier in Avalon. The military, as with the many smaller hotels that opened in Palm Springs following the war, did not provide any housing for civilian service workers, and pay for workers of color was often abysmally low. As a result, some blacks were forced to live outside of the city in unincorporated areas. Most, however, congregated in the city itself, but on land the city could not control. This was Section 14, the square-mile plot of Agua Caliente reservation land that lay immediately adjacent to downtown Palm Springs and Palm Canyon Drive, with its shops and hotels.[2]

Some Agua Calientes rented out land or housing to people of color denied housing elsewhere. As their own income was minimal, these rents were doubtless a useful source of revenue. Other tribal members simply allowed African Americans and Mexicans to build small cabins, shacks, or lean-tos on reservation land. Perhaps this was an act of charity. Perhaps also the Agua Calientes recognized these laborers as other people of color, like themselves, who had often faced discrimination and mistreatment by whites. A significant population of working class non-Indians, perhaps more than 4,500, soon occupied Section 14. This proved a source of constant conflict with the white city officials and resort owners who dominated Palm Springs.

Of course, other resort cities, like many larger cities, also were home to racial tensions, or exhibited discriminatory policies and urban planning. Santa Barbara, for example, a community that methodically constructed a Spanish fantasy city, simultaneously razed Mexican American houses and neighborhoods. The unique position of Palm Springs in this regard derived not from the exclusionary and exploitative nature of its urban planning policy—which was all too common—but instead from the singular fact that Palm Springs occupied Indian reservation land that the city could not fully control. As a result, city leaders regularly decried the "slum" they saw developing at the heart of what was supposed to be a picturesque resort town. The fact that this "slum" had been created as a direct result of their discriminatory policies seemed to elude them. The status of Section 14—and of workers who were needed, but not necessarily wanted—would remain a point of contention from World War II into the 1960s.[3]

Urban blight and racial strife hardly fit the escapist image city officials and promoters hoped to project. Even the local press, which placed the boosting of Palm Springs above all else, could not entirely gloss over the situation. One magazine ran an article on the Agua Calientes noting that many tourists found them quaint and picturesque. After spending time on the reservation, however, "you realize that what you see is squalor bred of poverty. You realize that it isn't quaint or picturesque at all." The greatest fear of local politicians and developers was that *Life* or another national magazine would arrive in Palm Springs and document the poverty at the heart of one of America's most famous resort towns. This drove them to action, though hardly to acts of humanitarian kindness. City leaders asserted that the land issue was resolved by a series of local and national decisions and actions that worked to the mutual benefit of all parties involved. Many Indians and other non-white residents of the town viewed the same developments in a profoundly different light—as a means of simply making them disappear, rather than remedying the problems from which they suffered.[4]

While Palm Springs had changed dramatically since the late nineteenth century, in some respects Anglo views of the Agua Calientes had not. The Indians were either ignored or simply overruled by people with more wealth and connections to political power. Such had been the case when Indian agent John McCallum had appropriated Agua Caliente water for his own farm and abortive real-estate development. The same had been true when the concession operated at the hot spring had been awarded to whites in the late nineteenth century. The Indians, however, were not entirely powerless. The Agua Caliente Reservation consisted of forty-seven and a half sections of land in the Coachella Valley, including nine sections that lay within or in the immediate vicinity of Palm Springs. Every even-numbered section of land in the Palm Springs area was theirs, no matter how often whites tried to cajole them into selling or tried to have the reservation lines redrawn. As a result, federal courts and the Bureau of Indian Affairs ensured that their water rights were upheld, much to McCallum's dismay. It also meant that they had the power to reject a government plan to incorporate Palm Canyon and the other "Indian Canyons" at the foot of Mount San Jacinto into a national monument. The tribe had been offered a paltry sum in exchange for land central to their spiritual beliefs and traditional subsistence.[5]

Whereas in the 1890s whites had coveted the Agua Calientes' water and their desert scenery in the 1920s, by the 1940s they desired Indian real estate. Section 14 and other areas could be exceedingly valuable if developed, and city leaders were determined to keep the town predominantly white. The U.S. Supreme Court had banned restrictive housing covenants in 1948, but that did not stop white homeowners and landowners from refusing to sell to African Americans or any other group they disdained. If white homeowners associations and realtors could collude to keep working-class neighborhoods white in a city such as Los Angeles, it was far easier to achieve the same ends in an affluent resort town. The unusual status of Section 14, however, required more elaborate measures.

The first means the city employed to vacate Section 14 was neglect. As Indian reservation land, Section 14 paid no taxes into city coffers. As a result, the city of Palm Springs refused to offer any municipal services to the tract. The city initially even refused water service, but in 1946 the Palm Springs Water Company installed a few water lines. Most residents still had to carry buckets of water back to their homes, or even subsist on runoff from Tahquitz Canyon, which flowed through town and into Section 14. Many homes had only an outhouse, and the city refused to provide garbage pickup—even as some whites used Section 14 as an illegal dump. Palm Springs officials could soon legitimately state that Section 14 was a menace to public health, though they refused to acknowledge the role they had played in its wretched state.[6]

In response to complaints, the city asserted that, if they were given authority over Indian land and presented with a long-term zoning plan by the Agua Calientes, the rehabilitation of Section 14 could begin. When granted some jurisdictional power over Section 14 by the Bureau of Indian Affairs, however, the city did not move to make improvements. It simply started issuing eviction notices. The city commenced burning houses in Section 14 in 1956. Purportedly, tenants would be eligible to rent low-income housing from the city. Yet these apartments, which were converted military barracks, were white-only. The city also decided not to take advantage of federal housing funds, which would have made it subject to federal regulations.[7]

At the same time, the Agua Calientes received Bureau of Indian Affairs approval to develop the master zoning plan the city had demanded, and the tribe commissioned the firm of Victor Gruen and Associates to complete it. The plan, which was unveiled in 1958, called for a "concentration of retail facilities in the heart of the Section, ringed by hotels and apartments, a Convention Center and golf course, bounded by a medium density residential development." According to the firm, this plan would succeed in "maintaining and intensifying the resort and recreational character of Palm Springs." Further, it would "add vitality to the City, strengthening its position as the focal point and center of activity in the Coachella Valley." Yet city officials, who had supposedly been awaiting a zoning proposal with eager anticipation, reacted with alarm. They feared that the plan would draw business away from Anglo-controlled downtown and leave Palm Springs with no tax base. Thus the city wanted the right to control the houses, inhabitants, and development of Section 14, but was opposed to any development that might actually improve the lot of the Agua Calientes and their non-Indian tenants.[8]

Transforming the Reservation into Real Estate

In the later 1950s, federal actions precipitated change in Section 14 and in Palm Springs as a whole. In 1959 President Eisenhower—who had vacationed regularly in Palm Springs and neighboring La Quinta, and bought a home in Palm Desert in 1957—signed the Equalization Act and the Indian Leasing Act. The Leasing Act allowed tribe members to lease their parcels for ninety-nine years, a great increase over the prior leasing schedule, which had been limited to leases of twenty-five years with the option to renew for an additional twenty-five. The Equalization Act allowed for collectively owned land to be divided into parcels of equal value that could then be distributed to all tribal members. Certain parcels, however, considered to be of special long-standing significance to the tribe, could not be allotted. They were instead set aside as tribal reserves "for the benefit and use of the band." These included the hot springs, San Andreas Canyon, Palm Canyon, Tahquitz Canyon, and Murray Canyon. The tribe wished that the canyons remain in their "rugged natural state," but hoped that they could be developed for tourist visitation, eventually achieving a status akin to national parks. The tribe had rejected national-park designation in the 1920s but clearly was not adverse to tourist development if it increased tribal revenues.[9]

While each tribal member had previously been granted a parcel of land within one of the various sections of the reservation, these parcels varied greatly in value. Some tribal members held title to land adjacent to downtown, while others held title to land on the sandy desert floor of the valley or on the rocky slopes of Mount San Jacinto. As a result, the value of individual parcels ranged from an appraised value of $74,500 to $629,000 in 1958. This inequality had hampered prior efforts at development and the distribution of tribal revenue. With this problem resolved and ninety-nine-year leases available, Agua Caliente reservation land was now of great value.[10]

The most visible manifestation of this was the new Spa Hotel, built atop the Agua Calientes' hot spring. Developer Sam Banowit leased the site from the tribe and hired Palm Springs architects Bill Cody and partners Donald Wexler and Richard Harrison. Cody had come to Palm Springs at age thirty after working for Cliff May, one of the most accomplished architects to design residences in what would come to be called the ranch-house style. Cody's first local commission had been the remodeling of cottages on the grounds of the Desert Inn. Later he served on the Palm Springs planning commission, supporting modernist projects when many locals still preferred Spanish-revival architecture. Due to financing issues, the spa facility was built first, and the hotel constructed later.

The final result was a five-story complex at the intersection of Indian Avenue and Tahquitz-McCallum Way. The rooms, clustered in a tower removed from Indian Avenue, were of unadorned, economical modernist design, recognizable anywhere in America as the style of a standard Holiday Inn. Public spaces and services were housed in a one-story structure to the front of the room tower, with the spa located above the hot springs, now piped into pools. Perhaps the most striking feature of the design was a long colonnade connecting the Spa to the street, and bisecting the one-story section of the complex. Alongside, in a channel lined with aqua tile, flowed a stream of water from the springs. Though he worked in the vocabulary of modernism, and in a style he described as "Desert Architecture," Cody's earlier exposure to Beaux-Arts design appeared in this aspect of the plan. The colonnade and water channel served as a striking axis for the complex, and reminded guests and passersby of the hot springs that had once sustained the Agua Calientes and drawn health seekers and tourists. A tribal publication claimed that where primitive bathing shacks had once stood, "the same identical springs bubble... with luxurious embellishments which rival the Roman baths of old and the outstanding spas throughout the world."[11]

Unfortunately, this new development played a larger role in white boosterism than it did in Indian reality. For decades, the Agua Calientes and their desert oasis had been sold to tourists as quaint reminders of the past, relics of an earlier California and Southwest. Now the Agua Calientes were made to play roles in a new narrative—one not of historical continuity, but rather of "progress." Americanized, taught business skills and capitalist values, these "new" Agua Calientes, proprietors of a resort hotel and other business ventures, were sold as a success story to corporate and conformist 1950s white America. Instead of whites adopting cultural elements from Indians, as Charles Lummis or Mary Austin had wished, now Indians had purportedly learned to be good American capitalists.

Though the Spa Hotel and other investments did prove successful, they did not result in immediate prosperity and power for the tribe. At the time the Spa was constructed in the early 1950s, tribal revenues averaged only fifty dollars per person per month. As it went only to certified members of the tribe, many of whom had married non-Indians or Indians who lacked tribal affiliation, this monthly income was paltry indeed. A tribal publication noted that while the Los Angeles Times might refer to the Agua Calientes as inhabitants of an "ermine lined Reservation," its residents knew that "one cannot eat dirt." The tribal council, which had replaced Joseph Patencio's traditional tribal chieftainship after his death, predicted that "there is hope for a bright future, but it will take a minimum of ten years before the Indians will be in a position to appreciate the value of their real property assets, and it will unquestionably take at least another quarter of a century until such full scale economic development takes place." That prediction would prove remarkably accurate.[12]

The Equalization Act required that guardians and conservators be appointed by the courts to oversee the distribution, leasing, and sharing of revenue derived from Indian lands. A group of pro-development Palm Springs whites, led by Superior Court Judge Hilton McCabe, were appointed to these positions. Complaints soon followed that tribal members were being forced to sell, that legal transactions were conducted without their knowledge, and that much of the revenue from leases and new development were going not to the Indians but instead to their white "guardians." The conservator arrangement was a boon to the city as well. The ethnic cleansing of

Section 14 could now continue, with the city claiming that the demolitions had been decreed to be in the Indians' best interest by their court-appointed guardians. Families were evicted and houses burned—sometimes without even notifying the occupants, who returned from work to find all their possessions incinerated.[13]

By 1961 the population of Section 14 had dropped to 1,727. This coincided with an exodus of black and Mexican residents from Palm Springs. Some moved outside the city limits to a new subdivision called Desert Highlands, which permitted people of color. More moved to Banning, or to the historically agricultural and working-class town of Indio. Many left the area entirely, settling in Riverside, San Bernardino, or Barstow. Another 235 homes were razed in 1965 and 1966. The wealthy resort city had successfully purged most poor people and nonwhites from its midst. Yet Section 14 and other tracts were still Indian land, and that fact portended much for the future.[14]

Mass Tourism in Postwar Palm Springs

Despite the conflict over Section 14, most tourists remained blissfully ignorant of the simmering racial problems in the resort they visited. The *Palm Springs Villager*, a magazine that began publication in February 1947, offered glowing coverage of the growing resort town, complete with articles on visiting celebrities, the latest fads in recreation and fashion, and vacation dream homes. Witty cover illustrations, reminiscent of the venerable *New Yorker*, depicted vacationers decorating cacti for Christmas, and other such Palm Springs scenes. The magazine offered a view of local life epitomizing "active leisure." One society wife, a self-described "outdoor girl," was depicted following her daily routine. This "routine" consisted of a morning climb in the mountains, followed by golf, a swim at the Palm Springs Tennis Club, and then a game of tennis.[15]

In addition to demonstrating how the resort wished to be seen, the magazine also illustrated what types of visitors the resort hoped to attract. The inaugural issue included coverage of a "desert honeymoon." Betty and Jack Boger, a young couple from Wheeling, West Virginia, had been selected by the ABC radio show "Bride and Groom" to enjoy a free week-long honeymoon in Palm Springs. The newlyweds were given deluxe accommodations, dinner at the Tennis Club, and horseback rides, and were showered with attention and gifts by local luminaries and visiting celebrities. The husband, a marine who had just returned from service in the South Pacific, was overwhelmed: "I still can't believe this is all true.... The town is just 'out of this world,' but if I am dreaming, please don't wake me up."[16]

These newlyweds were exemplars of the kind of tourists Palm Springs hoped to attract. Emergent middle-class citizens ready to relax, shop, and stargaze, the Bogers were the perfect demographic for the growing resort. Palm Springs, eager to be less exclusive, now welcomed travelers on a tight budget as well. The *Palm Springs Villager* also ran an article entitled "Five Days' Fun for $63.16: Two Girls on a Budget." It describes how two young stenographers from Compton and Hawthorne found accommodations and dining on the cheap and still enjoyed the sights Palm Springs had to offer. The magazine did, however, highlight the fact that the "girls" went to a local church on Sunday morning. Palm Springs was now ready to welcome a far larger swath of the traveling public—as long as they were suitably respectable.[17]

After the war, there were many more such tourists to visit. Postwar prosperity, increasing automobile ownership, and the booming population of Southern California ensured that visitation rose markedly. Western Airlines inaugurated regular service to Palm Springs in 1945, making the resort more accessible. Another key factor was the increasing affordability and use of air-conditioning. Just as the Santa Catalina Island Company strove to draw tourists in winter to what had primarily been a summer resort, Palm Springs developers and promoters hoped to draw tourists beyond the limited winter season. Palm Springs would remain predominantly a winter resort, but air-conditioning made fall and spring much more bearable for tourists. It also made Palm Springs far more bearable as a place of year-round residence.[18]

The permanent population of Palm Springs would grow from 3,434 to 7,660 between 1940 and 1950, and would surpass 10,000 by 1953. That year its seasonal residents totaled 35,000, more than half of whom came from California. In a shift from prewar winters, a majority of out-of-state seasonal residents now came from the Pacific Northwest, mainly the cities of Seattle and Portland, which had boomed during the war. Seasonals from the Northeast and Midwest continued to come as well, but they now made up a smaller percentage of total visitation. This likely reflected the growing population and prosperity of western states, but may have also resulted from an increased number of easterners travelling to Florida or Cuba. In 1958 the city counted 12,443 residents, with a seasonal winter population of 50,000, and an estimated total annual visitation of a half million.[19]

Nellie Coffman lived to see this postwar boom, but died on 10 June 1950. It was the end of an era. The occasion of her eightieth birthday on 3 November 1947 had garnered national media coverage, including an article in *Time* magazine. The Desert Inn would continue operation under the direction of her son, Earl, though he subsequently sold the hotel in 1955 to Marion Davies, the longstanding companion of William Randolph Hearst. The hotel was eventually torn down to make way for a retail development, the Desert Inn Fashion Plaza. Pearl McCallum McManus lived until 1966, when she died at the age of eighty-seven. Though she never attained the wealth that Coffman accrued, she had played a major role in the community. Though accused of being stingy, McManus nevertheless endowed the McCallum Desert Foundation, which gave millions of dollars to schools, charities, cultural institutions, and environmental causes. The foundation would continue to shape Palm Springs after her death. She had come a long way in eighty-seven years—from a survivor of a doomed pioneer family to a resort real-estate magnate who socialized with celebrities. In an interview conducted shortly before her death, she reflected, "I'm so glad I lived to see it all come out in the sunshine."[20]

Yet the Palm Springs that Coffman and McManus had presided over—a small resort for the very rich—had already given way to a larger, more egalitarian tourist town. The resort was evolving into a different sort of retreat, one that was more open, more democratic, and, as a result, less refined. Those looking for solitude in the desert would no longer find it here. What they found instead was postwar America, flush with prosperity, excited by new consumer goods and technology, and, above all, ready to play. Forms of leisure that had once been fads among the rich now spread to a much broader swath of society. Newcomers were instructed how to enjoy these new luxuries. The *Palm Springs Villager* ran an article entitled "How to Acquire a Sun Tan" which suggested what oils to use and how long to lie in the sun. Of course, sun-tanning advice could not supersede local boosterim; readers were warned that "Sunstroke is practically unknown here, but you could get enough sun to be uncomfortable."[21]

How observers reacted to this new resort was very much a matter of personal opinion. Journalist Neil Morgan derisively opined that Palm Springs in its postwar heyday was "the most conspicuous flowering of all that is vulgar and futile in the Southern California philosophy." On the other hand, for those with aspirations to the middle-class good life, the resort could seem entirely different. For them its allure extended far and wide. In 1947 the *Villager* received a letter from a woman named Nora Barker who had encountered a copy of the magazine during a hospital stay in Carlisle, West Australia. She wrote to relate that "the Nurses raved over it; romantic and novel, quite differently composed to our way of doing things; everything colorful and rich looking." These were appealing characteristics indeed.[22]

Desert Modern: Architectural Modernism in Palm Springs

Postwar Palm Springs offered outdoor recreation, Hollywood society, and lively nightlife to weekend travelers and vacation homeowners alike. It had contained all these elements before 1945 but now presented them in a decidedly modern setting. Indeed, perhaps no other resort would be so closely associated with architectural modernism. In this, Palm Springs differed starkly from Catalina, Santa Barbara, and Ojai, where Spanish revival or Mediterranean historicist architecture dominated. While Palm Springs already possessed a significant number of historicist structures—including the Desert Inn and El Mirador—its era of greatest popularity would witness the construction of a large number of modernist structures. Certainly, modernist architecture served to remind tourists that they had come to a trendsetting resort, more exciting perhaps than those older resorts. Modern architecture also "fit" the minimalist, monochromatic desert setting—so much so that many Palm Springs denizens would come to call modernist architecture "desert architecture." Many of the fundamental tenets and hallmarks of modernist design—the use of basic materials; structures that utilized natural light and were open to the outside, with outdoor spaces functioning as extensions of interior rooms; houses with open and flowing interiors, which were perfect for socializing—all these things made modernist design appealing in midcentury Palm Springs. Modified for less affluent and avant-garde communities, important elements of this modernism would appear elsewhere as well.

This did not mean that modernist structures were uniformly similar. Mid-twentieth-century modernism witnessed a division between rationalist and expressionist styles. Frank Lloyd Wright's later works, such as his Guggenheim Museum or the Marin County Civic Center, were often unabashedly expressionist, with stylized forms and striking colors. In contrast, Ludwig Mies van der Rohe's designs, such as his famed Seagram Building in Manhattan, were sleek, exacting constructions of metal and glass, beautiful in their simplicity and mathematical perfection.[23]

In addition to this stylistic division, modernist architecture in Palm Springs evidenced divergent approaches to landscape. Some architects attempted to make their buildings blend into the desert, becoming part of the natural environment. Others instead designed and sited structures that were clearly human constructions, distinct from the desert landscape. Such buildings, though located in the desert, were definitely not "of" it. Adopting different approaches, architects practicing in Palm Springs nevertheless attempted to address similar issues: Could architecture mediate a relationship between built and natural environments? Should architecture incorporate new technologies and the nation's postwar consumerist ethos? How could architects design structures that accommodated the casual life of a resort community?

Palm Springs would be indelibly marked by modernism, but the adoption of this architectural idiom was far from inevitable. Not all clients were necessarily well-disposed to modernist designs. Frank Sinatra, for example, who built his first home in Palm Springs in 1946, initially wanted a red-brick

Georgian mansion. His architects persuaded him to consider a modernist design, which he eventually accepted—though they acquiesced to his desire for a pool shaped like a piano. In fact, many of the city's political leaders favored Spanish-revival, Mediterranean, or Moorish architecture and tried to impose these styles in a way similar to that pursued with such fervor in Santa Barbara. That resort city had been severely damaged by an earthquake in 1925, and was reconstructed in an opulent Spanish-revival style. Their goal, as they saw it, was to preserve the "romantic, conservative beauty of the Village," and avoid a "honky-tonk appearance." Though Palm Springs city planning was stringently effective in some areas—most notably in its callous removal of nonwhites—it was never able to impose a historicist architectural "order" on the community.[24]

Perhaps this was because the cultural currents that had made Mission and Spanish revival so popular earlier in the century had subsided. By the 1950s Southern California no longer needed to sell itself with the urgency of its early boom years. More fundamentally, what it sold to the rest of the nation had changed. In the era of Charles Lummis, Southern California had presented itself as a pastoral retreat, an escape from urbanism, industry, and immigration where Anglo-Americans could reconnect with nature and tradition. By the 1920s, and certainly after World War II, Southern California, and Los Angeles in particular, sold itself instead as the city and region of tomorrow, where America's future could be lived today. Aspects of the earlier image endured, however, most particularly the access to nature, healthfulness, and leisure. In this sense, modernist architecture continued to reflect values present in some older regional architectural forms, most notably the turn of the century arts-and-crafts movement that had so marked communities such as Pasadena, and the startling modernism of structures created by San Diego architect Irving Gill.[25]

Like the earlier arts-and-crafts movement, Palm Springs modernism initially flourished owing to the patronage of wealthy easterners who wished to winter in Southern California. Their wealth not only made them potential clients, but also gave them the social status and security to be more open to modern architecture. Since most houses were designed as vacation homes, clients did not feel the need for staid respectability that might have dictated their architectural choices in an affluent neighborhood in New York, Chicago, or Seattle. Palm Springs had definite appeal for ambitious architects as well. The abundance of affluent clients was the town's most obvious attribute. Since many of these individuals owned more than one home, architects might enjoy the opportunity to design multiple residences or commercial structures for a single client and do so in different parts of the nation. Better still, architects could be certain that their houses would be seen by a national audience, whether in periodicals such as *Architectural Digest* and *Fortune*, or in celebrity magazines, films, and museum exhibitions.

Many of the new houses built in Palm Springs were stunning indeed. Surrounded by boulders and cacti, with huge windows and doorways opening to mountain and desert vistas, Palm Springs modernism seemed suited to the desert, spare and elegant. Richard Neutra's Kaufmann Desert House of 1946 was arguably the greatest modernist residence ever built in the community. Commissioned by the same Pittsburgh department store family that commissioned Frank Lloyd Wright to build Fallingwater, Neutra's design aimed to suit the landscape in a manner reminiscent of Wright's masterpiece. It did not, however, emulate Wright's Taliesin West outside Phoenix, which employed rustic wood and stone to lend a desert atmosphere. Edgar Kaufmann wanted a lighter, more open house than either Wright building. Neutra built a desert house, but his would be a modern "machine for living" in the International style. The second story consisted of an open-air "gloriette," a combination outdoor den, covered patio, and grandly scaled sleeping porch. The "gloriette" also circumvented local zoning laws that imposed a one-story limit on all residences. Downstairs, sleek wood, metal, and glass marked the house as an exquisite space for modern living, complete with master bedroom, living and dining rooms, kitchen, servants' quarters, covered patio, and pool.

The house opened into the landscape and offered vantage points to observe the desert and mountains. It also boasted overhangs, louvers, and radiant heating installed in the floor to maintain a comfortable temperature. The Kaufmann Desert House was indeed a desert house, but clearly modern and manmade, not a house that mimicked its surroundings or attempted to conceal itself as a natural feature of the landscape. A 1947 photograph of the Kaufmann Desert House by Julius Shulman became an iconic image for modernism, and for Palm Springs. The house and pool glow in the twilight dusk, while in the background rugged mountains fade into the hazy distance. The house looks like a machine dropped into the desert, polished and incongruous.[26]

A number of other houses also attempted to make the desert modern by merging architectural design with landscape. One especially accomplished architect to produce residences in this vein was Albert Frey, a native of Switzerland who had settled in Palm Springs, and had been the first follower of Le Corbusier to build in the United States. One of Frey's most striking commissions was the home he created for Raymond Loewy. Loewy was the most famous industrial designer in America, responsible for everything from the shape of Coca-Cola bottles to the corporate logos of Exxon and Shell, the Studebaker Avanti automobile, and the interior décor of Pan Am airplanes. Frey's Loewy House, also of 1946, adopted a low profile of natural wood and glass that opened onto a patio which in turn opened into the desert landscape. Boulders were built into the swimming pool, and the pool—to make the merging of indoor and outdoor complete—extended under retractable glass doors into the living room of the house. The result was remarkable, but was also a source of humor; no party was complete until some unsuspecting guest took a step backward and tumbled in. The *Palm Springs Villager* showcased the house as its home of the month in March 1947, asserting that it attained "a new height in home architecture."[27]

The two houses Frey built for himself in Palm Springs epitomized differing approaches to landscape and environment, as well as the division between rationalist and expressionist approaches to modernism. The first, constructed in 1940, was initially a small poolside pavilion of corrugated metal and cement, a collection of rationalist planes expanding into space and opening to the outdoors. While open to the desert, Frey's house was clearly an artificial construction. Additions in 1948 and 1953 remade the house in an aggressively expressionist style, sheathing it in metal and expanding its size. A new bedroom was installed atop the structure in the form of a metal cylinder with sheet-metal portholes jutting from its sides. Neighbors must have thought that B-movie aliens had landed on the roof.[28]

Frey's second house, constructed in 1963 and 1964, offered a dizzying contrast, built among boulders high above town on the side of Mount San

FIGURE 6.1 Richard Neutra's Kaufmann House, 1946. The photograph, taken by Julius Shulman, proved emblematic of Modernism and Palm Springs. © J. Paul Getty Trust. Used with permission. Julius Shulman Photography Archive, Research Library at the Getty Research Institute (2004.R.10).

Jacinto. The automobile-accessible side of the house, constructed on a platform that also suspended a pool above the garage, presented a wall of concrete block. The rest of the house instead merged into the rocky mountainside. The interior-floor elevation followed the hillside, and a large boulder pierced the wall of glass beside the bed. The Edris House, designed by E. Stewart Williams in 1954, also made use of natural boulders, placing the structure on the crest of a rocky outcrop. Sheathed in wood inside and out, the house presented a low profile to the landscape. Williams felt that a "building should grow out of its site, not look like a spaceship that has just landed." His design certainly followed that dictum, as did Frey's second home.[29]

Two houses designed by architect John Lautner were apparently intended to look precisely like spaceships recently landed in the desert. His 1968 Elrod House and 1979 Bob Hope residence embodied late modernist expressionism. The Elrod House, commissioned by interior designer Arthur Elrod, sat high on the slope of Mount San Jacinto. It contained some elements that connected it to the desert environment. Boulders found on site were incorporated into the final structure, and the house presented a relatively nondescript curving wall to the street. Inside, the house was anything but ordinary. A circular living room, sixty feet in diameter, offered sweeping views of the city below.

FIGURE 6.2 Albert Frey's Loewy House, 1946. A Palm Springs residence which literally opens to the outside. Note living room carpet in foreground. © J. Paul Getty Trust. Used with permission. Julius Shulman Photography Archive, Research Library at the Getty Research Institute (2004.R.10).

FIGURE 6.3 The Loewy House interior, bringing the outside in. Note boulder in swimming pool. © J. Paul Getty Trust. Used with permission. Julius Shulman Photography Archive, Research Library at the Getty Research Institute (2004.R.10).

FIGURE 6.4 Frey House II, 1963–64. Here Desert Modern seems to emerge out of the rock face of Mt. San Jacinto high above Palm Springs. © J. Paul Getty Trust. Used with permission. Julius Shulman Photography Archive, Research Library at the Getty Research Institute (2004.R.10).

A concrete dome pierced by clerestory windows was intended to evoke a desert flower and allowed in light while screening out the hottest late afternoon sun. The space was striking and would serve as a set for the 1971 film *Diamonds Are Forever*. Lautner later stated that Elrod had wanted a "party house," and he had certainly gotten one.[30]

If Elrod wanted a party house, Bob and Dolores Hope asked for an entertainment complex. Dolores Hope had been enchanted by the Elrod House, and the Hope House revisited the domed Elrod design, with a much larger dome intended to evoke the forms of the mountains nearby. Now, however, the dome was open to the sky and served to enclose a large courtyard. The space devoted to the couple's personal residence was relatively small, as most of the behemoth structure was intended to be used to entertain, feed, and potentially house hundreds of guests. When Dolores Hope's husband saw Lautner's design, he reportedly quipped that "at least when they come down from Mars they'll know where to go." Though Bob Hope consented to the project, Lautner and Dolores Hope had a difficult relationship. She repeatedly asked for changes that required redesigns. A devastating fire during construction also slowed building and resulted in a less ambitious design than Lautner's initial plan. He subsequently looked back on the project with regret, but the Hope residence nevertheless became a Palm Springs landmark.[31]

Of course, Palm Springs desert modern, whether intended to "fit" into the landscape or not, was rarely environmentally sensitive in ecological terms. Some houses included sophisticated techniques to mitigate desert heat. Most, however, relied heavily on air-conditioning to offset all that open glass. The *Palm Springs Villager* might claim that "the swimming pool is as much a part of the life of this desert country as the creosote bush, the dunes and the clean-cut mountain skyline," but the ubiquitous swimming pool was hardly a natural feature of the desert landscape. Pools, lawns, and golf courses required vast amounts of water to maintain. Palm Springs would draw groundwater from thirty-two wells, as well as from the Colorado River Aqueduct. Eventually it began trading water with the Southern California Metropolitan Water District to secure additional water from the California Aqueduct. Author and environmentalist Wallace Stegner, upon seeing photographs of one particularly striking desert house complete with swimming pool, told its architect that he thought he could undoubtedly "build a comfortable house in hell." Stegner did not mean this as a compliment: "The only reasons for building there were to let mad dogs and rich men go out in the midday sun, and to let them own and dominate a view they admired."[32]

While environmentalists might condemn desert modern, the masses would not. Here, it seemed, were houses that fully merged inside and outside, providing spaces for that essential component of Californian—and indeed middle-class American—life: leisure. While not everyone could have a Neutra masterpiece, many families could adopt aspects of Palm Springs modern. The Palm Springs chamber of commerce noted this with a marked lack of humility: "Palm Springs homes have opened a new era in architecture. 'The Palm Springs influence' can be noted in homes all over the country. Patios, sun decks, pools and barbecue areas bring the indoors outdoors—the outdoors indoors." According to the chamber, the "Desert Modern American Home" was the "indispensable asset" of Palm Springs.[33]

Perhaps the most striking manifestation of the "Palm Springs influence" was the backyard swimming pool, which before World War II had been largely an amenity for the wealthy. In 1949, there were ten thousand private swimming pools in the United States. By 1953, there would be six hundred swimming pools in Palm Springs—or one for every seventeen residents. The ratio would later drop to one pool for every five residents. Even more striking was the fact that nearly 470 of these pools had been constructed in less than six years. In 1959 there would be more than 250,000 private swimming pools in the United States—and a stunning 90,000 of these were located in the city of Los Angeles alone.[34]

Many subsequent modernist structures in Palm Springs would lack the refined simplicity and sensitivity that the best early works exhibited. Clashing colors, questionable décor, and oversized houses that dominated the landscape were all manifestations of what some critics have dismissed as "martini modern." These critics, however, missed the larger social and cultural function of this more mass-produced Palm Springs modern. Much like the art deco and streamline moderne architecture of the 1920s and 1930s, this architecture rendered modernism and modern life more comforting and approachable. Residences were equipped with a swimming pool and every imaginable consumer gadget—from endless kitchen gewgaws to automated sunbathing chairs that rotated to follow the sun's course across the sky. Such houses were livable and comfortable, even if occasionally silly, merging postwar prosperity and the California good life into a form that could be emulated elsewhere. This sunny, push-button modernism would epitomize Palm Springs at its height as a resort in the 1950s and 1960s.[35]

Modernism was by no means limited to residential structures. The Oasis Hotel, after all, had stood on Palm Canyon Drive since the early 1920s. For that matter, 1934 witnessed the construction on Palm Canyon Drive of the Kocher-Samson Building, a doctor's office with an apartment on the second floor. Designed by A. Lawrence Kocher and Albert Frey, the building was showcased in the 1935 Museum of Modern Art exhibition "Modern Architecture in California." Decades later, Frey would also design another landmark of commercial modernism, the Tramway Gas Station of 1963–65. The gas station roof, a wing-like structure arcing ninety-five feet over the gas pumps below, became an instant landmark and one of the first buildings most motorists from Los Angeles saw when driving into Palm Springs on Highway 111. After World War II, rapid growth resulted in the creation of a number of modernist structures along Palm Canyon Drive, further cementing its status as the axis and primary commercial thoroughfare for the resort town. With its double row of *Washingtonia* palm trees offering shade by day and lit at night by spotlights to illuminate the street, Palm Canyon became an integral component of the Palm Springs tourist experience. The commercial structures constructed along it also accelerated the spread of a modernist vernacular architecture in Palm Springs.[36]

Bullock's, the department-store chain that had marketed Palm Springs since the 1920s, opened a new store on Palm Canyon drive in 1947. Previously, the chain had operated a small location at the Desert Inn. Its new store, though still smaller than the stores in Los Angeles or Pasadena, clearly indicated the growing popularity of Palm Springs as a shopper's paradise. The design, by the firm of Wurdeman and Becket, adopted a resort-friendly moderne style. Significantly, this store, unlike the flagship Wilshire Boulevard location, still emphasized the pedestrian entrance on Palm Canyon Drive, a popular place for window shopping and star sightings. Ornamental screens and overhangs softened the bright desert light entering the building. Inside, bamboo and wicker furniture conveyed a resort atmosphere. A sundeck offered mountain views, and air-conditioning made shoppers comfortable. Other department stores followed. Robinson's constructed a more minimalist structure, also on Palm Canyon Drive, with metal columns and textured concrete block walls. Saks Fifth Avenue created another modernist structure, with a broad canopy over the entrance and a glass wall along the front. Yet this building also referenced the past; its roof beams jutted out beyond the walls, echoing the roof-supporting log *vigas* of adobe architecture, the iconic style of the Southwest.[37]

In addition to retailers, the large number of banks that opened or expanded operations in Palm Springs attested to the resort's growth and the increasing commerce conducted there. Promotional materials made use of these symbols of financial success, often depicting tourists gawking at cowboys sauntering down Palm Canyon Drive past the Bank of America, juxtaposing the Old and New Wests—though few cowboys had ever walked the streets of Palm Springs. This imagery advertised the combined sophistication and "westernness" of Palm Springs, but also served a local civic function, reminding residents just how far their community had come.

Some of these banks—almost all located along Palm Canyon Drive— also contributed to the accelerating modernist atmosphere of the resort. A symbol of local civic pride was the Coachella Valley Bank, opened in 1960. Designed by Stewart Williams, the pavilion-like structure, sheathed in bronze, was covered by a flat overhanging roof. Curved, tapering columns, which met at their bases as a seismic safety measure, rose to the roofline and recalled the architecture of Oscar Niemeyer's Brasilia. The entire structure sat on a raised platform in a pool of fountains. With a colonnade of graceful palm trees in front lining Palm Canyon Drive, the building attested to the prosperity of Palm Springs.[38]

Perhaps the most luxurious bank constructed in Palm Springs, however, was Victor Gruen and Associates' City National Bank of 1959, which boldly recalled Le Corbusier's masterpiece, the Ronchamp Chapel. The American version of Le Corbusier's mysterious religious shrine was placed by the road-side, opened with glass walls, and rendered casual and welcoming to pedestrians and drivers alike. A sweeping, curving roof, balanced atop walls and an oversized round column covered in aqua-blue tiles, covered the space within. The interior was as baroque as it was eclectic, containing surfaces covered in marble, walnut, and teak, with Italian chandeliers, German slate floors, Japanese grass wall coverings, and Rhodesian lion-hair draperies. The bank even included a scale built into the floor so health-conscious customers could keep track of their weight. Le Corbusier's chapel had been reborn as a temple of consumption, a fitting symbol for the California good life as epitomized in midcentury Palm Springs.[39]

Thunderbird Ranch and the Residential Golf Community

A central component of the good life in Palm Springs was "fun in the sun," defined as active outdoor recreation. Tennis and sunbathing were already common activities by the 1930s. Yet after World War II, Palm Springs would be increasingly dominated by outdoor sports and by institutions and facilities that encouraged them. Pearl McCallum McManus's Palm Springs Tennis Club was expanded, and other athletic social clubs were constructed. These served as social gathering places for vacation homeowners and regular tourists.

By far the most popular sport, however, and the one that proved most influential in Palm Springs, was golf. A small nine-hole course had been laid out near the Desert Inn in 1926 by Long Beach oilman Thomas O'Donnell. A golf fanatic, he constructed the course so that he and friends could enjoy the game while in Palm Springs. It opened to the public in 1944, shortly before his death. Cochran Ranch, another nine-hole course, was opened in 1946. While abundant land was available for courses, the essential ingredient—water—was more restricted and costly. In the shimmering heat of the Coachella Valley, the construction and maintenance of a green and manicured golf course was an expensive proposition indeed.[40]

In the late 1940s, a group of investors concocted a plan to fund the creation of such a course at Thunderbird Ranch. These were golfer Johnny Dawson, realtors Barney Hinkle and Tony Burke, and Frank Bogert, who had served as the publicist for El Mirador and then become manager of the Palm Springs chamber of commerce, as well as the proprietor of Thunderbird Ranch. Bogert would serve as manager of the new country club. Ironically, though, he never cared for golf, seeing it as an "old man's game." The plan attracted other investors, including Bob Hope and Bing Crosby. Together they would transform Thunderbird, one of the remaining dude ranches still operating in the area. Like Smoke Tree Ranch three decades before, Thunderbird would prove emblematic of Palm Springs, and aspects of it would be emulated many times over. The key to the Thunderbird scheme was to use real-estate revenue to fund construction of the golf course. Lots were sold along the fairway and around each green. Now a golf course itself would be a place of residence, merging family life and leisure into a form of urban planning and landscape design instantly recognizable in much of postwar American suburbia. The sale of these lots then financed the construction of the course, which included drilling a well 350 feet deep and spending twenty thousand dollars on grass seeds.[41]

The parcels sold quickly, with many being purchased by Hollywood stars. Lucille Ball and Desi Arnaz, for example, secured a prime lot. The CEO of Ford selected one just down the street. Like Smoke Tree Ranch, houses were required to adhere to a certain type—"one story, low, rambling" houses. While thus similar in basic form to the houses at Smoke Tree, the newer homes at Thunderbird largely eschewed desert rustic for desert modern, with glass and metal replacing wood and stucco. The same was true of the Thunderbird Clubhouse, designed by William Cody. Most lots in Smoke Tree Ranch had been sold to wealthy outsiders who would "winter" in Palm Springs for several months and not return until the following winter. Ownership patterns differed at Thunderbird Ranch. With faster transportation available, homeowners could now make more frequent visits of shorter duration. New homes were air conditioned, making them pleasant even in the hottest summer months. As a result, the number of "vacation" homeowners who actually spent much of the year in Palm Springs grew markedly. Eventually some would make it their permanent home.[42]

Thunderbird Ranch opened in 1950 and proved a great success, quickly becoming the premier postwar housing development in Palm Springs. The *Villager* hailed it as "a select, private membership country club unique in desert attractions," and "without doubt the most astounding addition to the many attractions that draw seasonal visitors and permanent home seekers to Palm Springs." That success would draw national interest. Other suburban golf communities would follow its restrictive membership policy and innovative development model. Many people who could never dream of buying a lot in Thunderbird could instead buy an emblem of the Palm Springs resort good life: Ford named its new sports car, introduced in 1955, the Thunderbird, and even offered a model painted "Thunderbird blue," the turquoise hue used on the country club's Native American–inspired logo. With long walks down fairways uncomfortable in hotter months, Thunderbird also introduced its own motorized vehicle, the "Thunderbus." This, a prototype of the golf cart, became a ubiquitous sight at American golf courses and resorts.

Most influential of all, however, was the development scheme Thunderbird had pioneered. The future landscape of the Coachella Valley, dotted with dozens of residential golf course clubs, was born with Thunderbird. The *Villager* opined that the club "has proved conclusively that there is a deep pool from which to draw, a pool of those who combine a love of golf with a penchant for the most comfortable and exquisite phase of desert living." Other golf clubs soon followed. Tamarisk Country Club opened within a year, on a site not far from Thunderbird. Another lavish club, Eldorado, would follow in Palm Desert in 1957, with former president Dwight D. Eisenhower becoming a member and homeowner. After finishing his presidential term, Eisenhower became something of a "retiree-in-chief," illustrating by example how postwar prosperity made retirement feasible and appealing for many older Americans. By 1958, the new Indian Wells Golf and Country Club could advertise a "Formal Invitation to Informal Living" and showcase modern residences and desert vistas. The model Thunderbird had created was now a set, replicable formula.[43]

The new golf courses made Palm Springs a compelling destination for avid golfers. New golf tournaments aided this growing reputation. The most famous of these was the Bob Hope Classic, inaugurated in 1960. This charity event was sponsored on national television by Chrysler, broadcasting to the nation images of idyllic golf courses and spectacular scenery. Much as America had come to know Catalina through newsreels and radio broadcasts of big-band music, televised golf would further popularize Palm Springs. Five clubs—Bermuda Dunes, Indian Wells, Eldorado, Tamarisk, and Thunderbird—served as venues for the event. Celebrity players included Bob Hope, Bing Crosby, Frank Sinatra, Phil Harris, Danny Thomas, Jimmy Stewart, Cary Grant, Perry Como, and Jerry Lewis. In 1964 former president Eisenhower donated a massive silver trophy, which was passed to the winner each year.[44]

The selling of real-estate lots to finance golf-course construction was copied all over the nation, making the residential country club a fixture of American suburbia. These country clubs, which emulated Thunderbird's development model, also exported components of Palm Springs life to the nation by creating communities centered on outdoor life and recreation. The houses in many of these developments, whether modernist, ranch-style, or historicist, were constructed to facilitate "outdoor living." Half a century after Charles Lummis and other writers had urged Americans to open their houses to the outside to enjoy the benefits of sunlight and fresh air, Americans from Long Island to Phoenix were building "California-style" houses and living the California dream, which had been transformed into the middle-class American dream. Charles Lummis no doubt would have scoffed at golf as an effete sport, but aspects of the mode of living he had championed for the "Great Southwest" were now spreading further than he could have ever imagined.

Though Palm Springs was now emulated across the nation, it retained elements that were unique. The desert landscape and warm temperatures, certainly, could not be replicated everywhere. The omnipresence of Hollywood in the Coachella Valley was also exceptional. By 1958, Bob Hope was honorary mayor of Palm Springs, actor Phil Harris was honorary mayor of Rancho Mirage, and Bing Crosby was the honorary mayor of Palm Desert. Walt Disney, who sold his house at Smoke Tree Ranch to raise money for the construction of Disneyland, remained a local fixture. One of Disney's 1960s nature films, *The Living Desert*, featured the Coachella Valley. It grossed more than six million dollars—a remarkable feat for a nature documentary.[45]

Neither could Palm Springs' wild nightlife be easily replicated. Las Vegas is more often associated with Rat Pack exploits, but Palm Springs offered a more intimate social scene, where celebrities, musicians, the traveling rich, and even the occasional ordinary tourist could interact. As early as the 1930s, the Hollywood set already gathered at the Chi Chi Club, a sort of Coconut Grove in the desert. Replete with numerous depictions of the "Chi Chi girl"—an attractive, topless, purportedly Polynesian young woman, the club featured entertainment and drinks. Desi Arnaz and other celebrities later performed at the Chi Chi. In the 1940s the Doll House, offering Mexican cuisine and décor, served the same function. Its owners, George and Ethel Strebe, advertised the restaurant as a place where guests could mingle in a casual atmosphere: "It's not a class restaurant in the sense of classifying people. The movie stars may be sitting alongside one of the Village pioneers. Gentile, Jew, Protestant and Catholic, clerk and tycoon, Indio rancher and San Francisco socialite make up a typical Doll House crowd."[46]

Other popular establishments included the Dunes and Romanoff's on the Rocks—a 1950s modernist block set atop a boulder outcrop—and all offered venues for performers to try out routines before heading for Las Vegas and the rest of the nation. Performers as varied as Peggy Lee, Liberace, Jerry Lewis, Nat King Cole, Eartha Kitt, and members of the Rat Pack could perform in a congenial, intimate setting, and tourists in turn could have much more interaction with celebrities than in Las Vegas, let alone in the security-conscious Hollywood of later decades. Despite the racial discrimination prevalent in local real estate, these clubs also provided an important opportunity for interracial entertainment and socialization, which had once been unthinkable. They must also have provided an opportunity for gays and lesbians to encounter each other in an atmosphere that was social, without being fully public, and far more tolerant than society as a whole.

From Resort to Retirement Community

The most significant change in Palm Springs in the 1960s and 1970s was the community's growing transformation from a resort into a residential community. The two fundamental developments that made this possible were the growing availability of more affordable housing and the arrival *en masse* of retirees. Once a stronghold for the highly affluent, by the 1950s more middling types could aspire to residence in Palm Springs. One of the first manifestations of this was the Blue Skies trailer park, opened in 1952. Owned by Bing Crosby, with streets named for film stars, the Blue Skies development offered a bit of Hollywood aura at a decidedly downscale price. Though perhaps tainted by negative connotations elsewhere, in Palm Springs a trailer park was simply an extension of the resort's vacation atmosphere. Airstream trailers were an admired modern design, and Palm Springs residents Lucille Ball and Desi Arnaz starred as a honeymooning couple seeing America by trailer in 1954's *The Long, Long Trailer*. Trailer parks would multiply in the Coachella Valley, from Palm Springs all the way to new resort developments on the shores of the Salton Sea.[47]

While trailer parks obviously offered inexpensive housing, most prospective buyers hoped to find a traditional house they could afford, and some inexpensive tract housing developments were laid out to meet this demand. For every Sinatra or Bob Hope there were less wealthy Hollywood actors, as well as many other professionals, who also wanted a home in the desert, even if it was simply a replica of the suburban tract housing that characterized much of Los Angeles County. The long-term solution, however, was the condominium, which first appeared in the late 1950s. Condominiums followed a model already set by co-op apartments, where residences were owned collectively. In condominiums they were owned individually. The city government of Palm Springs proved welcoming to this type of residential housing, which offered the prospect of more permanent residents than apartment dwellers. The city was the first in the state, and one of the first resorts in the nation, to legalize condominiums as a new form of vacation housing. Condominiums were also appealing to buyers who wanted a vacation residence but could not afford the upkeep required when away or the high membership fees of country clubs or resident associations such as those charged at Thunderbird or Smoke Tree Ranch. More than one family could jointly buy a condominium, paving the way for later "timeshare" developments, which were even more affordable. Not surprisingly, the "condo-ization" of Palm Springs was quickly followed by the growing popularity of condominiums at new ski resorts such as Vail, as well as established resorts such as Aspen.[48]

By 1970, new golf clubs, such as the Mission Hills Golf and Country Club and the Marrakesh Country Club, offered all the amenities of the older clubs, but in a residential setting that was entirely composed of condominiums. Even new luxury developments, like Deep Well Ranch, also offered condominiums. They also appealed to buyers on fixed incomes—retirees. "Snowbirds" could buy a vacation home for the winter, but, as Palm Springs and the Coachella Valley grew, gaining regular air service and a fully fledged hospital, the area grew in appeal as a place of permanent residence. Palm Springs Panorama, a housing development aimed at retirees, had begun advertising in 1965. The new Palm Springs convalescent hospital—designed by Albert Frey, an architect fully versed in modernist and ranch residential styles—designed it to look like an oversized, rambling ranch home. It was depicted in advertising photos with mountain vistas beyond, offering a comforting, residential image—old age as a vacation, rather than simply a decline.[49]

This redefinition of retirement would prove highly influential. Phoenix, Arizona, had Del Webb's Sun City, but the entire Coachella Valley, with its resort amenities, growing elderly population, and warm climate, held the potential of being a gargantuan "Sun City." In fact, Del Webb's original 1960 development had been a more traditional and much more modest retirement community. Webb even touted the availability of adjacent agricultural land for retirees who wished to raise their own crops or livestock. He had, however, severely misgauged what sort of lives buyers were now looking for on the retirement frontier. When lackluster sales threatened the project, Sun City was reconceived as a "resort city"—one that drew heavily from the model already emerging in Palm Springs, as well as the winter resorts around Phoenix.[50]

Despite this residential influx, tourism continued, and by the later 1960s Palm Springs began actively pursuing the growing convention market. Conventioneers were certainly an appealing demographic and could bring large numbers of tourists to Palm Springs throughout the year. Yet conventions became a big business in the 1970s, and Palm Springs began to lose convention bookings to more sizeable cities, including San Diego, which remade its downtown to accommodate ever-larger conventions. In Phoenix, Del Webb built the TowneHouse Hotel, which boasted the largest convention facility in Arizona. Webb's promotional materials asked prospective guests and convention organizers, "Where would you like to hold your next convention—in a conventional hotel or a hotel created specifically for conventions?" The largest conventions were increasingly drawn less by recreational amenities and more by easy and affordable airline access, the availability of convention meeting facilities, and huge hotels. Atlanta, for example, the newly ascendant capital of the Sunbelt South—but hardly a traditional tourist destination—pursued the convention market with great success in the 1960s and 1970s.[51]

---------- ✳ ----------

Though Palm Springs still drew tourists, by the 1970s it had lost some of its former luster. This did not indicate, however, that the resort town had languished. There were 5,146 swimming pools in the city by 1975, and that year taxable sales in the city totaled almost $25 million. Yet in the 1950s and 1960s, Palm Springs had been a national trendsetter, an exciting place to see and be seen. Conventioneers and retirees might fill local coffers, but they were not necessarily exciting. A Palm Springs Convention and Visitors Bureau report for 1975, entitled *Palm Springs: The Good Life City Holds its Own in a World Full of Uncertainty*, hardly indicated eager anticipation of an exciting future. More ominously, the Convention and Visitors Bureau found that visitors were complaining that Palm Springs had too many people, too much commercialism, and too much pollution. Some also found the resort boring, with too little to do, especially at night. The Hollywood nightlife that had once been a trademark largely decamped for Las Vegas, where gambling still drew those looking for risk taking, and ever-larger hotels began to draw conventioneers as well. If anything, the Coachella Valley became a destination for people recovering from recreational excess, as the Betty Ford Clinic began admitting rich addicts in the 1970s. Palm Springs tried to offer new amenities to enhance its reputation. An ambitious early example of this was the San Jacinto Tram, which began service in 1962. The tram had been championed for decades by Earl Coffman, who believed it would be a major attraction. The vertiginous ride up the sheer rock face of Mount San Jacinto, which carried passengers from desert heat to snow-covered fir trees on the world's longest aerial cable tram, was spectacular indeed. The tram, however, failed to meet usage projections. It could not serve as the sole reason to visit Palm Springs. By the 1970s, the growing perception that Palm Springs was moribund was evidenced by the derisive quip that the local average temperature, like the average age, was a "steady 88."[52]

Yet if Palm Springs was derided as stogy and behind the times, it also suffered from its own success. While La Quinta, located further southeast in the Coachella Valley near Indio, had offered an exclusive retreat for the rich since the founding of the La Quinta Inn in 1926, newer resort communities had sprung up in the desert. Cathedral City, Rancho Mirage, Palm Desert, and Indian Wells, each laid along the flanks of the San Jacinto Mountains, filled what had been open space separating Palm Springs and La Quinta. Each of these resorts attempted to replicate the atmosphere and amenities of Palm Springs. Unfortunately for Palm Springs, they succeeded only too well. As early as 1947, Palm Desert was already being advertised as "America's newest and finest desert resort community." The new community, carved from a ranch owned by actor Edgar Bergen, included the Shadow Mountain Club, which offered amenities similar to the Palm Springs Tennis Club, and a large lake created to serve as a swimming pool. This ranch had been remade in a style more lavish and green than the intentionally rustic, still desert-like Smoke Tree Ranch. Developers were quickly demonstrating that the elements of Palm Springs' postwar popularity could be replicated elsewhere. By 1949, Desert Hot Springs, located ten miles north of Palm Springs, already had two thousand residents. Gradually, the new resort communities only added to the sentiment that Palm Springs was old and tired, filled with once trendy modern architecture, which had lost favor there and elsewhere to the once more–revived Spanish revival.[53]

The growth of new resort communities also brought urban sprawl to the desert. This cluttered the vistas that had once drawn tourists, and the sheer number of swimming pools, irrigated lawns, and golf courses resulted in increased humidity and lessened visibility. Growing smog drifting eastward from Los Angeles and its teeming suburbs further worsened air quality. In some fundamental respects, Palm Springs had changed from a resort isolated from Los Angeles, an oasis removed from urbanism, to simply a far-flung suburb of the megalopolis. Catalina, located twenty-six miles off the coast, retained its isolation. Even Disneyland, surrounded by an earthen berm, attempted to hide the encroaching suburban sprawl that would lead Walt Disney to develop a new park outside Orlando.

By the end of the 1970s, it seemed that Palm Springs had reached the terminus of its resort journey. It had progressed from a health refuge to an exclusive resort for the elite, to a democratized resort for the middle class, and finally, to a retiree suburb. Like Catalina and Los Angeles, its political and economic elites almost always fought to ensure its whiteness and affluence, the hallmarks and prerequisites for leisure in Southern California. Even so, its visitors and residents proved more varied, and, over time, its resorts grew more tolerant and open. It was certainly far more accessible to middle-class tourists in the great age of affluence that followed World War II. Even the Agua Calientes, who faced such a hostile city government in the 1950s and 1960s, looked to the future with some tribal tourist infrastructure and profits in place, and the prospect of more to come.

Palm Springs had enjoyed a less linear trajectory than that of Catalina Island, which, despite all the efforts of William and Philip Wrigley, remained in fundamental respects a turn-of-the-century beach resort. Its primary attractions—a charming seaside village, beaches, glass-bottomed boats, sailing, fishing, hiking, and hunting—appeared early in the resort's history, and could not be augmented by new attractions. As a result, it grew less appealing and less relevant to tourists after World War II. What it offered instead was an escape to the pastoral past. Catalina would still draw tourists, but it drew people looking for a relaxing escape from the busting mainland. Its preservation as a conservation trust ensured its survival as a remnant of the past.

In contrast, Palm Springs in its postwar heyday seemed to offer tourists the future. With sunbathing, outdoor sports, scant clothing, avant-garde architecture, the latest technology, and endless opportunities for dining, socializing, and shopping, Palm Springs had indeed made the desert modern. What had begun as a retreat for the ill or those looking for solitary desert contemplation had become instead a desert paradise of consumption and leisure for middle-class white America. Yet as these attractions were successfully replicated by newer Coachella Valley resorts, Las Vegas, and other destinations, Palm Springs declined. More crucially, as the following chapter documents, aspects of Palm Springs life and leisure were made available to people across the nation. Backyard swimming pools, patios, and barbecues, houses that opened to the outside and made the backyard function as a social space for family and friends, as well as golf courses and more revealing attire—all these things had been popularized by Palm Springs, and were indelibly associated with Southern California. Thus, in the resort's very success, and its significance in the history of American culture, leisure, and urbanism, lay the seeds of its decline. Palm Springs had helped make America more like the resorts of Southern California, but Americans—and Southern Californians—were now less inclined to visit the resort. That story—of how so much of postwar suburbia came to resemble Palm Springs and Southern California—is the subject of the following chapter. As for Palm Springs itself, the future would bring unexpected changes there as well.

Chapter Seven

FROM RESORTS TO THE RANCH HOUSE

Southern California's Culture of Leisure and the Making of the Suburban Sunbelt

W HILE THE rise of Los Angeles, its resorts, its distinctive urbanism, and its florid culture of leisure drew national attention in the late nineteenth and early twentieth centuries, its development remained a largely regional phenomenon until after World War II. There were, however, portents of its coming national significance. These appeared in the most unexpected of places—the 1939 New York City World's Fair, and also in the mind of one of the nation's most famous architects, Frank Lloyd Wright. Together they offered two visions of the suburban nation soon to be born— one based on the technology of the future, and the other on the cultural ideals of the past.

Visitors to the 1939 World's Fair were treated to sweeping visions of an America to come. The central exhibit, located in the eighteen-story "Perisphere" at the heart of the fair, was an aerial overview of a city of the future. This city, a "perfectly integrated garden city of tomorrow" triumphantly named "Democracity," did not much resemble the city hosting the fair. While viewing this model for a city of one million residents, tourists were informed that "people do not live in the city proper." Instead, residents were "housed in a rim of garden apartments, in suburban developments, in satellite towns, or in the country." Beyond these zones of habitation were green belts and agricultural areas.[1]

After viewing the city of tomorrow, visitors could also see the transportation system of tomorrow, courtesy of General Motors. In the exhibit "Highways and Horizons," tourists were treated to another aerial view, this time of a national superhighway system: "The transportation arteries are seen as they pass by large cities—at superhighway intersections—in open and in mountainous country—at night—and in numerous other manifestations of the wonders of future vehicle transportation facilities." In this case, this particular prediction of the future really would come true in the form of the Interstate Highway System, inaugurated by President Dwight D. Eisenhower.[2]

Democracity, however, proved less accurate. It did correctly foresee a suburban future, but the future it envisioned was an urban planner's fantasy, carefully controlled and constructed, with a development pattern that owed much to the garden cities envisioned in Great Britain in the late nineteenth century. The actual future course of suburbia would follow a more distinctly American pattern, one less subject to the aims of environmental or urban planners, and more attuned to U.S.-style autonomy and free-range capitalism.

This new pattern was discernible in a model landscape constructed by Frank Lloyd Wright called Broadacre City. Wright first unveiled this model in New York in 1935 and elaborated on it further in his 1945 book, *When Democracy Builds*. He presented a radical plan to reshape relations between city and country, and to mediate between past and future. In it, there was no city, and no center—just a dispersed landscape of homes and agricultural land. It was a countryside stretched to continental proportions.

In this model, the most important structure was the single-family home, and each was allotted at least one acre of land. The implication was that virtually everyone in this imagined landscape was an agriculturalist, and that all of them must have a car. There was little evidence of communitarian structures, such as schools or government buildings. This was radical individualism in the form of urban planning.

As radical as this model seemed, Broadacre City appears far less outlandish from the perspective of the early twenty-first century. To see it in person, just catch a plane to Phoenix, and watch the planned communities, cotton fields, and sprawling suburban metropolis unfold beneath you. To be sure, Wright underestimated how much economics and the calculations of developers would dictate the development of postwar suburbia, and how much the personal automobile would dominate urban planning. For example, the "roadside markets" he designed and idealized as places for local farmers to sell produce look like nothing so much as fairly standard L.A. mini-malls. To note such deficiencies, however, does not in any way detract from the degree to which Wright correctly foresaw a decentralizing urge in postwar culture and suburban growth, one that aimed to reconnect ordinary families with nature, the outdoors, and an idealized agrarian past. Indeed, he tied this urge to one of the oldest ideas in American history—the frontier—and his model was proof of how powerful its attraction remained.

Broadacre City, according to Wright, was where Americans—or at least one kind of Americans—would settle on a "New Frontier," with the individual family home its essential unit: "In this Free City coming of age the individual home of the individual family-group will be far more directly related to land-scape, transport, distribution of goods, publicity and all cultural opportunity than at present. But it is the Home that will enjoy a freedom and freshness of life from within that no civilization has ever attained or could ever attain until now." Wright asserted that "this greater free city for the Individual" would be the "City of Democracy," where Usonians—Wright's invented term for U.S. citizens—would be permanently marked with the vitality of the frontier: "Usonians! Your pioneer days are not yet over! Perhaps Pioneer days are never, should never, be over.... The White man must pioneer again along the New Frontier!" Though his call was racially problematic, Wright correctly foresaw the powerful cultural forces that, once unleashed, would radically alter the American landscape.[3]

From Southern California to the Sunbelt

World War II was a watershed moment for Palm Springs as it evolved from a small, elite retreat to a destination for modern mass tourism. It continued to develop in the postwar era, becoming both a residential model and a place for residence and retirement. While the resort helped shape the appearance and culture of postwar suburbia, it and all of Southern California were also affected by larger political, economic, and demographic forces that facilitated the emergence of a new, distinctive American region, the Sunbelt. One way to trace the development of this region is simply to document its meteoric growth. Arizona contained less than half a million residents in 1940, but by 2005 metropolitan Phoenix alone contained 3.8 million. By the first decade of the twenty-first century, Phoenix was poised to supplant Philadelphia as the fifth largest city in the nation, and Detroit, the industrial metropolis of the Midwest, was in danger of falling off the list of the nation's ten largest cities and being replaced with San Jose, the hub of Silicon Valley. Other cities in the southern tier of U.S. states also experienced rapid growth in the six decades following World War II. Houston and Dallas grew from cities of less than 400,000 in 1940 to metropolitan areas of more than 5,000,000 in Houston and nearly 6,000,000 in Dallas. Atlanta grew from a city of 300,000 to a metro-politan area of 5,000,000. Miami grew from a city of 172,000 to a metropolitan area of 5,400,000. Southern California continued to grow as well. By 2005 the region from Santa Barbara south to San Diego contained more than twenty million residents.[4]

Yet population figures, however impressive, do not in themselves explain why the Sunbelt grew so dramatically. At the most basic level, the growth that had begun in Los Angeles in the 1880s and the growth that occurred in cities across the Sunbelt after 1945 bore some similarity. In both cases, new arrivals were drawn by jobs, inexpensive land and housing, or the opportunity to begin life anew. Unlike those earlier migrants, however, the later, larger wave enjoyed more benefits than merely inexpensive rail transportation. Many would have their own transportation, in the form of automobiles. Some were also already acquainted with the region, since so many military personnel had trained or been stationed in the Southwest during World War II.[5]

More importantly, the federal government, with far more resources than any local chamber of commerce or individual booster, actively aided the creation of a new mass suburbia across the United States, particularly in the Sunbelt. This began during the war, with the G.I. Bill of 1944. The G.I. Bill offered educational grants, low-interest mortgages, and business loans for returning servicemen. By 1947 the Veteran's Administration was paying the tuition of nearly fifty percent of all male college students. By 1960, more than five million homes had been financed through the Veteran's Administration. Yet this federal housing program would be dwarfed by another assistance initiative, the Federal Housing Administration (FHA) loan system. FHA loans began during the New Deal, but were expanded after the war. With FHA loans, the federal government made it far easier to buy a house—applicants could put less than ten percent down, and would have thirty years to pay off the mortgage. This became the standard terms for most private home loans as well. Previously, prospective home buyers had to have cash on hand to buy houses outright, or at least cover a much larger down payment. Unsurprisingly, this meant that a much smaller proportion of Americans were homeowners, and a much larger number of those who were built their houses themselves. This had been true in the working-class suburbs of Los Angeles, such as South Gate. Most residents built houses from scratch or used kits from Sears and other builders who could ship the house materials from lumberyards to the nearest train station.[6]

The federal government, both through direct military employment and indirect employment through massive defense contracts, also created large numbers of jobs in many cities in the Sunbelt. In Los Angeles, for example, World War II–employment and production soon shifted to fighting the cold war with the Soviet Union. By the 1960s, aerospace manufacturers employed 500,000 workers, more than 40 percent of Los Angeles County's total industrial workforce.[7]

In addition to employment and new forms of housing assistance, the government also created the new Interstate Highway System. The Federal

Highway Act of 1956, signed by President Eisenhower, inaugurated the largest single public-works program in American history. The government expended $76 billion to build forty-one thousand miles of interstate to create the original system, later expanded further. The interstate system was designed for defense purposes, but it had a vast impact on American society. It favored cars and trucks over trains for freight and long-distance passenger transport, and the passenger car over mass transit. It made Americans even more mobile and facilitated suburban growth. Between home loans and freeways, the federal government was a primary architect of a new kind of urbanism. The government obviously aided suburbanization, but the development that followed was on such a vast scale, and so unlike traditional patterns of suburbanization, that some historians argue that it was not really suburbia at all—instead, it was a radically new form of urbanism, decentered, sprawling, and mixing places of residence and work. In this sense, however, it had one clear historical precedent and model—the distinctive urban form of greater Los Angeles.[8]

In the later 1940s, however, this new urban/suburban landscape did not yet entirely resemble the resort architecture or culture of a place such as Palm Springs, or affluent suburbs of L.A. At Levittown on Long Island, Park Forest outside Chicago, or Lakewood, the largest new suburban development in the nation in this era, located south of Los Angeles and adjacent to a Douglas Aircraft factory, the houses were tiny in comparison to later suburban standards. Though developers sometimes said that these homes had been designed in "Small California House" style, they mostly employed traditional architectural styles, such as colonial revival or Cape Cod, and bore little resemblance to the sprawling ranch-style homes in Palm Springs. They did differ from the bungalows of a generation or two before in one key respect: bungalows were usually placed in small, narrow lots, perpendicular to the street. These houses were instead oriented parallel to the street, presenting a longer horizontal façade to public view. Larger models might feature an attached garage at one end, and lots were generally larger than older bungalow lots.[9]

Still, furnishings were modest, amenities such as fireplaces or large patios were rare, and golf courses, country clubs, and backyard swimming pools were nonexistent. Developers, worried above all about affordability, cut every possible corner. Houses were placed closer to streets to save on piping, and planting strips were eliminated so that curbs and sidewalks could be constructed as single sections of concrete. At Lakewood, instead of creating independent fire and police departments, the newly incorporated community of eighty thousand saved costs by contracting with Los Angeles County to provide services, and this "Lakewood System" became a popular regional and national model for developers.[10]

By the time another decade had passed, however, everything would change. The houses became much larger. Backyard pools and resort-style residential golf courses dotted the suburban landscape. And ranch houses, in innumerable variations, were ubiquitous. Buyers could purchase a "California-style" house in the suburbs of New York, Chicago, New Orleans, or any other sizeable city. How and why had this happened?

To understand this process—how the growth of postwar suburbs spurred the development of the Sunbelt, and how California-inspired architecture and urbanism became a national template for development, one must look at this emerging region in closer detail. It might seem that a likely candidate for a case study of this process would be Las Vegas. Yet Las Vegas is not an entirely satisfactory example. Its early growth as a gambling destination was driven largely by Southern Californians, rendering it in many ways a recreational suburb of Los Angeles. Its emergence as a major population center came later than most other growing Sunbelt cities, and occurred in part because rising housing costs in California forced an exodus out of the state in the 1990s.

Another example might be Miami or one of the other large cities in Florida. South Florida, like Southern California, clearly profited by selling leisure, and was undoubtedly influenced by earlier developments in Southern California, where Florida was often perceived as a rival recreational and residential destination. Its resorts and especially its retirement communities drew a significant new population to the state after World War II. The single most famous tourist landmark in Florida, Disney World is an import on a grandiose scale from Southern California. Yet Florida too is an imperfect example—its initial resort and residential development began in the 1920s, driven by wealthy wintering Northerners. This first boom was waylaid by disastrous hurricanes in 1926 and 1928, and then by the Depression. Large urban growth came later, particularly after the civil-rights era, and cities such as Miami in many respects replicated the problematic race relations of the South, albeit made more diverse by the arrival of Cubans and residents from other Caribbean nations. Further, development in Florida, unlike in earlier Southern California, often took place in a vacuum—vast tracts of open wetland converted into suburbia through backroom deals between corporations and state politicians. In most northeastern and Midwestern states, zoning is controlled by townships. In most southern and western states, zoning is controlled at the county level. In Florida it is controlled instead at the state level. Development in Florida in the postwar era, as in the 1920s, was often not a local process, nor a direct result of local urban boosterism.[11]

To find an urban encapsulation of Sunbelt emergence, one must locate a place in which the push for development was primarily local, and in which tourism played an important role. It also must have begun its ascent immediately during and after the war, in that short span in which postwar suburbia did not in fact closely resemble Southern California resort culture. This eliminates cities in the Southeast, where true Sunbelt growth could not begin in earnest until after the social and political pangs of integration and the civil-rights movement. One excellent candidate is the largest city in the interior Southwest—Phoenix. Like Dallas, Houston, Atlanta, or Orlando, it is a monument to the largest migration in American history—one that had begun in the late nineteenth century in Southern California, and by the 1950s, 1960s, and 1970s had spread eastward to encompass a vast new region stretching across the southern tier of U.S. states.

The development of Phoenix shares many parallels with the rise of both Los Angeles and Southern California resorts. Its boosters were no less avid, and it relied heavily on resorts and tourists in its early development. Like Los Angeles, it would also lure migrants with defense-industry jobs following World War II. Federal funds like these were crucial—federal dams, highways, and home loans gave Phoenix developers and promoters access to funds that turn of the century L.A. boosters could scarcely have imagined—it was Southern California's development model on financial steroids. It would replicate and propagate many aspects of Southern California's earlier development and urbanism, and serve as a crucible for the politics, culture, and architecture of the Sunbelt, which made many aspects of Southern California's urbanism and culture a national phenomenon. The city would also give rise to a new political movement, first championed at a national level by senator and presidential candidate Barry Goldwater. His personal career, and the movement he helped create, were deeply rooted in the history of the U.S.-Mexico borderlands, the Southwest, and Anglo promotion of the region. Phoenix would also serve as a central point of popularization for the ubiquitous architectural form of postwar suburbia—the ranch house. To understand the popularity of the ranch house and Sunbelt suburbia, one must explore the careers of two very different architects—Frank Lloyd Wright and Cliff May. Examining the seemingly disparate but in fact interconnected ascents of Phoenix, Goldwater, and the ranch house illuminates the origins of the Sunbelt and postwar suburbia, and their deep connection to Southern California's frontier of leisure.

Phoenix and the Valley of the Sun

In the winter of 1933, America's most infamous architect came to the desert. Like so many Anglos before him, Frank Lloyd Wright came to the Southwest hoping for renewal, reinvention, and a new life. His career had been in decline for decades, and his public reputation had been severely damaged when he, a married man, fled the country in 1909 with Mamah Borthwick Cheney, a client's wife. He was not new to the Southwest—Wright had designed houses in Los Angeles in the 1920s, and had contributed to the design of the Biltmore Resort near Phoenix. Wright had been less than impressed with the rich eccentrics, batty celebrities, and transplanted Midwesterners of booming 1920s Los Angeles, commenting famously that it seemed to him that at some point the continent had been tilted on its side, and all the loose pieces had rolled to Southern California.

Sparsely populated southern Arizona, however, entranced him. Charles and Warren McArthur and their brother, Albert, who had been one of Wright's students, envisioned a luxurious resort for rich easterners in the desert, something far grander than the Desert Inn or Oasis Hotel in Palm Springs. Wright shared their ambitions, claiming that "there could be nothing more inspiring to an architect on this earth than that spot of pure desert in Arizona." The building, Wright wrote, was "meant to embody all worthwhile about natural architecture," and to "grow up out of the desert by way of desert materials," taking the saguaro cactus as its unifying motif.[12] Of course, the actual construction of the hotel fell short of such ideals, devolving into the usual squabbling over money and time. Albert McArthur was the primary architect of the final product, the Arizona Biltmore, even though the resort continues to tout its connection to Wright. William Wrigley, initially just one of several investors, took over the property entirely as costs rose, buying out the resort's other owners. Despite its early troubles, the resort went on to great success, and Wrigley's son Philip later built a home adjacent to the resort, dividing his time between Phoenix and Catalina. It also was the only major resort in Phoenix to accept Jewish guests, as the El Mirador in Palm Springs had first done in the 1920s. In Phoenix, this exclusion lasted far longer, through the 1950s and beyond at some resorts, most notably the Camelback Inn.[13]

For his part, Wright's prophesying in the desert did contain one element of truth. During his stay in Phoenix, Wright foresaw that Americans would be drawn to the desert Southwest. He noted that Victor Hugo wrote that "the desert is where God is and Man is not." Americans, however, were deciding to make God's landscape their own. Wright believed that the Arizona desert would "make the playground for these United States someday."[14]

That was not the case in 1933, when Wright selected a high mesa twenty-six miles from Phoenix, a tract overlooking a vast panorama of desert. He claimed that the view was "a look over the rim of the world." Here, away from his Wisconsin home, Wright and his apprentices reenacted one of the oldest and most potent dreams in Euro-American history. Like the Puritans in Massachusetts, the Mormons in Nauvoo, and even Walt Disney in Anaheim, Wright believed that given isolation and enough virgin land, he could create the world anew. He would find that goal no less elusive than any of the others who pursued it.

FIGURE 7.1 Taliesin West. This home, constructed by Frank Lloyd Wright and his apprentices, would increasingly serve as his primary residence, the location of his "Fellowship" for architectural training, and also served as the place in which he resurrected his career. Photograph by the author.

It might seem difficult to entertain any similarities between Frank Lloyd Wright and Charles Fletcher Lummis, yet they had more in common than diminutive stature and oversized egos. Both men arrived in the region in flight from eastern woes. Both also built houses as statements of individuality, which at the same time aimed to blend architecture with local culture and landscape. Even though they were born within a decade of each other—Wright in 1867, and Lummis in 1859—their careers followed very different chronological trajectories. When Lummis began his "tramp" to Los Angeles in 1885, he was twenty-five and at the forefront of a movement just beginning. By the time Wright arrived in Arizona to construct a house as a winter residence and setting for his fellowship of apprentices, he was already older than Lummis had been at his death. His prairie-school houses lay decades in the past, and his architecture had been surpassed by International-style modernism. Fallingwater, the house he built for the Kaufmann family that would restore his international fame, was as yet unbuilt. Further, times had changed. Southern California was already thickly populated. The Arizona desert, as of yet, was not. He would live to see that change dramatically by the end of his long life in 1959.

Like countless settlers before him, Wright purchased the plot at the government land office and began to plan his new winter home. A well drilled nearly five hundred feet deep brought up hot but potable water. Aided by about thirty apprentices and his third wife Olgivanna, Wright oversaw construction of his new compound. Built of desert boulders and redwood, with canvas roofs to maximize cooling, Taliesin West became a local landmark, and was one of Wright's most famous architectural triumphs. Wright loathed historicist or revivalist architecture, yet his compound came complete with a movie theater disguised as a kiva, and he described his home as a place that "belonged to the desert as if it had stood there for centuries." Initially, the landscaping surrounding the house included local cacti, but repeated encounters with cactus needles led Wright to re-landscape using bougainvillea and other flowering plants. The home and grounds still echoed the surrounding desert landscape, but the reflecting pools and patches of lawn portended the direction of much of the future development in the area.[15]

Resorts such as the Biltmore might incorporate cacti as themes in decoration, but cacti possessed limited appeal as actual landscaping plants. Lush lawns, flowers, fountains, reflecting pools, and, of course, swimming pools were far more likely to grace resort grounds, just as they did in many resorts in Palm Springs. In fact, this denial of desert conditions played an important role in the rivalry between Phoenix and neighboring Tucson. Though Tucson was the older and larger community at the beginning of the twentieth century, Phoenix possessed a larger water supply and a predominantly Anglo population that more easily gained favor with the federal government. The Newlands Reclamation Act of 1902, which authorized the use of federal funds for irrigation projects, provided a crucial early example of this. The Roosevelt Dam on the Salt River, completed in 1911, was only the first of many federal dam and irrigation projects that would permit the growth of Phoenix.

The community and its boosters also possessed an irrepressible flair for showboating. The road constructed to facilitate the building of the dam was promptly rechristened the Apache Trail and promoted as a diverting desert drive for auto tourists. A photographic booklet created to promote the route showcased mountain and canyon vistas, ancient cliff dwellings, and desert flora—"a garden of strange growth." The booklet also unintentionally illustrated the social costs of dam construction. Apaches, who had been displaced from fertile river bottomlands now submerged, instead camped on the shores of Roosevelt Lake. One caption of a photograph of an Apache seated in front of his shelter blithely proclaimed that "where Geronimo's wild raiders once rode, this warrior now takes the sun." Once greatly feared, Apaches were now presented as just one more group of cheerful Arizona recreationalists. The Indian in the photograph, however, wrapped in a blanket and warily eying the photographer, appears tired and dejected. Like the Anglo resort and real-estate developers of Southern California, Phoenix boosters blithely used Native Americans and Mexicans when it suited them, but were just as likely to push them out of the way if they stood in the way of "progress," or, more simply, material gain. With water, federal aid, and relentless promotion, Phoenix surpassed Tucson in population by 1920.[16]

Local tourism promoters chose distinctive marketing strategies. Tucson sold itself as a desert city, while Phoenix showcased the lush gardens and lawns of its resorts. Like Los Angeles, Phoenix used water to create the fiction of Midwestern greenery, and even tropical verdure, in an arid environment. These different approaches reflected divergent civic cultures. Tucson embraced conservation and an awareness of scarcity early on. Phoenix instead emphasized unlimited growth and the assumption that technology and federal money would always provide water. While in hindsight Tucson's approach was obviously more environmentally sustainable, it was not so obvious in the heady days of federal reclamation and wonders such as Boulder (later Hoover) Dam. American will and technological know-how, it seemed, could conquer the desert.

The Phoenix-Arizona club, created in 1923, sold the city in national magazines such as *Better Homes and Gardens* as "Delightful Phoenix, the Garden Spot of the Southwest." While showcasing dude ranches and resorts and the potential of Phoenix as a winter playground, local boosterism enlisted homeowners as well. In an effort to emulate the verdant, cultivated greenery of Pasadena, still a winter tourist destination, Phoenix homeowners were urged to "do away with the desert" by planting grass, roses, and other ornamental landscaping.[17]

While Tucson promoted its Spanish and Mexican past, and its hotels often adopted Spanish-revival architecture, those in Phoenix more often adopted art deco or other "modern" styles. This was true of the Arizona Biltmore Hotel, which, like Lloyd Wright's Oasis Hotel in Palm Springs, utilized modern architecture to facilitate luxurious desert leisure. The Biltmore, like late nineteenth-century resort hotels in Southern California such as the Hotel Raymond in Pasadena and the Hotel Del Coronado in San Diego, served as a nucleus for surrounding tourist, residential, and commercial development. Some of this development was historicist, such as "Old Town" Scottsdale, which adopted an "Old West" theme to attract tourists, but most of it was contemporary, proof that Phoenix was a booming modern metropolis, not a quaint desert retreat.[18]

At the state level, the most effective tool for regional promotion was *Arizona Highways*, begun in 1921 as a newsletter for the Arizona Highway Department, highlighting road construction in the state. By 1945 it had developed into a regional promotional magazine, not unlike *Land of Sunshine, Sunset,* or

FIGURE 7.2 As in Palm Springs, the desert landscape surrounding Phoenix was presented as exotic but nonthreatening, and as a "garden," rather than as the arid wasteland earlier generations of Americans had perceived much of the Southwest to be. Russell Todd, "Apache Trail: The Wonder Trip through Oldest America." Southern Pacific Rail Road. Special Collections, Hayden Library, Arizona State University.

Westways, the magazine of the Automobile Club of Southern California. It contained articles extolling the recreational possibilities of the state's spectacular natural scenery, complimented by photographs taken by a range of photographers, from Ansel Adams to amateur photographers including Barry Goldwater. The magazine, like the urban boosterism of Phoenix, would play a key role in drawing new residents after World War II.[19]

The Salt River Valley, rebranded as the "Valley of the Sun," would grow from a group of winter resorts to a booming regional metropolis. It also continued its tradition of seizing on federal largess whenever possible. In the early twentieth century, this had facilitated the development of water and irrigation. By the 1930s, 1940s, and 1950s, federal money would instead be used to construct houses. When President Franklin Roosevelt unveiled the original National Housing Act in 1934, which would later be greatly expanded as the FHA loan program, many bankers and builders reacted with caution or hostility. Here, it seemed, was yet another example of creeping economic federalism.

In Phoenix, however, the reception was warmer. Del Webb, the owner of a large construction company and a housing developer who would later create

FIGURE 7.3 Promoters of Phoenix used both Native Americans and the new
lake created by Roosevelt Dam as attractions for tourists, even when the Apache
pictured here seemed to be in anything but a celebratory mood. Russell Todd,
"Apache Trail: The Wonder Trip through Oldest America." Southern Pacific Rail
Road. Special Collections, Hayden Library, Arizona State University.

Sun City, and Carl Bimson, the president of Valley National Bank, both foresaw the potential of these federal loans to aid homebuyers, banks and builders,
and metropolitan Phoenix. Webb's firm eagerly and indiscriminately snagged
government contracts, particularly during World War II. One of the largest was
a contract to construct the Poston internment camp for Japanese Americans,

which at full capacity was the third largest "city" in Arizona. For Webb, the FHA program was yet another federal windfall. Bimson, for his part, even traveled the country speaking before other banking and business groups in support of the New Deal program. Bimson bragged that the "Valley National Bank has consistently pioneered in the FHA program which has meant so much to the state as a whole in stimulated business and increased employment." This was no idle boast. Valley National Bank, which was only a small regional bank in the 1930s, ranked fifth in the nation out of more than eight thousand banks that made these new housing loans. Later, when the G.I. Bill and VA loans facilitated home ownership for veterans, Valley National Bank created a special "Veteran's Division" to help guide former servicemen into homeownership. By the 1960s, Valley National Bank was the largest bank in the intermountain West. The consequences of all this for the bank, for developers such as Webb, and for the accelerating growth of Phoenix were obvious.[20]

Though Wright would maintain his Wisconsin house, also called Taliesin, Arizona became a semi-permanent home for him, and he would die there in 1959. Two years before that he had returned to Chicago, the city where he had first risen to prominence, along with writer Carl Sandburg, another famous son. Both had been invited back to Chicago by U.S. Steel and toured construction sites that demonstrated the ongoing vitality of the "world's most dynamic city." In public both men were duly impressed by these projects and the economic energy of the city. Wright once again bragged of his ambition to build a mile-high skyscraper in Chicago. Sandburg claimed that he felt a resurgence in civic spirit that reminded him of the heady days of the Columbian Exposition of 1893. Yet a telling moment occurred later, during a television interview on Chicago's educational channel. As the moderator signed off after a boosterist discussion about the city's future, Wright, thinking that the microphones had been switched off, turned to Sandburg and said, "We'd better get out of here, Carl, before somebody starts telling the truth."[21]

Wright's remark highlighted a growing if still largely unspoken unease in Chicago, decades before the Midwest, the industrial heartland of America, was pejoratively nicknamed the rustbelt. Young people, particularly soldiers returning from World War II, were moving south and west, to new jobs, often in defense industries, and to new housing developments that were transforming former agricultural landscapes around Los Angeles, Phoenix, Dallas, and other cities. The census of 1960 determined that Los Angeles had supplanted Chicago as the nation's second-largest city. The Sunbelt migration was well underway. The iconoclastic Wright, who returned to Arizona, and Sandburg, who had moved to North Carolina, were early examples of this migration, and were representative of the increasing numbers of older Americans who would redefine retirement and remake Florida and other balmy regions of the United States.

Making the Regional National: Cliff May and the California Ranch House

Another architect, Cliff May, far less renowned than Wright but arguably no less influential, would be responsible for the iconic style of architecture so many Sunbelt residents chose for their homes—the ranch house. As early as 1906, author Herbert Croly noticed houses in suburban Los Angeles with "long low lines, and with the roof overhanging and dominating the upright members." These houses, according to Croly, "remind one of the lines and proportions of the ranch houses [of early California]." The term "ranch house," however, was first formally applied in the 1920s to a vernacular style found across the region, functional in plan and rustic in both use of materials and also often in setting—rural rather than urban. Henry H. Saylor, the editor of *American Architect*, named this style in 1925, noting that it had been largely obscured by the massive proliferation of bungalows, Spanish revival, and other historicist styles in California, many of which he dismissed as "mere affectations." He was more laudatory of this new "ranch" style: "It never put forth any great claims of merit, it never really entered the lists to establish itself as the vogue. Apparently it just grew, naturally, inevitably, a logical result of meeting definite needs in the most direct, workmanlike manner possible with the materials at hand."[22]

Any formal lineages for this architectural style remain unclear. The one-story, rambling horizontality of most ranch houses certainly owed something to Wright's earlier prairie-school houses. The sliding glass doors, patios, and large windows opened these houses to the outside, and made yards part of the social and living space of the house. In this regard, they echoed aspects of turn-of-the-century bungalows, designed to take advantage of California's temperate climate. The flowing, open interiors and expanses of glass also reflected aspects of modernist design. The "rustic" exterior and interior elements, particularly those with a western theme, drew upon the homes built at Smoke Tree Ranch and other resorts, and those in turn perhaps echoed the earlier "Adirondack" camp and vacation houses built in upstate New York and elsewhere in the Northeast and Midwest. Yet May, the most prolific architect to design in ranch style, did not acknowledge any of these architectural forerunners. For him, the ranch home was an indigenous product of the environment and history of California.[23]

May in fact began his career not as an architect, but rather by designing "Monterey" furniture, derived from Craftsman and mission revival designs, which was highly popular during the 1920s. When he began building houses in San Diego in 1932, he was entirely self-taught: "At the time, I didn't know what I was doing, I was just building houses, the kind of houses I thought they should be." He sold the first house he built, furnished with furniture he had created, for $9,500. He built a second house in 1933, and it appeared in *Architectural Digest*.[24]

Working as both architect and contractor, May garnered further success rapidly, and by the mid-1930s had built more than fifty modest homes in the city and elsewhere in Southern California. These early homes fell into two basic varieties. One May termed a "Mexican hacienda," and these utilized tile roofs, rough-hewn timbering, and coarse plaster that echoed traditional adobe homes. The other, which May called an "early California rancheria," featured wood shingle roofs and wooden exteriors, mirroring agricultural homes and buildings constructed in California in both the Mexican and U.S. eras.[25]

When asked to define the ranch house, his only criteria were that it be one story, and "not a box" but "stretched out somewhat." According to May, "If it lives like a ranch house, it is a ranch house." The mode of living the ranch house permitted was all-important: "The ranch house was this informal way of living, the old California way." The ranch house was also "an informal way of living out of doors." Patios and verandas were essential, as was privacy—verandas opened onto backyards and courtyards, not front yards exposed to the street.[26]

Over the course of his career, May personally designed or built more than a thousand homes in the United States, Mexico, Europe, and Australia, and his designs for low-cost ranch houses were used by licensed contactors to build at least eighteen thousand houses after World War II. The number of tract houses that borrowed from May was many times larger still. By the mid-1950s, perhaps as many as eight in every ten suburban tract houses being constructed in the nation were built in ranch style, many directly or indirectly based on his designs.[27] During the 1930s his houses were featured in periodicals including *Sunset*, *American Home*, and *California Arts and Architecture*, and his regional and national reputation grew. After World War II, May conceived of using one of his planned houses as a prototype—an "After the War House," highlighting the possibilities his designs could offer in the postwar era. The result was the 1948 featuring of just such a house as a "Pace-Setter House" in *House Beautiful*, in the first issue of that magazine printed in color and the only issue to focus exclusively on a single home. The magazine also included special sections offering advice on how to adapt the design to hot or cold climates, and how best to construct a more economical version for the budget-conscious. In 1950 *Better Homes and Gardens* selected another of May's ranch houses for the magazine's exhibit on the Avenue of American Homes at the Chicago Lake Front Fair. In 1953 May formed the Ranch House Supply Corporation and began selling licenses and home plans to numerous builders and contractors in California, the Southwest, and the Southeast, ensuring that his houses would dot the landscape of the Sunbelt.[28]

His houses also won awards that brought national attention to his work, including prizes in 1947, 1952, and 1953 from the National Association of Home Builders. Other accolades included an award from *House and Home* magazine in 1956, the "Hallmark House" award from *House and Garden* in 1958, and the Builder of the Year Award from the Congress of Building Contractors Association of California in 1963. May's influence also included connections to publishing, with May serving as staff consultant for construction to *House Beautiful. Sunset Magazine* also published two house pattern books featuring his ranch designs. He even designed the headquarters for *Sunset Magazine*, constructing an office building in Menlo Park, California, that was essentially an oversized ranch house, and designed a home for its owner and publisher, Lawrence William Lane. Frank Lloyd Wright later visited the *Sunset* building, and while he had a few complaints—the Mexican tile floors, for example, were a tripping hazard for an octogenarian—he was remarkably effusive in praising it. He liked the lobby, particularly its views out into the lawn and garden. Overall, Wright opined, "It's well planned, and the ideas are good, and the proportions are simple and I would say it's one of the best efforts I've seen in modern times." Coming from Wright, this was high praise indeed.[29]

May's houses were also truly radical. American homebuilders and home-buyers have long been dedicated traditionalists where residential architecture is concerned. Part of this no doubt springs from the nation's longstanding vernacular architectural styles, which vary from region to region. Another reason, however, is economic. "Traditional" houses held their value; anything too new, or too radical, might not have as much resale value. Ranches lacked imposing facades, porticoes, gables, columns, and other architectural status symbols. California homebuyers might see a ranch as an extension of local vernacular tradition, but the same was not true for homebuyers elsewhere. This makes the popularity of the style all the more surprising. The only other example of a nontraditional building style sweeping the nation had happened a half century earlier, and also began in Los Angeles and other West Coast cities—the style of house called the California bungalow. Bungalows, like ranches, offered homebuyers a simpler, more casual way of life, more open and attuned to the outdoors. In that earlier era, Midwesterners had imagined relocating to Los Angeles and buying a bungalow with palm or orange trees in the yard. Now, with the ranch, people would continue to relocate, but the architecture and lifestyle could relocate as well.[30]

A sixth-generation Californian, May was born in San Diego in 1908. May's mother, Beatrice Magee May, was the daughter of a California woman, Victoria de Pedrorena, and Henry Magee, a member of a New York state militia that stationed in California after annexation. Beatrice May regaled him with stories of their Californio ancestors, the de Pedrorena and Estudillo families. Though their rancho lands were long since lost, their homes in Old Town San Diego, Casa de Estudillo and Casa de Pedrorena, still stood, and the Estudillo home drew tourists as a museum and as the purported site of "Ramona's marriage place." Further, May spent most of the summers of his childhood at his aunt Jane Magee's ranch property, located on the lands of the Rancho Santa Margarita y Las Flores in northern San Diego County, once owned by Pío Pico, last governor of Mexican Alta California. The ranch's holdings were greatly reduced from its nineteenth-century cattle rancho heyday, but it remained a sizeable agricultural operation, mostly growing lima beans. It also contained two nineteenth-century adobe homes, the Rancho San Margarita and the Las Flores Adobe. Here, even more than in his family's homes in Old Town, May could experience the architectural world and agricultural landscape of his Californio ancestors, and it left a lasting imprint.[31]

The Spanish missions also featured heavily as landmarks in May's childhood. His parents took him and their other children to Easter and Christmas masses at Mission San Louis Rey and San Juan Capistrano. They had been married in Mission San Luis Rey, and May would be married to his first wife, Jean Lichty, at Mission San Diego in 1932. With Jean, May would have four children, and she played an active role in his subsequent homebuilding career. May recalled that his family knew all the mission fathers, and that "the thick walls and the deep sanctuaries and the tile floors and the tile roofs...were all just a part of our boyhood and childhood."[32]

The architecture and history—real and romanticized—of his Californio ancestors profoundly influenced May. The region's past permeated his houses. The romanticized pastoral of genteel leisure that had entranced Charles Lummis and made such an impression on many Anglos would, through May, come to influence postwar suburbia in complex ways. The two *Sunset Magazine* ranch-house pattern books featuring his designs—both still available in print in the early twenty-first century—used the del Valles' rancho adobe Camulos as a key model of the original "ranch house." These books even used photos of Camulos that may have been taken by Charles Lummis. Significantly, while *Sunset* magazine was aimed at western readers, its books were marketed nationally.[33]

May asserted that ranch style was a longstanding vernacular tradition in California, one that he traced back to his ancestors. For May, the ranch style home offered functionality, space, comfort, and above all privacy: "I mean, to me, ranch living was just the only way to go. It was spread out. You had cross-ventilation in every room and a fireplace in every room. Every room had privacy. The walls were thick. You couldn't hear people. You couldn't hear noise. You had shutters you could close up and make it dark if you wanted to sleep."[34]

When May began designing homes in the style that came to be known as ranch, he was "rebelling against...the 'box' house," the basic shape of most eastern houses, and the design of most of the new homes in San Diego in the 1920s and 1930s, as well as the new homes in Levittown, New York in the 1940s. May cared little for this form, and for all "the houses of the East, from Cape Cod to the thousands of houses that Bill [William J.] Levitt and his associates built right after World War II. They're all variations of the box...with a garage in the back. I think Bill's big contribution was putting the garage in front and making the house look bigger."[35] May also had little interest in what he perceived as passing vogues for particular types of houses, arguing that his houses instead harkened back to the distant past: "The ranch house, I think, goes back to the first primitive people who came to this part of the country, and from there it goes back to the first primitive people who were in Spain and Andalusia...and the warm belt all around the world."[36]

May presented the ranch house as the embodiment of regional history, built to open out into nature, and to bring nature into daily life, by making the patio and backyard part of the social space of the house. May pointedly did not include Frank Lloyd Wright's prairie-school houses as predecessors of the ranch style. Whether this was due to regional chauvinism, or because May, who had not been formally trained in architecture, was simply unaware of Wright's prairie-school houses, remains unclear. Wright's later Usonian houses, designed for affordability, certainly influenced the development of ranch houses. Alfred Levitt, one of the sons in Levitt & Sons, had observed Wright constructing a Usonian home on Long Island in 1937, and Alfred subsequently designed the first generation of houses at Levittown. The first model, a Cape Cod of only 750 square feet, included radiant heating in the floor, as well as other aspects of Wright's designs. May did come to know Wright once his career was underway, and he visited the architect numerous times at Taliesin West.[37]

For May, the ranch house was wholly a western phenomenon, a product of regional history and climate. *Sunset* magazine, which had been published by the Southern Pacific Railroad since 1898, used this regional emphasis of the ranch house for its own purposes. After decades of serving as a regional boosterist magazine, promoting California and the West for settlement, agriculture, and industry, the magazine remade itself as World War II drew to a close. The magazine was purchased by Lawrence William Lane, an advertising executive who had previously worked for *Better Homes and Gardens*, and he reconceived the publication as "The Magazine of Western Living." Instead of selling the West to the East, *Sunset* would serve as a guidebook for living—and living well—in the postwar West. After the war, the magazine published a series of designs for innovative houses, all designed by western architects. A new book division began publishing in 1946, and one of the first titles was *Sunset Western Ranch Houses*, published that year. It sold out its initial run of fifty thousand copies quickly, and more printings followed.[38] This book, followed by *Western Ranch Houses by Cliff May* in 1958, offered a variety of house patterns and models drawn from May-designed homes, and also offered histories of the ranch house.

These histories—like the houses—sold the region as effectively as anything Charles Lummis, his magazine, or his own southwestern home had even done. Lummis had written that Southern California was the "chosen country," a place populated in large part by people who had chosen to relocate there, and who had the resources to do so. In a preface to the second book, *Sunset* offered its view of May's houses and the lifestyle they promised to create. His houses offered a mode "for living that fits comfortably into the Western scene and brings the reassuring feeling of continuity with the past." The book, rather than being merely a portfolio of house designs, was a "collection of ideas in one kind of Western living."[39]

The *Sunset* ranch house books presented May's houses as authentic outgrowths of the vernacular architecture of Southern California, and they did indeed draw heavily upon Californio rancho houses, such as the ones owned by his family. Yet they also drew heavily on the invented past of Southern California, of *Ramona*, Lummis, and the entire booster class of an earlier era. A quote from Helen Hunt Jackson's *Ramona* appeared in both books, extolling Californio culture: "It was a picturesque life, with more of sentiment and gayety in it, more also that was truly dramatic, more romance, than will ever be seen again on these sunny shores. The aroma of it all lingers there still; industries and inventions have not yet slain it; it will last out its century." The 1958 book also utilized a quote from Hubert Howe Bancroft, who described the Californios much as Lummis had:

> Absolutely unconfined socially and politically ... master of all their eyes surveyed, the beautiful earth and its fruits as free as its sweet air and sunshine, lands unlimited, cattle on a thousand hills, with ready-made servants to tend them; born here, basking here, with none to molest or make afraid; to shrive; with heart full and stomach full; how could they be else than happy, than lovers of home and country.[40]

This sense of freedom and autonomy not only echoed Lummis's idealization of Californio life, it ignored the often brutal labor relations that underlay the rancho system. Its eulogizing of unfettered freedom also suggested the political rhetoric of a later era, one that would arise in the new suburbs of the postwar Sunbelt, suspicious of government and any attempts to limit freedom—at least freedom for some. The May ranch house, above all, offered

FIGURE 7.4 Cover of the first *Sunset Western Ranch Houses* book, published in 1946. The cover image features one of Cliff May's many home designs drawing on California rancho and adobe architectural forms. Through May, variations of this regional architecture would appear in suburbs across the United States. Image courtesy of Hennessey + Ingalls.

freedom of movement and independence—it was an architectural distillation of the pioneer ethos, as well as the social atomization it could engender. It echoed the powerful lure of the Californio rancho fantasy, of leisure and complete independence, that Bancroft and Lummis believed rancho families had enjoyed.

The same book also utilized Jackson's description of Rancho Camulos, the rancho Jackson fictionalized as the home of Ramona, and her description echoed the same language used to praise May's houses for their utilization of outdoor space: "The house was of adobe, low, with a wide veranda on the three sides of the inner court, and a still broader one across the entire front, which looked to the south. These verandas, especially those on the inner court, were supplementary rooms to the house. The greater part of the family life went on in them. Nobody stayed inside the walls, except when it was necessary." May and other developers linked these houses to the houses and supposed lifestyle of the Californio past. Much of Los Angeles and its suburbs had in fact been mission and then rancho land, and developers were only too happy to allow homeowners to buy their own little parcel of the romanticized mission and Mexican past.[41]

May utilized this sales strategy as well at his first tract development, named Riviera Ranch, which was located in Brentwood, in west Los Angeles. Advertisements sold houses at Riviera Ranch as "Exclusive Early California Ranches in a Planned Community on the Last of the Great California Ranchos, San Vicente y Santa Monica." Each home promised "the romantic charm of early-day California life," but with thoroughly modern amenities. Homeowners could keep horses in a rustic setting like the ranchos of old, yet live in houses that thoughtfully incorporated auto garages into the home, integrating cars and driving into the experience of living in a May house. *House Beautiful* showcased the home May built for his family at Riviera Ranch in an article entitled "Meet a Family that Really Knows How to Live." Several home, garden, and architectural magazines jostled to showcase houses in the development, one of very few constructed during World War II. Riviera Ranch heightened May's national visibility at a crucial moment. Readers were hungry for the postwar world and wondered what the future might hold. Opening magazines such as *House Beautiful* and *Better Homes and Gardens*, readers were presented with lush distillations of the California dream, rendered in architectural form. After the war, that dream would spread across the continent, to one suburb after another.[42]

The most explicit link between past and present was the patio, the "key" to his house plans—the place where, according to *Western Ranch Houses by Cliff May*, "the pleasures of indoor-outdoor living have been enjoyed for more than a century." Like May's homes, these structures focused social life in the interior or in walled outdoor areas, with little interaction with the surrounding landscape or streetscape: "It was for this inner court that the Spaniards reserved the real beauties of architectural details and planting... toward the public the house presented an emblematic façade, but on the inside was an oasis of trees and flowers, occasionally graced with a fountain." Of course, May's ranch-house patios differed markedly from the patios of the past.

While the patios at adobe rancho homes were undoubtedly social spaces, they were also very much places of labor and production. May's house patios were instead solely for the purposes of leisure and private family socialization and relaxation. Many also featured something that would have been utterly alien at a rancho—a swimming pool.[43]

May's erasure of labor extended further than the patio. He read it directly into the histories of the adobe homes he emulated. He asserted that the ranch style and plan had endured because

> the plan has been shaped by the materials. The materials are native, and they go well with the community. And they're cheap. So that's the thing we are having trouble with right now: everything costs too much. Of course, it's labor that makes it cost now. In the old days, labor was free. . . . They got their labor for nothing. One day of their life they contributed towards building their house.

Certainly, many Californios had built their own residences. Yet for the rancho elite, or the mission priests who preceded them, labor had been performed not by them but by Indian workers, often under varying degrees of coercion or duress. Such workers might well have challenged May's valuation of their "free" labor.[44]

While linking his ranch homes firmly to the landscape of Southern California, May and the *Sunset* pattern books also asserted that this regional style could be readily exported and adapted elsewhere. One example, showcased in the 1958 *Sunset* book, was a home he had built in Missouri, where "half a continent away from its birthplace," the "ranch house looks serenely at home," adapted to a more variable climate. More insulation, double-paned windows, and heavier framing to support a roof covered in snow addressed winter issues, as did a radiant heating system under the flagstone patio to keep it snow-free and useable as much of the time as possible: "after a snow storm, when the entire countryside is white, this patio is bare and dry and, if the sun is out, surprisingly comfortable." For summers, full air conditioning abated the heat and humidity of the Midwest. With these adjustments, May's houses could be—and were—constructed across the nation, becoming as ubiquitous as the bungalows of half a century earlier.[45]

In the variety of May ranch-house patterns, plans, and examples included in the *Sunset* books, the ranch house was presented as a link between past and present that would be able to absorb modern innovations while still remaining comfortable and familiar. The bungalows constructed several decades earlier had likewise included new plumbing technologies and kitchen appliances while simultaneously promising buyers a return to a simpler life. Indeed, as modernist architect Albert Frey had proven in his many ranch-style

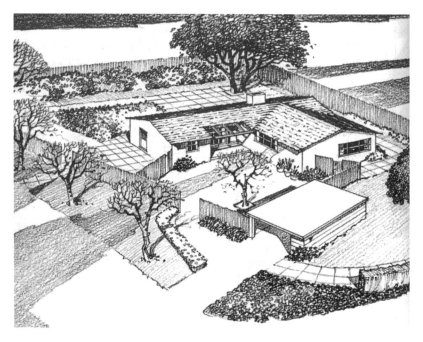

FIGURE 7.5 A house pattern illustration from *Western Ranch Houses by Cliff May*, 1958. Like many of May's designs, this one utilized outdoor areas as recreational and social space, particularly the large, private patio secluded from the street. Image courtesy of Hennessey + Ingalls.

homes at Smoke Tree Ranch in Palm Springs—homes May likely was familiar with—home buyers embraced new technologies and designs when they were sheathed in the rustic familiarity of ranch style. Others noted this as well. As early as 1936, *Sunset* described May as an architect who "captures the past in structures that please the present." The title of an article in *House Beautiful* a decade later was more succinct: "A House Can Be Modern and Not Look It."[46]

Many of May's later designs, in terms of form, function, and amenities, consisted largely of modernist interiors camouflaged by exteriors embracing the vernacular or historicist architecture of California and the Southwest. In this way, the houses of both Frey and May, like Wright's prairie-school houses, the turn-of-the-century bungalows that appeared across Southern California, and the Spanish-revival homes that followed by the 1920s, all addressed similar underlying concerns. Each attempted to demonstrate how to make a house harmonize with its surrounding landscape, how to make it innovative yet not alien, how to draw outside spaces into the home and take advantage of yards and a balmy climate, and above all how to facilitate family socialization through private leisure. The architectural appearance of the homes changed, but the cultural imperatives that underlay them remained remarkably constant.[47]

Though May was a hugely significant figure in the architectural development of postwar suburbia, the houses May designed personally were never financed through FHA or VA loans—his early homes were so modest that buyers paid cash, and his later homes, mostly designed for the wealthy, were paid for by buyers for whom cost was no concern. May's designs, however, whether constructed by him, by licensed contractors, or by developers who simply pilfered his ideas, proved immensely popular with homebuyers who did utilize government financing. Many of these homes were far less luxurious, carefully planned, or well-appointed than May's houses. Mass production, adapted from wartime industrialization, meant that a variety of building materials, from concrete to aluminum siding, were inexpensive and plentiful. Plywood, vinyl flooring, and Formica countertops made these homes less architecturally distinctive, but also made them far less expensive to build, particularly on a large scale. This lower cost of construction, in addition to the FHA and VA loan programs, made suburban houses far more affordable. The spiraling prosperity of the postwar decades, and the 1950s in particular, also played a key role. The nation's gross national product doubled between 1946 and 1956, and doubled again by 1970. Median family income doubled from 1949 to 1973. Families that could not afford a ranch home in 1948 could do so a decade later. Here, then, lies the confluence of explanations for the transformation of suburbia, from the first small, Cape Cod–style houses at Levittown to the far larger ranch homes that followed.[48]

———————————— ✹ ————————————

The first place this happened on a large scale was Phoenix. Local developer John F. Long, aiming to give his new suburban development, Maryvale (named for his wife, Mary), an edge over surrounding developments, traveled to California to inspect May's designs. He went west because he believed that "California is the trend setter, the Midwest has no ideas." All of the homes in Maryvale, twenty-five thousand in total, would be designed in ranch styles derived from May. The development eventually housed more than a hundred thousand residents, mostly migrants from the east who relocated to Phoenix to take jobs in postwar defense industries. Horizontal layouts, with backyards ample enough for a pool, were the norm. These houses were far less palatial than May's largest home designs, but they carried the same ideas and the same cachet of California and California-style living. When model homes first opened at Maryvale in 1955, one of the homes showcased General Electric's latest electric kitchen, complete with refrigerator, stove, oven, and dishwasher. GE's commercial spokesman, actor Ronald Reagan, arrived to promote the kitchen as thousands of prospective homebuyers passed through.[49]

FIGURE 7.6 Prospective homebuyers at a 1955 open house in Maryvale inspect a new way of life. When completed, Maryvale became home to one hundred thousand residents. It was also the first of many large housing developments in the United States built entirely in ranch style. Courtesy of John F. Long Properties, LLLP. Phoenix, Arizona.

The Rise of Barry Goldwater and the Regional Origins of the New Right

These new ranch-house suburbs were crucibles of a new leisure culture derived from Southern California. They were likewise political crucibles, where a wide range of political movements, from second-wave feminism, to post–*Silent Spring* and Earth Day environmentalism, to the New Right took shape. Reagan would be the most famous and successful product of conservative suburban politics, but his predecessor, Arizona senator and 1964 presidential candidate Barry Goldwater, is perhaps an even more instructive example. While other historians have capably documented the origins and growth of the new conservative movement that emerged in the Sunbelt, such as Lisa McGirr in her 2001 book *Suburban Warriors: The Origins of the New American Right*, they have not always acknowledged the deep links between this postwar political movement and a longer regional history in the Southwest. In the Southeast, the uneasy links between the New Right and that region's troubled history of segregation, racism, and states' rights were perhaps more obvious. The career of Barry Goldwater illustrates that the New Right in the southwestern Sunbelt also exhibited connections to much older regional history.

Goldwater was born in 1909, the grandson of Jewish immigrants who had moved to Los Angeles. They relocated to Gila City, in the future state of

Arizona, in the 1860s, and by the early 1870s owned a goods store in Phoenix, and later opened a second store in Prescott. In so doing, they were following a very old pattern—families of *conversos*, Jews who had converted to Catholicism, had long been prominent merchants in the Spanish and Mexican Southwest. Morris Goldwater, an uncle of Barry's, was elected mayor of Prescott in 1878. His younger brother Baron made a new store in Phoenix a success, transforming it from a goods store to a department store that catered to women. In 1907 he married Josephine Williams, a native of Illinois who came to Arizona in her twenties hoping to recuperate from tuberculosis. They were married in an Episcopalian service, and their eldest son, Barry Morris Goldwater, was born on 1 January 1909. His mother was an avid outdoor recreationalist, and she taught her children to hunt, fish, and camp. She also drove them west to Santa Monica during the summers, vacationing at the beach while Phoenix sweltered. Josephine also encouraged Barry's interest in photography, through which he documented his interest in and affection for the landscapes and cultures of the Southwest.[50]

In addition to photographing Native Americans, Goldwater also participated in a more dubious act of cultural appropriation. In the 1920s a group of young Anglo men in Prescott had donned Native American attire and begun performing annual dances adapted from native ceremonies. This led to the creation of a fraternal "tribe," the "Smokis," which Goldwater was invited to join when he was in his early thirties in 1941. Southwestern writer Mary Austin, an early contributor to *Land of Sunshine* who had relocated from Los Angeles to Santa Fe, saw this act as a worthy adoption of authentic Southwestern culture. It was, not coincidentally, exactly the same sort of cultural cross-dressing Charles Lummis had engaged in, remaking himself first as a Pueblo Indian and later as a Californio "Don Carlos." Goldwater saw the dances as harmless, and seemed to think they were a sort of homage to Native American values and traditions. Native Americans, unsurprisingly, were less impressed. Even the *Los Angeles Times*, hardly a consistent champion of respect for Native Americans, dismissed the dances as a "thoroughly offensive, objectionable and indefensible exhibition of bad taste." Goldwater remained a member of the group, even though its dances were later terminated. His romantic attachment to Native American cultures and Southwestern landscapes linked him, however problematically, with the long history of romanticized boosterism in the region.[51]

The regional booster strain in Goldwater's character resurfaced repeatedly in his career. Goldwater made his family department store a success through designing and selling "Purely Southwestern" clothes to a national market. The most popular design was the "branding iron" line—cattle brands on white cloth that first appeared on women's blouses and were later used on towels, glassware, and even wrapping paper. Other western clothing lines

FIGURE 7.7 Goldwater's fashion show at the Biltmore Hotel, 1946. *Arizona Highways*, February 1946.

included denim dresses and women's clothes sold in desert colors. While he enjoyed design, running the retail chain bored Goldwater. It also sometimes caused great strain—in the late 1930s the pressures of opening a new store led to what his wife—and subsequent political opponents—termed a nervous breakdown. Goldwater denied he had experienced anything that severe, though he also suffered bouts of depression. When one hit, he would disappear into the desert to explore and enjoy his photography habit. He also enjoyed alcohol, and freely admitted to his copious drinking. If Goldwater displayed a Lummis-like flair for promotion, he also seemed to share some less positive traits with him as well.[52]

Goldwater's Department Store also put on fashion shows at the Biltmore and other area resorts, drawing business from tourists and residents alike, just as Bullock's and other Los Angeles stores had done in Palm Springs. In 1934, Goldwater married a customer he first met at one such fashion show, Margaret "Peggy" Johnson, from Muncie, Indiana, whose parents wintered in Arizona. Tourism had made Los Angeles a metropolis, and Goldwater thought that tourism could free Arizona from its dependency on the federal government. He believed that "the natural thing to which to turn was the capitalization of our climate, our natural beauties, and the romance of our desert."[53]

As a rising figure in Phoenix's economic, political, and cultural circles, he also proved a tireless booster for Phoenix and the Valley of the Sun. He taught a "tourist information" class to help local merchants cater to visitors. He joined the chamber of commerce, later serving as president and also joining the chamber's "Royal Order of Thunderbirds," created to "work for the glorious future of Phoenix." He also served on the board of the Heard Museum, the YMCA, the Boys' Club of Phoenix, and two hospitals.[54]

Goldwater would also use his own photographic skills to help promote the city and state. *Arizona Highways* began publishing color photographs in 1938, and Goldwater proved an avid contributor to the magazine. He thought that photographs could help demonstrate his belief that "God got about 114,000 square miles out of heaven and let it fall down here in Arizona."[55] He emulated Ansel Adams and Edward Weston, and he became friends with Adams. His wife, who had studied art in New York City, helped him compose his photographs of landscapes and Native Americans. In 1940 he took a long trip on the Colorado River, retracing the route of the Powell Expedition—over the objections of Peggy, then pregnant with their third child. The trip, made in small wooden boats, involved significant dangers, and when he reached Lake Mead he became only the seventy-first person known to have made the journey along the length of the Colorado. He later published the photos from it in *Arizona Highways*. He also made a film, "Shooting Grand Canyon Rapids," featuring his exploits. Goldwater traveled the state screening the film, and this gave him an early opportunity for public speaking and earning him some notoriety as a public figure. He also left a more lasting memento of his journey along the Colorado itself. After crossing into Arizona through Glen Canyon, later submerged by Lake Powell, he carved an inscription on the canyon wall: "ARIZONA WELCOMES YOU."[56]

By the time World War II arrived, Arizona was doing exactly that. Phoenix, a small city of 65,000 in 1940, would nearly double to nearly 107,000 by 1950, and quadruple again to 439,000 by 1960. With good-paying jobs and inexpensive housing, migrants poured into the Valley of the Sun. Author Ivan Doig, whose father relocated from Montana to Arizona to take a wartime job at Alcoa, recalled an overwhelming sense of opportunity and prosperity that pervaded the region: "Surely this, the state of Arizona humming and buzzing with defense plants and military bases installed for the war, this must be the craved new world, the shores of Social Security and the sugar trees of overtime." In addition to factories constructed by Alcoa and Goodyear, boosters hoped to attract "clean" industries, such as electronics and aviation, rather than old smokestack industries such as steel that had polluted eastern cities. Goldwater pushed for aviation development in particular, aiding the construction of Sky Harbor Airport in Phoenix.[57] Goldwater also enjoyed piloting planes and subsequently joined the Aviation Country Club of California, composed of a group of flying aficionados. As a result, he became an acquaintance of another member of the same group—architect Cliff May. Motorola opened a plant in 1948 and would become the largest employer in the state. By 1955 the three largest sources of income for Phoenix were manufacturing, agriculture, and tourism.[58]

In the torrid Sonoran Desert, the advent of mass air-conditioning proved crucial. Advances in air-conditioning made company executives more confident that the climate would be tolerable, and more and more corporations arrived. In 1952 banker Carl Bimson argued that its impact could not be overemphasized. It eliminated seasonal fluctuations in visitation and business activity. Further, Bimson noted that it created an entirely new local industry devoted to the "manufacturing and servicing of air conditioning equipment." Barry Goldwater asserted in 1960 that air-conditioning had become ubiquitous in Phoenix: "At most, only 200 homes in the city are without it." Goldwater was likely counting only Anglo households, and not Mexican or African American ones, in such a pronouncement. For middle-class Phoenicians, however, air conditioning did become essentially universal. A Valley National Bank promotional booklet from the mid-1960s asserted that "refrigeration, once considered a luxury, has now become so popular as to be in the same class as a "two-car family."[59]

Like countless western boosters before him, Goldwater pursued the promotion of Phoenix and Arizona with great enthusiasm. A 1960 article in *Newsweek* examined the growth "miracle" in Arizona and showcased Goldwater's enthusiasm: "Barry Goldwater sums up the booster spirit of Phoenix and all Arizona. 'Before I die,' the senator says, 'Phoenix will be one of the five or six biggest cities in the U.S. There is no stopping this state.'" By the time of his death in 1998, his prediction had been proven accurate.[60]

In addition to his photography, Goldwater made more films extolling Arizona in the 1960s. *The Story of Arizona and Sun City* promoted the state as a whole, but emphasized Sun City, which Goldwater claimed was "America's most famous resort-retirement community," which offered residents recreation and companionship, cures for the "lonesomeness" of retirement. This film, like Del Webb's copious promotional materials, made no mention of the prior history of the Sun City site, other than to state it arose from former cotton fields. Those cotton fields belonged to the Southwest Cotton Company, a subsidiary of Goodyear Tire and Rubber. Sun City was in fact built atop Marinette, Southwest Cotton's company town for Mexican field laborers. The laborers and the town were erased, but they lived on—in name only—in this new community of retirement leisure: one of Sun City's recreation centers was named Marinette.[61]

Another film, *Land of Giants*, presented both Southwestern scenery and Goldwater's version of state history. He hailed Anglo pioneers who endured droughts, floods, and violence, but "they stuck on!" The film made no mention, however, of the U.S.-Mexico War, which, along with the Gadsden Purchase, had brought the future state into the union. Showcasing state scenery, particularly the new reservoir created by the Glen Canyon Dam, Goldwater claimed to be a conservationist, and complained about litter and smog in contemporary Arizona. He concluded by urging viewers to visit and live in his state, and to tackle current and future problems to keep Arizona a "land of giants." His closing summary of the state's history was succinct and revealing: "We tamed it. We did it by ourselves—and proud of it." All the federal funding and initiatives that had created Roosevelt Dam, Lake Powell, and innumerable jobs connected to World War II and the cold war were ignored, as was all the labor provided by Mexicans and Native Americans. Only the storied Anglo pioneer heritage remained.[62]

Phoenix and its burgeoning population readily embraced the urban model Los Angeles had pioneered, building a sprawling, decentered city navigated by cars and filled with lush vegetation kept green by water imported from elsewhere. Single-story ranch homes were the ideal residential form for this new Sunbelt city, and they would sprout in other Sunbelt cities, as well as suburbs from Dallas to Chicago. The Goldwaters moved into a ranch-style home in 1957 and named it "Be-nun-i-kin," Navajo for "house on top of a hill." Goldwater oversaw the design of the home, constructed in the shape of

FIGURE 7.8 A new era begins in Phoenix. The cover of the February 1946 issue of *Arizona Highways* depicts a returned soldier with his wife in front of their new home in the city, at the beginning of more than a half-century of growth.

an arrowhead and built with sandstone from the Navajo Reservation. By this time, Goldwater had already made the leap from retail sales and management to politics. In 1949 a pro-reform slate of candidates took over the Phoenix City Council. Goldwater was one of the reformers. Republicans began their statewide takeover as well in what had been a Democratic state, aided by all the new arrivals.[63]

Goldwater then ran for the U.S. Senate, and it was this first campaign for a seat in Washington that illustrated a constant tactic of all his subsequent campaigns—selling himself to voters by selling Arizona and the Southwest. In his 1952 campaign for the Senate, rather than using photos of himself, he instead used some of his own scenic photos of Arizona, connecting the landscape to his political views and family history. This strong identification with Arizona and the West would be a hallmark of his failed 1964 presidential bid and a subsequent campaign that retuned him to the Senate. His television ads featured Monument Valley and sounded more than a little like the narration of a film trailer for a John Ford western:

> There is a great message in this beautiful land. Barry Goldwater is, above all else, a product of the land he loves. He has unrolled his bed on Arizona's wind-chilled mesas. Roamed her forests and valleys. And explored the yawning depths of her sheer canyons. And he learned. There was a great message in that beautiful, raw-boned land. Self-reliance. Hard work. Rugged, determined, stick-to-getherness. These are the words Barry Goldwater has taken to the nation. The lessons of a great State that still remembers its fierce struggle for survival. Arizona's lesson is America's lesson. But much of America has forgotten. That's why Barry Goldwater must be returned to the U.S. Senate. From Tombstone to Boston...from Kayenta to Detroit...Arizona's strong true words are needed now, more than ever before.[64]

The use of such western language and images would lead critics to call Goldwater the Marlboro Man, but that carping did not dent the success of his strategy. This rhetoric, a nostalgic paean for the supposed pioneer ethos of an earlier era, obviously ignored all the ways in which the settlers of Arizona and the West had been anything but self-reliant. The federal government had sold the land, paid for the construction of railroads, roads, and freeways, and built vast dams and canals to water the West's cities and agriculture. It had commissioned the factories and financed the houses many Arizonans worked and lived in. This factual history, however, did not interfere with the myth. Ronald Reagan and other conservatives would employ similar rhetoric from the 1950s through the rest of the twentieth century.[65]

Just as Sunbelt conservatives willfully ignored the central role of the federal government in the development of their region, they likewise ignored the consequences of all their boosterist rhetoric. Inveterate booster Charles Lummis had railed against the growth that swamped Los Angeles, causing traffic jams and endangering the historicist vision he imagined for the city. He died, however, before his beloved Arroyo Seco was entombed in cement and the new Pasadena Freeway sent cars hurtling by only yards from his home. Frank Lloyd Wright was infuriated when the state of Arizona had the temerity to run tall, high-voltage transmission lines directly in front of Taliesin West, carrying electricity to Phoenix but obstructing his view of the Sonoran Desert. Those power lines carried electricity generated by the burning of coal at vast new power plants on the Navajo Reservation, destined to power the air conditioners of Phoenix. Phoenix prospered by selling desert living and desert vistas, but the desert was only made habitable by despoiling the scenic landscapes Goldwater's photographs and Lummis's prose extolled. Subsequent residential and commercial development would begin to obscure the desert landscape around Phoenix itself. Even Goldwater was forced to abandon his abhorrence of government regulations when housing development threatened to engulf the desert ranges around Phoenix, and he came to support development limits on the flanks of Camelback Mountain and other peaks.[66]

From Southern California to a Suburban Nation

By this time, however, development had already led to rapid growth in many cities across the Sunbelt and in newer suburbs surrounding eastern cities. Cliff May had been correct—the ranch-style house could be adapted to other regions, and developers and individual homeowners did so on a vast scale. Chicago, the city Wright had fled decades earlier, was one example, and would itself would be touched by this process. As it lost residents to the newer cities of the Sunbelt, some of its residents, especially suburban ones, incorporated elements of Sunbelt leisure and living into their midcentury suburban culture.

By the summers of the late 1950s, the latest fad was backyard barbecue grilling, where the household patriarch strove to cook out successfully without immolating a family meal or himself. Sensing a profit to be made, grocery chains and hardware stores offered barbecuing lessons so that suburban husbands could keep up with their neighbors. Basements were remade into faux-Polynesian tiki rooms, and prosperity, paid vacation time, and inexpensive gas and accommodations made vacation travel accessible to more families than ever before. By far the most common form of leisure, however, was watching television. Families gathered around the television, watching programming that, like movies, often originated in Southern California. Such families were in the audience when Walt Disney unveiled his Anaheim theme park on television in 1955.[67]

Increasingly, leisure time and family time were synonymous. Parents were expected to play and socialize with their children and with other parents and their children. The primary venue for this leisure was the private backyard, rather than public parks, pools, or beaches. Patios and barbecues proliferated in suburban neighborhoods, transplanting a Southern California model of the backyard as a family room, at least in clement weather. Backyard swimming pools spread more slowly, both because of cost and cold winters. These, however, spread too as construction costs fell. Above-ground pools with vinyl sides were the cheapest solution, but for dug, sunken pools, which conferred more social status, the breakthrough was gunite, a form of sprayed concrete that could be molded into curving shapes. The first architect to pioneer this new construction technique had in fact been Frank Lloyd Wright, who used it to construct the curving spiral form of the Guggenheim Museum in New York. With gunite, any middle-class home could have what had once been a preserve of the rich and resorts.

Ranch houses soon spread across the country. One Chicago developer, Gene Dreyfus, made clear that new suburban ranch homes were the embodiment of American family values: "The most important room in any home is the family room.... There, natural materials might be used—rich woods to capture warmth from controlled lighting—soft earth colors to carry the relaxed, informal atmosphere through full glass walls which lead to a huge patio area." Such patios, according to Dreyfus, "offer an opportunity for family togetherness which too often is lacking in modern-day living."[68] His physical description of interior living space and outdoor patio could have been applied to many of the most striking modernist residences in Palm Springs. Now, however, instead of resort leisure for the privileged few, the ranch house offered leisure as a way of life, crucial to the happiness of the modern middle-class family.

Mass production and less expensive building materials had already lowered costs and allowed the construction of larger ranch homes. Another architectural innovation, however, developed in California to cope with hilly lots, also played an important role. This was the "split-level" home. By folding the ranch house floor plan in on itself, placing bedrooms above and social space below, the footprint of the house itself—and the lot required to contain house and yard—could be reduced. This meant a denser concentration of houses, and thus more money for developers. It also further reduced costs for homebuyers, and as a result new amenities, such as fireplaces and family or recreation rooms, could become more common. The "rec room" also offered a location for the television, while preserving the living room for more formal entertaining.

The split-level soon became synonymous with suburbia. The ranch style endured, inside and out, but the split-level made ranch-style living available to a far larger population of prospective homebuyers, and since most split-levels included a basement, they also functioned as a regional adaptation of the California-style ranch to less temperate climates. With living room, dining room, and kitchen on one level, bedrooms a few stairs up and a family room a few stairs down, the split-level maintained the informality and flowing interior of the ranch house. The new house style was wildly popular. *House Beautiful* summarized its appeal as "spaciousness, and not simply the illusion of space . . . soaring, singing spaces that have been made possible in our time." The magazine also extolled the extensive use of floor-to-ceiling sliding glass doors and windows through which "interior and exterior melt into one." In 1953, 88 percent of new homes constructed in the United States were one-story ranch homes, usually atop a concrete slab or crawlspace. By 1956, two-story split-levels had already overtaken them.[69]

Closing the Frontier of Leisure

By the mid-1950s, the original buyers of small suburban houses—mostly young couples with (or soon to have) children—were joined by a new class of homebuyers. These buyers were less motivated by needs for a larger home, but rather by the perceived need to move to neighborhoods that would remain white-only. The civil rights movement and integration efforts in the 1950s focused on the South, but whites in the North were already moving out of neighborhoods that were—or might become—racially mixed. White flight, fueled by racial fears and aided by FHA and VA loans, played a decisive role in middle-class migration to the suburbs.

In Los Angeles, and in the postwar suburbia that emulated it, private was consistently privileged over public. This led to two systems at the federal and local level for funding housing construction and facilitating recreation—one private and the other public. Government money flowed to banks and developers through the VA and FHA loan programs and facilitated the construction of homes that were almost always single-family residences built on open land in suburban areas, while government-funded public-housing projects, almost always multifamily buildings and sometimes behemoth in scale, were built in inner cities. Private suburbia was overwhelmingly white; public housing projects were not. Likewise, all those cheap gunite pools also guaranteed that most white swimmers would swim in backyards or private suburban swimming or golf clubs, and not in the municipal pools that were flashpoints of civil rights activism and racial conflict, as they had been decades before in Los Angeles.[70]

It was such modest homes as the split-level ranch in which the glamorous lifestyles of a resort would be transformed into the family recreation of overwhelmingly white suburban neighborhoods. Cultural critics and intellectuals from Jane Jacobs to Jack Kerouac considered these new suburbs banal, boring, and conformist. Environmentalists likewise decried suburbia, not for its banality, but rather because suburban sprawl was devouring open space and agricultural land. Malvina Reynolds's 1962 song, "Little Boxes," gave voice to both these critques:

> Little boxes on the hillside,
> Little boxes made of ticky tacky,
> Little boxes on the hillside,
> Little boxes all the same.

The cultural and class message was clear. Anyone who bought such a house was tasteless, conformist, and, ultimately, boring.

Californian author Joan Didion shrewdly observed that these sorts of houses, even when much larger and more luxurious, raised difficult and ultimately inescapable issues of class and taste. Her observation on this point arose from a political spat in California, one that originated in the decision of Governor Ronald Reagan and his wife Nancy to live not in the storied Victorian governor's mansion in Sacramento, but instead in a new home, a ranch house near the American River. Democrats railed against the extravagance of the large home, even though many professed never to have actually seen it. After extended political squabbling, construction was halted in 1975, the year Reagan left office, never having moved into the house he commissioned. Didion, however, noted that the house itself was not particularly extravagant. It was not one of Cliff May's luxurious designs, replete with natural materials and thoughtfully arranged interior and outdoor spaces. The "slate" countertops were vinyl; the "redwood" doors and beams were actually plain lumber stained red; the "adobe" walls were plastered cement block; the house boasted a recreation room and wet bar that could be found in countless Californian and American homes by the 1970s. And that, Didion noted, was in fact the point. To suggest that many—if not most—middle-class California voters lacked taste was a point the political class of Sacramento could not make. Didion wrote that she had "seldom seen a house so evocative of the unspeakable."[71]

What had once been a preserve of the rich at resorts had been remade into the most common type of housing built in the decades following World War II. The elite had become the ubiquitous—and lost its cachet in the process. Like Palm Springs, which had lost visitation when so much of the Sunbelt was remade in its image, the ranch house suffered a similar fate. If seemingly everyone had one, then it could not be that special or desirable after all. Yet becoming banal, even passé, was in a sense proof of the triumph of this architectural style and the suburban leisure culture it represented. Homeowners in the 1980s and 1990s reverted to a preference for more traditional housing styles, such as colonial or English Tudor, but Spanish revival also returned in vast new subdivisions in Phoenix, Orange County, Las Vegas, Florida, and many other locales. Ronald Reagan moved on from the unloved and unlived-in ranch house in Sacramento, but he and Nancy Reagan still maintained their restored rancho adobe home near Santa Barbara and touted its connection to the "Old West" and frontier California.[72]

Further, the suburban leisure culture the ranch house represented likewise endured. Leisure and recreation, which were central to the social structure and identity of Los Angeles, became a hallmark of suburban life. Leisure—for those who had access to it—became in some ways a more important marker of identity than labor. Nature and outdoor recreation remained important as well, even as suburbia sprawled over natural landscapes and devoured natural resources, and Sunbelt migration brought millions of Americans into areas prone to environmental hazards—wildfires, hurricanes, droughts, and earthquakes. For that matter, dependence on the automobile and the comfort of air-conditioning meant that many suburbanites actually experienced nature with increasing rarity. Far from bringing a regular taste of the rugged frontier and strenuous outdoor exercise to domestic life, mass suburbia instead aided the growing problem of inactivity and obesity in America. It also heightened the nation's dependence on imported oil, as drivers would painfully discover in the oil shocks of the 1970s. Such criticisms, however, lay decades in the future in the 1950s, and in that era the suburbs were embraced by the middle class as a perfect merging of city and country, just as Los Angeles had been half a century earlier.[73]

Park and playground planners in Los Angeles and other cities in the Progressive Era had hoped to bring nature into the city in the form of green spaces for public play. Suburbanization turned this inside out on a massive scale, instead bringing the city out into nature and placing play and socialization in private backyards rather than public parks or pools. Perhaps it is not surprising that these new kinds of cities and suburbs attempted to incorporate nature and leisure not at the city or community level but rather at the level of the individual home and family, domesticating nature. From the bungalow to the ranch house and beyond, emphasis was placed on the single family and single-family dwelling, not a larger sense of civic culture or community.

In Los Angeles this turn inward, away from a sense of community involvement and responsibility, directly affected public policy. The city had long lagged in preserving parks and recreational space, and had long tried to prevent nonwhites from accessing them. The civil rights movement and the election of Tom Bradley, the city's first African American mayor, in 1973, augured changes, and African Americans and others did see increases in spending for recreational amenities in their neighborhoods.

In 1978, however, California voters passed Proposition 13, which rolled back property taxes on residential and commercial real estate. This proposition, a landmark of conservative political ascendancy in the state, also represented the fundamental triumph of private over public in Southern California and the state as a whole. The ballot measure proved popular among homeowners during an economic downturn, though many likely thought little about its consequences. One unintended consequence would be the death of the California ranch house. The new tax system, which required developers to build infrastructure, led developers to build two-story homes with a smaller footprint—and cost—than ranch homes. Another consequence was a vast reduction in tax revenues, beginning California's long slide into debt that crippled the state by 2009. As a result, state, county, and city governments slashed spending. Parks and recreation budgets were gutted, as they could not compete with law enforcement, education, and medical care for scarce government funds. What made matters even worse was that these funds were cut so soon after nonwhites and the poor finally began to benefit from them.[74]

Unsurprisingly, this devastated parks and recreation programs in poor areas. Recreation centers and pools were closed. By the 1980s some parks were left derelict, abandoned by many whites as terra incognita, purportedly inhabited only by the homeless, drug dealers, and gang members. James Hadaway, director of the Los Angeles Department of Recreation and Parks, publicly stated that half of the city's parks were located in gang territories. A survey found that half of city residents were afraid to enter parks in their own neighborhoods.[75]

Park staff in more affluent areas worked to maintain programs and facilities by raising fees and soliciting donations from the surrounding neighborhoods. "Quimby" funds, which assessed fees on certain construction projects, provided some park funding, but primarily benefited Westside L.A., where much more residential construction took place. A 1983 study demonstrated this growing "recreation gap." It found that recreation centers in middle class and affluent neighborhoods, despite cuts, had 59 percent more staff, were able to provide 74 percent more hours of classes per week, and served 123 percent more children and adolescents than those in poor areas. Further, families and children in more affluent neighborhoods were far more likely to have their own backyards and swimming pools, or access to private pools.[76]

Much of the expansion of parkland that did come after Proposition 13 was not in the form of traditional parks, but rather in the form of "open space." Tracts of undeveloped land, particularly in the Santa Monica Mountains, were set aside as natural areas to preserve habitat and provide hiking trails. Unfortunately, the state funding system that provided money for the acquisition of land for urban parks or open space often pitted advocates of one against the other. Open-space proponents affiliated with environmental advocacy groups often proved more adept at securing these "Prop K" funds. Some proponents of open space, residents of affluent neighborhoods such as Pacific Palisades and Malibu, adjacent to the Santa Monica Mountains Recreation Area, also proved less interested in the plight of poor immigrant communities in Los Angeles, which lacked even small parks and received marginal benefits from open space acquisitions in the Santa Monicas. Homeowners adjacent to open-space acquisitions, by contrast, could enjoy not only greater access to recreation—they could also enjoy a hefty uptick in the resale value of their properties.[77]

Proposition 13, for all of its impact, was just one example of a much larger phenomenon. It manifested the collective turn inward by white suburbanites—away from the street and toward the backyard or patio, and away from community and toward the nuclear family. This helps explain the fundamental misapprehensions of the modern Southwest, and much of modern America. Technology, affluence, and inexpensive labor allowed Anglo southwesterners to misinterpret both their relationship to nature and their relationship to the nation—ignoring how technology, federal largess, and the labor of others made the development of their region possible. By the 1990s, nine out of ten housing construction workers in the booming Sunbelt state of Texas were identified as "Mexican," and contractors and homebuyers alike did not seem to mind if such workers were documented or not as long as the labor they provided was inexpensive. The use of immigrant labor, a hallmark of the Southwest since at least the 1870s, spread across the nation by 2000. Sunbelt suburbia had inherited the booster regional and recreational ideology of the Southwest, but it also inherited much more as well. It inherited the housing segregation that already existed in Los Angeles and many other U.S. cities, even though suburbs gradually grew more racially diverse later in the twentieth century. It also inherited and perpetrated the older and often coercive labor system of the Southwest, based on citizenship and race.[78]

From the individual misrepresentations and misunderstandings of Lummis and Jackson, waxing poetic at Rancho Camulos about the rancho system, to Anglos in the early twenty-first century ranting about "illegals," Anglo-Americans have largely ignored and occluded the labor of others who helped make the development of the urban Southwest and Sunbelt suburbs possible. Perhaps there is no greater illustration of this willful ignorance than the spectacle of an Anglo-American homeowner, ensconced in a lavishly landscaped Spanish-revival house in the suburbs of Phoenix, railing against the federal government and undocumented workers—the very entities most responsible for the growth of that metropolis, and the construction and maintenance of such houses.[79]

From Los Angeles to Santa Catalina, to Palm Springs, to Phoenix and other Sunbelt cities, who provided labor, and who enjoyed leisure, said much about issues of race, class, power, and politics. The leisure culture of Southern California resorts had been institutionalized in postwar suburbia, but so had their problematic labor relations. In this way, the resorts and leisure culture of Southern California shaped their own region, the Sunbelt, and much of American suburbia, for good and ill. At their best, they facilitated the oldest of all American preoccupations—the pursuit of happiness, and the freedom so many Americans associated with it. Yet they also posed more vexing questions: how much freedom, and for whom? In this sense, they were inextricably connected to the oldest questions and dilemmas of the American historical experience. The answers they found could be limiting and excluding, as at the beaches of Los Angeles in the 1920s and the all-white suburbs of the 1950s. Yet they could also arrive at other answers, more open, more welcoming, and filled with possibilities that the original architects of Southern California's frontier of leisure could never have imagined.

EPILOGUE

The View from
Mount San Jacinto

I N 1998 the future ended at Tomorrowland. The original Tomorrowland, created in the 1950s and modified in the 1960s and 1970s, with its
energy-saving People Movers and simulated moon landings, seemed
dated. To bring it up to date, the park installed a new Tomorrowland, based
upon one constructed at Disneyland Paris. This new Disneyland attraction eschewed predictions of the future in favor of imagined futures past.
Nostalgic, playful rides and themes borrowing from H. G. Wells and Jules
Verne replaced confident predictions of the American future. Since 1998 that
future has only grown more cloudy. Rides based upon the actual concerns
of the twenty-first-century future—climate change, terrorism, pandemics,
religious fanaticism, and genocide—would hardly make for a carefree day at
an amusement park.[1]

The beginning of the twenty-first century proved especially unforgiv-
ing to Los Angeles and California. With troubled public schools, soaring
poverty rates, a dysfunctional state government, acrimonious battles over
immigration, natural disasters from fires to earthquakes, and soaring real-
estate prices that sent the middle class fleeing to Phoenix, Las Vegas, and
Seattle, things seemed grim indeed. Those soaring home values proved
to be the basis of yet another real-estate bust, one of many dating back
to the 1880s. Similar slumps afflicted Las Vegas and Phoenix. This time,
however, the consequences were not merely regional, but international.
Bloated mortgages, based on inflated real-estate prices and swollen further
by a variety of questionable financing schemes, were turned into commodities bought and traded on Wall Street and purchased by investors
worldwide. Replicated in other cities across the nation, and unnoticed
by lax government regulators, this global real-estate bubble burst in the
fall of 2008, triggering the worst global economic crisis since 1929. The

storied Levitt & Sons, which had constructed Levittown, was just one of many housing companies laid low by the crisis. Instead of a model of the future, L.A. seemed to have become a poster child for all of America's contemporary problems. Perhaps the California dream had finally reached its end. An article in the *New York Times* quoted a professor at Berkeley who pronounced its demise: "In the end, we do not know for sure whether the California public really wants the California dream anymore.... The population is too diverse to have a common vision of what it wants to provide to everyone. Some people want the old dream, some want the gated privatized version, and some would like to secede and get away from it all."[2]

Not just California, but perhaps even the entire Sunbelt, which had boomed for half a century, appeared to be in dire trouble. If more than half a century earlier an exodus had begun in the rust belt, perhaps Los Angeles, Las Vegas, and Phoenix were in danger of becoming the centers of a new post-Sunbelt "dust belt," its regional growth machine stymied and its residents soon to flee. Urban planners and environmentalists also proclaimed the end of sprawl and far-flung suburbs. Americans would finally be forced to live within their means in dense housing near city centers. While such theories are plausible, they are also unlikely. The oil crisis of the 1970s made nary a dent in the suburbanization of the nation, nor did it slow the accelerating migration to the Sunbelt. Economic conditions and serious environmental concerns notwithstanding, the desire to own one's own house, to have a yard, and to live where and how one pleases are very old urges in American culture. Those who bet against the continued growth of Los Angeles, California, or the Sunbelt may well be disappointed. For that matter, despite their problematic environmental impact, American-style suburbs have sprung up around the globe since 2000—and polling consistently indicates that most people in most countries would rather live in a free-standing house. Affluent Chinese, for example, can now live in vaguely Mediterranean McMansions and shop in stucco-covered pedestrian malls. Shanghai has an entire suburban district designed in American style. Suburban China even has several "Palm Springs," among multiple suburban developments that adopted names evocative of California's culture of leisure. However much California's frontier of leisure had been tarnished, its lure remained as potent as ever.[3]

For that matter, there has never been a singular California "dream." There have been many. Even small resort communities such as Avalon or Palm Springs contained wide varieties of opinion about their present and future, and they witnessed fights over what the exact nature of their futures would be. Indeed, the frontier of leisure imagined by Anglo-Americans in the late nineteenth century still survives, offering opportunities and political and economic power to individuals and groups that its original architects could scarcely have imagined.

———————✴———————

This book took as its starting point an examination of tourism and promotion in Southern California. Yet Southern California was also advertised as a place of residence, and as a place to make a living. As this study demonstrates, there was much more to Southern California tourism than just Disneyland. It transcended its tourist phase, and this book has aimed to do the same.

Leisure and its promotion made Southern California a distinct American region. Helen Hunt Jackson, author of *Ramona*, and Carey McWilliams, perhaps the most trenchant observer of the region in the twentieth century, both called Southern California an "island on the land." Though it was connected to the rest of the state and nation, for them it remained a place apart. Santa Catalina was literally an island, but in a sense Palm Springs was as well. Both resorts offered an escape from Los Angeles and the rest of Southern California, which might have seemed exotic to people elsewhere, but for residents was the place where they lived and worked. Catalina and Palm Springs were islands of private leisure within a larger region shaped by leisure, offering an idealized vision of regional history and nature to visitors. Yet these islands—the resorts and the larger region—were not truly divorced from the nation as a whole. Each resort shaped the region, offering models of leisure and living. And they, like Los Angeles and Southern California, shaped the nation as well.

In Southern California, leisure drew tourists who became residents. In this they reflected the basic desires of people in any place, and at any time, all of whom require a means of making of living, hope to find enjoyment and fulfillment in life, and want a place to call home. These residents persisted in their tourist habits in the ways they traveled in Southern California, ventured to Catalina and Palm Springs, and even in they ways they related to the city of Los Angeles. Yet if leisure helped define an emerging region, the leisure of Southern California, remade into rhetorical, social, and material forms, also shaped the twentieth-century development of the United States. Modes of play, forms for building resorts, houses, and suburbs, ways of experiencing and thinking about nature, ways of living—Southern California's frontier of leisure proved influential indeed.

This book has also aimed to demonstrate the problematic aspects of leisure alongside its potentialities. Southern California's frontier of leisure was dependent on nonwhite and noncitizen labor, and the region would remain dependent on that labor in the twenty-first century. It linked leisure with whiteness and wealth, and divided residents into two classes—the leisured and the laboring. Leisure thus became synonymous with segregation and seclusion, and those social urges would carry forward from the resorts of

Southern California to the suburbs of Sunbelt America. Charles Fletcher Lummis had urged Americans to adopt aspects of the cultures of the Southwest into a modernizing United States. The adoption of the labor system of an older and decidedly unromantic Southwest was certainly one of the most troubling aspects of Southern California's development. The fact that leisure was offered as a central allure to white newcomers but often withheld from other inhabitants of the region is perhaps its most unfortunate aspect.

This study has explored paired counterpoints in Southern California history: the booster rhetoric of leisure and its urban reality; the island of Santa Catalina and the oasis of Palm Springs; the appetite for leisure versus the need for labor. These opposites nevertheless resolve into a whole. A rhetoric of leisure helped create resorts that served as unique manifestations of leisure. That leisure, however imperfectly, was then incorporated into Los Angeles itself. The identification of Southern California with leisure was unique. Its usefulness as a tool of regional economic and demographic development was apparent. This study has attempted to elucidate its other uses as well.

Southern Californians used leisure to mediate a new relationship with nature and with regional history. They utilized it to create or popularize new styles of residential architecture, from the bungalow to Spanish revival, and from modernism to the ranch house. They constructed new urban forms such as the residential golf community, new varieties of individual, social, and family recreation, and new modes of living. As a result, Catalina and Palm Springs were far more than merely regional resorts, and the suburban landscapes of Los Angeles, Phoenix, and the Sunbelt were much more than just new housing developments. They were manifestations of how Americans in one region—and, eventually, other regions—attempted to create satisfying ways to live and play in the later nineteenth and twentieth centuries. The search for a relationship with nature and a sense of community, the desire for a useable past, and the hope for a better future—none of these are unique to Los Angeles, Southern California, the Sunbelt, or the United States. The solutions Southern Californians proposed to these universal human dilemmas were sometimes unique. This book has attempted to elucidate what those solutions were, what they meant for residents of the region, and why they often had such potent appeal far beyond the boundaries of Southern California.

---　✳　---

This book began at Disneyland, the magic kingdom constructed by Walt Disney, one of a long succession of Anglo-Americans who saw in Southern California a malleable landscape, awaiting whatever form they wished to mold it into. It concludes at another location in the tourist landscape of Southern California, Mount San Jacinto, which rises above Palm Springs. Here one can read a very different history of the region: a narrative of tradition rather than invention, and of stability despite continued change. The Agua Calientes held on in Palm Springs, fending off Anglos who tried to seize their land, water, and mountain canyons. They had also adapted to a tourist economy, albeit one that rarely paid well. By the 1970s it seemed that the tribe and its resort community had settled into stasis as a staid retiree suburb. In reality, the resort community was about to change radically, and would return to the vanguard of American leisure. The transformations in late twentieth-century Palm Springs were instigated by groups long oppressed, ignored, or rendered invisible. By the end of the century, the older social and economic order would be overturned, and Palm Springs remade, by forces resort founders Nellie Coffman or Pearl McCallum McManus could hardly have imagined. In the process, a new era was born, one in which Palm Springs would again shape national ideas about leisure. This era in Palm Springs history would be dominated by mass gay and lesbian tourism, and by Indian gaming, sanctioned by federal and state law.

The Gay Frontier of Leisure in Palm Springs

The emergence of Palm Springs as a gay tourist mecca defies easy explanation, though local history and comparisons with the history of other tourist destinations offer some possible answers to this phenomenon. The most common perception has been that gay tourism was a result of the "Hollywood effect." Gays and lesbians have been a part of filmmaking from its formative era, and bohemian Hollywood proved far more tolerant than broader society—at least for those blessed with money, talent, or physical attractiveness. Just as gay Hollywood frequented Palm Springs, so too did other homosexuals as well. F.B.I. director J. Edgar Hoover, for example, long rumored to be gay, was a regular guest at the Desert Inn in the 1940s. Like Hoover, most gays and lesbians, whether in Hollywood or elsewhere, remained firmly closeted until the last decades of the twentieth century. Many popular tourist spots—New Orleans, Key West, Las Vegas—offer an escape from usual social mores, and the anonymity of a tourist setting meant that gay and lesbian tourists could pursue social or sexual homosexual contact in Palm Springs with little fear of being discovered when they returned home. As at Catalina in the late nineteenth century, Palm Springs offered a "safe" place to engage in behavior that was not accepted or would be considered dangerous in other contexts.[4]

The growth of Palm Springs as a lesbian tourist destination does have at least one clear origin: the Dinah Shore Golf Tournament, which began in 1972. David Foster, president of Colgate-Palmolive, inaugurated the tournament as a way to reach female consumers, who were central to the company's successful product line. It also proved wildly popular with spectators and television viewers. A Colgate-Palmolive executive boasted that the Colgate Dinah Shore Winner's Circle Championship "immediately catapulted women's golf into the top ranks of big-money sports—in size of audience as well as prize money." As with Chrysler's sponsorship of the broadcast of the Bob Hope Classic, a major corporation and national television coverage further popularized the sport and the resort. Golf proved popular with many women, but perhaps especially so with many lesbians. Numerous other lesbian social events were organized around the Shore Tournament and other golf events. By the 1980s, these had become public and open, making Palm Springs' growing reputation as a friendly destination for gays and lesbians more widespread.[5]

Another possibility is that gay tourism in Palm Springs reflects broader trends in the history of tourism. Early American resorts, from Newport to Saratoga Springs, had been exclusive—limited to the wealthy and to the white. Jews were excluded, and sometimes Catholics were as well. The new resorts of the American West, from Colorado Springs to Monterey and the hotels of Pasadena and San Diego, operated on the same exclusionary model. Over time, however, these resort areas opened to a broader swath of society. Both Catalina and Palm Springs followed this general trajectory. For that matter, some subsequent tourist attractions, such as Coney Island, drew primarily a middle- and working-class clientele.

Until resorts and attractions became more welcoming, excluded groups created their own spaces of leisure. Perhaps the most famous example was the "Borscht Belt," the hotels and camps in the Catskill Mountains of New York. Wealthy WASPS retreated to the Adirondacks in summer, and, as the Jewish population of New York became more affluent, they created their own resorts in the upstate mountains. The Catskills resort region emulated many aspects of the older Adirondack resort culture, but was also influenced by Jewish culture, including vaudeville. In Los Angeles excluded groups also strove to create their own spaces of leisure, such as Val Verde, the "Black Palm Springs." Perhaps then gays and lesbians, increasingly visible, vocal, and newly appreciated as consumers, functioned as racial or ethnic groups once had. Palm Springs could therefore be understood as simply the gay-specific manifestation of a broader Southern California resort and tourist culture.[6]

While any of these theories may help explain the emergence of Palm Springs as a popular destination for gay and lesbian vacationers, they do not entirely explain one of the most striking aspects of Palm Springs after 1980—its increasing popularity as a gay residential community. This is particularly remarkable in light of the resort city's earlier history, when Palm Springs' political leaders had demonstrated a near-maniacal obsession with maintaining the residential whiteness of their community. Why would this same community prove more tolerant of gay and lesbian homeowners? Certainly, affluent gays and lesbians were able to buy houses simply because, unlike most African Americans or Mexicans, they had the money to purchase them. Money certainly would have trumped the discriminatory attitudes of some homeowners and developers. At a broader civic level, selling housing to gays and lesbians might have seemed a good investment. As Palm Springs real-estate values slumped in the 1980s, gays may have been perceived as effective agents of gentrification. The rediscovery, restoration, and burgeoning resale value of many modernist structures, from houses to stores and hotels, owed much to gays and lesbians who found modernist architecture appealing after the postmodern and increasingly historicist architecture that dominated the 1980s. The reevaluation of Palm Springs modernism spurred a strong resurgence in local real estate. In this respect, Palm Springs paralleled the trajectory of Miami Beach, where historic preservationists and real estate buyers "rediscovered" the art-deco architecture of the neighborhood prior to its resurgence as a gay-friendly tourist destination. If city leaders did indeed see selling to gays and lesbians as a canny civic investment, their decision would reap generous dividends. For that matter, many gay and lesbian tourists returned to shop for prospective houses after vacationing in Palm Springs, reflecting a pattern that went all the way back to the first California booster efforts of the 1870s aimed at vacationers who could return as new residents.[7]

There remains yet another possibility, one that resonated with Palm Springs' melancholy early history. The specter that had stalked so many of the health refugees traveling to Southern California after 1870 had been tuberculosis. This dread disease had drawn some of the first Anglo visitors to Palm Springs and would remain its primary reason for existence until World War I. As the 1980s began, a new disease became the subject of national and global fears: acquired immune deficiency syndrome, or AIDS. This viral disease, which had emerged in Africa, would decimate a generation of gay men in the United States. AIDS was incurable, and until the late 1990s no medicines were able to significantly slow its terrible progress. What medicines were available were exorbitantly expensive. For infected gay men in San Francisco—which was both the epicenter of the disease and one of the nation's most expensive housing markets—or in Los Angeles or other cities, options were limited. One choice, an increasingly popular one as infected patients began to live longer after diagnosis, was for them to sell their homes and move somewhere less expensive, where savings would allow them to live independently and with some degree of dignity for as long as possible.

Palm Springs became a common destination for these AIDS sufferers. Here they could live in a balmy climate that might prove comforting. They could inhabit a community that was increasingly open to them, with an existing network of gay organizations and charities that offered assistance. They could also live as gay men in a community of gays and lesbians, enjoying a level of social and psychological support that would be rare elsewhere. Palm Springs had entered the twentieth century as an oasis of refuge for the ailing. Despite all the changes that remade it, it left the century as a health oasis again.

Indian Gaming and the Agua Calientes Ascendant in Palm Springs

It is difficult to imagine a transformation more striking than that of the Agua Calientes over the course of the twentieth century. They had entered the century as a small band centered on the oasis at the center of their patchwork of tribal landholdings. Unlike the Tongva at Santa Catalina, they managed to hold on to most of their land, despite the designs of irrigationists, national-monument proponents, and real-estate developers. After their removal, the Tongva reasserted their presence in the late twentieth century by recreating their ocean-going heritage and participating in archaeological projects on Catalina. The Agua Calientes had remained at their oasis without such disruption and attempted the transition to a tourist economy. They charged admission to bathe in their spring and to hike in their palm canyons. They took work at resorts, hotels, and restaurants. Despite the highly problematic way it was administered, leasing and equalization of land claims gradually provided revenue for tribal members. Certainly, the Agua Calientes, whether at the Spa Hotel or elsewhere, played a highly visible role in Palm Springs, one unlike that at any other contemporary resort. Obviously Anglo-American tourists encountered Native Americans when traveling on the Navajo Reservation or at some national parks. Perhaps only Santa Fe offered a comparable urban tourist setting where Indians played such a prominent role in the tourist experience. The fact remained, however, that the Agua Calientes, like Native Americans at other tourist sites who provided craft goods, labor, or "atmosphere," unfortunately usually played the part of characters in a play written by someone else.

All this changed in the late twentieth century due to a confluence of events in the Coachella Valley, in California, and across the nation. In Palm Springs, white city officials had tried to assert municipal control over Indian lands. While not entirely successful in gaining official recognition of municipal authority, those efforts nevertheless resulted in the "ethnic cleansing" of Section 14, the contested square mile of reservation land at the heart of the resort community. The state of California sometimes pursued tactics similar to those of the city of Palm Springs. Intense lobbying from the state ensured passage of a congressional law in 1955 that granted the California state government criminal jurisdiction over Indian reservations. Beginning in the 1950s, in the pursuit of assimilation, the U.S. Congress adopted a policy of "termination." In a series of acts, tribes were stripped of their federal status, and their reservations divided up among tribal members. In 1958 Congress passed the California Rancheria Act, which stripped federal recognition from approximately forty tribal groups and reservations in California.[8]

While the state and federal governments moved toward increased control of Indian lands—and their dispersal to white purchasers—events elsewhere in the nation were moving along a different track. In the 1976 case *Bryan v. Itasca County*, the U.S. Supreme Court affirmed that states did have criminal and civil jurisdiction over Indian tribes, but not regulatory jurisdiction. In 1979 a Florida court in the case of *Seminole Tribe v. Butterworth* applied the Supreme Court's 1976 decision to Indian bingo. According to this ruling, the state had no authority to prohibit Indian gaming. The national ruling that would indicate the full implications of this legal interpretation would come a decade later—and originate in a case concerning tribal lands of other Cahuillas near those of the Agua Calientes. The state of California sued to stop gaming in the form of bingo and poker on the Cabazon Reservation, located in the San Gorgonio Pass at the northwestern end of the Coachella Valley. The U.S. Supreme Court sided with the tribe, agreeing that regulatory authority, including the regulation of gaming on tribal lands, was a matter of tribal rather than state jurisdiction.

As a result, the 1987 case of *California v. Cabazon Band of Mission Indians* paved the way for gaming on Indian land. The following year Congress passed the Indian Gaming Regulatory Act, which formalized federal regulation of Indian gaming and created three classes of games. "Class I" gaming consisted of traditional forms of Indian gaming and social gaming for winnings of minimal value. "Class II" gaming consisted of bingo and similar games. "Class III" gaming included Las Vegas–style forms such as slot machines, casino games, and the racing of dogs or horses. Only this last category could be regulated by states, as tribes and states would have to enter into mutually agreed compacts for Class III gaming to take place.[9]

Initially, the state of California tried to maintain a firm grip on casino gaming. This was exemplified by the 1998 Pala Compact, backed by Governor Pete Wilson, which permitted some casino games, but only if the Pala tribe of San Diego County agreed to a substantial increase in state oversight. This, critics feared, would reduce reservations to the status of "quasi-municipalities." For other tribes, the choice was clear—sign compacts and keep gaming, but only at the expense of lost sovereignty, or keep sovereignty—and lose the gaming that provided tribal income.[10]

The response of other California tribes was immediate. They decided to campaign for a statewide proposition, the Tribal Government Gaming and Economic Self-Sufficiency Act. Collecting signatures proved easy, and what became known as Proposition 5 easily won approval in the elections of November 1998, despite opposition advertisements funded by Nevada casino interests. The California Supreme Court, however, subsequently ruled the ballot initiative unconstitutional in a case brought by the AFL-CIO. Labor unions already had a rocky relationship with Indian gaming operations, which were not subject to federal labor laws, and this lawsuit did not bode well for the future. In September 1999, fifty-eight tribes signed gaming compacts with the state of California. These compacts, negotiated by Governor Gray Davis, were far more generous than those offered by his predecessor. Tribes could operate slot machines and offer casino card games and gambling, but would have to abide by limitations on the number of slot machines, share revenues with the state, and meet environmental and labor requirements. Critics assailed the compacts as far too lenient.[11]

The Agua Calientes had decided to follow their own course during this process. Even before the California Supreme Court ruled Proposition 5 unconstitutional, the tribe had begun to collect signatures for a new proposition for the April 2000 elections—one that would amend the state constitution to allow Indian gaming on Indian terms. The prospect of voter approval of this proposition was credited with Governor Davis's willingness to expand gaming and the types of gaming offered at Indian casinos in an effort to circumvent another proposition. The Agua Calientes eventually signed a compact as well, and the state legislature approved a new constitutional amendment to be placed on the April 2000 ballot. This was Proposition 1A, Gambling on Tribal Lands.[12]

Tribal representatives from across the state gathered in Palm Springs to plan their electoral strategy. The previous proposition had passed easily, but that had been in a general election. This would instead be a primary, with a smaller number of voters. Those voters were likely to be older and whiter than in a general election. They were also more likely to be conservative Christians, drawn to the polls to support a ballot measure banning gay marriage in the state. Las Vegas casinos, however, did not bankroll an opposition ad campaign this time. For that matter, the California Republican Party endorsed the gaming proposition. The measure passed by an even larger margin than the previous measure. Perceptions of Indian gaming were strongly positive among every major demographic group polled in the state.[13]

The passage of Proposition 1A transformed Indian gaming in California, and in the process Palm Springs and the Coachella Valley. The Agua Calientes operated two casinos in the vicinity. In addition to a casino in Rancho Mirage, their flagship was the Spa Resort Casino, an $85 million

Spanish-revival behemoth built near the refurbished Spa Hotel and opened in November of 2003. The tribal Web site boasted of the transformations the casinos had wrought: "Before the Agua Caliente Band of Cahuilla Indians opened their first casino in a tent next to the Spa Resort Hotel in Palm Springs, the Tribe was unable to even qualify for a credit card at Kmart. Now...the Tribe has a hotel, two casinos, a golf resort, and another hotel under construction.[14] Other tribes also constructed or expanded existing gaming facilities in the Coachella Valley. These included the Morongo Band of Mission Indians' Casa Morongo at Cabazon, the Fantasy Springs Casino operated at Indio by the Cabazon Band of Mission Indians, and the Augustine Casino, operated at Coachella by the Augustine Band of Mission Indians. The Agua Calientes, however, had become the dominant gaming force in the region and one of the most visible—and vocal—tribes in the state. Indian gaming spread in other states as well. By 2008 Indian gaming produced revenues of $25 billion nationwide, dwarfing the $12 billion in gaming revenues generated by Las Vegas. After initially fighting the expansion of Indian gaming, Las Vegas casino companies decided cooperation was more profitable and entered into partnerships and casino-managing agreements with various tribes.[15]

With power and wealth for their four hundred members came scrutiny and criticism for the Agua Calientes and other gaming tribes. Some accused tribes of behaving like moneyed special interests, and the role of tribal money was a source of contention in the gubernatorial recall campaign of 2003 that resulted in the removal of Governor Gray Davis and his replacement with actor Arnold Schwarzenegger. The Agua Calientes, like other tribes, were accused of flouting environmental laws. The issue of labor and unionization proved especially contentious in the Agua Calientes' two casinos. While some tribes allowed the unionization of casino workers, the Agua Calientes, led by tribal chairman Richard Milanovich, a staunch Republican, did not. They were also accused of paying their predominantly Mexican and Latino workforce poorly. These and other charges angered some liberals and progressives who had once supported Indian gaming. One particularly caustic article published in the months after the opening of the Spa Resort Casino was entitled "Bury My Heart at Agua Caliente."[16]

Gays and lesbians, newly empowered and numerous, suffered some bad press as well. The "White Party," which began as a social gathering for gay men in 1989, had evolved into a sprawling weekend-long festival by the late 1990s, annually drawing more than twenty-five thousand attendees. This party, often held on Easter weekends, also witnessed a number of overdoses from illegal drugs and other behavior that drew police scrutiny and community criticism. An effort to end the White Party, however, resulted in a voter backlash that forced out the incumbent city government and witnessed the election of openly gay and African American city councilman Ron Oden as mayor of Palm Springs in 2003.[17]

Oden's election warranted national and international press coverage. Regardless of his sexual orientation, Oden was in many ways representative of Southern Californians. He had been born in Detroit and grew up in the San Fernando Valley after his parents relocated to Southern California. He came to Palm Springs in 1989 after divorcing his wife. He immediately felt that the desert landscape was home—here he could be himself and recover from the emotional turmoil of his past life. This same sense of rejuvenation and freedom had enthralled Charles Lummis when he first arrived in the Southwest a century earlier, just as it had many other migrants to the region. Oden also proved to be an avid booster of tourism and economic and community development, like so many Southern Californian business and political figures before him.

Yet Oden's election was significant in a city and region with such a troubled history of race, labor, and class relations. It did signal a true change, and Oden seemed to recognize this fact. At his inauguration, he did something no previous Palm Springs mayor had ever done—he invited the tribal chairman of the Agua Calientes, Richard Milanovich, to share the stage with him. The two men standing together, one Native American, the other African American and gay, now politically and economically the most influential figures in Palm Springs, reflected how radically the society, culture, and power structure of the community had changed. Gay tourists and residents and the Agua Calientes may not have understood each other as individuals with much in common. Yet both groups profited from the unforeseen consequences of Southern California's frontier of leisure.[18]

In Palm Springs, as at other resort communities, fights over land, labor, and acceptable tourist behavior were nothing new. Newly flush with revenue, their tribal sovereignty reaffirmed by the courts and popular opinion, the Agua Calientes now possessed the power to shape the future of Palm Springs. The appearance of downtown, the density and characteristics of future housing developments, the role gaming would play in the resort's future—these were all things that once would have been determined solely by an Anglo-American elite, but would now be decided in a substantial way by Native Americans. Not perhaps since the 1920s, when the formidable Nellie Coffman and Pearl McCallum McManus operated the Desert Inn and Oasis Hotel, had anyone held comparable power to shape the future of the resort town.

Of course, Palm Springs in the early twenty-first century was a profoundly different place from what it had been a lifetime before. It was now a small city of more than 42,000 in a desert valley filled with other resort communities and a resident population of nearly 280,000. Yet the Agua Calientes could now essentially dictate terms to whites on reservation land, just as whites so often had to them. The monthly payments for land leases were raised dramatically, forcing out some white homeowners. The new Spa Resort Casino was constructed as the tribe desired, flouting some city zoning laws. The casino lay in Section 14, and the Agua Calientes could build the structure however they wished. Some whites fretted that the town was destined to become another Las Vegas, losing the charm of a small resort. Casino employees complained about wages and the lack of affordable insurance for dependents, which had become so costly that some had been reduced to using medical welfare programs.[19]

Many Agua Calientes responded to such criticism with disdain. They had been ignored, oppressed, and dispossessed by whites for decades. Now that they had money and power, whites, who had ignored them when they were poor and weak, found them a threat. It is perhaps unfair to expect that the newly empowered Agua Calientes would behave as model business proprietors or as the collective embodiment of an "ecological Indian" stereotype invented by whites. Whatever the nature of their actions, the irony of Indians being accused of the sort of tactics once leveled against the Santa Catalina Island Company under the Bannings and Wrigleys was rich indeed. The "Golden Checkerboard" of Palm Springs and the Coachella Valley had proven golden once more. After more than a century of Anglo-American boosterism, however, it had finally proven golden for its original inhabitants.[20]

In addition to their new casinos, the Agua Calientes began planning an imposing new museum in Section 14, near their hotel and flagship casino. Their original Agua Caliente Cultural Museum was located next to the Palm Springs Historical Society, which was housed in the relocated and restored McCallum adobe. Both would be dwarfed by this new edifice, which would showcase the history and culture of the Agua Calientes. The new building design, created by the same lead architect who had overseen the construction of the National Museum of the American Indian in Washington, DC, was intended to evoke Agua Caliente basketry and pottery, and to blend into the surrounding desert landscape. The museum could also tout its status as an official affiliate of the Smithsonian Institution. Certainly this new facility will be a tourist attraction and a source of pride for tribal members. Yet the museum will serve another function, one suited to Southern California's complex past. Though only a small group in a vast urbanized region, the Agua Caliente's museum and tribal revenues will allow them to play a role in the future shaping of Southern California and the region's shared history.[21]

Since the late nineteenth century, whites had used Indians as characters in a regional narrative. This narrative presented Indians, like Mexican Americans, as relics of the past divorced from the unpleasant history of the Anglo-American annexation of California and the lingering tensions of a border region. To be sure, these "relics" might have useful attributes that whites could adapt, but they almost always remained fundamentally part of the past, markers of how far Anglo California had traveled since the days of the missions. Later, during World War II and after, Los Angeles was transformed from a regional city to a national and international one, and this growth included the development of a restive underclass. This social discontent engendered a new narrative, one that largely eschewed the historic "quaintness" of Indians or Mexican Americans and instead presented them as nonthreatening—assimilated, modern, and amenable.

Cast against this Anglo-American narrative were other narratives. Some were simply narratives of survival, such as those constructed by Native Americans across the Southwest who adapted their crafts to access an emergent cash economy, Santa Catalina fishermen who became sportfishing guides, or Agua Calientes who used knowledge of their land and its flora and fauna to serve as tour guides. Still others, such as the del Valles, who had entranced Charles Lummis and claimed a prominent role in the mythology of *Ramona* and the Mission Play, constructed another narrative—one that strengthened their claim on the past, but also asserted a role in the present. The del Valles had indeed survived and sometimes even prospered. The new Agua Caliente Museum was a twenty-first-century heir to the del Valle strategy, albeit one created by a group with far more wealth and political clout.

The boosters of Southern California had relentlessly themed the region as a health resort, a respite from urbanism, and a frontier of leisure. They had achieved this by utilizing the landscapes and cultures of Southern California, repackaged and sold for the consumption of tourists and new residents. They had recast Southern California as a new realm of leisure for white Americans, and the houses, recreational areas, and resorts they had created all reflected this race-based recreation. This process had been adopted at resorts such as Catalina, where the Bannings and Wrigleys gave boosterism architectural form. It also appeared in Palm Springs, and would be used again with great success at Disneyland. What was new, however, was the identity of those now utilizing those techniques to remake a tourist locale in Southern California, as well as the larger identity and history of the region. Is it possible that in the foreseeable future large swaths of Palm Springs may be architecturally refashioned and rethemed in a Native American mold? Design plans undertaken by the tribe to redevelop and rejuvenate Section 14 suggest just such a possibility. Instead of a saga of breathless change, the Agua Calientes will tell the story of Palm Springs as one of continuity and survival, using techniques that are hallowed regional traditions. The fact that they are now being employed by Native Americans attests to how profoundly Southern California has changed since the 1870s, and how far removed it is from the place Anglo-Americans thought they had found so long ago.[22]

Notes

INTRODUCTION

1. For examples of the range of perspectives on the history and significance of Disneyland, see John M. Findlay, *Magic Lands: Western Cityscapes and American Culture after 1940* (Berkeley: University of California Press, 1992); Eric Avila, *Popular Culture in the Age of White Flight: Fear and Fantasy in Suburban Los Angeles* (Berkeley: University of California Press, 2004); Michael Steiner, "Frontierland as Tomorrowland: Walt Disney and the Architectural Packaging of the Mythic West," *Montana: The Magazine of Western History* 48, no. 1 (Spring 1998): 2–17; Richard Francaviglia, "Walt Disney's Frontierland as an Allegorical Map of the American West," *Western Historical Quarterly* 30, no. 2 (Summer 1999): 155–82; Karal Ann Marling, ed., *Designing Disney's Theme Parks: The Architecture of Reassurance* (Montreal: Canadian Centre for Architecture, 1997); and Lynn Y. Weiner, "'There's a Great Big Beautiful Tomorrow': Historic Memory and Gender in Walt Disney's 'Carousel of Progress,'" *Journal of American Culture* 20, no. 1 (Spring 1999): 111–16. The Carousel of Progress was added to Tomorrowland after its debut at the New York World's Fair of 1964.

2. The evolving promotion of Southern California is traced in Clark Davis, "From Oasis to Metropolis: Southern California and the Changing Context of American Leisure," *Pacific Historical Review* 61, no. 3 (May 1992): 357–86.

3. A motley band of Southern Californians actually occupied Baja California border communities in 1910 and 1911, and Anglos looted Tijuana. See D. W. Meinig, *The Shaping of America: A Geographical Perspective on 500 Years of History*, vol. 3, *Transcontinental America, 1850–1915* (New Haven, CT: Yale University Press, 1998), 66.

4. The best study of regional promotion in this era is David Wrobel, *Promised Lands: Promotion, Memory, and the Creation of the American West* (Lawrence: University Press of Kansas, 2002).

5. "Population, County of Los Angeles," in Leonard Pitt and Dale Pitt, *Los Angeles A to Z: An Encyclopedia of the City and County* (Berkeley: University of California Press, 1997), 403.

6. The volumes of Kevin Starr's *Americans and the California Dream* series most relevant to this book are *Americans and the California Dream, 1850–1915* (New York: Oxford University Press, 1973); *Inventing the Dream: California through the Progressive Era* (New York: Oxford University Press, 1985); *Material Dreams: Southern California through the 1920s* (New York: Oxford University Press, 1990), and *Golden Dreams: California in an Age of Abundance, 1950–1963* (New York: Oxford University Press, 2009). Mike Davis acknowledges this sunshine/noir dichotomy in his *City of Quartz: Excavating the Future in Los Angeles* (New York: Verso, 1990) and *Ecology of Fear: Los Angeles and the Imagination of Disaster* (New York: Metropolitan, 1998).

7. Conceptualizing, contextualizing, and historicizing Los Angeles and California proved a popular activity at the end of the twentieth century and the beginning of the twenty-first, as the state observed the sesquicentennial of the Gold Rush and statehood. For example, see the "Historicizing the City of Angels" review essays published in the *American Historical Review* in 2000: Robert A. Schneider, "The Postmodern City from an Early Modern Perspective," *American Historical Review* 105, no. 5 (December 2000): 1668–75; Michael E. Engh, SJ, "At Home in the Heteropolis: Understanding Postmodern L.A.," *American Historical Review* 105, no. 5 (December 2000): 1676–82; and Catherine Coquery-Vidrovich, "Is L.A. a Model or a Mess?," *American Historical Review* 105, no. 5

(December 2000): 1683–91. Melody Graulich, ed., "California Dreaming," special issue, *Western American Literature* 34, no. 2 (Summer 1999) also provides a variety of literary and personal perspectives on the history of the state and city.

8. Carey McWilliams, *Southern California: An Island on the Land* (Santa Barbara, CA: Peregrine Smith, 1973), 377.

9. A signature compilation of this school is Allen J. Scott and Edward W. Soja, eds., *The City: Los Angeles and Urban Theory at the End of the Twentieth Century* (Berkeley: University of California Press, 1996).

10. Elaine Tyler May, *Great Expectations: Marriage and Divorce in Post-Victorian America* (Chicago: University of Chicago Press, 1980). William Leach presents mass consumerism as a transformative late-nineteenth-century event in *Land of Desire: Merchants, Power, and the Rise of a New American Culture* (New York: Pantheon, 1993); and Jackson Lears presents the same era as a key moment in *Fables of Abundance: A Cultural History of Advertising in America* (New York: Basic, 1994). For a longer historical perspective of consumerism, see Richard L. Bushman, *The Refinement of America: Persons, Houses, Cities* (New York: Knopf, 1992). For modernism and its relationship to the rise of Los Angeles, see David Alan Karnes, "Modern Metropolis: Mass Culture and the Transformation of Los Angeles, 1890–1950" (PhD diss., University of California, Berkeley, 1991). Works that have informed my own view of modernism and the emergence of modern thought, culture, and society include Marshall Berman, *All That Is Solid Melts Into Air: The Experience of Modernity* (New York: Simon and Schuster, 1982); and Stephen Kern, *The Culture of Time and Space, 1880–1918* (Cambridge, MA: Harvard University Press, 1983); as well as Carl E. Schorske's works *Fin-de-Siècle Vienna: Politics and Culture* (New York: Vintage, 1981); and *Thinking With History: Explorations in the Passage to Modernism* (Princeton: Princeton University Press, 1998), which eloquently attest to the complexity of "modernity."

11. Loren Baritz, *The Good Life: The Meaning of Success for the American Middle Class* (New York: Alfred A. Knopf, 1989), 96.

12. Lary May, *Screening Out the Past: The Birth of Mass Culture and the Motion Picture Industry* (New York: Oxford University Press, 1980). May asserts that Hollywood transformed the old frontier into a new one of creativity, and made living in Los Angeles a permanent vacation, with celebrities becoming "leisure experts" instructing the rest of America how to embrace leisure—and how to enjoy it "correctly." See also Neal Gabler, *An Empire of Their Own: How the Jews Invented Hollywood* (New York: Doubleday, 1989); and Richard Schickel, *D. W. Griffith: An American Life* (New York: Simon and Schuster, 1984); as well as Dona Polan, "California Through the Lens of Hollywood," and Norman M. Klein, "Gold Fevers: Global L.A. and the Noir Imaginary," both in *Reading California: Art, Image, and Identity, 1900–2000*, ed. Stephanie Barron, Sheri Bernstein, and Ilene Susan Fort (Los Angeles: Los Angeles County Museum of Art and University of California Press, 2000), 129–52 and 389–409.

13. McWilliams, *Southern California*, 8.

14. See Douglas Monroy, *Thrown Among Strangers: The Making of Mexican Culture in Frontier California* (Berkeley: University of California, 1990); Lisbeth Haas, *Conquests and Historical Identities in California, 1769–1936* (Berkeley: University of California Press, 1995); and Ramón Gutiérrez and Richard J. Orsi, eds., *Contested Eden: California before the Gold Rush* (Berkeley: University of California Press, 1998) for historical perspectives on Los Angeles and Southern California before U.S. annexation, and continuities connecting the Spanish, Mexican, and U.S. eras. William Deverell's *Whitewashed Adobe: The Rise of Los Angeles and the Remaking of Its Mexican Past* (Berkeley: University of California Press, 2004) is particularly relevant for this subject.

15. Eric Hobsbawm, *The Age of Capital, 1848–1875* (New York: Vintage, 1996); Denis E. Cosgrove, *Social Formation and Symbolic Landscape* (Totowa, NJ: Barnes and Noble, 1985).

16. Thorstein Veblen, *The Theory of the Leisure Class: An Economic Study in the Evolution of Institutions* (New York: MacMillan, 1899). One example of this often grim view of tourism is Hal K. Rothman's *Devil's Bargains: Tourism in the Twentieth-Century American West* (Lawrence: University Press of Kansas, 1998). Some other works suggest ways to move beyond solely a critique of tourism to a broader understanding of recreational leisure and tourist promotion. These include Findlay, *Magic Lands*; David M. Wrobel, *Promised Lands: Promotion, Memory, and the Creation of the American West* (Lawrence: University Press of Kansas, 2002); Dona Brown, *Inventing New England: Regional Tourism in the Nineteenth Century* (Washington, DC: Smithsonian Institution Press, 1995); and Cindy S. Aron, *Working at Play: A History of Vacations in the United States* (New York: Oxford University Press, 1999).

17. A few historians have already shown the potential of studies that consider leisure's possibilities rather than merely its costs. Lizabeth Cohen's *Making a New Deal: Industrial Workers in Chicago, 1919–1939* (Cambridge, UK: Cambridge University Press, 1990) demonstrates that working-class people could experience leisure in the form of consumption of mass-cultural products such as film and radio, yet not lose their ethnic, racial, or working-class identity in the process. Roy Rosenzweig, *Eight Hours for What We Will: Workers and Leisure in an Industrial City, 1870–1920* (Cambridge, UK: Cambridge University Press, 1983) utilizes resident recreational leisure to analyze middle- and working-class social development in Worcester, Massachusetts. His emphasis on the leisure of nonaffluent residents, rather than vacationists, allows him to avoid the social criticism that seems to overtake so many studies of tourism. Two studies of Southern California offer particular insights about the usefulness of leisure as a subject of analysis. Matt Garcia, *A World of Its Own: Race, Labor, and Citrus in the Making of Greater Los Angeles, 1900–1970* (Chapel Hill: University of North Carolina Press, 2001) documents the racial and class inequalities of citrus agriculture, yet demonstrates that leisure in the form of social events at dance halls and regional theater productions provided opportunities for interaction across race and class lines. Becky Nicolaides, *My Blue Heaven: Life and Politics in the Working-Class Suburbs of Los Angeles, 1920–1965* (Chicago: University of Chicago Press, 2002) offers insights into the role recreation and leisure played in community formation and identity among working-class whites in Los Angeles.

18. Arguably the two American cities with histories most akin to that of Los Angeles—at least as places developed through tourism—are Miami and Las Vegas. Miami certainly promoted its balmy climate and "Spanish" atmosphere; its development as a tourist destination nevertheless began later than Los Angeles's, and did not precipitate an equivalent amount of urban growth. While Spanish Revival hotels opened in St. Augustine in the 1880s, Spanish Revival architecture would not find favor in Miami until after World War I. Though obviously important to the history of American leisure, Florida also lacked Hollywood, and film promoted Los Angeles, its resort culture, and its residential and recreational modes of living to an unrivaled degree. The ultimate proof of this fact may well be the creation of Walt Disney World near Orlando, which effectively imported Southern California tourism to Florida. For comparative analyses of Los Angeles and Miami, see William Deverell, Greg Hise, and David C. Sloane, eds., "Orange Empires," special issue, *Pacific Historical Review* 68, no. 2 (May 1999). David J. Weber analyzes the spread of Spanish Revival as an architectural and cultural phenomenon in Southern California, Florida, and elsewhere in "The Spanish Legacy," in *The Spanish Frontier in North America* (New Haven, CT: Yale University Press, 1992), 335–60. Las Vegas emerged as a travel destination well after Miami, and did not evolve into a large metropolitan area until the late twentieth century. Though it unquestionably became a trendsetter for American tourism, Las Vegas began as an outlet for the recreational appetites of Southern California, and arguably functioned primarily as a

recreational suburb of Los Angeles for decades before drawing a truly national audience. See Eugene P. Moehring, *Resort City in the Sunbelt: Las Vegas, 1930–2000*, 2d ed. (Reno: University of Nevada Press, 2000); and Hal Rothman, *Neon Metropolis: How Las Vegas Started the Twenty-First Century* (New York: Routledge, 2002).

19. Mary P. Ryan, *Civic Wars: Democracy and Public Life in the American City during the Nineteenth Century* (Berkeley: University of California Press, 1997) offers a useful analysis of urban public spaces. For a broad, though dated, history of American recreation, see Foster Rhea Dulles, *A History of Recreation: America Learns to Play*, 2d ed. (New York: Appleton-Century-Crofts, 1965).

20. It is important to state at the outset of a book that considers issues of race and ethnicity that there are no entirely satisfactory terms available to describe the identity of the "Anglo" and "Latino" residents of Southern California. Many English-speaking whites are not of English descent, and therefore not "Anglo." Neither is "white" useful, as many Mexicans and Latin Americans of predominantly European descent are also "white." "Hispanic" is considered inappropriate by some people of Native American, mestizo, and mulatto ancestry. "Latino" is commonly used to describe all the Spanish- and Portuguese-speaking inhabitants of the Americas, though some people of Mexican origin or descent prefer to be called Chicana/o, while others consider themselves Mexican Americans. None of these terms, however, were in common usage for much of the era covered by this book, and all, to some degree, describe more recent ethnic identities. Spanish-speaking inhabitants of nineteenth-century California called themselves Californios, while the inhabitants of New Mexico often referred to themselves as Hispanos. Here I generally use those regional names when discussing the nineteenth century, and "Mexicans" when discussing both Mexican Americans and Mexican immigrants in the twentieth century.

21. The concept of an "island community" is elaborated in Robert H. Wiebe, *The Search for Order, 1877–1920* (New York: Hill and Wang, 1967). For an analysis of eastern antimodernism, see T. J. Jackson Lears, *No Place of Grace: Antimodernism and the Transformation of American Culture, 1880–1920* (New York: Pantheon, 1981).

22. William Cronon, *Nature's Metropolis: Chicago and the Great West* (New York: W. W. Norton, 1991). Racial conflict over natural resources was sometimes also a facet of the Conservation movement. See Louis Warren, *The Hunter's Game: Poachers and Conservationists in Twentieth-Century America* (New Haven: Yale University Press, 1999); and Karl Jacoby, *Crimes Against Nature: Squatters, Poachers, Thieves, and the Hidden History of American Conservation* (Berkeley: University of California Press, 2001).

23. The standard, elite-oriented history of American environmental thought is Roderick Nash, *Wilderness and the American Mind*, 4th ed. (New Haven, CT: Yale University Press, 2001). A helpful corrective to this view that considers popular culture is Jennifer Price, *Flight Maps: Adventures with Nature in Modern America* (New York: Basic Books, 1999).

24. Greg Hise examines how planning decisions of the past continue to influence the city of the present in *Magnetic Los Angeles: Planning the Twentieth-Century Metropolis* (Baltimore: Johns Hopkins Press, 1997). Carol O'Connor places the development of Los Angeles into a regional context in "A Region of Cities," in *The Oxford History of the American West*, ed. Clyde A. Milner II, Carol A. O'Connor, and Martha A. Sandweiss (New York: Oxford University Press, 1994), 535–63.

25. The standard history of American suburbia is Kenneth T. Jackson, *Crabgrass Frontier: The Suburbanization of the United States* (New York: Oxford University Press, 1985). Robert Fishman traces the rise of suburbia in Britain and the U.S., and its problematic culmination in Los Angeles, in *Bourgeois Utopias: The Rise and Fall of Suburbia* (New York: Basic Books, 1987).

26. Though I do not always agree with his conclusions, Lewis Mumford's *The City in History: Its Origins, its Transformations, and its Prospects* (New York: Harcourt, Brace & World, 1961) is an excellent overview of the long history of suburbs in human history. For more recent examinations of suburbs, see Kevin M. Kruse and Thomas J. Sugrue, eds., *The New Suburban History* (Chicago: University of Chicago Press, 2006); and Mary Corbin Sies, "North American Suburbs, 1880–1950: Cultural and Social Reconsiderations," *Journal of Urban History* 27, no. 3 (March 2001): 313–46.

CHAPTER 1

1. Charles F. Lummis, *A Tramp across the Continent* (New York: Charles Scribner's Sons, 1892; repr., Lincoln: University of Nebraska Press, 1982), 269. Cajon Pass remains a primary route into Southern California, as it was subsequently traversed by Interstate 15, connecting Southern California and Las Vegas.

2. Richard Henry Dana, *Two Years before the Mast and Twenty-Four Years After* (New York: P. F. Collier and Son, 1937), 170.

3. Amy S. Greenberg, "Domesticating the Border: Manifest Destiny and the 'Comforts of Life' in the U.S.-Mexico Boundary Commission and Gadsden Purchase, 1848–1854," in *Land of Necessity: Consumer Culture in the United States–Mexico Borderlands*, ed. Alexis McCrossen (Durham, NC: Duke University Press, 2009), 83–112.

4. D. W. Meinig, *The Shaping of America: A Geographical Perspective on 500 Years of History*, vol. 3, *Transcontinental America, 1850–1915* (New Haven, CT: Yale University Press, 1998), 116, 119.

5. Samuel Bowles, *Our New West: Records of Travel Between the Mississippi River and Pacific Ocean* (Hartford, CT: Hartford Publishing Company, 1869), 362. Bowles's earlier travel account bypassed the region entirely, sailing past Southern California and instead landing at Acapulco, where he brooded upon the "pitiful civilization" and "mulattoish race" of Mexico; see Samuel Bowles, *Across the Continent: A Summer's Journey to the Rocky Mountains, the Mormons, and the Pacific States* (Springfield, MA: Samuel Bowles, 1865), 374; George A. Crofutt, *Crofutt's New Overland Tourist and Pacific Coast Guide*, vol. 1 (Chicago: Overland, 1878), 245.

6. Charles Nordhoff, *California: For Health, Pleasure, and Residence: A Book for Travellers and Settlers* (New York: Harper and Brothers, 1873), 18.

7. Ibid., 11. See also John E. Baur, "Charles Nordhoff, Publicist Par Excellence," *Ventura County Historical Society Quarterly* 19 (Summer 1974); John E. Baur, *The Health Seekers of Southern California, 1870–1900* (San Marino, CA: Huntington Library, 1959); Judith W. Elias, *Los Angeles: Dream to Reality, 1885–1915* (Los Angeles: Santa Susana Press and California State University, Northridge Libraries, 1983), and Norman M. Klein, "The Sunshine Strategy: Buying and Selling the Fantasy of Los Angeles," in *20th Century Los Angeles: Power, Promotion, and Social Conflict*, ed. Norman M. Klein and Martin J. Schiesl (Claremont, CA: Regina, 1990), 1–38.

8. Nordhoff, *California*, 137–39, 155–56. Wilson's Indian agent report is reprinted in John Walton Caughey, ed., *The Indians of Southern California in 1852* (San Marino, CA: Huntington Library, 1952), 21–23.

9. J. M. Guinn, "Early California Industries that Failed," *Out West*, May 1908, 418–19. For a broader discussion of intersections between the antebellum South and the West, see Henry Nash Smith, *Virgin Land: The American West as Symbol and Myth* (Cambridge, MA: Harvard University Press, 1950).

10. *Nation*, December 5, 1872, 369; Baur, "Charles Nordhoff," 6; Lawrence Clark Powell, *California Classics: The Creative Literature of the Golden State* (Los Angeles: W. Ritchie, 1971), 19.

11. P. C. Remondino, *The Mediterranean Shores of America: Southern California; Its Climatic, Physical, and Meteorological Conditions* (Philadelphia: F. A. Davis, 1892); Charles Dudley Warner, *Our Italy* (New York: Harper & Brothers, 1902), 147. Matt Garcia discusses the promotion and development of what he terms the "ideal country life" in *A World of its Own: Race, Labor, and Citrus in the Making of Greater Los Angeles, 1900–1970* (Chapel Hill: University of North Carolina Press, 2001). Douglas Cazaux Sackman links the promotion and development of California to the citrus industry in *Orange Empire: California and the Fruits of Eden* (Berkeley: University of California Press, 2005).

12. Baur, *Health Seekers*, ix.

13. For the history of eastern resorts, see Theodore Corbett, *The Making of American Resorts: Saratoga Springs, Ballston Spa, Lake George* (New Brunswick, NJ: Rutgers University Press, 2000); and Jon Sterngass, *First Resorts: Pursuing Pleasure at Saratoga Springs, Newport, and Coney Island* (Baltimore: Johns Hopkins University Press, 2001). Ronald G. Pisano provides an insightful collection of artistic representations of late Victorian eastern leisure in *Idle Hours: Americans at Leisure, 1865–1914* (Boston: Little, Brown, 1988).

14. Santa Barbara's Arlington Hotel and early tourism history is examined in Kathryn M. Lang, "From Refuge to Resort: Tourism and Recreation, 1870s–1920s" in Rochelle Bookspan, ed., *Santa Barbara by the Sea* (Santa Barbara, CA: McNally and Loftin, West, 1982), 164–184. For promotional materials advertising the Mission Inn, see the series of pamphlets in the Ephemera Collection, Seaver Center for Western History Research, Natural History Museum of Los Angeles County, Los Angeles. For a discussion of Miller's career, see Zona Gale, *Frank Miller of Mission Inn* (New York: D. Appleton-Century, 1938).

15. Elias, *Los Angeles*, 4. For an example of how the new Raymond Hotel was promoted to prospective tourists, see "The Raymond and its Surroundings," pamphlet, ca.1886, Ephemera Collection, Seaver Center.

16. Amy T. Bridges, "Journal Kept on Fourth Raymond Excursion from Massachusetts to California," 22 May 1882, Manuscripts Collection, Huntington Library, San Marino, California. It should be noted that due to irregular capitalization and poorly defined punctuation marks, it is difficult to tell the difference between commas, periods, and dashes in these journals. In addition, some entries were written days or weeks after the events they describe. Other entries appear to have been written over several days, although they are dated only once.

17. Amy T. Bridges, "Journal Kept on a Raymond Excursion from Massachusetts to California and Return, Including a Three-Month Stay at the Raymond Hotel in South Pasadena, the Del Monte Hotel, and San Francisco, Etc," 21 December 1886–16 February 1887 passim., Manuscripts Collection, Huntington Library.

18. Ibid., 21 December 1886.

19. Ibid., 16 February 1887.

20. Ibid., 12 February, 3 March 1887; Meinig, *The Shaping of America*, 3:51; Frances S. Borton, "Handbook of the Glenwood Mission Inn," Ephemera Collection, Seaver Center; Gale, *Frank Miller of Mission Inn*.

21. Borton, "Handbook of the Glenwood Mission Inn," 49; "Easter Sunrise Pilgrimage to Father Serra Cross, Mt. Rubidoux," ca. 1914, Ephemera Collection, Seaver Center.

22. Bridges, "Journal Kept on a Raymond Excursion," 24 February 1887.

23. Ibid., 21 December 1886; Bridges, "Journal Kept on Fourth Raymond Excursion," 7 May 1882.

24. Bridges, "Journal Kept on a Raymond Excursion," 16 February 1887. Nevertheless, Phoebe S. Kropp's " 'All Our Yesterdays': The Spanish Fantasy Past and the Politics of Public Memory in Southern California, 1884–1939" (PhD diss., University of California,

San Diego, 1999) amply demonstrates the commodification of Indian cultures that could occur as a result of tourism or urban expositions.

25. For general information about Lummis's life and career, I have relied upon Mark Thompson, *American Character: The Curious History of Charles Fletcher Lummis and the Rediscovery of the Southwest* (New York: Arcade, 2001); Turbesé Lummis Fiske and Keith Lummis, *Charles F. Lummis: The Man and his West* (Norman: University of Oklahoma Press, 1975); Edwin R. Bingham, *Charles F. Lummis: Editor of the Southwest* (San Marino, CA: Huntington Library, 1955); and—to a lesser degree because of its relentlessly hagiographical tone—Dudley Gordon, *Charles F. Lummis: Crusader in Corduroy* (Los Angeles: Cultural Assets, 1972).

26. Fiske and Lummis, *Charles F. Lummis*, 39–40.

27. Ibid., 49–51; Thompson, *American Character*, 120.

28. Charles F. Lummis, *The Land of Poco Tiempo* (New York: Charles Scribner's Sons, 1893), 1; Martin Padget, "Travel, Exoticism, and the Writing of Region: Charles Fletcher Lummis and the 'Creation' of the Southwest," *Journal of the Southwest* 37 (Fall 1995): 433; Marta Weigle and Barbara A. Babcock, eds., *The Great Southwest of the Fred Harvey Company and the Santa Fe Railway* (Phoenix: Heard Museum, 1996), 2; *Out West*, February 1905.

29. The superficial connection between California and the interior Southwest continues in the twenty-first century in the form of rapid bus tours of "California" for European and Asian tourists. In addition to California sights such as Los Angeles, San Francisco, the Big Sur coast, and Yosemite, these tourists are also taken to Las Vegas and the Grand Canyon, which are also considered "California" attractions. Cultural geographer J. Valerie Fifer discusses the competition between various cities and states in the western tourist market in *American Progress: The Growth of the Transport, Tourist, and Information Industries in the Nineteenth Century West, Seen through the Life and Times of George A. Crofutt, Pioneer and Publicist of the Transcontinental Age* (Chester, CT: Globe Pequot, 1988). The classic study of tourism in the American West remains Earl S. Pomeroy, *In Search of the Golden West: The Tourist in Western America* (New York: Knopf, 1957). See also Hal K. Rothman, *Devil's Bargains: Tourism in the Twentieth-Century American West* (Lawrence: University Press of Kansas, 1998), and Marguerite S. Shaffer, *See America First: Tourism and National Identity, 1880–1940* (Washington: Smithsonian Institution Press, 2001). For an analysis of the intersections between tourism, western scenery, and national culture, see Anne Farrar Hyde, *An American Vision: Far Western Landscape and National Culture, 1820–1920* (New York: New York University Press, 1990). A variety of analyses of the efforts of the Santa Fe Railway and Fred Harvey Company to promote the Southwest can be found in Weigle and Babcock, *The Great Southwest*.

30. See Edward W. Said, *Orientalism* (New York: Pantheon, 1978); Padget, "Travel, Exoticism," 448. The analysis of Anglo authors' representations of southwestern cultures proved especially popular in the 1990s. See, for example, Leah Dilworth, *Imagining Indians in the Southwest: Persistent Visions of a Primitive Past* (Washington, DC: Smithsonian Institution Press, 1996); Margaret D. Jacobs, *Engendered Encounters: Feminism and Pueblo Cultures, 1879–1934* (Lincoln: University of Nebraska Press, 1999); Barbara A. Babcock, "'A New Mexican Rebecca': Imaging Pueblo Women," *Journal of the Southwest* 32, no. 4 (Winter 1990), 400–437; and Barbara A. Babcock, "Bearers of Value, Vessels of Desire: The Reproduction of the Reproduction of Pueblo Culture," *Museum Anthropology* 17, no. 3 (October 1993): 43–57.

31. Martin Padget, *Indian Country: Travels in the American Southwest, 1840–1935* (Albuquerque: University of New Mexico Press, 2004), 116; *Out West*, June 1893; Lummis, *Land of Poco Tiempo*, 40; Charles F. Lummis, *Flowers of our Lost Romance*

(Boston: Houghton Mifflin, 1929), 257; Charles F. Lummis, *Mesa, Cañon and Pueblo* (New York: Century, 1925), 272, 430–34. For more on the development of what Sylvia Rodriguez terms the southwestern "enchantment industry," see her "Tourism, Whiteness, and the Vanishing Anglo," in *Seeing and Being Seen: Tourism in the American West*, ed. David M. Wrobel and Patrick T. Long (Lawrence: University Press of Kansas, 2001), 194–210. See also Chris Wilson's excellent analysis of New Mexico's historical and architectural tourist fictions in *The Myth of Santa Fe: Creating a Modern Regional Tradition* (Albuquerque: University of New Mexico Press, 1997).

32. For an example of this escapism in Lummis's work, see *Land of Poco Tiempo*, 57–58. William Alexander McClung discusses Anglo antimodern escapism in Southern California in *Landscapes of Desire: Anglo Mythologies of Los Angeles* (Berkeley: University of California Press, 2000). For a broader view of the Southwest as an Anglo-American antimodern refuge, see "Escape to Taos" (409–24) and "Left Bank of the Rio Hondo" (425–34) in William H. Goetzmann and William N. Goetzmann, *The West of the Imagination* (New York: Norton, 1986); and Charles C. Eldredge, Julie Schimmel, and William H. Truettner, *Art in New Mexico, 1900–1945: Paths to Taos and Santa Fe* (Washington, DC: National Museum of American Art, Smithsonian Institution, 1986).

33. Charles F. Lummis, "As I Remember," ca. 1928, Lummis Collection, Braun Research Library, Southwest Museum of the American Indian, Autry National Center, Los Angeles. This manuscript, dictated by Lummis near the end of his life, was intended as the nucleus of a future autobiography, and consists of a variety of episodic reminiscences. Long after Lummis's death, Turbesé Lummis Fiske began work on a biography of her father. She rearranged the pages of the manuscript and interspersed her own annotations and commentary within it. Fiske died before the project was completed, and her brother Keith utilized information from "As I Remember" when he completed their book, *Charles Fletcher Lummis: The Man and His West*. The original pagination of the manuscript appears to have been incomplete, and after Fiske's reediting of the original, pages are out of order, and existing pagination is irregular or often absent. Typed page numbers are listed when present, but they do not correspond to any order within the manuscript. While most annotations and stylistic corrections appear to be by Fiske, some may also have been made by Lummis or his secretary. I have used the text of the original, Lummis-dictated manuscript whenever possible.

34. "Land Classification Map of Part of S.W. California, Atlas Sheet No. 73 (C), Expeditions of 1875 & 1878 Under the Command of 1st Lieut. Geo. M. Wheeler, Corps of Engineers, U.S. Army," Surveys West of 100th Meridian 70 C (3)–77, Braun Library; Charles F. Lummis, *The Home of Ramona* (Los Angeles: Lummis, 1888).

35. Fiske and Lummis, *Charles F. Lummis*, 29–32, 41–42.

36. Lummis, *Land of Poco Tiempo*, 1.

37. See David E. Shi, *The Simple Life: Plain Living and High Thinking in American Culture* (New York: Oxford University Press, 1985). See also Daniel T. Rodgers, "Play, Repose, and Plenty," in *The Work Ethic in Industrial America, 1850–1920* (Chicago: University of Chicago Press, 1978), 94–124.

38. Emily K. Abel, *Suffering in the Land of Sunshine: A Los Angeles Illness Narrative* (New Brunswick, NJ: Rutgers University Press, 2006).

39. Meinig, *The Shaping of America* 3:66; Thompson, *American Character*, 178–82. See also the discussion of Lummis and the *Land of Sunshine* in Franklin Dickerson Walker, *A Literary History of Southern California* (Berkeley: University of California Press, 1950).

40. Lummis, "As I Remember," 238, Lummis Collection, Braun Research Library.

41. *Out West*, May 1907. For a detailed analysis of the magazine, see relevant portions of Bingham, *Editor of the Southwest*. The magazine format interspersed articles, Lummis's editorial pieces, and untitled short essays, and Lummis sometimes adopted pseudonyms

to fill issues with few outside contributors. All quotes from the magazine are by Lummis unless otherwise noted.

42. Information for *Land of Sunshine* and *Out West* is derived from the *Land of Sunshine* and *Out West* materials included in the Lummis Collection, Braun Research Library. The magazine materials consist of boxes of correspondence and business records, and a box containing rolls of mailing lists. These rolls, printed on the back of ballot sheets, are extremely fragile, with the exception of those from 1903, which were printed on more durable paper which I could unroll and examine. As I have estimated the total number of subscribers in 1903 as roughly five thousand, and magazine records indicate approximately three thousand cancellations at this time, I assume that total subscriptions could have been eight thousand at the beginning of the year. Subscriptions may have been significantly higher before Lummis's outspoken criticism of the Spanish-American War, but incomplete records and the poor condition of those that remain make this difficult to determine.

43. This list of subscribers is derived from the subscription rolls for 1903.

44. Lummis, "As I Remember," 3, 241–42, Lummis Collection, Braun Library.

45. I am indebted to Denise S. Spooner for her interpretation of *Land of Sunshine* as a shelter magazine in "Something There Is That Loves a Wall: Constructing the Landscape of Community in Southern California," a paper presented at the Los Angeles History Research Group, 10 April 2004.

46. Lummis, *Land of Sunshine*, May 1896, 261; *Land of Sunshine*, May 1897, 261.

47. *Land of Sunshine*, July 1901); See the article "Where the Date Palm Grows," *Land of Sunshine*, August 1900, for an example of the promotional literature about the desert published in the magazine.

48. Lummis, "Right Hand of the Continent," *Out West*, August 1902, 151. Lummis's serialized "Right Hand of the Continent" ran for an extended number of issues.

49. Lummis, "Right Hand of the Continent" *Out West*, August 1902, 154; Lummis, "Right Hand of the Continent," *Out West*, March 1903, 305; Lummis, *Out West*, September 1908, 243. Here and elsewhere Lummis, like some other white Americans of his era, expressed a belief in racial theories of climate, especially the idea that a harsh climate could stunt cultural development, while a benign one could foster it.

50. See, for example, Frances Jennings, *The Invasion of America: Indians, Colonialism, and the Cant of Conquest* (Chapel Hill: University of North Carolina Press, 1975); and Wilcomb E. Washburn, "The Moral and Legal Justifications for Dispossessing the Indians," in *Seventeenth-Century America: Essays in Colonial History*, ed. James M. Smith (Chapel Hill: University of North Carolina Press, 1959), 15–32. For discussions of the negative consequences of mission revival, see relevant portions of Douglas Monroy, *Thrown among Strangers: The Making of Mexican Culture in Frontier California* (Berkeley: University of California Press, 1990); and George J. Sánchez, *Becoming Mexican American: Ethnicity, Culture, and Identity in Chicano Los Angeles, 1900–1945* (Berkeley: University of California Press, 1993).

51. For an unflattering view of the land acquisitions pursued by Amado Chaves's family in northern new Mexico, see William deBuys, *Enchantment and Exploitation: The Life and Hard Times of a New Mexico Mountain Range* (Albuquerque: University of New Mexico Press, 1985), 171–92.

52. Lummis, *The Home of Ramona*.

53. For more on the novel and the tourism it spawned, see Dydia DeLyser, *Ramona Memories: Tourism and the Shaping of Southern California* (Minneapolis: University of Minnesota Press, 2005).

54. Dydia DeLyser analyzes del Valle promotion of Rancho Camulos in "Ramona Memories: Fiction, Tourist Practices, and Placing the Past in Southern California," *Annals of the Association of American Geographers* 93 (December 2003): 886–908. Richard Griswold

del Castillo provides a fascinating view of the del Valles in "The del Valle Family and the Fantasy Heritage," *California History* 59, no. 1 (Spring 1980): 2–15. See also Cecelia Rasmussen, "Del Valle Family Played a Starring Role in Early California," *Los Angeles Times*, November 11, 2001. Genaro M. Padilla discusses the social prestige nostalgia could sometimes grant to Californios and New Mexico Hispanos in *My History, Not Yours: The Formation of Mexican American Autobiography* (Madison: University of Wisconsin Press, 1993).

55. "The Mission Play—Second Season," [1913], Ephemera Collection, Seaver Center. Lummis discusses Lucretia del Valle's role in fundraising for the Landmarks Club in "As I Remember," and the donation cards for "Candle Day," a fundraiser arranged by del Valle at Mission San Gabriel, are held in the Landmarks Club membership card box, Lummis Collection, Braun Research Library.

56. For broad discussions of the dynamism of the Southwest, which Lummis and other Anglos ignored, see Edward H. Spicer, *Cycles of Conquest: The Impact of Spain, Mexico, and the United States on the Indians of the Southwest, 1533–1960* (Tucson: University of Arizona Press, 1962); and D. W. Meinig, *Southwest: Three Peoples in Geographical Change, 1600–1970* (New York: Oxford University Press, 1971).

57. A collection of critical letters can be found in the *Out West* box of the Lummis Collection, Braun Research Library.

58. For examples of Lummis's repudiation of U.S. imperialism, see *Land of Sunshine*, August 1897; *Land of Sunshine*, August 1899; *Land of Sunshine*, March 1898; Carl C. Marshall, Battle Creek, Mich., to Charles Lummis, Los Angeles, 21 March 1899, Lummis Collection, Braun Research Library.

59. F. L. Wilmot, Chillicothe, Ill., to Charles Lummis, Los Angeles, 28 July 1900, Lummis Collection, Braun Research Library, Southwest Museum.

60. Fiske and Lummis, *Charles Lummis*, 100–102, 131–37. For general information on home life at El Alisal, I have relied upon this work as well as Thompson, *American Character*.

61. Thompson, *American Character*, 278–86.

62. Lummis, Diary, 23 November 1909, Lummis Collection, Braun Research Library.

63. Bingham, *Charles F. Lummis*, 24–26; *Out West*, May 1907; Gintaras Valiulis, "The Southwest Museum: A Community Preserves Indian Culture," *Southern California Quarterly* 66, no. 4 (Winter 1984): 352.

64. Lummis, "The Southwest Museum," *Out West*, May 1907, 390, 396, 407, 405. The prickly relationship between Lummis and various Progressive women's groups in Los Angeles—and their divergent views of museums, mission restoration, and other projects—are examined in Anastasia Christman's "The Best Laid Plans: Women's Clubs and City Planning in Los Angeles, 1890–1930" (PhD diss., University of California, Los Angeles, 2000). The clubwomen's municipal museum project achieved fruition with the construction of the Los Angeles County Museum of History, Science, and Art in Exposition Park. That structure later became part of the Natural History Museum of Los Angeles County.

65. Fiske and Lummis, *Charles F. Lummis*, 122–24; 146–50; Lummis, "Journal," 15 February 1913, Special Collections, Young Research Library, University of California, Los Angeles, Los Angeles. Lummis kept an extensive daily journal, dictated to a secretary, containing information about his activities and opinions. His diary, written in his own hand, contains more mundane information, such as household finances, as well as much more personal information, including his romantic conquests, recorded in Spanish or Greek for secrecy; Fiske and Lummis, *Charles Lummis*, 203–5; "The Southwest Museum" (Los Angeles: Southwest Museum, 1919), Special Collections, UCLA.

66. James W. Byrkit uses the term "Southwest Mausoleum" in "Land, Sky, and People: The Southwest Defined," *Journal of the Southwest* 34 (Fall 1992), 373. The Southwest Museum

merged with the Autry Museum of Western Heritage in 2004. The product of the merger, the Autry National Center, stabilized and seismically retrofitted the Southwest Museum building, but its future use and purpose remained unclear in 2010.

67. Lummis, *Out West* 22 (May 1905), 351–52.

68. Fiske and Lummis, *Charles Lummis*, 210–24; Kevin Starr, *Inventing the Dream: California through the Progressive Era* (New York: Oxford University Press, 1985), 124–27.

69. For a discussion of the later, New Mexico-centered Southwest cult that succeeded Lummis, see Lois Palken Rudnick, *Utopian Vistas: The Mabel Dodge Luhan House and the American Counterculture* (Albuquerque: University of New Mexico Press, 1996); and Flannery Burke, *From Greenwich Village to Taos: Primitivism and Place at Mabel Dodge Luhan's* (Lawrence: University Press of Kansas, 2008).

70. Lisbeth Haas, "Regional Culture," in *Conquests and Historical Identities in California, 1769–1936* (Berkeley: University of California Press, 1995), 138–64; Kenneth A. Erickson, "Ceremonial Landscapes of the American West," *Landscape* 22 (Autumn 1977): 39–47.

71. Thompson, *American Character*, 293.

72. Lary May argues that film served a crucial role in the emergence of an American culture of recreation, with celebrities playing the part of "leisure experts," instructing the masses to embrace leisure, but also to enjoy it "correctly." See Lary May, *Screening Out the Past: The Birth of Mass Culture and the Motion Picture Industry* (New York: Oxford University Press, 1980).

73. The architecture of the new city hall is discussed in David Gebhard and Robert Winter, *Los Angeles: An Architectural Guide* (Salt Lake City: Gibbs Smith, 1994), 246–47.

CHAPTER 2

1. Galen Cranz, *The Politics of Park Design: A History of Urban Parks in America* (Cambridge, MA: MIT Press, 1982); William H. Wilson, *The City Beautiful Movement* (Baltimore: Johns Hopkins University Press, 1989). Much of what has been written about the "national" history of urban parks in the United States has in fact focused primarily on East Coast cities such as New York and Boston. While Midwestern cities such as Chicago or Cleveland are also sometimes examined, cities of the American West or South have received less scholarly scrutiny. While New York and other northeastern cities are clearly important models, the history of park development in these cities may not be fully instructive for the creation of parks elsewhere.

2. Roy Rosenzweig and Elizabeth Blackmar, *The Park and the People: A History of Central Park* (Ithaca, NY: Cornell University Press, 1992); Witold Rybczynski, *A Clearing in the Distance: Frederick Law Olmsted and America in the Nineteenth Century* (New York: Scribner, 1999). Even today, though it is far less restricted than it was in the nineteenth century, Central Park arguably serves less as a civic commons than as a communal backyard for the wealthy who live near it. After deteriorating badly during the fiscal crises New York City faced in the 1970s, the park now flourishes due to prodigious philanthropic fundraising. Yet many other parks in the city system, not fortunate enough to be surrounded by millionaires, languish due to a lack of funds. See *New York Times*, November 22, 1999, "Neighbors Give Central Park a Wealthy Glow."

3. William H. Wilson, *The City Beautiful Movement*, 184–85; Terence Young, *Building San Francisco's Parks, 1850–1930* (Baltimore: Johns Hopkins University Press, 2004); Diana Elaine Lindsay, *Our Historic Desert: The Story of the Anza-Borrego Desert, the Largest State Park in the United States of America* (San Diego, CA: Copley, 1973), 86–97.

4. Robert Fishman, *Bourgeois Utopias: The Rise and Fall of Suburbia* (New York: Basic Books, 1987), 155–81, passim.

5. Anthony D. King, *The Bungalow: The Production of a Global Culture*, 2d ed. (New York: Oxford University Press, 1995).

6. Janet Ore, *The Seattle Bungalow: People and Houses, 1900–1940* (Seattle: University of Washington Press, 2005). Ore expertly examines the appeal of the bungalow in another West Coast city and the tensions between its idealizations and its daily lived experience.

7. Carl Abbott discusses the histories and the cultural and political implications of "bungalow belt" neighborhoods in western cities in *How Cities Won the West: Four Centuries of Urban Change in Western North America* (Albuquerque: University of New Mexico Press, 2008), 138–49.

8. Phoebe S. Kropp deftly explores Spanish revival in both residential and tourist forms in *California Vieja: Culture and Memory in a Modern American Place* (Berkeley: University of California Press, 2006).

9. Robert Fogelson, *The Fragmented Metropolis: Los Angeles, 1850–1930* (Cambridge, MA: Harvard University Press, 1967).

10. Some of the national trends that helped produce the pastoral vision of Los Angeles are discussed in Peter J. Schmitt, *Back to Nature: The Arcadian Myth in Urban America* (New York: Oxford University Press, 1969).

11. Frank J. Taylor, *Land of Homes* (Los Angeles: Powell, 1929), 33, 59.

12. Ibid., 60, 61.

13. Ibid., 61, 67.

14. Scott L Bottles, *Los Angeles and the Automobile: The Making of the Modern City* (Berkeley: University of California Press, 1987); Harry Carr, *Los Angeles: City of Dreams* (New York: D. Appleton-Century, 1935), 387–88.

15. For more on white working-class neighborhoods, see Becky M. Nicolaides, *My Blue Heaven: Life and Politics in the Working-Class Suburbs of Los Angeles, 1920–1965* (Chicago: University of Chicago Press, 2002).

16. Al Goldfarb, *100 Years of Recreation and Parks, City of Los Angeles: An Overview* (Los Angeles: Recreation and Parks Department, 1988); Burton L. Hunter, *The Evolution of Municipal Organization and Administrative Practice in the City of Los Angeles* (Los Angeles, Parker, Stone and Baird, 1933); Fred G. Crawford, *Organizational and Administrative Development of the City of Los Angeles, During the Thirty-Year Period July 1, 1925–September 30, 1955.* Los Angeles: School of Public Administration, University of Southern California, 1955.

17. Mary Katherine Gibson, "The Changing Conception of the Urban Park in America: The City of Los Angeles as a Case Study" (master's thesis, UCLA, 1977), 29–32.

18. Griffith published a work arguing for the value of urban parks and bemoaning the condition of his gift to the city. See Griffith J. Griffith, *Parks, Boulevards, and Playgrounds* (Los Angeles: Prison Reform League, 1910), Rare Book Collection, Huntington Library, San Marino, California.

19. Charles Lummis, *Los Angeles and her Makers: A Record* (Los Angeles: Out West, 1907), 244–45; quoted in Mike Davis, *Ecology of Fear: Los Angeles and the Imagination of Disaster* (New York: Metropolitan, 1998), 63n5.

20. The plan is reprinted in its entirety in Greg Hise and William Deverell, *Eden by Design: The 1930 Olmstead-Bartholomew Plan for the Los Angeles Region* (Berkeley: University of California Press, 2000). Mike Davis also analyzes the plan in *Ecology of Fear*, 61–67.

21. B. P. Gruendyke, "Los Angeles County Department of Parks and Recreation" (typescript), 1946, Departmental History Files, County of Los Angeles Department of Parks and Recreation, Los Angeles. See also Ellis McCune, *Recreation and Parks* (Los Angeles: Haynes Foundation, 1954).

22. For the history of urban planning and zoning in Los Angeles, see Greg Hise, *Magnetic Los Angeles: Planning the Twentieth-Century Metropolis* (Baltimore: Johns Hopkins

University Press, 1997); and Greg Hise, "'Nature's Workshop': Industry and Urban Expansion in Southern California, 1900–1950," *Journal of Historical Geography* 27 (Spring 2001): 74–92; Nicolaides, *My Blue Heaven*, 50; and Leonard Pitt and Dale Pitt, *Los Angeles A to Z: An Encyclopedia of the City and County* (Berkeley: University of California Press, 1997), 93. Robert M. Fogelson examines the history of racially restrictive covenants and zoning in *Bourgeois Nightmares: Suuburbia, 1870–1930* (New Haven: Yale University Press, 2005).

23. Dominick Cavallo, *Muscles and Morals: Organized Playgrounds and Urban Reform, 1880–1920* (Philadelphia: University of Pennsylvania Press, 1981); Goldfarb, *100 Years of Recreation and Parks;* Hunter, *The Evolution of Municipal Organization*. See also Mark Wild, *Street Meeting: Multiethnic Neighborhoods in Early Twentieth-Century Los Angeles* (Berkeley: University of California Press, 2005), 99–106.

24. Charles Lincoln Edwards, "An Outline of Nature Study, Showing the Plan and Practice in the Los Angeles Public Schools," reprinted in *Popular Science Monthly*, April 1914. Edwards was director of nature-study in the Los Angeles City Schools. See also *Health Supervision in Los Angeles City Schools*, pamphlet, n.d., Ephemera Collection, Los Angeles, Downtown-E, Seaver Center for Western History Research, Natural History Museum of Los Angeles County, Los Angeles.

25. George Hjelte, *The Development of a City's Public Recreation Service, 1904–1962* (Los Angeles: Public Service, 1978); *Report, 1930–32*, City of Los Angeles Department of Playground and Recreation, Special Collections, Young Research Library, University of California, Los Angeles.

26. *Report of the Playground Commission, City of Los Angeles, 1 December 1908 to 30 June 1910*, Huntington Library.

27. *Annual Report of the Department of Playground and Recreation, City of Los Angeles, 1930*, 33, Special Collections, UCLA.

28. For analyses of race in Los Angeles, particularly the experience of African Americans, see Susan Anderson, "A City Called Heaven: Black Enchantment and Despair in Los Angeles," in *The City: Los Angeles and Urban Theory at the End of the Twentieth Century*, eds. Allen J. Scott and Edward W. Soja, (Berkeley: University of California Press, 1996): 336–64; Quintard Taylor, *In Search of the Racial Frontier: African Americans in the American West, 1528–1990* (New York: Norton, 1998); Lawrence B. de Graaf, Kevin Mulroy, and Quintard Taylor, eds., *Seeking El Dorado: African Americans in California* (Los Angeles: Autry Museum of Western Heritage, 2001); and Walter Nugent, *Into the West: The Story of its People* (New York: Knopf, 1999).

29. Annual reports of the Department of Playgrounds, and later the Los Angeles Department of Recreation and Parks, Special Collections, UCLA, and Archive, City of Los Angeles Department of Recreation and Parks, Los Angeles. Both archives hold incomplete sets of this departmental publication. The near total absence of nonwhite children, particularly African American children, in publications from the 1910s to the 1940s is striking. They appear occasionally in the 1950s and 1960s, but in publications printed after the election of Mayor Tom Bradley in 1973, photos of nonwhite children often outnumber photos of white children. The same general pattern is visible in the unorganized collection of historic photographs of people and recreation in Los Angeles parks contained in the Los Angeles Department of Recreation and Parks Archive.

30. Quintard Taylor, *In Search of the Racial Frontier*, 223.

31. A total of 84,230 residents of the "Western South" states of Arkansas, Missouri, Oklahoma, and Texas are estimated to have relocated to California in the 1920s; see James N. Gregory, *American Exodus: The Dust Bowl Migration and Okie Culture in California* (New York: Oxford University Press, 1989), 6; Charlotta A. Bass, *Forty Years: Memoirs from the Pages of a Newspaper* (Los Angeles: C. A. Bass, 1960), 55.

32. Andre Keil, *Swimming at the Park Pool: A History of Aquatics in the City of Los Angeles* (Los Angeles: City of Los Angeles, Recreation and Parks, 1994), 9; *Annual Report of the Board of Park Commissioners,* City of Los Angeles, 1928, Special Collections, UCLA; Los Angeles City Council Minutes, 7 July 1927, also 1929, Los Angeles City Archives; Douglas Flamming, telephone interview by author, 31 October 2002. In 2002 Professor Flamming, an historian at the Georgia Institute of Technology, was completing a book on the history of African Americans in Los Angeles, *Bound for Freedom: Black Los Angeles in Jim Crow America* (Berkeley: University of California Press, 2005). He generously shared his research on the history of segregation and black recreation in the city and region. For more on the national history of swimming and segregation, see Jeff Wiltse, *Contested Waters: A Social History of Swimming Pools in America* (Chapel Hill: University of North Carolina Press, 2007). For a history of swimming pools, see Thomas A. P. van Leeuwen, *The Springboard in the Pond: An Intimate History of the Swimming Pool* (Cambridge, MA: MIT Press, 1998).

33. Stella Elizabeth Hartman, "A Study of Leisure-Time Habits of Young Men and Young Women in Los Angeles" (master's thesis, University of Southern California, 1942), 47. A frenzy of backyard-pool construction occurred in the 1950s. In 1949, there were 10,000 private residential pools in the nation. By 1959, there were 250,000, and 90,000 of these—more than a third of the total—were located in Los Angeles (Keil, *Swimming at the Park Pool,* 32).

34. Keil, *Swimming at the Park Pool,* 9.

35. The case was *Ethel Prioleau v. Board of Playground and Recreation Commissioners,* S.P. 285104. Copies of the court's judgment, as well as communications between the City Council, City Attorney, and the Board of Playground and Recreation Commissioners are contained in City Council File 1636 (1931), Los Angeles City Archives.

36. Michael Hurley, telephone interview by author, 30 October 2002. Mr. Hurley is an urban planner who has conducted extensive research on the history of parks and recreation in Pasadena; Flamming interview. See also "Suit Accusing Coach of Racism Stirs Bitter Memories of Pool's Past,"*Los Angeles Times,* April 16, 2001.

37. For an examination of mid-century California beach culture, see Kirse Granat May, *Golden State, Golden Youth: The California Image in Popular Culture, 1955–1966* (Chapel Hill: University of North Carolina Press, 2002).

38. Pitt and Pitt, *Los Angeles A to Z,* 41–42; beach attendance figure from *Annual Report of the Department of Playground and Recreation, City of Los Angeles,* 1928, 15, "Old Department History" file, Los Angeles Department of Recreation and Parks.

39. Flamming interview.

40. Bass, *Forty Years,* 55, 69; Flamming interview. Though Bass states that the Valentine beating occurred in 1928, it appears that the correct date was 1920.

41. "Resort Was an Oasis for Blacks until Racism Drove Them Out." *Los Angeles Times,* July 21, 2002.

42. Flamming interview; Hurley interview; see also the beach photos in the Shades of L.A. Archive, Los Angeles Public Library, Los Angeles. This collection of photographs from family albums—Latino, Asian, African American, Native American, and more—is an exceptional resource for documenting the history of recreation in Los Angeles.

43. Douglas Flamming interview; Charles Dinnijes Withers, "Problems of Mexican Boys" (master's thesis, University of Southern California, 1942), 83. This survey also found that teenaged Mexican American boys who arrived at some dance halls attired in flamboyant *pachuco* suits and long hair were denied admittance, while the same boys were permitted when sporting more conservative clothes and hairstyles; Arthur Verge, interview by author, San Marino, California, 1 November 2003. Verge, a member of the Los Angeles History Research Group, was a lifeguard in Los Angeles County, and is an acquaintance

of a number of retired Mexican American and African American Los Angeles lifeguards. For the evidence of continuing beach segregation, see N. S. Johnson, Director, County of Los Angeles Department of Parks and Recreation, to Kenneth Hahn, Los Angeles County Supervisor, 15 August 1967. Attached is a letter from Johnson to Sydney Wolfe, chairperson of employee grievance committee, 11 August 1967, Kenneth Hahn Collection, Huntington Library.

44. Laura Pulido, interview by author, San Marino, California, 1 November 2003. Pulido is a member of the Los Angeles History Research Group, and recalled these ersatz picnics on Westside lawns from her own family history.

45. "Forgotten Oasis of Freedom Val Verde, the Black Palm Springs," *Los Angeles Times*, March 2, 1994,

46. Ibid., "Val Verde to Get Pool," *Los Angeles Examiner*, November 28, 1938, *Los Angeles Examiner* Clippings Collection, "Parks," Archival Research Center, Doheny Library, University of Southern California.

47. "Val Verde County Park Now Open for Summer Season," *Los Angeles Sentinel*, June 20, 1946; "Hollywood Spotlight," *Los Angeles Sentinel*, July 3, 1946; "Social Notebook—Gay Cavaliers at Val Verde," *Los Angeles Sentinel*, July 11, 1946; *Los Angeles Times*, "Forgotten Oasis of Freedom Val Verde," March 2, 1994. Another retreat for African Americans was Murray's Dude Ranch, located near Victorville. One of the first integrated dude ranches in the nation, it served as a filming location for African American westerns, including 1938's "The Bronze Buckaroo" and "Harlem Rides the Range." The property was later bought by singer Pearl Bailey and her husband Louis Bellson. See "In Prejudiced Era, Ranch Welcomed Dudes of All Colors," *Los Angeles Times*, February 22, 2004.

48. City council minutes, 14 October 1937, Los Angeles City Archives.

49. "Today's Leisure," Department of Playground and Recreation, 1938, Special Collections, UCLA.

50. *Department of Playground and Recreation, City of Los Angeles, Annual Financial Report, Fiscal Year Ending June 30, 1936; Department of Playground and Recreation, Annual Report, 1937*, Special Collections, UCLA.

51. The definitive history of the Los Angeles Plaza is William David Estrada, "Sacred and Contested Space: The Los Angeles Plaza" (PhD diss., UCLA, 2003).

52. "Pershing Square Park," Histories—P, Los Angeles Department of Recreation and Parks Archives. See also William McClung, *Landscapes of Desire: Anglo Mythologies of Los Angeles* (Berkeley: University of California Press, 2000), 142–53.

53. The growth in nonwhite population, and concerns of "problems" as a result of this growth, prompted the city planning commission to complete a series of maps of all "foreign-born and colored populations." See *Accomplishments, 1943*, Board of Planning Commissioners, City of Los Angeles, Los Angeles Chamber of Commerce Collection, Carton 72, Archival Research Center, USC; Mel Scott, *Cities are for People: The Los Angeles Region Plans for Living* (Los Angeles: Pacific Southwest Academy, 1942); *Report on Master Plan of Parks, County of Los Angeles (Unincorporated Area)*, Regional Planning Commission, Los Angeles County Regional Planning District [ca. 1945], County of Los Angeles Department of Parks and Recreation; Quintard Taylor, *In Search of the Racial Frontier*, 254.

54. *Excerpts from Echo Park Study*, 1950, John Anson Ford Collection, Huntington Library.

55. Evidence that Hahn and Ford quickly began collaborating is suggested by a report prepared in early 1953 for the board of supervisors by B. P. Gruendyke, superintendent of the Department of Parks and Recreation. This report listed the status of all local and neighborhood parks, regional parks, and golf courses. It also estimated the cost of carrying out minimal development at undeveloped parks ($2,580,900), and partial

or complete development at parks that already possessed some facilities ($8,068,528); see B. P. Gruendyke to Los Angeles Board of Supervisors, 2 March 1953, Los Angeles Department of Recreation and Parks. For pool attendance, see, for example, a news release from the office of Kenneth Hahn, 11 September 1974, stating that free summer swimming lessons in public pools had attracted more than 187,000 participants that summer (Hahn Collection, Huntington Library).

56. For an excellent examination of black Angelenos since World War II, see Josh Sides, *L.A. City Limits: African American Los Angeles from the Great Depression to the Present* (Berkeley: University of California Press, 2003).

CHAPTER 3

1. *The Columbia Encyclopedia*, 5th ed., 1993, s.v. "Santa Barbara Islands" and "Santa Catalina Island"; William Stanford White and Steven Kern Tice, *Santa Catalina Island: Its Magic, People, and History* (Glendora, CA: White Limited Editions, 1997), 9–10. The history of Catalina has not been extensively studied. A few local histories of the island have been published, and they are cited here. One scholarly work is Gary Steven Okun, "Avalon, California: Structure and Function of an Island Town" (master's thesis, UCLA, 1976).

2. Studies of eastern resorts, urban recreation areas, and tourist destinations range from local histories to social, cultural, and environmental studies. For early resorts, see Jon Sterngass, *First Resorts: Pursuing Pleasure at Saratoga Springs, Newport, and Coney Island* (Baltimore: Johns Hopkins University Press, 2001); and Theodore Corbett, *The Making of American Resorts: Saratoga Springs, Ballston Spa, Lake George* (New Brunswick, NJ: Rutgers University Press, 2000). See also John F. Kasson, *Amusing the Million: Coney Island at the Turn of the Century* (New York: Hill and Wang, 1978); Stefan Kanfer, *A Summer World: The Attempt to Build a Jewish Eden in the Catskills, from the Days of the Ghetto to the Rise and Decline of the Borscht Belt* (New York: Farrar, Straus & Giroux, 1989); Emil R. Salvini, *The Summer City by the Sea: Cape May, New Jersey; An Illustrated History* (Belleville, NJ: Wheal-Grace, 1995); Philip G. Terrie, *Contested Terrain: A New History of Nature and People in the Adirondacks* (Syracuse, NY: The Adirondack Museum and Syracuse University Press, 1997); Myra B. Young Armstead, *"Lord, Please Don't Take Me in August": African Americans in Newport and Saratoga Springs, 1870–1930* (Urbana: University of Illinois Press, 1999); and Karen Dubinsky, *The Second Greatest Disappointment: Honeymooners, Heterosexuality, and the Tourist Industry at Niagara Falls* (New Brunswick, NJ: Rutgers University Press, 1999).

3. Adelaide LeMert Doran, *The Ranch that was Robbins': Santa Catalina Island; A Source Book* (Los Angeles: A. H. Clark, 1963), 40–42.

4. For the history of the native inhabitants of Catalina, the Spanish and Mexican eras, and the early American era, I have relied upon Doran, *The Ranch that was Robbins'*, 38–50, relevant portions of W. W. Robinson, *Southern California Local History: A Gathering of the Writings of W. W. Robinson*, ed. Doyce B. Nunis Jr. (Los Angeles: Historical Society of Southern California, 1993), and to a lesser degree White and Tice, *Santa Catalina Island*, 9–20.

5. Doran, *The Ranch that was Robbin's*, 54–81.

6. Donald Chaput, "The Civil War Military Post on Catalina Island," *Southern California Quarterly* 75 (Spring 1993), 37–50.

7. In one of the earliest and most popular western guidebook series, Catalina is described only as a place "with some gold mines, and great numbers of sheep and goats." The island's only apparent tourist value was as a misty vista visible from Santa Monica beach (Geo. A. Crofutt, *Crofutt's New Overland and Pacific Coast Guide*, vol. 1 [Chicago: Overland, 1878], 245, 247).

8. Dayelle H. Kittredge (Wiley), "Diary of a Trip to Santa Catalina Island," 1870, Jack London Collection, Huntington Library, San Marino, CA.

9. *The Island of Santa Catalina, Los Angeles County California*, San Francisco: H. M. Newhall, [1885], 1–11, 12, 14–15, Ephemera Collection, Seaver Center for Western History Research, Natural History Museum of Los Angeles County, Los Angeles.

10. *Early Avalon*, 4, 7, n.d., Catalina Island Museum Archives, Avalon, California. This anonymous manuscript is both typescript and handwritten, with some pages missing. This manuscript was donated to the Catalina Island Museum in the early 1950s, shortly after its founding. It was apparently written by a longtime resident intending to write a history of Catalina, and most of the manuscript is comprised of chronologically arranged quotations and articles from island newspapers. It contains the only remaining references to articles in Avalon's earliest newspapers; unfortunately, no copies of the newspapers appear to have survived. I verified that the manuscript's references to *Los Angeles Times* articles are correct, and I have assumed that the references to the other newspapers are correct as well. Shatto's real-estate venture is recounted in "Early Days in California: Santa Catalina Island, Chapter VIII," *Los Angeles Times*, May 19, 1918. For more on the history of sheep grazing on the island, see a reminiscence by a Catalina sheepherder, Eloi J. Amar, *Sheepherder's Shack at El Rancho Escondido*, 1962, G. Natural History File, Catalina Island Museum Archives.

11. The naming of Avalon for the fictional Avilion is mentioned in White and Tice, *Santa Catalina Island*, 26. (It is unclear if Shatto intentionally changed Tennyson's spelling or simply used a more conventional spelling for the Arthurian locale.) For a discussion of Shatto's plans at the time he purchased the island, see American Photogravure Company, *Picturesque Los Angeles County, California* (Chicago: Fred'k Weston, 1887), 9–10. Catalina had emerged as a tourist attraction by the late 1880s, and thus warranted mention in guidebooks to the region. See, for example, Walter Lindley and J. P. Lindley, *California of the South: Its Physical Geography, Climate, Resources, Routes of Travel, and Health Resorts* (New York: D. Appleton, 1888).

12. *Early Avalon*, 25, 30; "Early Days in California: Santa Catalina Island, Chapter VIII," *Los Angeles Times*, May 12, 1918.

13. *Early Avalon*, 32, 34; "Altadenan Recalls Early Avalon Era," *Los Angeles Times*, May 22, 1955; "Pasadena Pioneer Paid Tribute for 'Y' Work," *Pasadena Star News*, June 14, 1952, clipping, G. Personages—Catalina—Elms Family File, Catalina Island Museum Archives.

14. "Early Days in California: Santa Catalina Island, Chapter VIII," *Los Angeles Times*, May 12, 1918.

15. Ibid.

16. *Early Avalon*, 124; "Early Days in California: Santa Catalina Island, Chapter IX," *Los Angeles Times*, May 19, 1918.

17. *Early Avalon*, 151–53.

18. The ambivalent attitudes with which many Americans perceived leisure is discussed in Cindy S. Aron, *Working at Play: A History of Vacations in the United States* (New York: Oxford University Press, 1999); and Daniel T. Rogers, *The Work Ethic in Industrial America, 1850–1920* (Chicago: University of Chicago Press, 1974).

19. Banning Company, *Santa Catalina Island, California* (Los Angeles: McBride, 1910) and *Santa Catalina Island* (Los Angeles: M. Rieder, 1905), Special Collections, Young Research Library, UCLA.

20. Hancock Banning Jr., *The Banning Family in Southern California*, UCLA Oral History Archives, Special Collections, UCLA; Doran, *The Ranch that was Robbins'*, 70–87, 100–111; Alma Overholt, *The Catalina Story: Compiled and Edited under the Auspices of the Catalina Island Museum Society* (Avalon, CA: Catalina Island Museum Society, 1962).

Overholt was the publicist of the Santa Catalina Island Company for decades. For a discussion George Shatto's efforts in Catalina within the larger history of early resort and real-estate development in greater Los Angeles, see Glenn S. Dumke, *The Boom of the Eighties in Southern California* (San Marino, CA: Huntington Library, 1944).

21. "Early Days in California: Santa Catalina Island," *Los Angeles Times*, May 19, 1918; Banning, *The Banning Family in Southern California*. Banning Company ships first provided intermittent passenger service to Catalina as early as 1881. See John M. Houston, *Accounts and Stories of Old San Pedro: Including Early Excursion Ships to Santa Catalina* (San Pedro, CA: San Pedro Historical Publications, 1978).

22. For a discussion of tourism development in the twentieth century West, as well as the history of ski resorts in the region, see Hal K. Rothman, *Devil's Bargains: Tourism in the Twentieth-Century American West* (Lawrence: University Press of Kansas, 1998); and Susan Rhoades Neel, ed., "Tourism and the American West," special issue, *Pacific Historical Review* 65 (Fall 1996).

23. U.S. Bureau of the Census, *Fourteenth Census of the United States, 1920*. Vol 1, *Population* (Washington, DC: Government Printing Office, 1921), 354; "Catalina's Population Shows Steady Increase" *Catalina Islander*, April 1930, 23. The Catalina Island Museum Archives contain the full run of this newspaper. Copies of the enumeration rolls for the 1900, 1910, and 1920 federal censuses are on file at the Catalina Island Museum Archives. Perhaps these discrepancies resulted from other enumerators counting some seasonal island occupants at residences on the mainland. If so, they may have been removed from the total count for Catalina.

24. Doran, *The Ranch that was Robbins'*, 100–111.

25. *Los Angeles Times*, August 16, 1909; *Early Avalon*, 19.

26. *Early Avalon*, 18; *Los Angeles Times*, July 15, 1909; Squirrel "Duke" D'Arcy, interviewed by Chuck Liddell, Joe Guin, and Lloyd Rathburn, 25 February 1976, Catalina Island Museum Society Oral History Program, Catalina Island Museum Archives.

27. See Banning Company Collection, box 5, "Business Papers," folder 4, Huntington Library. For legal paperwork and documentation pertaining to several unauthorized attempts to land at Catalina; Banning, *The Banning Family in Southern California*; *Los Angeles Times*, June 15, 1887; Dumke, *The Boom of the Eighties*, 225.

28. For a discussion of boat access to the island and the Bannings' efforts to maintain control of it, see James Zordich, "Santa Catalina Island Company: The First Quarter Century." *Water Lines*, 1st quarter, 1994, Catalina Island Museum Archives. (*Water Lines* is the employee magazine of the Santa Catalina Island Company.)

29. William Banning to E. H. Brewster, Al. Carraher, J. E. Mathewson, Wm. Hunt, Jr., Dr. G. Roscoe Thomas, W.S. Wright, and J. Lane, 1 December 1908, typescript memo with handwritten annotations, G. History, Banning Era File, Santa Catalina Museum Archives.

30. For an audit conducted by the California Railroad Commission as part of this suit, as well as other legal papers, see *Audit, California Railroad Commission*, [1915], box 5, Banning Company Collection, Huntington Library.

31. Los Angeles County Liquor License, certified 11 August 1893 for William, Joseph, and Hancock Banning, box 5, Banning Company Collection, Huntington Library. For opposition to alcohol, see an 1895 petition signed by forty-eight Avalon residents—all of whom appear to be Anglo—requesting that the Los Angeles County Board of Supervisors reject an application for a saloon in the community (box 5, Banning Company Collection, Huntington Library).

32. *Joseph Banning Memo*, 15 August 1913, box 5, Banning Company Collection, Huntington Library. Banning noted that the "liquor element" had claimed that only permanent residents could vote in the upcoming referendum. "Avalon City Council Minutes," 3, 9, 11, 19 July 1913; 12 September 1913; 7 March 1919; 25 April 1919; 10 August 1919, Frederick

Baker Collection, Special Collections, UCLA; Joseph B. Banning, *Memorandum of Policy*, typescript, 16 January 1911, box 5, Banning Company Collection, Huntington Library.

33. Banning, *The Banning Family in Southern California*.

34. *Catalina Islander*, January 1, 1943; April 29, 1971, G. Personages-Catalina-Adargo Family File, Catalina Island Museum Archives.

35. W. L. Scofield, *Fish Bulletin 96, California Fishing Ports*, State of California Department of Fish and Game, 1954, 180, Bowron Collection, Huntington Library.

36. Charles Frederick Holder, "The Glass-Bottom Boat" *National Geographic*, September 1909. Holder claimed that the glass-bottomed-boat craze began in Avalon when locals saw the glass-bottomed box he used to peer under the surface of the ocean. An associate of George Shatto, however, asserted that one of Avalon's fishermen came up with the idea on his own. See "Early Days in California: Santa Catalina Island, Chapter VIII," *Los Angeles Times*, May 12, 1918. See also "Glass Bottom Cruising," *Catalina Islander*, July 1940, 4.

37. *Santa Catalina Island: Winter and Summer* (Los Angeles: Wilmington Transportation Company, [1895?]); Banning, *The Banning Family in Southern California*; Ernest Windle, *Windle's History of Santa Catalina Island* (Avalon, CA: Catalina Islander, 1931), 93; *Santa Catalina Island—Ever Grand, Attractive, and Unique—The Season of 1896*, pamphlet, Banning Company Collection, box 5, Huntington Library.

38. Mary Elise Groff (Jenkins) to Gregory Groff, 12 August 1898. Groff (Lewis Augustine) Collection, Huntington Library.

39. *Early Avalon*, 20; "Early Days in California: Santa Catalina Island," *Los Angeles Times*, May 19, 1918.

40. *Early Avalon*, 19.

41. Harry Carr, *Los Angeles: City of Dreams* (New York: D. Appleton-Century, 1935), 301.

42. Banning, *The Banning Family in Southern California*; Carey McWilliams, *Southern California: An Island On the Land* (Pasadena, CA: Peregrine Smith, 1973), 147; White and Tice, *Santa Catalina Island*, 73–77. Though Holder thought himself the model gentleman sportsman, Mike Davis amply illustrates the hooliganism that resulted from some Valley Hunt Club outings, and the racist and elitist views that underlay Holder's conservation ideology. See Mike Davis, *Ecology of Fear: Los Angeles and the Imagination of Disaster* (New York: Metropolitan, 1998), 221–28.

43. Charles Frederick Holder, *Santa Catalina, an Isle of Summer: Its History, Climate, Sports and Antiquities* (San Francisco: Murdock, 1895), 42, 95–96; *Life in the Open: Sport with Rod, Gun, Horse, and Hound in Southern California* (New York: G. P. Putnam's Sons, 1906); *The Channel Islands of California: A Book for the Angler, Sportsman, and Tourist* (Chicago: A. C. McClurg, 1910), v. The essential text on the Progressive Era conceptualization of American masculinity is Gail Bederman, *Manliness and Civilization: A Cultural History of Gender and Race in the United States, 1880–1917* (Chicago: University of Chicago Press, 1995).

44. Charles Fletcher Lummis, "In the Lion's Den," *Out West*, August 1903, 215–16.

45. Henry Van Dyke, "Devastating the Fisheries of Southern California," 18 April 1913, typescript, Catalina Island Museum Archives. See also Connie Y. Chiang, *Shaping the Shoreline: Fisheries and Tourism on the Monterey Coast* (Seattle: University of Washington Press, 2008).

46. *Annual Tournaments, The Tuna Club—Catalina Island, California—1898–1916*, Ephemera Collection, Seaver Center; Doran, *The Ranch that was Robbins'*, 123–24. For an analysis of the intersections of class and conservation, see Louis S. Warren, *The Hunter's Game: Poachers and Conservationists in Twentieth-Century America* (New Haven, CT: Yale University Press, 1997), and Karl Jacoby, *Crimes against Nature: Squatters, Poachers, Thieves, and the Hidden History of American Conservation* (Berkeley: University of

California Press, 2001). Warren also discusses the cult of masculinity that glorified the hunt in the late nineteenth and early twentieth centuries.

47. *Los Angeles Times*, June 23, 1894; April 21, 1909; Captain George Farnsworth to Governor Olson, quoted in Santa Catalina Island Company press release, June 1940, Catalina Island Museum Archives. For a larger discussion of California marine conservation, see Arthur F. McEvoy, *The Fisherman's Problem: Ecology and Law in the California Fisheries, 1850–1980* (New York: Cambridge University Press, 1986). According to the 1880 U.S. Census, Avalon's diverse population was typical for California fishing communities. Fully 92% of the state's fishermen were categorized as immigrants. This figure likely included some California-born Mexican Americans. McEvoy argues that marine conservation began in nineteenth-century California as an attempt to drive Chinese immigrants from fisheries.

48. Ralph Bandini, *Veiled Horizons: Stories of the Big Game Fish of the Sea* (New York: Derrydale, 1939), 26–27.

49. Doran, *The Ranch that was Robbins'*, 30–37, 95–98.

50. "Locally Famous Woman Dies on Catalina Island," *Los Angeles Times*, 1915, clipping in G. Personages—Catalina—Pesciado File, Catalina Island Museum Archives; "Early Days in California: Santa Catalina Island, Chapter IX," *Los Angeles Times*, May 1, 1918. See also White and Tice, *Santa Catalina Island*, 184.

51. *Catalina Jew Fish*, September 14, 1889.

52. Ibid.

53. Bureau of Marine Fisheries, "The Commercial Fish Catch of California for the Year 1947 with an Historical Review 1916–1947," *Fish Bulletin* 74, State of California Department of Natural Resources, Division of Fish and Game, 1949, 183–84, Fletcher Bowron Collection, Huntington Library.

54. *Permit to Land at Santa Catalina Island for the Purpose of Fishing*, box 5, Banning Company Collection, Huntington Library; Charlton Lawrence Edholm, "The Seaward Suburbs of Los Angeles," *Out West*, May 1909, 459.

55. See, for example, Sylvia Lawson Covy, "The Paths of Catalina," *Overland Monthly*, June 1896; Covy, "Catalina. In an Island Hollow," *Overland Monthly*, September 1896; Marion Pruyn, "Santa Catalina," *Overland Monthly*, June 1897; Leavenworth Macnab, *Overland Monthly*, October 1898; and Neil C. Wilson, "Santa Catalina," *Overland Monthly*, July 1910.

56. George Wharton James, *Traveler's Handbook to Southern California* (Pasadena, CA: G. W. James, 1904), 210; Charles A. Keeler, *Southern California* (Los Angeles: Santa Fe Railroad, 1902), 63.

57. Thomas S. Hines identifies the lodge at Two Harbors as a Gill building in *Irving Gill and the Architecture of Reform* (New York: Monacelli, 2000). For an analysis of mission revival, see Phoebe S. Kropp, California Vieja: Culture and Memory in a Modern American Place (Berkeley: University of California Press, 2006); and William Alexander McClung, *Landscapes of Desire: Anglo Mythologies of Los Angeles* (Berkeley: University of California Press, 2000).

58. Charles Frederick Holder, *The Adventures of Torqua: Being the Life and Remarkable Adventures of Three Boys, Refugees on the Island of Santa Catalina (Pimug-Na) in the Eighteenth Century* (Boston: Little, Brown, 1902).

59. Catalina appeared in the first issue of *Land of Sunshine*, and remained a regular feature for the full run of the magazine. See "Southern California Resorts," June 1894; "Southern California Points of Interest," April 1899; "Southern California as a Summer Resort," May 1899; "A California Aquarium and Zoölogical Station," July 1899; "Royal Sport," December 1900; "The Resorts of Southern California," July 1901; "California Summer Resorts," July 1903; and "The Seaward Suburbs of Los Angeles," May 1909.

60. *La Fiesta de Los Angeles, 1895 Official Program* (Los Angeles: Union Photo-Engraving, 1895) and P. Maurice McMahon, *Romance de la Fiesta de Los Angeles* (Los Angeles, 1895), Ephemera Collection, Seaver Center.

61. *Hotel Register, Avalon House*, June 1890—September 1894, Huntington Library. The hotel register maintained by the Avalon House, a small hotel owned independently of the SCIC, demonstrates this pattern. Guests were overwhelmingly from Los Angeles or other parts of Southern California. The great majority of guests arrived from June to September. Aside from a small increase in the spring—perhaps seasonal residents arriving before their cabins or homes were ready for occupation—occupancy the rest of the year was minimal. The small number of visitors in fall and winter did include a noticeably higher percentage of Easterners, however. This pattern persisted throughout the Banning era. See, for example, William Banning to Frank Karr, 21 November 1910, Banning Company Collection, box 5, Huntington Library. Banning hoped Karr would loan the SCIC $7,500 because taxes had proven higher than expected. See also William Banning to Union Hardware and Metal Co., 6 December 1910, Banning Company Collection, box 5, Huntington Library. Upon receiving a request to settle an outstanding debt, Banning asked to continue paying interest on the debt until it could be paid off the following autumn.

62. *Audit, California Railroad Commission*, [1915], box 5, Banning Company Collection, Huntington Library. This audit was conducted in response to the suit brought by Avalon merchants J. H. Miller and E. Donaldson; Joseph B. Banning, *Memorandum of Policy*, typescript, 16 January 1911, boxes 5, 6; Hancock Banning to Mrs. J. B. (Katherine) Banning, 26 December 1917, box 5, Banning Company Collection. Huntington Library.

63. William Banning to Joseph Banning, 13 April 1909, mentions an offer from a group of investors. William Banning to E. Cole, 3 January 1916, contains offer to sell the island east of the Isthmus. *Personal Memorandum*, 20 December 1916, suggested creating a trust, box 5, Banning Company Collection, Huntington Library.

64. 3, 31 December 1915, *Avalon City Council Minutes*, Frederick Baker Papers, UCLA Special Collections; Banning, *The Banning Family in Southern California*; Doran, *The Ranch that was Robbins'*, 109–11; Zordich, "Santa Catalina Island Company," 14–15. The standard history of early auto tourism in the United States is Warren James Belasco, *Americans on the Road: From Autocamp to Motel, 1910–1945* (Cambridge, MA: MIT Press, 1979). John Ott discusses auto tourism in "Landscapes of Consumption: Auto Tourism and Visual Culture in California, 1920–1940," in *Reading California: Art, Image, and Identity, 1900–2000*, ed. Stephanie Barron, Sheri Bernstein, and Ilene Susan Fort (Los Angeles: Los Angeles County Museum of Art, 2000), 51–68.

65. Materials pertaining to the sale of Catalina, the SCIC, and the Banning Company to William Wrigley, can be found in box 1 of the Banning Company Collection, Huntington Library.

CHAPTER 4

1. Business records pertaining to the sale of Catalina Island to William Wrigley can be found in Banning Company Collection, box 1, Huntington Library, San Marino, California. See also James Zordich, "Santa Catalina Island Company: The First Quarter Century," *Water Lines*, 1st quarter 1994, Catalina Island Museum Archives, Avalon, California.

2. Hancock Banning Jr., *The Banning Family in Southern California*, UCLA Oral History Archives, Special Collections, Young Research Library, University of California, Los Angeles, Los Angeles.

3. Alison Wrigley-Rusack, "William Wrigley, Jr. and Santa Catalina Island, Part I," *Water Lines* 3d quarter 1986, Catalina Island Museum Archives. For more on advertising,

department stores, the Columbian Exposition, and American society and culture in the late nineteenth and early twentieth centuries, see William Leach, *Land of Desire: Merchants, Power, and the Rise of a New American Culture* (New York: Pantheon, 1993); T. J. Jackson Lears, *Fables of Abundance: A Cultural History of Advertising in America* (New York: Basic Books, 1994); Roland Marchand, *Advertising the American Dream: Making Way for Modernity, 1920–1940* (Berkeley: University of California Press, 1985); and Robert W. Rydell, *All the World's a Fair: Visions of Empire at American International Expositions, 1876–1916* (Chicago: University of Chicago Press, 1984).

4. "Catalina Under New Management," *Catalina Islander*, February 18, 1919; Wrigley-Rusack, "William Wrigley, Jr. and Santa Catalina Island," *Water Lines*, 3d quarter 1986), 12. The Catalina Island Museum Archives contain a full run of this newspaper and this periodical.

5. "Catalina Under New Management," *Catalina Islander*, February 18, 1919.

6. *Los Angeles Examiner*, [February 1919], Catalina Island Museum Archives.

7. See, for example, the following issues of the *Catalina Islander*: "Catalina Advancement," December 26, 1923, "Avalon Gets Water," April 2, 1924, "More About that Water," April 9, 1924, and "Water Shortage Confronts Avalon; Becoming Serious," February 26, 1948; Alma Overholt, *The Catalina Story: Compiled and Edited under the Auspices of the Catalina Island Museum Society* (Avalon, CA: Catalina Island Museum Society, 1962) 54.

8. "Catalina's Population Shows Steady Increase," *Catalina Islander*, April 23, 1930; U.S. Bureau of the Census, *Fourteenth Census of the United States, 1920*. Vol. 1, *Population* (Washington, DC: Government Printing Office, 1921), 354; *Fifteenth Census of the United States, 1930*. Vol. 2, Part 1, *Population* (Washington, DC: Government Printing Office, 1932), 280; *Sixteenth Census of the United States*. Vol. 1, *Population* (Washington, DC: Government Printing Office, 1942), 124; *Sixteenth Census of the United States*. Vol. 2, *Characteristics of the Population* (Washington, DC: Government Printing Office, 1943), 580; Federal Writers' Project, Works Progress Administration, *Los Angeles: A Guide to the City and its Environs*, 2d ed. (New York: Hastings House, 1951), 375–78.

9. In 1937, for example, the *Catalina Islander* reported that of twenty resident births on the island, six were Mexicans; Malcom Renton, *Black People Who Have Lived on Santa Catalina Island*, interview, 30 November 1990, Catalina Island Museum Archives. St. Catherine Hotel chef Rodney Jefferson appears in an Avalon newspaper article, "St. Catherine Hotel Chef Tells How to Prepare Swordfish Steak," *Catalina Islander*, October 28, 1931. The career of airplane mechanic Nat Laws is discussed in "Four Generations: A Family Mirrors Roots of Black L.A.," *Los Angeles Times*, August 22, 1982. See G. Personages—Catalina—Black File, Catalina Island Museum Archives. For an example of African American vacation notices, see "Pastor, Bride Honeymoon on Catalina Island," *Los Angeles Sentinel*, June 27, 1946.

10. Bill Bushing, "Santa Catalina Island Company: 1919–1944," *Water Lines*, 2d quarter 1994, 4; John M. Houston, *Accounts and Stories of Old San Pedro* (Harbor City, CA: Economy, 1978).

11. Banning, *The Banning Family in Southern California*. See also Samuel Butler, interview, UCLA Oral History Archive, UCLA Special Collections. Butler was a longtime Wrigley employee who worked on several of the major Catalina construction projects of the 1920s, and was also employed at other Southern California resorts.

12. Federal Writers' Project, *Los Angeles*, 375–78.

13. Bushing, "Santa Catalina Island Company," 9.

14. Charlotte Bronte Herr, *Their Mariposa Legend: A Romance of Catalina* (Pasadena, CA: Post, 1921), 1.

15. William Wrigley, Jr. Enterprises, Advertising Division, *Catalina's Yesterdays: A Glimpse into the Life of the Ancient Dwellers on the Magic Isle* (Avalon, CA: Santa Catalina Island Company, 1926), 2, 1; Overholt, *The Catalina Story*, 60–65.

16. Mary Austin, *California: The Land of the Sun* (London: Adam and Charles Black, 1914), 48–49.

17. Nellie E. Dashiell, *Catalina: A Poem* (Washington, DC: Dashiell, 1924), 1–6.

18. "Photographs—California, 1922," Album of Mr. and Mrs. Humm and Mr. and Mrs. Hassenfluh's trip to California, January 1922, created by Mrs. Humm, Institute for the Study of the American West, Autry National Center, Los Angeles. Unfortunately, the couples' first names are not recorded in the album.

19. Charles Barnard, "On Santa Catalina Island, the Kings of Swing Held Sway," *Smithsonian*, October 1991: 159–60; William Wrigley, Jr. Enterprises, Advertising Division, *Catalina, California's Magic Isle* (Avalon, CA: Santa Catalina Island Company, 1926); "Wrigley Ocean Marathon, *Catalina Islander*, September 20, 2002; "Outboard Motor Race Held on Lee Side of Island," *Catalina Islander*, January 18, 1928; Banning, *The Banning Family in Southern California*.

20. Charles C. Grossman, *The Wonder City: Los Angeles* [1931], Ephemera Collection, Seaver Center for Western History Research, Natural History Museum of Los Angeles County, Los Angeles. This booklet contains a large amount of statistics and other information provided by the All-Year Club. For a concise history of the All-Year Club, see Leonard Pitt and Dale Pitt, *Los Angeles A to Z: An Encyclopedia of the City and County* (Berkeley: University of California Press, 1997), 276–77

21. Charles C. Grossman, *The Wonder City: Los Angeles*. For more on regional industrial development, see Greg Hise, "'Nature's Workshop': Industry and Urban Expansion in Southern California, 1900–1950," *Journal of Historical Geography* 27, no. 1 (January 2001): 74–92.

22. Charles C. Grossman, *The Wonder City: Los Angeles*; *Los Angeles County, Sportland*, Los Angeles Junior Chamber of Commerce, 1928, Ephemera Collection, Seaver Center.

23. *Wireless*, October 4, 1913, Catalina Island Museum Archives. The file "G. Motion Picture Production—Movie" contains a variety of clippings and lists discussing films made at Catalina.

24. For information on individual celebrities who frequented Catalina, see the file "Celebrities—General," Catalina Island Museum Archives; Harry Carr, *Los Angeles: City of Dreams* (New York: D. Appleton-Century, 1935), 310.

25. *A Picture Tour of Catalina Island: California's Magic Isle* (Avalon, CA: Wix-Hastell, 1927), 16; *Catalina Islander*, December 24, 1924; Julia Braun Kessler, "As We Were in Avalon," *California History* 63, no. 1 (Winter 1984): 76.

26. 1 February 1932, "Avalon City Council Minutes," Frederick Baker Papers, UCLA Special Collections; Patricia Anne Moore, *The Casino: Avalon, Santa Catalina Island, California* (Avalon, CA: Catalina Island Museum Society, 1979), 59–61; History—Prohibition, in file "G. Avalon—History—General," Santa Catalina Island Museum Archives.

27. Braun, "As We Were in Avalon," 72–76; Ernest Windle, *Windle's History of Santa Catalina Island* (Avalon, CA: Catalina Islander, 1931), 63. See also Moore, *The Casino*.

28. Barnard, "On Santa Catalina Island," 160; Ray Miller and Jo Miller, *Catalina!: "...Wish You Were Here"* (Avalon, CA: Evergreen, 1993), 59; Yellowstone attendance figures from Paul Schullery, *Searching for Yellowstone: Ecology and Wonder in the Last Wilderness* (Boston: Houghton Mifflin, 1997), 135; Carr, *Los Angeles: City of Dreams*, 308.

29. For information on individual celebrities who frequented Catalina, see the file "Celebrities—General," Catalina Island Museum Archives; Carr, *Los Angeles: City of Dreams*, 310. For a description of the social world of Hollywood in this era, see Otto Friedrich, *City of Nets: A Portrait of Hollywood in the 1940's* (Berkeley: University of California Press, 1997).

30. See Lary May, *Screening Out the Past: The Birth of Mass Culture and the Motion Picture Industry* (New York: Oxford University Press, 1980).

31. Bushing, "Santa Catalina Island Company," 11.

32. Press release, Santa Catalina Island Company Publicity Department, [ca. 1935], G. Personages, Catalina—P. K. Wrigley file, Catalina Island Museum Archives. This file also contains a series of memos from Wrigley detailing his concerns about unauthorized postcards; File: "Events—Chicago World's Fair; Exhibit," Catalina Island Museum Archives.

33. For a description and photograph of Neutra's ticket office, see Thomas S. Hines, *Richard Neutra and the Search for Modern Architecture: A Biography and History* (New York: Oxford University Press, 1982).

34. Bushing, "Santa Catalina Island Company," 14.

35. E. S. to John Anson Ford, Lettergram, [1947], John Anson Ford Collection, Box 41, Parks and Recreation, folder B 18, Huntington Library.

36. For an example of Catalina's promotion in the new postwar age of passenger air travel, see *It's Sun Country Vacation Time Again!*, American Airlines pamphlet, 1946, Institute for the Study of the American West. Air fare and visitation figures from 1950 and a discussion of regional promotion are found in Federal Writers' Project, *Los Angeles*, 137–45, 375–78. See also Bushing, "Santa Catalina Island Company," 14.

37. Philip Wrigley to Alma Overholt, 16 June 1947, G. Personages, Catalina—P. K. Wrigley File, Catalina Island Museum Archives; *The Isthmus*, Santa Catalina Island Company, [1938], Ephemera Collection, Seaver Center.

38. Philip K. Wrigley to Alma Overholt, 12 August 1947, Personages, Catalina—P. K. Wrigley File, Catalina Island Museum Archives; Federal Writers' Project, *Los Angeles*, 375–78; Bushing, Santa Catalina Island Company," 11; Malcom J. Renton, "The SCIC's Third Quarter Century: 1944–1969," *Water Lines*, 3d quarter 1994, 6.

39. Philip Wrigley to Alma Overholt, 12 August 1947, Catalina Island Museum Archives.

40. Songs and lyrics compiled by Catalina Island Museum. See G. Music—Songs about Avalon File and G. Music—General—Big Bands file, Catalina Island Museum Archives.

41. Federal Writers' Project, *Los Angeles*, 375–78; Outing Bureau of the Automobile Club of Southern California, *Log of the Peninsula of Lower California*, 1930; *The Mexican Year Book for 1922–23* (Los Angeles: Times-Mirror, 1922); both items in Ephemera Collection, Seaver Center; *San Diego Union*, October 1, 1887, quoted in Glenn S. Dumke, *The Boom of the Eighties in Southern California* (San Marino, CA: Huntington Library, 1944), 154.

42. *Cruise to Mexico in Luxury and Comfort on Big Ocean Liners* (Los Angeles: Peck-Judah Travel Bureau, 1936); *Mexico Adventure Tours: Three Suggested Itineraries Off the Beaten Path* (Los Angeles: Southern California Tourist Bureau, [1935]); *Coronado Islands*, pamphlet, all in Ephemera Collection, Seaver Center.

43. *Along the Roads of Romance Land: An Illustrated Guide to the Charm Spots in and Around Mexico City Which May Be Readily Reached by the Motorist*, Monte Carlo Cigarettes, El Department de Tourismo, Mexico, D. F., 1936; *Agua Caliente: Carefree, Dutyfree in Old Mexico*, pamphlet, Ephemera Collection, Seaver Center.

44. Dina Berger, *The Development of Mexico's Tourism Industry: Pyramids by Day, Martinis by Night* (New York: Palgrave Macmillan, 2006), 1–10; 15.

45. Berger, *The Development of Mexico's Tourism Industry*, 61.

46. For more on vice tourism in Mexico, see Eric Michael Schantz, "From the *Mexicali Rose* to the Tijuana Brass: Vice Tours of the United States–Mexico Border, 1910–1965" (PhD diss., University of California, Los Angeles, 2001). The career of the casino boats is discussed in Vickey Kalambakal, "The Battle of Santa Monica Bay," *American History* 37 (Spring 2002): 36–40. For the early history of Las Vegas, and an overview of America's gambling appetites, see John M. Findlay, *People of Chance: Gambling in American Society from Jamestown to Las Vegas* (New York: Oxford University Press, 1986).

47. For an examination of the creation of Disneyland, see John M. Findlay, *Magic Lands: Western American Cityscapes after 1940* (Berkeley: University of California Press, 1992).
48. These surveys included studies composed of interviews of visitors to Catalina and others that consisted of mailed questionnaires sent to recent visitors. Questions sometimes varied, but usually concerned length of stay, type of accommodation, mode of transportation, money spent, and place of origin. All surveys are of non-California residents. *Bureau Registrants' Survey, Catalina Island Visitors, November 1946–March 1947*, All-Year Club of Southern California, 1947; *Bureau Registrant's Survey, Catalina Island Visitors, June–July 1947*, All-Year Club of Southern California, 1947; *Survey of Catalina Island Visitors Spring and Summer, 1947*, All Year Club of Southern California, 1947; *Bureau Registrants' Survey, Catalina Island Visitors, September–November 1947*, All-Year Club of Southern California, 1947; *Bureau Registrants' Survey, Catalina Island Visitors, December 1947–February 1948*, All-Year Club of Southern California, 1948, ser. 5: Reports and Surveys on Southern California Tourism, 1920–1976, box 48, Greater Los Angeles Visitors and Convention Bureau (All-Year Club of Southern California) Collection, 1900–1980, Special Collections, Oviatt Library, California State University, Northridge.
49. *Guide Book Survey of California Visitors*, All-Year Club of Southern California, 1937, ser. 5, box 49; *Survey of Southern California Visitors Over 50 Years of Age*, 1942, ser. 5, box 51, Greater Los Angeles Visitors and Convention Bureau (All-Year Club of Southern California) Collection, Special Collections, California State University, Northridge.
50. *Preliminary Tabulation, Fall 1956 Disneyland Registrants*, All-Year Club of Southern California, 1957, 20, ser. 5, box 49, Greater Los Angeles Visitors and Convention Bureau (All-Year Club of Southern California) Collection, Special Collections, California State University, Northridge.
51. Barnard, "On Santa Catalina Island," 164–67; *Los Angeles Times*, November 30, 1986.
52. Renton, "The SCIC's Third Quarter Century," 6, 8–9.
53. Doug Lombard quoted in "Other Personal Remembrances of Philip K. Wrigley," *Water Lines* Special Anniversary Edition, December 1994; Renton, "The SCIC's Third Quarter Century," 8.
54. "Memo," 17 February 1974, folder: 1.34.1.10; Seymour Greben, "Santa Catalina Island: A Planning and Development Proposal," 29 May 1974, attached to correspondence, Seymour Greben to Kenneth Hahn, 19 August 1974, Folder 1.34.1.11, "Catalina Island," both box 19: Parks and Recreation, Correspondence, Chronological, 1974, Kenneth Hahn Collection, Huntington Library. Seymour Greben was director of parks and public recreation for Los Angeles County. His Catalina correspondence was with Kenneth Hahn, a Los Angeles County supervisor.
55. Seymour Greben, "Santa Catalina Island: A Planning and Development Proposal," 29 May 1974, 1, attached to correspondence, Seymour Greben to Kenneth Hahn, 19 August 1974, Hahn Collection, Huntington Library.
56. Greben, "Santa Catalina Island: A Planning and Development Proposal." Some criticized Los Angeles County for this easement, as even the county admitted that lost tax revenue from the SCIC would have been enough money to purchase and develop twenty-five public parks on the mainland. See "Santa Catalina Island: An Interim Development Proposal," 21 August 1974, attached to correspondence, Seymour Greben to Kenneth Hahn, 19 August 1974, Folder 1.34.1.11, "Catalina Island," box 19: Parks and Recreation, Correspondence, Chronological, 1974, Hahn Collection, Huntington Library. See also a critical article by Philip Fradkin in the *Los Angeles Times*, November 24, 1974.
57. Charles Frederick Holder, *Santa Catalina, an Isle of Summer: Its History, Climate, Sports, and Antiquities* (San Francisco: Murdock, 1895), 42; *Fodor's Los Angeles* (New York: Fodor's Travel Publications, 1993), 177. The transformation of Southern California and its impact on the promotion of tourism is traced in Clark Davis, "From Oasis to

Metropolis: Southern California and the Changing Context of American Leisure," *Pacific Historical Review* 61, no. 3 (May 1992). The rhetoric and imagery used to promote the region in the early twentieth century is analyzed in Tom Zimmerman, "Paradise Promoted: Boosterism and the Los Angeles Chamber of Commerce," *California History* 64, no. 1 (Winter 1985). Catalina's more recent history offers intriguing parallels with Cape May, one of the nation's oldest resorts, a beach community located at the southern tip of New Jersey. Initially a whaling village, it became an exclusive retreat for affluent Philadelphians early in the nineteenth century. When railroads made Cape May more accessible in the 1860s, it became a popular destination for a much larger number of urbanites. By the late nineteenth century, however, the elite had decamped for Newport, Rhode Island, while the masses headed for the wider beaches and amusement parks of Atlantic City. After languishing for much of the twentieth century, Cape May experienced a remarkable renaissance beginning in the 1970s. Economic stagnation had left a large assemblage of exuberant Victorian architecture preserved relatively intact. Cape May boomed again, with its primary amenity and tourist industry resource no longer its beachfront, but instead its restored architecture and tourists' nostalgia for an earlier era; see Emil R. Salvini, *The Summer City by the Sea: Cape May, New Jersey; An Illustrated History* (Belleville, NJ.: Wheal-Grace, 1995); and Charles A. Stansfield Jr., "Cape May: Selling History by the Sea," *Journal of Cultural Geography* Vol. 11 (Fall/Winter 1990): 25–37.

58. "Catalina (Pimu) Island Field Archaeology Project," UCLA Archaeology Field Program, http://www.archaeology.ucla.edu/programs/north-america/u.s.-california-pimu-catalina-island-archaeological-project/; "Recent Projects and Endeavors by Tongva," Gabrieleno/Tongva Tribal Council of San Gabriel, http://www.tongva.com/.

CHAPTER 5

1. The existing historiography of Palms Springs and resort development in the Coachella Valley prior to World War II is quite limited. Local histories include Katherine Ainsworth, *The McCallum Saga: The Story of the Founding of Palm Springs* (Palm Springs, CA: Palm Springs Desert Museum, 1973), which recounts the history of the first white settlers in the area, though it does so while glossing over some of the less flattering aspects of their history. Ed Ainsworth, *Golden Checkerboard* (Palm Desert, CA: Desert-Southwest, Inc., 1965), tells the complex and contentious history of Indian and Anglo land and water claims and ownership in the Coachella Valley. The paternalistic tone that pervades the book limits its usefulness, however. An excellent corrective to both of these older sources is Ryan M. Kray, "The Path to Paradise: Expropriation, Exodus, and Exclusion in the Making of Palm Springs," *Pacific Historical Review* 73 (2004), 85–126. A more recent book, critical of the community's environmentally unsustainable development, is Peter Wild, *Tipping the Dream: A Brief History of Palm Springs* (Johannesburg, CA: Shady Myrick Research Project, 2007). A master's thesis and a dissertation have also focused on Palm Springs. Thomas A. Jensen, "Palm Springs, California: Its Evolution and Functions" (Master's thesis, UCLA, 1954) offers a geographical analysis of Palm Springs' development as a resort. Rachel Dayton Shaw, "Evolving Ecoscape: An Environmental and Cultural History of Palm Springs, California, and the Agua Caliente Indian Reservation, 1877–1939," (PhD diss., University of California, San Diego, 1999), presents an environmental history of Palm Springs, focusing primarily on water issues. Important sources for the history of the Agua Calientes include Harry C. James, *The Cahuilla Indians: The Men Called Master* (Los Angeles: Westernlore, 1960); Lowell John Bean, *Mukat's People: The Cahuilla Indians of Southern California* (Berkeley: University of California Press, 1972); and George

Harwood Phillips, *Chiefs and Challengers: Indian Resistance and Cooperation in Southern California* (Berkeley: University of California Press, 1975). Two recent photographic surveys of Palm Springs architecture are Adèle Cygelman, *Palm Springs Modern: Houses in the California Desert* (New York: Rizzoli, 1999); and Alan Hess and Andrew Danish, *Palm Springs Weekend: The Architecture and Design of a Mid-Century Oasis* (San Francisco: Chronicle, 2001).

2. Francisco Patencio, *Stories and Legends of the Palm Springs Indians* (Los Angeles: Times Mirror, 1943), 81–82; Bean, *Mukat's People*, 17–18.

3. Stephen Bowers, *A Remarkable Valley and an Interesting Tribe of Indians*, San Buena Ventura, CA: 1888.

4. Patencio, *Stories and Legends,* 58; Bean, *Mukat's People*, 18; Shaw, "Evolving Ecoscape," 41–42; 56–57.

5. W. W. Robinson, *The Story of Riverside County* (Los Angeles: Title Insurance and Trust Company, 1957), 29–30; Ed Ainsworth, *Golden Checkerboard*, 62–63.

6. Ainsworth, *The McCallum Saga*, 1–46.

7. Ainsworth, *The McCallum Saga*, xiii–xiv; Will Bowart, *The McCallum Centennial* (Palm Springs: Palm Springs Historical Society, 1984).

8. Ainsworth, *The McCallum Saga*, 128–32.

9. Bowart, *The McCallum Centennial*; Frank Bogert, interview by author, Palm Springs, California, 26 August 2003. Even Bogert, who considered himself a friend of Pearl McCallum McManus, readily admitted that she could be "a miserly witch." Arriving in Palm Springs as a teenager in 1921 to herd horses, Bogert held a variety of jobs in the Palm Springs tourist industry over several decades, served as mayor of the city, and wrote a history of Palm Springs. As a young man, he also met Charles Lummis, and remembered his trademark green corduroy suit. The interview took place in his home in Palm Springs.

10. J. Kellogg, Mecca, CA, to Williams Lawrence Paul, 17 March 1921, "First Official Bulletin Issued by International Festival of Dates Association, Indio, California, 1921," 50, Williams Lawrence Paul Papers, Special Collections, UCR.

11. The *Coachella Valley Submarine*, Special Chamber of Commerce Edition, 1919, offers a boosterist view of the local date industry (Ephemera Collection, Seaver Center for Historical Research, Natural History Museum of Los Angeles County, Los Angeles).

12. *Palm Springs: The Oasis of Delight*, Hugh Evans and Company, ca. 1930, Ephemera Collection, Seaver Center; Elizabeth W. Richards, *A Look Into Palm Springs' Past*, Santa Fe Federal Savings and Loan Association, [1960], History and Genealogy Department, Richard J. Riordan Central Library, Los Angeles; "Walled Oasis of Biskra: An Interpretation of the American Desert in the Algerian Manner," Charles S. Jones, 1928, Special Collections, Young Research Library, University of California, Los Angeles.

13. For a discussion of Ruskin, the romantic movement, and the evolving aesthetic interpretation of nature in Europe and the United States, see Simon Schama, *Landscape and Memory* (New York: Knopf, 1995).

14. For analysis of the changing perceptions of deserts in American culture, including a discussion of John C. Van Dyke, see Patricia Nelson Limerick, *Desert Passages: Encounters with the American Deserts* (Albuquerque: University of New Mexico Press), 1985.

15. John C. Van Dyke, *The Desert: Further Studies in Natural Appearances* (New York: Charles Scribner's Sons, 1901); Peter Wild, "John. C. Van Dyke and the Desert Aestheticians," in *The Opal Desert: Explorations of Fantasy and Reality in the American Southwest* (Austin: University of Texas Press, 1999), 75–87; Charles Lummis, *Out West*, November 1901, 372. See also John C. Van Dyke, *The Secret Life of John C. Van Dyke: Selected Letters*, ed. David W. Teague and Peter Wild (Reno: University of Nevada Press, 1997); and John C. Van Dyke, *The Autobiography of John C. Van Dyke: A Personal*

Narrative of American Life, 1861–1931, ed. Peter Wild (Salt Lake City: University of Utah Press, 1993).

16. Marjorie Belle Bright, *Nellie's Boardinghouse: A Dual Biography of Nellie Coffman and Palm Springs* (Palm Springs, CA: ECT, 1981), 12–14; Bowers, "A Remarkable Valley," 4.

17. Wayland H. Smith, "California Indians to Date," *Out West*, February–March 1909, 143.

18. Shaw, "Evolving Ecoscape," 250–62.

19. David Cathers, *Gustav Stickley* (London: Phaidon, 2003), 107–16; George Wharton James, *The Wonders of the Colorado Desert* (Boston: Little, Brown, 1911), 287–88.

20. Bright, *Nellie's Boardinghouse*, 20–23.

21. Ibid., 30.

22. Ernie Pyle, *Ernie Pyle's Southwest* (Palm Desert, CA: Desert-Southwest, 1965), 90; Elizabeth Coffman Kieley and Thomas Kieley, interview by author, Palm Springs, California, 25 August 2003. Elizabeth Coffman Kieley was the granddaughter of Nellie Coffman; Thomas Kieley served on the Palm Springs city council. The interview took place in their home. After our interview Mr. Kieley took me on a tour of Smoke Tree Ranch, where their house was located.

23. Frank Bogert interview. The primary study of health migrants in Southern California remains John E. Baur, *The Health Seekers of Southern California, 1870–1900* (San Marino, CA: Huntington Library, 1959). A recent study that emphasizes the degree to which nineteenth-century Americans believed some environments to be healthful and others perilous is Conevery Bolton Valenčius, *The Health of the Country: How American Settlers Understood Themselves and their Land* (New York: Basic Books, 2002).

24. Emily K. Abel, *Suffering in the Land of Sunshine: A Los Angeles Illness Narrative* (New Brunswick, NJ: Rutgers University Press, 2006), recounts the about-face of regional promoters in Southern California who had long courted tuberculosis victims but later began to shun them.

25. *The Desert Inn: Where Desert and Mountains Meet*, Palm Springs, 1920, Ephemera Collection, Seaver Center; *Santa Catalina Island—Ever Grand, Attractive, and Unique— The Season of 1896*, Banning Company Collection, box 5, Huntington Library, San Marino, California; Bright, *Nellie's Boardinghouse*, 112; Frank Bogert interview.

26. A. Ross Bourne, "Some Major Aspects of the Historical Development of Palm Springs between 1880 and 1938, and in Addition a Continuation of the Historical Changes in the Indian Land Problem and Four Cultural Institutions until 1948" (Master's thesis, Occidental College, 1953), 15. Bright, *Nellie's Boardinghouse*, 136–37; Thomas A. Jensen, "Palm Springs, California: Its Evolution and Functions" (Master's thesis, UCLA, 1954), 86.

27. Bright, *Nellie's Boardinghouse*, 89.

28. Bright, *Nellie's* Boardinghouse, 94–96.

29. *The Oasis: Palm Springs, California*, pamphlet, no date, Ephemera Collection, Seaver Center.

30. Bogert interview; *El Mirador: In the Garden of the Sun*, pamphlet, n.d.; *El Mirador: America's Foremost Desert Resort*, pamphlet, 1934, Ephemera Collection, Seaver Center.

31. Frank Bogert interview.

32. Hess and Danish, *Palm Springs Weekend*, 116–20; Katherine Ainsworth, *The McCallum Saga*, 192–93.

33. Tony Burke, *Palm Springs: Why I Love You* (Palm Desert, CA: Palmesa, 1976); Ted Salmon, *From Southern California to Casco Bay* (San Bernardino, CA: San Bernardino, 1930).

34. Hess and Danish, *Palm Springs Weekend*, 25, 84–86.

35. Ernest Young, *North American Excursion* (London: Edward Arnold, 1947), 263–64, 261.

36. J. Smeaton Chase, *Our Araby: Palm Springs and the Garden of the Sun* (Pasadena, CA: Star-News, 1920), 5.

37. Chase, *Our Araby*, 20. Hal K. Rothman discusses this progression of tourist development in *Devil's Bargains: Tourism in the Twentieth-Century American West* (Lawrence: University Press of Kansas, 1998).

38. Chase, *Our Araby*, 23–24. The history of Jackson Hole is the subject of M. Lawrence Culver, "Resorting to Tourism: The Town and the Valley of Jackson, Wyoming, through the 1950s" (Master's thesis, Utah State University, 1997).

39. Chase, *Our Araby*, 51–52; Mary Austin, *The Lands of the Sun* (Boston: Houghton Mifflin, 1927), viii; J. Smeaton Chase, "Desert Park in Prospect," *Palm Springs News*, April 12, 1933, Palm Springs Public Library, Palm Springs, California; *Riverside County: Its Hotels and Resorts*, Riverside County Chamber of Commerce, 1935, Ephemera Collection, Seaver Center.

40. *Desert Magazine*, May 1929, September 1929, December 1929, July 1930. For a history of this periodical, as well as of changing American attitudes about deserts, see Peter Wild, *Desert Magazine: The Henderson Years* (Johannesburg, CA: The Shady Myrick Research Project, 2004).

41. *Desert Magazine*, April 1930.

42. *The Desert*, Bullock's Department Store, Los Angeles, ca. 1927, Ephemera Collection, Seaver Center.

43. *Palm Springs: The Oasis of Delight*, Hugh Evans and Company, ca. 1930; *"Our Araby" Palm Springs, Merito Vista*, pamphlet, ca.1935, Ephemera Collection, Seaver Center; Elizabeth and Thomas Kieley interview.

44. *Palm Springs Life*, The Chaffey Company, Inc., 1938, 54, Ephemera Collection, Seaver Center; *The Palm Springs and Desert Resort Area Story*, Palm Springs Chamber of Commerce, 1955, Special Collections, UCR.

45. *Palm Springs Life*, The Chaffey Company, Inc., 1938; Kieley Interview.

46. *Palm Springs Life*, The Chaffey Company, Inc., 1938, ad for Smoke Tree Ranch on page 37; Hess and Danish, *Palm Springs Weekend*, 60–65.

47. Thomas S. Hines, *Richard Neutra and the Search for Modern Architecture: A Biography and History* (New York: Oxford University Press, 1982), 121–24.

48. "Palm Springs Life," The Chaffey Company, Inc, 1938, 49; Katherine Ainsworth, *The McCallum Saga*, 191; Bright, *Nellie's Boardinghouse*, 178–79.

49. While histories present this as a united act, the decision to burn the roundhouse, as well as bury the band's sacred bundle, may have been controversial at the time. Agua Caliente Ray Patencio, for example, regretted the loss of these material connections to the traditional past, and thought that with them more traditions might have survived. Ray Patencio Oral History Interview, 20 May 2005, Agua Caliente Cultural Museum.

50. Bright, *Nellie's Boardinghouse*, 177.

51. Ed Ainsworth, *Golden Checkerboard*, 66–67; Elizabeth and Thomas Kieley interview.

CHAPTER 6

1. Peter Wild, *Tipping the Dream: a Brief History of Palm Springs* (Johannesburg, CA: Shady Myrick Research Project, 2007); Elizabeth Coffman Kieley and Thomas Kieley, interview by author, Palm Springs, California, 25 August 2003; *Palm Springs Villager*, May–June 1948, 18–19. The complete run of the *Villager* and the periodicals that succeeded it, such as *Palm Springs Life*, are held in the collections of the Palm Springs Public Library, Palm Springs, California.

2. Elizabeth and Thomas Kieley interview; Frank Bogert, interview by author, Palm Springs, California, 26 August 2003.

3. Ryan M. Kray, "The Path to Paradise: Expropriation, Exodus, and Exclusion in the Making of Palm Springs," *Pacific Historical Review* 73 (2004): 97. Kray's article provides

the best and most comprehensive history available of Section 14, and racial segregation in Palm Springs.

4. *Palm Springs Villager*, May–June 1948, 12; Frank Bogert interview. Bogert served as a city councilman and mayor in Palm Springs in this period, and at the time of our conversation continued to assert that the city's actions were for the good of the tribe and the non-Indian residents of Section 14. For a decidedly slanted view of the history of Section 14 as a successful example of progress and mutual cooperation, see Ed Ainsworth, *Golden Checkerboard* (Palm Desert: Desert-Southwest, 1965). Kray's "The Path to Paradise" is the best corrective to this biased and boosterist view.

5. Thomas A. Jensen, "Palm Springs, California: Its Evolution and Functions" (Master's thesis, UCLA, 1954), 194.

6. Kray, "The Path to Paradise," 96–100.

7. Kray, "The Path to Paradise," 98–102; 104–05.

8. Kray, "The Path to Paradise," 104–06; "Progress in Section 14," in *1962 Progress Report*, Agua Caliente Band of Mission Indians, unpaginated booklet, 1962, Special Collections, Rivera Library, University of California, Riverside.

9. "Progress in Preserving Reserves," in *1962 Progress Report*, Agua Caliente Band of Mission Indians, 1962, Special Collections, UCR.

10. See "Progress in Equalization," in *1962 Progress Report*, Agua Caliente Band of Mission Indians, 1962, Special Collections, UCR.

11. *Palm Springs the Town and Club Magazine, 1960–1961 Annual Pictorial*, 71–83, Palm Springs Public Library; "Progress in Leasing," in *1962 Progress Report*, Agua Caliente Band of Mission Indians, 1962, Special Collections, UCR; *The Story of Palm Springs Reservation*, Agua Caliente Band of Mission Indians, 1952, Special Collections, UCR. This description of the Spa predates construction of the hotel.

12. Jensen, "Palm Springs, California," 202; "Progress in Equalization," in *1962 Progress Report*, Agua Caliente Band of Mission Indians, 1962, Special Collections, UCR.

13. Kray, "The Path to Paradise," 106–109; 118.

14. Kray, "The Path to Paradise," 109; 111. Kray's article provides the most detailed study available of the clearance of Section 14.

15. *Palm Springs Villager*, February 1947, 6; Christmas cactus appeared on cover of December 1947 issue.

16. *Palm Springs Villager*, February 1947, 16–17.

17. *Palm Springs Villager*, December 1947, 10–11.

18. For the expansion of tourism, particularly family auto tourism, after 1945, see Susan Sessions Rugh, *Are We There Yet?: The Golden Age of American Family Vacations* (Lawrence: University Press of Kansas, 2008). For the history of air conditioning, see Gail Cooper, *Air-Conditioning America: Engineers and the Controlled Environment, 1900–1960* (Baltimore: Johns Hopkins University Press, 1998); and Marsha E. Ackermann, *Cool Comfort: America's Romance With Air-Conditioning* (Washington, DC: Smithsonian Institution Press, 2002).

19. *Palm Springs Villager*, May–June 1948, 20; Jensen, "Palm Springs, California," 85, 114–15; *Palm Springs Villager Annual Pictorial*, September 1958, 15.

20. *Palm Springs Villager*, June 1952; Marjorie Belle Bright, *Nellie's Boardinghouse: A Dual Biography of Nellie Coffman and Palm Springs* (Palm Springs, CA: ECT, 1981), 185–86; Katherine Ainsworth, *The McCallum Saga: The Story of the Founding of Palm Springs* (Palm Springs, CA: Palm Springs Desert Museum, 1973), 224; Will Bowart, The McCallum Centennial (Palm Springs: Palm Springs Historical Society, 1984).

21. *Palm Springs Villager*, February 1948, 18–19.

22. Neil Morgan, *Westward Tilt: The American West Today* (New York: Random House, 1963), 126; quoted in Kerwin L. Klein, "Frontier Tales: The Narrative Construction of

Cultural Borders in Twentieth-Century California," *Comparative Studies in Society and History* 34, no. 3 (July 1992): 466; *Palm Springs Villager*, December 1947, 6.

23. I am indebted to Thomas S. Hines for his analysis of the rationalist/expressionist division within modernism.

24. Frank Bogert interview; Adèle Cygelman, *Palm Springs Modern: Houses in the California Desert* (New York: Rizzoli, 1999), 72; *Palm Springs Villager*, October 1948, 17.

25. Thomas S. Hines, *Irving Gill and the Architecture of Reform* (New York: Monacelli, 2000).

26. Thomas S. Hines, *Richard Neutra and the Search for Modern Architecture: A Biography and History* (New York: Oxford University Press, 1982), 200–204.

27. Joseph Rosa, *Albert Frey, Architect* (New York: Rizzoli International, 1990), 71–72; *Palm Springs Villager*, March 1947.

28. Rosa, *Albert Frey*, 60–61, 72–73.

29. Ibid., 120; Cygelman, *Palm Springs Modern*, 86–93.

30. Frank Escher, ed., *John Lautner, Architect* (London: Ellipsis, 1994), 159–65.

31. Ibid., 211–18.

32. *Palm Springs Villager*, April 1952, 40; Elizabeth and Thomas Kieley interview; Wallace Stegner, *Where the Bluebird Sings to the Lemonade Springs: Living and Writing in the West* (New York: Random House, 1992), 77, 78.

33. "The Palm Springs and Desert Resort Area Story," Palm Springs Chamber of Commerce, 1955, Special Collections, UCR.

34. Jensen, "Palm Springs, California," 182–83; Andre Keil, *Swimming at the Park Pool: A History of Aquatics in the City of Los Angeles*, City of Los Angeles, Recreation and Parks, 1992,

35. Cygelman, *Palm Springs Modern*, 56.

36. Rosa, *Albert Frey*, 35–36, 119; Cygelman, *Palm Springs Modern*, 12; "Palm Canyon Drive," *Palm Springs Villager Pictorial*, September 1958.

37. Alan Hess and Andrew Danish, *Palm Springs Weekend: The Architecture and Design of a Mid-Century Oasis* (San Francisco: Chronicle, 2001), 112–16, 125–27.

38. Ibid., 120–24.

39. Ibid., 126–31.

40. *Palm Springs Villager*, March 1952, 13–16.

41. Frank Bogert interview; *Palm Springs Villager*, October 1950, 3; *Palm Springs Villager*, January 1951, 24; *Palm Springs Villager*, November 1950, 3.

42. *Palm Springs Villager*, January 1951, 24.

43. *Palm Springs Villager*, March 1951, 3; *Palm Springs Villager Annual Pictorial*, September 1958, 47; *Palm Springs Life*, February 1965, 23. For an overview of the new golf developments around Palm Springs, see "The Making of America's Country Club Capital," *Palm Springs Life Annual Pictorial*, 1960–61, 41–65.

44. *Palm Springs Life*, February 1965, 33–40.

45. *Palm Springs Villager*, October 1948, 34; *Palm Springs Life*, July 1965, 33–34.

46. *Palm Springs Villager Annual Pictorial*, September 1958, 32.

47. Elizabeth and Thomas Kieley interview.

48. Frank Bogert interview; Elizabeth and Thomas Kieley interview. The growing popularity of vacation homes and condominiums at western ski resorts is traced in Hal K. Rothman, *Devil's Bargains: Tourism in the Twentieth-Century American West* (Lawrence: University Press of Kansas, 1998); see also Annie Gilbert Coleman, *Ski Style: Sport and Culture in the Rockies* (Lawrence: University Press of Kansas, 2004).

49. *Palm Springs Life*, September 1970, 8–9, 23; *Palm Springs Life*, December 1965, 3, 67.

50. *Your Del Webb's Sun City Tour Guide*, ca. 1960, Special Collections, Hayden Library, Arizona State University. For a fuller analysis of Sun City, see John M. Findlay, *Magic Lands: Western Cityscapes and American Culture After 1940* (Berkeley: University of California Press, 1992).

51. Frank Bogert interview; *Del Webb's TowneHouse*, undated pamphlet, Newton Rosenzweig Collection, Arizona Historical Foundation. Susan G. Davis discusses the growth of regional convention tourism in "Landscapes of Imagination: Tourism in Southern California," *Pacific Historical Review* 68, no. 2 (May 1999), 173–191. The role of tourism in Atlanta's development is the subject of Harvey K. Newman, *Southern Hospitality: Tourism and the Growth of Atlanta* (Tuscaloosa: University of Alabama Press, 1999).

52. *Palm Springs Life Annual Desert Progress Issue*, 1975–76, 18, 42–47, 51; Elizabeth and Thomas Kieley interview.

53. *Palm Springs Villager*, October 1947, 15; L. W. Coffee, *Desert Hot Springs*, 1949, box: Riverside County, folder 3, Ephemera Collection, Seaver Center.

CHAPTER 7

1. Sylvia Harris Monaghan, *Going to the Fair: A Preview of the New York World's Fair 1939* (New York: Sun Dial, 1939).

2. Ibid., 47.

3. Frank Lloyd Wright, *When Democracy Builds* (Chicago: University of Chicago Press, 1945), vii, 37, 56, 113.

4. Population figures for cities from the 1940 census, "Table 17: Population of the 100 Largest Urban Places: 1940," available online at: http://www.census.gov/population/www/documentation/twps0027/tab17.txt. Arizona state population from 1940 census, "U.S. Population, Vol. 1, Number of Inhabitants," 89. Available online at: http://www2.census.gov/prod2/decennial/documents/33973538v1ch03.pdf. Post-2000 population estimates from "July 1, 2005 Population estimates for Metropolitan, Micropolitan, and Combined Statistical Areas," available online at: http://www.census.gov/population/www/estimates/Estimates%20pages_final.html.

5. Historical studies analyzing the growth of the Sunbelt region include Richard M. Bernard and Bradley R. Rice, eds., *Sunbelt Cities: Politics and Growth since World War II* (Austin: University of Texas Press, 1983); Raymond A. Mohl, ed., *Searching for the Sunbelt: Historical Perspectives on a Region* (Knoxville: University of Tennessee Press, 1990); Janet Rothenberg Pack, ed., *Sunbelt/Frostbelt: Public Policies and Market Forces in Metropolitan Development* (Washington, DC: Brookings Institution Press, 2005); and Bruce J. Schulman, *From Cotton Belt to Sunbelt: Federal Policy, Economic Development, and the Transformation of the South, 1938–1980* (New York: Oxford University Press, 1991).

6. For a succinct summary of the creation and evolution of the FHA loan system, see Robert Fishman, *Bourgeois Utopias: The Rise and Fall of Suburbia* (New York: Basic Books, 1987), 174–77. For broader examinations of suburban house financing and construction before and after World War II, and its place as a component of larger consumer culture, see Lizabeth Cohen, *A Consumer's Republic: The Politics of Mass Consumption in Postwar America* (New York: Vintage, 2004) and Becky M. Nicolaides, *My Blue Heaven: Life and Politics in the Working-Class Suburbs of Los Angeles, 1920–1965* (Chicago: University of Chicago Press, 2002).

7. D. J. Waldie documents the aerospace suburbs of his childhood in *Holy Land: A Suburban Memoir* (New York: W. W. Norton, 1996). The figures for aerospace employment in Southern California come from his essay "Lost in Aerospace: Inhabiting a Future Long since Past," *Huntington Frontiers*, Fall/Winter 2007, 5.

8. For an overview and analysis of debates within the historiography of suburbia, see Mary Corbin Sies, "North American Suburbs, 1880–1950: Cultural and Social Reconsiderations" *Journal of Urban History* 27, no. 3 (March 2001), 313–46.

9. Fishman, *Bourgeois Utopias*, 176–77.

10. Dolores Hayden, *Building Suburbia: Green Fields and Urban Growth, 1820–2000* (New York: Vintage, 2004), 138–46.

11. Michael Gannon, *Florida: A Short History* (Gainesville: University Press of Florida, 1993); Ted Steinberg, *Acts of God: The Unnatural History of Natural Disaster in America*, 2d ed. (New York: Oxford University Press, 2006), 51–63; Witold Rybczynski, *Last Harvest: How a Cornfield became New Daleville; Real Estate Development in America from George Washington to the Builders of the Twenty-First Century, and Why We Live in Houses Anyway* (New York: Scribner, 2007), 32.

12. Frank Lloyd Wright, *An Autobiography* (New York: Duell, Sloan and Pearce, 1943), 305, 307.

13. Robert Alan Goldberg, *Barry Goldwater* (New Haven, CT: Yale University Press, 1995), 89.

14. Wright, *An Autobiography*, 309, 308.

15. Charles E. Aguar and Berdeanna Aguar, *Wrightscapes: Frank Lloyd Wright's Landscape Designs* (New York: McGraw-Hill, 2002), 242–44.

16. Russell Todd, *Apache Trail: The Wonder Trip through Oldest America*, Southern Pacific Rail Road, n.d., Special Collections, Hayden Library, Arizona State University. The Apache image is photo SPC 44–75.13.

17. Michael F. Logan, *Desert Cities: The Environmental History of Phoenix and Tucson* (Pittsburgh, PA: University of Pittsburgh Press, 2006), 104.

18. For a history of the growth and development of Phoenix, see Bradford Luckingham, *Phoenix: The History of a Southwestern Metropolis* (Tucson: University of Arizona Press, 1989).

19. Peter Iverson, *Barry Goldwater: Native Arizonan* (Norman: University of Oklahoma Press, 1997), 22–25.

20. Carl A. Bimson, *How Arizona Showed Them*, Arizona Historical Foundation, Arizona State University; Carl A. Bimson, "Veterans Loans," addresses by Carl A. Bimson, 1946–1951. Arizona Historical Foundation, Arizona State University; Valley National Bank, *About Arizona . . .*, 5th ed., ca. 1965, Arizona Historical Foundation.

21. Alan Ehrenhalt, *The Lost City: The Forgotten Virtues of Community in America* (New York: Basic Books, 1995), 57.

22. Croly quoted in Fishman, *Bourgeois Utopias*, 160–61; Saylor quoted in John Mack Faragher, "Bungalow and Ranch House: The Architectural Backwash of California," *Western Historical Quarterly* 32, no. 2 (Summer 2001): 163.

23. For more on the history of the ranch style—and its connections to older bungalow styles—see Faragher, "Bungalow and Ranch House."

24. Daniel P. Gregory, *Cliff May and the Modern Ranch House* (New York: Rizzoli, 2008), 31.

25. "The California Ranch House, Cliff May," interview by Marlene L. Laskey, 1984, UCLA Oral History Program, 195–96; Mary A. van Balgooy, "Designer of the Dream: Cliff May and the California Ranch House," *Southern California Quarterly* 86 (2004): 131–33.

26. "The California Ranch House, Cliff May," interview by Marlene L. Laskey, 195–96, 197; 190–92; Gregory, *Cliff May and the Modern Ranch House*, 22.

27. Van Balgooy, "Designer of the Dream," 138.

28. "The California Ranch House, Cliff May," interview by Marlene L. Laskey, 212–17; vii–ix; van Balgooy, "Designer of the Dream," 137.

29. "The California Ranch House, Cliff May," interview by Marlene L. Laskey, vii–ix, 198; Sunset Magazine, *Sunset Western Ranch Houses* (San Francisco: Lane, 1946); Sunset Magazine, *Western Ranch Houses by Cliff May* (San Francisco: Lane, 1958); Gregory, *Cliff May and the Modern Ranch House*, 117.

30. Rybczynski, *Last Harvest*, 207–8.

31. "The California Ranch House, Cliff May," interview by Marlene L. Laskey, 7–8; van Balgooy, "Designer of the Dream," 128–29.

32. Gregory, *Cliff May and the Modern Ranch House*, 26; "The California Ranch House, Cliff May," interview by Marlene L. Laskey, 28.

33. Gregory, *Cliff May and the Modern Ranch House*, 68.

34. "The California Ranch House, Cliff May," interview by Marlene L. Laskey, 29.

35. Ibid., 169.

36. Ibid., 163.

37. Sunset Magazine, *Sunset Western Ranch Houses*; Sunset Magazine, *Western Ranch Houses by Cliff May*; Rybczynski, *Last Harvest*, 159–60; "The California Ranch House, Cliff May," interview by Marlene L. Laskey, 47–48.

38. "The California Ranch House, Cliff May," interview by Marlene L. Laskey, 209.

39. Sunset Magazine, *Western Ranch Houses by Cliff May*, 7.

40. Ibid., 10, 12.

41. Ibid., 10, 12.

42. Van Balgooy, "Designer of the Dream," 133, 136; Gregory, *Cliff May and the Modern Ranch*, 23.

43. Ibid., 19.

44. "The California Ranch House, Cliff May," interview by Marlene L. Laskey, 166.

45. Sunset Magazine, *Western Ranch Houses by Cliff May*, 74–75.

46. Gregory, *Cliff May and the Modern Ranch House*, 23; "A House Can Be Modern and Not Look It," *House Beautiful*, October 1945, 109–15.

47. Van Balgooy, "Designer of the Dream," 137.

48. Cohen, *A Consumer's Republic*, 121.

49. For the history of Maryvale, see Alan Hess, *The Ranch House* (New York: Harry N. Abrams, 2004.

50. Iverson, *Barry Goldwater*, 3–7.

51. Ibid., 162–67.

52. Goldberg, *Barry Goldwater*, 54–55.

53. Iverson, *Barry Goldwater*, 18.

54. Goldberg, *Barry Goldwater*, 52.

55. Iverson, *Barry Goldwater*, 52.

56. Goldberg, *Barry Goldwater*, 35–54; *Desert Film Presents: Shooting Grand Canyon Rapids*, Arizona Historical Foundation, Arizona State University; Barry M. Goldwater, *A Journey Down the Green and Colorado Rivers 1940* (Phoenix, AZ: H. Walker, 1940), 43–44.

57. Iverson, *Barry Goldwater*, 57–58.

58. Ibid., 25.

59. *Evolution of the Arizona Economy*, October, 1952, "Addresses of Carl A. Bimson, 1951–1954," 50, Arizona Historical Foundation; "Rising Phoenix: 'Miracle' in Arizona," *Newsweek*, January 4, 1960, 46; Valley National Bank, *About Arizona . . .*, 5th ed., ca. 1965, Arizona Historical Foundation.

60. "Rising Phoenix: 'Miracle' in Arizona," *Newsweek*, January 4, 1960, 49.

61. Sun City Historical Society, *Memories of the Sun Cities: Marinette Preceded Sun City*; *Sun Cities Area Historical Society History 101*, DTO Sun City 8, Special Collections, Hayden Library, Arizona State University.

62. *The Story of Arizona and Sun City* and *Land of Giants*, Arizona Historical Foundation.

63. "Admirers Buy Goldwater Home," *Arizona Republic*, May 24, 2000.

64. Iverson, *Barry Goldwater*, 131.

65. For an example of this "Marlboro Man" imagery, see the postcard reproduced in the image portfolio between pages 178 and 179 in Goldberg, *Barry Goldwater*.

66. For more on Goldwater's conservation efforts, see Gary Driggs, *Camelback: Sacred Mountain of Phoenix* (Tempe: Arizona Historical Foundation, 1998).

67. Ehrenhalt, *The Lost City*, 82–83.

68. Ibid., 194.

69. Ibid., 204–5.

70. Eric Avila examines the linkages between suburbanization and white flight in *Popular Culture in the Age of White Flight: Fear and Fantasy in Suburban Los Angeles* (Berkeley: University of California Press, 2004).

71. Joan Didion, *The White Album* (New York: Simon and Schuster, 1979), 73.

72. For more on shifting tastes in American house styles, see John Archer, *Architecture and Suburbia: From English Villa to American Dream House, 1690–2000* (Minneapolis: University of Minnesota Press, 2005).

73. Robert A. Beauregard amply critiques suburbs and suburbanization in *When America Became Suburban* (Minneapolis: University of Minnesota Press, 2006); and Adam Rome examines both the environmental damage wrought by suburbanization as well as the environmental movements that arose from it in *The Bulldozer in the Countryside: Suburban Sprawl and the Rise of American Environmentalism* (New York: Cambridge University Press, 2001).

74. For an analysis of Proposition 13, see Peter Schrag, "The Spirit of 13," *Paradise Lost: California's Experience, America's Future* (New York: New Press, 1998), 129–87; Rybczynski, *Last Harvest*, 209.

75. Hit by the same budget cuts, Los Angeles County considered selling or leasing park land for development. The county did allow the construction of a hotel and restaurant at Bonelli Regional Park, though a larger development plan was abandoned in the face of a public outcry. See " 'Dead' Urban Parks Need Revitalization," *Los Angeles Times*, April 25, 1989; statement on parks and gang territories from "Parks That Pay Their Own Way," *Los Angeles Times*, April 17, 1984; survey is discussed in "The Dead Parks: Insufficient Funding, Drugs and Violence Drive Many Away from City Recreation Areas," *Los Angeles Times*, September 3, 1987; see also "The Sad Decline and Fall of Urban Parks," *Los Angeles Times*, March 19, 1989.

76. *City of Los Angeles Department of Recreation and Parks, 1980 Annual Report*, Los Angeles Department of Recreation and Parks Archives. For the statistics on disparities in recreation, see Denise L. Lawrence, *The Recreation Gap: How Los Angeles City Recreation Areas in the Central Park Five Area and in Suburban Communities have been Affected by Recent Budget Cuts* (Los Angeles: Urban Project, University of Southern California, 1984).

77. For information on urban parks and open-space preservation in Los Angeles in recent decades, see Jennifer Wolch, John P. Wilson, and Jed Fehrenbach, "Parks and Park Funding in Los Angeles: An Equity Mapping Analysis," *Urban Geography* 26 (2005); and *Cornfield of Dreams: A Resource Guide of Facts, Issues and Principles*, Department of Urban Planning, University of California, Los Angeles, 2000, online at http://www.sppsr.ucla.edu/dup/research/Section1.pdf. See also Mike Davis, *Ecology of Fear: Los Angeles and the Imagination of Disaster* (New York: Metropolitan, 1998), 77–91; and William Fulton, *The Reluctant Metropolis: The Politics of Urban Growth in Los Angeles* (Point Arena, CA: Solano, 1997).

78. Mark Friedberger discusses the role of undocumented workers in home construction in "Development, Politics, and the Rural-Urban Fringe in North Texas," *Southwestern Historical Quarterly* 109 (2006).

79. For longer histories of regional labor systems in the Southwest based on race and citizenship, see William Deverell, *Whitewashed Adobe: The Rise of Los Angeles and the Remaking of its Mexican Past* (Berkeley: University of California Press, 2004); Neil Foley, *The White Scourge: Mexicans, Blacks, and Poor Whites in Texas Cotton Culture* (Berkeley:

University of California Press, 1997); and Douglas Monroy, *Thrown among Strangers: The Making of Mexican Culture in Frontier California* (Berkeley: University of California Press, 1990). For the history of immigration to the region and its effects, see David G. Gutiérrez, *Walls and Mirrors: Mexican Americans, Mexican Immigrants, and the Politics of Ethnicity* (Berkeley: University of California Press, 1995).

EPILOGUE

1. Michael Steiner, "Frontierland as Tomorrowland: Walt Disney and the Architectural Packaging of the Mythic West," *Montana: The Magazine of Western History* 48, no. 1 (Spring 1998): 2–17.
2. Bruce E. Cain quoted in "Pinch of Reality Threatens the California Dream," *New York Times*, July 22, 2009.
3. Witold Rybczynski, *Last Harvest: How a Cornfield became New Daleville; Real Estate Development in America from George Washington to the Builders of the Twenty-First Century, and Why we Live in Houses Anyway* (New York: Scribner, 2007), 144–46; Daisy Nguyen, "Architects Create American-Style Suburbs Overseas," Associated Press, 2008; "One City Nine Towns," ChinaTravel.com, http://www.chinatravel.com/shanghai/attraction/one-city-nine-towns/.
4. *Palm Springs Villager*, May–June 1948, 16; Frank Bogert interview; Marne Campbell, interview by author, Pasadena, California, 15 April 2004. Bogert only became aware of Palm Springs' emergence as a gay tourist destination in the 1990s. Research on the origins of gay tourism in Palm Springs has proven difficult due to a lack of source material. The ONE Institute and Archives, which are affiliated with the University of Southern California and are the oldest archival collection of gay and lesbian material in Los Angeles, contain a selection of community periodicals and guides from Palm Springs. All of these materials, however, were produced after 1980 and do not appear to discuss the earlier history of Palm Springs as a gay or lesbian tourist destination. Marne Campbell, then a UCLA doctoral candidate and native of Palm Springs who I interviewed for this project, was aware of some businesses that catered to gays in the 1980s, such as Daddy Warbucks, a gay bar in Cathedral City. While she could not provide any other specific information on the origins of gay and lesbian tourism in Palm Springs, she agreed that each of the theories I propose here are plausible explanations.
5. *Palm Springs Life*, April 1975, 56.
6. The Palm Springs *Desert Sun* newspaper published a series of articles examining the gay and lesbian tourism boom in the 1990s. See "Gay Tourism Boosts Economy," *Desert Sun*, February 2, 1996; "Gay Market Drawing National Recognition," *Desert Sun*, March 30, 1996; "Desert Environment has Always Extended an Open Invitation," *Desert Sun*, April 1, 1996.
7. Frank Bogert interview. The restoration of Art Deco structures and the revival of Miami Beach in the late twentieth century sparked a subsequent effort to revitalize Miami's neglected mid-century modernist resort architecture. See "Push to Make Old Buildings Cool Again in Miami Beach," *New York Times*, May 16, 2004. Indeed, the real-estate revival of Palm Springs and Miami Beach proved so remarkable that by the early twenty-first century gay buyers began to look for more affordable communities elsewhere. One example was Wilton Manors, Florida, which was evolving as a more middle-class gay community; a middlebrow suburb rather than a resort. See "Newest Gay Mecca is Less of Key West, More of Mayberry," *New York Times*, May 15, 2004. Gay and lesbian retirees, mirroring established demographic patterns among heterosexuals, began relocating to gay and gay-friendly Sunbelt retirement communities as well. These included residential subdivisions near St. Petersburg, Florida and in North Carolina's Blue Ridge Mountains, a resort in

Santa Fe, and retirement-community apartment buildings in Phoenix and Los Angeles. As of 2004 another developer was planning a gay retirement community in Palm Springs. See "Gray and Gay? These Communities Want You," *Washington Post*, May 31, 2004.

8. For the contested history of Section 14, see Ryan M. Kray, "The Path to Paradise: Expropriation, Exodus, and Exclusion in the Making of Palm Springs," *Pacific Historical Review* 73 (2004): 85–126; Michael Lombardi, *Long Road Traveled I: From the Treaty of Temecula to the Pala Compact*, California Nations Indian Gaming Association Web site, www http://www.cniga.com/facts/History_of_CA_Gaming_Part_1.pdf. This document provides a useful chronology of the evolution of Indian gaming, but does so from a decidedly pro–tribal gaming perspective. For more on the history of termination, see Michael C. Walch, "Terminating the Indian Termination Policy," *Stanford Law Review* 35, no. 6 (July 1983): 1181–1215. A chart listing the year and name of each tribe or groups of tribes and reservations terminated can be found on page 1187.

9. *Indian Gaming*, Minnesota Department of Public Safety Web site, http://www.dps.state.mn.us/alcgamb/gamindev.html.

10. Lombardi, *Long Road Traveled I*.

11. Michael Lombardi, *Long Road Traveled II: Tribal Self-Sufficiency and the Battle for Proposition 1A*, California Nations Indian Gaming Association Web site, http://www.cniga.com/facts/History_of_CA_Gaming_Part_2.pdf; *Overview*, California Nations Indian Gaming Association Web site, http://www.cniga.com/overview/index.php.

12. Lombardi, *Long Road Traveled II*; and Michael Lombardi, *Long Road Traveled III: California Indian Self Reliance and the Battle for 1A*, California Nations Indian Gaming Association Web site, http://www.cniga.com/facts/History_of_CA_Gaming_Part_3.pdf.

13. Lombardi, *Long Road Traveled III*.

14. Agua Caliente Band of Cahuilla Indians Web site, http://www.aguacaliente.org/TribalEnterprises/tabid/60/Default.aspx.

15. David Treuer, "An American Indian's Journey in the Land of Indian Casinos," *Slate*, August 11, 2009, http://www.slate.com/id/2222879/entry/2222910/.

16. Robert Lovato, "The Big Gamble," *Salon*, February 16, 2004, http://www.salon.com/tech/feature/2004/02/16/agua_caliente/index.html; "Tribes Fear Backlash to Prosperity," *Los Angeles Times*, May 3, 2004; Marc Cooper, "Bury My Heart at Agua Caliente," *LA Weekly*, April 30, 2004.

17. "Drug Overdoses Raise Concerns about White Party," *Desert Sun*, April 6, 1999; "Making Gay Black History," *The Advocate*, February 17, 2004.

18. Interview with Palm Springs Mayor Ron Oden, Palm Springs City Hall, July 21, 2006.

19. U.S. Census Bureau, 2000 Census American FactFinder, http://factfinder.census.gov; "County Growth Fourth in State," *Palm Springs Desert Sun*, March 10, 2000.

20. "The Point Is, They Are Willing to Share," *Los Angeles Times*, February 24, 2004. This article offers a more positive view of the Agua Caliente's new prosperity and political clout.

21. Agua Caliente Cultural Museum Web site, *The Agua Caliente Cultural Museum Capital Campaign*, http://www.accmuseum.org/page3.html.

22. Gruen Associates, Economics Research Associates, and J. F. Davidson Associates, Inc., *Section 14: Master Development Plan, Specific Plan for the Agua Caliente Band of Cahuilla Indians*. September 1995, 3d revision July 1996, Palm Springs Public Library.

Selected Bibliography

Primary Sources

ARCHIVES AND COLLECTIONS

Agua Caliente Cultural Museum. Palm Springs, California.
Archival Research Center, Doheny Library, University of Southern California. Los Angeles.
    Los Angeles Chamber of Commerce Collection
    Los Angeles Examiner Clippings Collection
Arizona Historical Foundation, Arizona State University. Tempe, Arizona.
    Barry Goldwater Collection
    Carl Bimson Collection
Braun Research Library, Southwest Museum of the American Indian, Autry National Center. Los Angeles.
    Charles Fletcher Lummis Collection
    George Wharton James Collection
Catalina Island Museum Archives. Avalon, California.
City of Los Angeles Department of Recreation and Parks. Los Angeles City Hall.
County of Los Angeles Department of Parks and Recreation. Vermont Avenue County Building, Los Angeles.
Ephemera Collection, Seaver Center for Western History Research, Natural History Museum of Los Angeles County. Los Angeles.
Greater Los Angeles Visitors and Convention Bureau (All-Year Club of Southern California) Collection, 1900–1980, Special Collections, Oviatt Library, California State University, Northridge. Los Angeles.
Getty Research Institute Special Collections, Los Angeles.
    Julius Shulman Photography Archive
Huntington Library, San Marino, California.
    Banning Company Collection
    Groff (Lewis Augustine) Collection
    Jack London Collection
    John Anson Ford Collection
    Kenneth Hahn Collection
Institute for the Study of the American West, Autry National Center. Los Angeles.
    Rosenstock Collection
Los Angeles City Archives, Records Management Division, Office of Los Angeles City Clerk.
ONE Institute and Archives, University of Southern California. Los Angeles.
Palm Springs Historical Society. Palm Springs, California.
Palm Springs Public Library. Palm Springs, California.
Richard J. Riordan Central Library. Los Angeles
    Historic Photograph Collection
    Shades of L.A. Photograph Archive
Special Collections, Hayden Library, Arizona State University, Tempe.
Special Collections, Rivera Library, University of California, Riverside.

Special Collections, Young Research Library, University of California, Los Angeles.
    Frederick Baker Collection
    Lloyd Wright Collection
    Richard Neutra Collection
    UCLA Oral History Archives

PUBLISHED SOURCES

American Photogravure Company. *Picturesque Los Angeles County, California.* Chicago: Fred Weston, 1887.

Austin, Mary. *California: The Land of the Sun.* London: Adam and Charles Black, 1914.

———. *The Lands of the Sun.* Boston: Houghton Mifflin, 1927.

Bandini, Ralph. *Veiled Horizons: Stories of the Big Game Fish of the Sea.* New York: Derrydale, 1939.

Banning Company. *Santa Catalina Island, California.* Los Angeles: Banning Company and McBride Press, [1910]. Special Collections, UCLA.

Bass, Charlotta A. *Forty Years: Memoirs from the Pages of a Newspaper.* Los Angeles: C. A. Bass, 1960.

Bowers, Stephen. *A Remarkable Valley and an Interesting Tribe of Indians.* San Buena Ventura, CA: 1888.

Bowles, Samuel. *Across the Continent: A Summer's Journey to the Rocky Mountains, the Mormons, and the Pacific States.* Springfield, MA: Samuel Bowles, 1865.

———. *Our New West: Records of Travel Between the Mississippi River and Pacific Ocean.* Hartford, CT: Hartford Publishing Company, 1869.

Carr, Harry. *Los Angeles: City of Dreams.* New York: D. Appleton-Century, 1935.

Caughey, John Walton, ed. *The Indians of Southern California in 1852.* San Marino, CA: Huntington Library, 1952.

Chase, J. Smeaton. *Our Araby: Palm Springs and the Garden of the Sun.* Pasadena, CA: Star-News, 1920.

Crofutt, Geo. A. *Crofutt's New Overland Tourist and Pacific Coast Guide,* vol. 1. Chicago: Overland, 1878.

Dana, Richard Henry. *Two Years before the Mast and Twenty-Four Years After.* New York: P. F. Collier & Son, 1937.

Dashiell, Nellie E. *Catalina: A Poem.* Washington, DC: Dashiell, 1924.

Edwards, Charles Lincoln. "An Outline of Nature Study, Showing the Plan and Practice in the Los Angeles Public Schools." Reprinted in *Popular Science Monthly,* April 1914.

Federal Writers' Project, Works Progress Administration. *Los Angeles: A Guide to the City and its Environs.* 2d ed. New York: Hastings House, 1951.

Goldwater, Barry M. *A Journey down the Green and Colorado Rivers 1940.* Phoenix, AZ: H. Walker, 1940.

Griffith, Griffith J. *Parks, Boulevards, and Playgrounds.* Los Angeles: Prison Reform League, 1910. Huntington Library.

Herr, Charlotte Bronte. *Their Mariposa Legend: A Romance of Southern California.* Pasadena, CA: Post, 1921.

Hjelte, George. *The Development of a City's Public Recreation Service, 1904–1962.* Los Angeles: Public Service, 1978.

Holder, Charles Frederick. *The Adventures of Torqua: Being the Life and Remarkable Adventures of Three Boys, Refugees on the Island of Santa Catalina (Pimug-Na) in the Eighteenth Century.* Boston: Little, Brown, 1902.

———. *The Channel Islands of California: A Book for the Angler, Sportsman, and Tourist.* Chicago: A. C. McClurg, 1910.

———. *Life in the Open: Sport with Rod, Gun, Horse, and Hound in Southern California.* New York: G. P. Putnam's Sons, 1906.

———. *Santa Catalina, an Isle of Summer: Its History, Climate, Sports, and Antiquities.* San Francisco: Murdock, 1895.

James, George Wharton. *Traveler's Handbook to Southern California.* Pasadena, CA: G. W. James, 1904.

———. *The Wonders of the Colorado Desert.* Boston: Little, Brown, 1911.

Keeler, Charles A. *Southern California.* Los Angeles: Santa Fe Railroad, 1902.

Lindley, Walter, and J.P Lindley. *California of the South: Its Physical Geography, Climate, Resources, Routes of Travel, and Health Resorts.* New York: D. Appleton, 1888

Lummis, Charles F. *Flowers of Our Lost Romance.* Boston: Houghton Mifflin, 1929.

———. *The Home of Ramona.* Los Angeles: Lummis, 1888.

———. *The Land of Poco Tiempo.* New York: Charles Scribner's Sons, 1893.

———. *Los Angeles and her Makers: A Record.* Los Angeles: Out West, 1907.

———. *Mesa, Cañon and Pueblo: Our Wonderland of the Southwest, its Marvels of Nature, its Pageant of the Earth Building, its Strange Peoples, its Centuried Romance.* New York: Century, 1925.

———. *A Tramp across the Continent.* New York: Charles Scribner's Sons, 1892. Reprinted with an introduction by Robert E. Fleming. Lincoln: University of Nebraska Press, 1982.

Nordhoff, Charles. *California: For Health, Pleasure, and Residence.* New York: Harper and Brothers, 1873.

Patencio, Francisco. *Stories and Legends of the Palm Springs Indians.* Los Angeles: Times Mirror, 1943.

Remondino, P. C. *The Mediterranean Shores of America: Southern California; Its Climatic, Physical, and Meteorological Conditions.* Philadelphia: F.A. Davis, 1892.

Richards, Elizabeth W. *A Look Into Palm Springs' Past.* Santa Fe Federal Savings and Loan Association, [1960]. History and Genealogy Department, Richard J. Riordan Central Library.

Salmon, Ted. *From Southern California to Casco Bay.* San Bernardino, CA: San Bernardino, 1930.

Santa Catalina Island. Los Angeles: M. Rieder, 1905. Special Collections, UCLA.

Scott, Mel. *Cities are for People: The Los Angeles Region Plans for Living.* Los Angeles: Pacific Southwest Academy, 1942.

Southern California Research Council. *The Challenge of Leisure: A Southern California Case Study.* Report 15 from the Southern California Research Council. Claremont: Pomona College, 1967. Rare Book Collection, Huntington Library.

Southwest Museum. *The Southwest Museum.* Los Angeles: Southwest Museum, 1919. Special Collections, UCLA.

Sunset Magazine. *Sunset Western Ranch Houses.* In collaboration with Cliff May. San Francisco: Lane, 1946.

———. *Western Ranch Houses by Cliff May.* San Francisco: Lane, 1958.

Taylor, Frank J. *Land of Homes.* Los Angeles: Powell Publishing Company, 1929.

Van Dyke, John C. *The Autobiography of John C. Van Dyke: A Personal Narrative of American Life, 1861–1931.* Edited by Peter Wild. Salt Lake City: University of Utah Press, 1993.

———. *The Desert: Further Studies in Natural Appearances.* New York: Charles Scribner's Sons, 1901.

Warner, Charles Dudley. *Our Italy.* New York: Harper and Brothers, 1902.

William Wrigley, Jr. Enterprises, Advertising Division. *Catalina, California's Magic Isle.* Avalon, CA: Santa Catalina Island Company, 1926.

———. *Catalina's Yesterdays: A Glimpse into the Life of the Ancient Dwellers on the Magic Isle.* Avalon, CA: Santa Catalina Island Company, 1926.

Wilmington Transportation Company. *Santa Catalina Island: Winter and Summer*. Los
    Angeles: Wilmington Transportation Company, ca. 1895.
Windle, Ernest. *Windle's History of Santa Catalina Island*. Avalon, CA: Catalina Islander, 1931.
Wright, Frank Lloyd. *An Autobiography*. New York: Duell, Sloan and Pearce, 1943.
————. *When Democracy Builds*. Chicago: University of Chicago Press, 1945.
Young, Ernest. *North American Excursion*. London: Edward Arnold, 1947.

UNPUBLISHED SOURCES

Agua Caliente Band of Mission Indians. *The Story of Palm Springs Reservation*. Agua Caliente
    Band of Mission Indians, 1952. Special Collections, UCR.
————. *1962 Progress Report*. Agua Caliente Band of Mission Indians, 1962. Special
    Collections, UCR.
Banning, Hancock Jr. *The Banning Family in Southern California*. Transcript. UCLA Oral
    History Archives, Special Collections, UCLA.
Bridges, Amy T. "Journal Kept on Fourth Raymond Excursion from Massachusetts to
    California," 1882. Manuscripts Collection, Huntington Library.
————. "Journal Kept on a Raymond Excursion from Massachusetts to California and Return,
    Including a Three-Month Stay at the Raymond Hotel in South Pasadena, the Del Monte
    Hotel, and San Francisco, Etc," 1886–87. Manuscripts Collection, Huntington Library.
California Nations Indian Gaming Association. "Overview." California Nations Indian
    Gaming Association Web site, http://www.cniga.com/overview/index.php.
D'Arcy, Squirrel "Duke." Interview by Chuck Liddell, Joe Guin, and Lloyd Rathburn,
    25 February 1976. Catalina Island Museum Society Oral History Program, Catalina
    Island Museum Archives.
Early Avalon. Manuscript, n.d. Catalina Island Museum Archives, Avalon, California.
Excerpts from Echo Park Study. 1950. John Anson Ford Collection, Huntington Library.
Gruen Associates, Economics Research Associates, and J. F. Davidson Associates, Inc.
    *Section 14: Master Development Plan, Specific Plan for the Agua Caliente Band of Cahuilla
    Indians*. September 1995, 3d revision July 1996. Palm Springs Public Library.
Gruendyke, B. P. *Los Angeles County Department of Parks and Recreation*. Typescript.
    1946. Departmental History Files, County of Los Angeles Department of Parks and
    Recreation, Los Angeles.
Hotel Register, Avalon House. June 1890–September 1894. Huntington Library.
Humm, Mrs. "Photographs—California, 1922." Photograph Album, 1922. Institute for the
    Study of the American West, Autry National Center.
Jones, Charles S. *Walled Oasis of Biskra: An Interpretation of the American Desert in the
    Algerian Manner*, Charles S. Jones, 1924. Special Collections, UCLA.
Liemert Plaza Park History. Histories—L, City of Los Angeles Department of Parks and
    Recreation Archives.
Lombardi, Michael. *Long Road Traveled I: From the Treaty of Temecula to the Pala Compact*.
    California Nations Indian Gaming Association Web site, http://www.cniga.com/facts/
    History_of_CA_Gaming_Part_1.pdf.
————. *Long Road Traveled II: Tribal Self-Sufficiency and the Battle for Proposition 1A*.
    California Nations Indian Gaming Association Web site, http://www.cniga.com/facts/
    History_of_CA_Gaming_Part_2.pdf.
————. *Long Road Traveled III: California Indian Self Reliance and the Battle for 1A*.
    California Nations Indian Gaming Association Web site, http://www.cniga.com/facts/
    History_of_CA_Gaming_Part_3.pdf.
Lummis, Charles Fletcher. "Journal," 1913. Special Collections, UCLA.
————. *As I Remember*, ca. 1927. Lummis Collection, Braun Research Library, Southwest
    Museum of the American Indian, Autry National Center.

May, Cliff, *The California Ranch House*. Interview by Marlene L. Laskey. UCLA Oral
    History Program, 1984.

Palm Springs Chamber of Commerce. *The Palm Springs and Desert Resort Area Story*. 1955.
    Special Collections, Rivera Library, University of California, Riverside.

Patencio, Ray, Oral History Interview, May 20, 2005. Agua Caliente Cultural Museum.

Pershing Square Park. Histories—P, Los Angeles Department of Recreation and Parks
    Archives.

Picture Tour of Catalina Island: California's Magic Isle. Avalon, CA: Wix-Hastell, 1927.

Renton, Malcom. *Black People Who Have Lived on Santa Catalina Island*. Interview by
    Catalina Island Museum, 30 November 1990. Catalina Island Museum Archives.

Todd, Russell. *Apache Trail: The Wonder Trip through Oldest America*. Southern Pacific Rail
    Road, n.d. Special Collections, Hayden Library, Arizona State University.

Van Dyke, Henry. *Devastating the Fisheries of Southern California*. Typescript. 18 April 1913.
    Catalina Island Museum Archives.

Your Del Webb's Sun City Tour Guide. Ca. 1960. Special Collections, Hayden Library,
    Arizona State University.

GOVERNMENT DOCUMENTS

Avalon City Council Minutes. 1913–1932. Frederick Baker Collection, Special Collections, UCLA.

Los Angeles Board of Park Commissioners. *Annual Report of the Board of Park
    Commissioners*. City of Los Angeles, 1928. Special Collections, UCLA.

Los Angeles Board of Planning Commissioners. *Accomplishments, 1943*. Board of Planning
    Commissioners, City of Los Angeles. Los Angeles Chamber of Commerce Collection,
    Carton 72, Archival Research Center, USC.

Los Angeles City Council Minutes, 1900—1950. Los Angeles City Archives.

Los Angeles County Regional Planning Commission. *Report on Master Plan of Parks, County
    of Los Angeles (Unincorporated Area)*. Regional Planning Commission, Los Angeles
    County Regional Planning District [ca.1945]. County of Los Angeles Department of
    Parks and Recreation.

Los Angeles Department of Playground and Recreation. *Annual Report of the Department of
    Playground and Recreation, City of Los Angeles*. 1928. "Old Department History" file, Los
    Angeles Department of Recreation and Parks.

———. *Annual Report of the Department of Playground and Recreation, City of Los Angeles,
    1930*. Special Collections, UCLA.

———. *Report, 1930–32*. City of Los Angeles Department of Playground and Recreation.
    Special Collections, UCLA.

———. *Department of Playground and Recreation, City of Los Angeles, Annual Financial
    Report, Fiscal Year Ending June 30, 1936*. Special Collections, UCLA.

———. "Department of Playground and Recreation, Annual Report, 1937." Special
    Collections, UCLA.

———. *Today's Leisure*. Department of Playground and Recreation, 1938. Special
    Collections, UCLA.

Los Angeles Department of Recreation and Parks. *City of Los Angeles Department of
    Recreation and Parks, 1980 Annual Report*. Los Angeles Department of Recreation and
    Parks Archives.

Los Angeles Playground Commission. *Report of the Playground Commission, City of Los
    Angeles, December 1, 1908 to June 30, 1910*. Huntington Library.

Minnesota Department of Public Safety. *Indian Gaming*. Minnesota Department of Public
    Safety Web site, http://www.dps.state.mn.us/alcgamb/gamindev.html.

Prioleau v. Board of Playground and Recreation Commissioners, S.P. 285104. City Council
    File 1636 (1931), Los Angeles City Archives.

U.S. Department of Commerce, Bureau of the Census. *Fourteenth Census of the United States, 1920*. Vol. 1, *Population*. Washington, DC: Government Printing Office, 1921.

———. *Fifteenth Census of the United States, 1930*. Vol. 2, Part 1, *Population*. Washington, DC: Government Printing Office, 1932.

———. *Sixteenth Census of the United States*. Vol. 1, *Population*. Washington, DC: Government Printing Office, 1942.

———. *Sixteenth Census of the United States*. Vol. 2, *Characteristics of the Population*. Washington, DC: Government Printing Office, 1943.

———. 2000 Census American FactFinder, http://factfinder.census.gov.

NEWSPAPERS

Avalon (CA) Catalina Islander
Avalon (CA) Catalina Island Wireless
Los Angeles Examiner
Los Angeles Sentinel
Los Angeles Times
Palm Springs (CA) Desert Sun
Palm Springs (CA) News
Pasadena Star News
Washington Post

PERIODICALS

Desert Magazine
Land of Sunshine/Out West
Nation
National Geographic
Newsweek
Overland Monthly
Palm Springs Life
Palm Springs Villager

INTERVIEWS BY AUTHOR

Bogert, Frank. Interview by author, 26 August 2003, Palm Springs, California.

Campbell, Marne. Interview by author, 15 April 2004, Pasadena, California.

Flamming, Douglas. Telephone interview by author, 31 October 2002.

Hurley, Michael. Telephone interview by author, 30 October 2002.

Kieley, Elizabeth Coffman, and Thomas Kieley. Interview by author, 25 August 2003, Palm Springs, California.

Oden, Ronald. Interview by author, 21 July 2006, Palm Springs, California.

Pulido, Laura. Interview by author, 1 November 2003, San Marino, California.

Verge, Arthur. Interview by author, 1 November 2003, San Marino, California.

Secondary Sources

PUBLISHED SOURCES

Abbott, Carl. *How Cities Won the West: Four Centuries of Urban Change in Western North America*. Albuquerque: University of New Mexico Press, 2008.

———. *The Metropolitan Frontier: Cities in the Modern American West*. Tucson: University of Arizona Press, 1993.

Abel, Emily K. *Suffering in the Land of Sunshine: A Los Angeles Illness Narrative*. New Brunswick, NJ: Rutgers University Press, 2006.

Ackermann, Marsha E. *Cool Comfort: America's Romance with Air-Conditioning*. Washington, DC: Smithsonian Institution Press, 2002.

Aguar, Charles E., and Berdeanna Aguar. *Wrightscapes: Frank Lloyd Wright's Landscape Designs*. New York: McGraw-Hill, 2002.

Ainsworth, Ed. *Golden Checkerboard*. Palm Desert, CA: Desert-Southwest, 1965.

Ainsworth, Katherine. *The McCallum Saga: The Story of the Founding of Palm Springs*. Palm Springs, CA: Palm Springs Desert Museum, 1973.

Anderson, Susan. "A City Called Heaven: Black Enchantment and Despair in Los Angeles." In *The City: Los Angeles and Urban Theory at the End of the Twentieth Century*, edited by Allen J. Scott and Edward W. Soja, 336–64. Berkeley: University of California Press, 1996.

Archer, John. *Architecture and Suburbia: From English Villa to American Dream House, 1690–2000*. Minneapolis: University of Minnesota Press, 2005.

Armstead, Myra B. Young. *"Lord, Please Don't Take Me in August": African Americans in Newport and Saratoga Springs, 1870–1930*. Urbana: University of Illinois Press, 1999.

Aron, Cindy S. *Working at Play: A History of Vacations in the United States*. New York: Oxford University Press, 1999.

Avila, Eric. *Popular Culture in the Age of White Flight: Fear and Fantasy in Suburban Los Angeles*. Berkeley: University of California Press, 2004.

Babcock, Barbara A. "Bearers of Value, Vessels of Desire: The Reproduction of the Reproduction of Pueblo Culture." *Museum Anthropology* 17, no. 3 (October 1993): 43–57.

———. "'A New Mexican Rebecca': Imaging Pueblo Women." *Journal of the Southwest* 32, no. 4 (Winter 1990): 400–437.

Baritz, Loren. *The Good Life: The Meaning of Success for the American Middle Class*. New York: Alfred A. Knopf, 1989.

Barnard, Charles. "On Santa Catalina Island, the Kings of Swing Held Sway." *Smithsonian*, October 1991: 153–67.

Baudrillard, Jean. *America*. Translated by Chris Turner. London: Verso, 1988.

Baur, John E. "Charles Nordhoff, Publicist Par Excellence." *Ventura County Historical Society Quarterly* 19 (Summer 1974): 2–11.

———. *The Health Seekers of Southern California, 1870–1900*. San Marino, CA: Huntington Library, 1959.

Bean, Lowell John. *Mukat's People: The Cahuilla Indians of Southern California*. Berkeley: University of California Press, 1972.

Beauregard, Robert A. *When America Became Suburban*. Minneapolis: University of Minnesota Press, 2006.

Becker, Jane S. *Selling Tradition: Appalachia and the Construction of an American Folk, 1930–1940*. Chapel Hill: University of North Carolina Press, 1998.

Bederman, Gail. *Manliness and Civilization: A Cultural History of Gender and Race in the United States, 1880–1917*. Chicago: University of Chicago Press, 1995.

Belasco, Warren James. *Americans on the Road: From Autocamp to Motel, 1910–1945*. Cambridge, MA: MIT Press, 1979.

Berger, Dina. *The Development of Mexico's Tourism Industry: Pyramids by Day, Martinis by Night*. New York: Palgrave Macmillan, 2006.

Berman, Marshall. *All That Is Solid Melts Into Air: The Experience of Modernity*. New York: Simon and Schuster, 1982.

Bernard, Richard M. and Bradley R. Rice, eds. *Sunbelt Cities: Politics and Growth since World War II*. Austin: University of Texas Press, 1983.

Bingham, Edwin R. *Charles F. Lummis: Editor of the Southwest*. San Marino, CA: Huntington Library, 1955.

Bookspan, Rochelle, ed. *Santa Barbara by the Sea*. Santa Barbara, CA: McNally and Loftin, West, 1982.

Boorstin, Daniel J. *The Image; or, What Happened to the American Dream*. New York: Atheneum, 1962.

Bottles, Scott J. *Los Angeles and the Automobile: The Making of the Modern City*. Berkeley: University of California Press, 1987.

Bowart, Will. *The McCallum Centennial*. Palm Springs: Palm Springs Historical Society, 1984.

Bright, Marjorie Belle. *Nellie's Boardinghouse: A Dual Biography of Nellie Coffman and Palm Springs*. Palm Springs, CA: ECT, 1981.

Brown, Dona. *Inventing New England: Regional Tourism in the Nineteenth Century*. Washington, DC: Smithsonian Institution Press, 1995.

Burke, Flannery. *From Greenwich Village to Taos: Primitivism and Place at Mabel Dodge Luhan's*. Lawrence: University Press of Kansas, 2008

Burke, Tony. *Palm Springs: Why I Love You*. Palm Desert, CA: Palmesa, 1976.

Bushing, Bill. "Santa Catalina Island Company: 1919–1944." *Water Lines*, 2d quarter 1994.

Bushman, Richard L. *The Refinement of America: Persons, Houses, Cities*. New York: Knopf, 1992.

Byrkit, James W. "Land, Sky, and People: The Southwest Defined." *Journal of the Southwest* 34 (Fall 1992): 257–387.

Cavallo, Dominick. *Muscles and Morals: Organized Playgrounds and Urban Reform, 1880–1920*. Philadelphia: University of Pennsylvania Press, 1981.

Chaput, Donald. "The Civil War Military Post on Catalina Island." *Southern California Quarterly* 75 (Spring 1993): 37–50.

Chiang, Connie Y. *Shaping the Shoreline: Fisheries and Tourism on the Monterey Coast*. Seattle: University of Washington Press, 2008.

Cocks, Catherine. *Doing the Town: The Rise of Urban Tourism in the United States, 1850–1915*. Berkeley: University of California Press, 2001.

Cohen, Lizabeth. *A Consumer's Republic: The Politics of Mass Consumption in Postwar America*. New York: Vintage, 2003.

———. *Making a New Deal: Industrial Workers in Chicago, 1919–1939*. Cambridge, UK: Cambridge University Press, 1990.

Coleman, Annie Gilbert. *Ski Style: Sport and Culture in the Rockies*. Lawrence: University Press of Kansas, 2004.

Cooper, Gail. *Air-Conditioning America: Engineers and the Controlled Environment, 1900–1960*. Baltimore: Johns Hopkins University Press, 1998.

Coquery-Vidrovich, Catherine. "Is L.A. a Model or a Mess?" *American Historical Review* 105, no. 5 (December 2000): 1683–91.

Corbett, Theodore. *The Making of American Resorts: Saratoga Springs, Ballston Spa, Lake George*. New Brunswick, NJ: Rutgers University Press, 2000.

Cosgrove, Denis E. *Social Formation and Symbolic Landscape*. Totowa, NJ: Barnes and Noble, 1985.

Cathers, David. *Gustav Stickley*. London: Phaidon, 2003.

Cranz, Galen. *The Politics of Park Design: A History of Urban Parks in America*. Cambridge, MA: MIT Press, 1982.

Cronon, William. *Nature's Metropolis: Chicago and the Great West*. New York: W. W. Norton, 1991.

Cygelman, Adèle. *Palm Springs Modern: Houses in the California Desert*. New York: Rizzoli, 1999.

Davis, Clark. "From Oasis to Metropolis: Southern California and the Changing Context of American Leisure." *Pacific Historical Review* 61, no. 3 (May 1992): 357–86.

Davis, Mike. *City of Quartz: Excavating the Future in Los Angeles*. New York: Verso, 1990.

————. *Ecology of Fear: Los Angeles and the Imagination of Disaster*. New York: Metropolitan, 1998.

Davis, Susan G. "Landscapes of Imagination: Tourism in Southern California." *Pacific Historical Review* 68, no. 2 (May 1999): 173–91.

DeBuys, William. *Enchantment and Exploitation: The Life and Hard Times of a New Mexico Mountain Range*. Albuquerque: University of New Mexico Press, 1985.

De Graaf, Lawrence B., Kevin Mulroy, and Quintard Taylor, eds. *Seeking El Dorado: African Americans in California*. Los Angeles: Autry Museum of Western Heritage, 2001.

DeLyser, Dydia. "Ramona Memories: Fiction, Tourist Practices, and Placing the Past in Southern California." *Annals of the Association of American Geographers* 93 (December 2003): 886–908.

————. *Ramona Memories: Tourism and the Shaping of Southern California*. Minneapolis: University of Minnesota Press, 2005.

Deverell, William. *Whitewashed Adobe: The Rise of Los Angeles and the Remaking of Its Mexican Past*. Berkeley: University of California Press, 2004.

Deverell, William, Greg Hise, and David C. Sloane, eds. "Orange Empires." Special issue, *Pacific Historical Review* 68, no. 2 (May 1999).

Didion, Joan. *The White Album*. New York: Simon and Schuster, 1979.

Dilworth, Leah. *Imagining Indians in the Southwest: Persistent Visions of a Primitive Past*. Washington, DC: Smithsonian Institution Press, 1996.

Doran, Adelaide LeMert. *The Ranch that was Robbins': Santa Catalina Island; A Source Book*. Los Angeles: A. H. Clark, 1963.

Driggs, Gary. *Camelback: Sacred Mountain of Phoenix*. Tempe, AZ: Arizona Historical Foundation, 1998.

Dubinsky, Karen. *The Second Greatest Disappointment: Honeymooners, Heterosexuality, and the Tourist Industry at Niagara Falls*. New Brunswick, NJ: Rutgers University Press, 1999.

Dulles, Foster Rhea. *A History of Recreation: America Learns to Play*. 2d ed. New York: Appleton-Century-Crofts, 1965.

Dumke, Glenn S. *The Boom of the Eighties in Southern California*. San Marino, CA: Huntington Library, 1944.

Eco, Umberto. *Travels in Hyper Reality: Essays*. Translated by William Weaver. San Diego, CA: Harcourt Brace Jovanovich, 1986.

Ehrenhalt, Alan. *The Lost City: The Forgotten Virtues of Community in America*. New York: Basic Books, 1995.

Eldredge, Charles C., Julie Schimmel, and William H. Truettner. *Art in New Mexico, 1900–1945: Paths to Taos and Santa Fe*. Washington, DC: National Museum of American Art, Smithsonian Institution, 1986.

Elias, Judith W. *Los Angeles: Dream to Reality, 1885–1915*. Los Angeles: Santa Susana Press and California State University, Northridge Libraries, 1983.

Engh, Michael E., SJ. "At Home in the Heteropolis: Understanding Postmodern L.A." *American Historical Review* 105, no. 5 (December 2000): 1676–1682.

Erickson, Kenneth A. "Ceremonial Landscapes of the American West." *Landscape* 22 (Autumn 1977): 39–47.

Escher, Frank, ed. *John Lautner, Architect*. London: Ellipsis, 1994.

Faragher, John Mack. "Bungalow and Ranch House: The Architectural Backwash of California." *Western Historical Quarterly* 32, no. 2 (Summer 2001): 149–73.

Fifer, J. Valerie. *American Progress: The Growth of the Transport, Tourist, and Information Industries in the Nineteenth Century West, Seen through the Life and Times of George A. Crofutt, Pioneer and Publicist of the Transcontinental Age*. Chester, CT: Globe Pequot, 1988.

Findlay, John M. *Magic Lands: Western Cityscapes and American Culture after 1940*. Berkeley: University of California Press, 1992.

———. *People of Chance: Gambling in American Society from Jamestown to Las Vegas*. New York: Oxford University Press, 1986.

Fishman, Robert. *Bourgeois Utopias: The Rise and Fall of Suburbia*. New York: Basic Books, 1987.

Fiske, Turbesé Lummis, and Keith Lummis. *Charles F. Lummis: The Man and his West*. Norman: University of Oklahoma Press, 1975.

Flamming, Douglas. *Bound for Freedom: Black Los Angeles in Jim Crow America*. Berkeley: University of California Press, 2005.

Fodor's Los Angeles. New York: Fodor's Travel Publications, 1993.

Fogelson, Robert M. *Bourgeois Nightmares: Suburbia, 1870–1930*. New Haven, CT: Yale University Press, 2005.

———. *The Fragmented Metropolis: Los Angeles, 1850–1930*. Cambridge, MA: Harvard University Press, 1967.

Foley, Neil. *The White Scourge: Mexicans, Blacks, and Poor Whites in Texas Cotton Culture*. Berkeley: University of California Press, 1997.

Francaviglia, Richard. "Walt Disney's Frontierland as an Allegorical Map of the American West." *Western Historical Quarterly* 30, no. 2 (Summer 1999): 155–82.

Friedberger, Mark. "Development, Politics, and the Rural-Urban Fringe in North Texas." *Southwestern Historical Quarterly* 109 (2006): 358–83.

Friedrich, Otto. *City of Nets: A Portrait of Hollywood in the 1940's*. Berkeley: University of California Press, 1997.

Fulton, William. *The Reluctant Metropolis: The Politics of Urban Growth in Los Angeles*. Point Arena, CA: Solano, 1997.

Gabler, Neal. *An Empire of Their Own: How the Jews Invented Hollywood*. New York: Doubleday, 1989.

Gale, Zona. *Frank Miller of Mission Inn*. New York: D. Appleton-Century, 1938.

Gannon, Michael. *Florida: A Short History*. Gainesville: University Press of Florida, 1993.

Garcia, Matt. *A World of its Own: Race, Labor, and Citrus in the Making of Greater Los Angeles, 1900–1970*. Chapel Hill: University of North Carolina Press, 2001.

Gebhard, David. *An Exhibition of the Architecture of R. M. Schindler*. Santa Barbara: University of California, Santa Barbara, 1967.

———. *Schindler*. New York: Viking, 1972.

Gebhard, David, and Robert Winter. *Los Angeles: An Architectural Guide*. Salt Lake City: Gibbs Smith, 1994.

Goetzmann, William H., and William N. Goetzmann, *The West of the Imagination*. New York: Norton, 1986.

Goldberg, Robert Alan. *Barry Goldwater*. New Haven, CT: Yale University Press, 1995.

Goldfarb, Al. *100 Years of Recreation and Parks, City of Los Angeles: An Overview*, Los Angeles: Recreation and Parks Department, 1988.

Gordon, Dudley. *Charles F. Lummis: Crusader in Corduroy*. Los Angeles: Cultural Assets, 1972.

Graulich, Melody, ed. "California Dreaming." Special Issue, *Western American Literature* 34 (Summer 1999).

Greenberg, Amy S. "Domesticating the Border: Manifest Destiny and the 'Comforts of Life' in the U.S.-Mexico Boundary Commission and Gadsden Purchase, 1848–1854." In *Land of Necessity: Consumer Culture in the United States–Mexico Borderlands*, edited by Alexis McCrossen, 83–112. Durham, NC: Duke University Press, 2009.

Gregory, Daniel P. *Cliff May and the Modern Ranch House*. New York: Rizzoli, 2008.

Gregory, James N. *American Exodus: The Dust Bowl Migration and Okie Culture in California*. New York: Oxford University Press, 1989.

Griswold del Castillo, Richard. "The del Valle Family and the Fantasy Heritage." *California History* 59 (Spring 1980): 2–15.

Gutiérrez, David G. *Walls and Mirrors: Mexican Americans, Mexican Immigrants, and the Politics of Ethnicity*. Berkeley: University of California Press, 1995.

Gutiérrez, Ramón, and Richard J. Orsi, eds. *Contested Eden: California before the Gold Rush*. Berkeley: University of California Press, 1998.

Haas, Lisbeth. *Conquests and Historical Identities in California, 1769–1936*. Berkeley: University of California Press, 1995.

Hayden, Dolores. *Building Suburbia: Green Fields and Urban Growth, 1820–2000*. New York: Vintage, 2004.

Hess, Alan. *The Ranch House*. New York: Harry N. Abrams, 2004.

Hess, Alan, and Andrew Danish. *Palm Springs Weekend: The Architecture and Design of a Mid-Century Oasis*. San Francisco: Chronicle, 2001.

Hines, Thomas S. *Irving Gill and the Architecture of Reform*. New York: Monacelli, 2000.

————. *Richard Neutra and the Search for Modern Architecture: A Biography and History*. New York: Oxford University Press, 1982.

Hise, Greg. *Magnetic Los Angeles: Planning the Twentieth-Century Metropolis*. Baltimore: Johns Hopkins Press, 1997.

————. " 'Nature's Workshop': Industry and Urban Expansion in Southern California, 1900–1950." *Journal of Historical Geography* 27, no. 1 (January 2001): 74–92.

Hise, Greg, and William Deverell, *Eden by Design: The 1930 Olmstead-Bartholomew Plan for the Los Angeles Region*. Berkeley: University of California Press, 2000.

Hobsbawm, Eric. *The Age of Capital, 1848–1875*. New York: Vintage, 1996.

Hoffman, Peter R. "Tourism and Language in Mexico's Los Cabos." *Journal of Cultural Geography* 12, no. 2 (Spring/Summer 1992): 77–92.

Houston, John M. *Accounts and Stories of Old San Pedro: Including Early Excursion Ships to Santa Catalina*. Harbor City, CA: Economy, 1978.

Hunter, Burton L. *The Evolution of Municipal Organization and Administrative Practice in the City of Los Angeles*. Los Angeles: Parker, Stone and Baird, 1933.

Hyde, Anne Farrar. *An American Vision: Far Western Landscape and National Culture, 1820–1920*. New York: New York University Press, 1990.

Iverson, Peter. *Barry Goldwater: Native Arizonan*. Norman: University of Oklahoma Press, 1997.

Jackson, Kenneth T. *Crabgrass Frontier: The Suburbanization of the United States*. New York: Oxford University Press, 1985.

Jacobs, Margaret D. *Engendered Encounters: Feminism and Pueblo Cultures, 1879–1934*. Lincoln: University of Nebraska Press, 1999.

Jacoby, Karl. *Crimes against Nature: Squatters, Poachers, Thieves, and the Hidden History of American Conservation*. Berkeley: University of California Press, 2001.

James, Harry C. *The Cahuilla Indians: The Men Called Master*. Los Angeles: Westernlore, 1960.

Jennings, Frances. *The Invasion of America: Indians, Colonialism, and the Cant of Conquest*. Chapel Hill: University of North Carolina Press, 1975.

Kalambakal, Vickey. "The Battle of Santa Monica Bay." *American History* 37 (Spring 2002): 36–40.

Kanfer, Stefan. *A Summer World: The Attempt to Build a Jewish Eden in the Catskills, from the Days of the Ghetto to the Rise and Decline of the Borscht Belt*. New York: Farrar, Straus & Giroux, 1989.

Kasson, John F. *Amusing the Million: Coney Island at the Turn of the Century*. New York: Hill and Wang, 1978.

Kearns, Gerry, and Chris Philo, eds. *Selling Places: The City as Cultural Capital, Past and Present*. Oxford: Pergamon, 1993.

Kern, Stephen. *The Culture of Time and Space, 1880–1918*. Cambridge, MA: Harvard University Press, 1983.

Kessler, Julia Braun. "As We Were in Avalon." *California History* 63, no. 1 (Winter 1984): 71–76.

King, Anthony D. *The Bungalow: The Production of a Global Culture.* 2d ed. New York: Oxford University Press, 1995.

Klein, Kerwin L. "Frontier Tales: The Narrative Construction of Cultural Borders in Twentieth-Century California." *Comparative Studies in Society and History* 34, no. 3 (July 1992): 464–90.

———. "Frontier Products: Tourism, Consumerism, and the Southwestern Public Lands, 1890–1990." *Pacific Historical Review* 62, no. 1 (February 1993): 39–71.

Klein, Norman M. "Gold Fevers: Global L.A. and the Noir Imaginary." In *Reading California: Art, Image, and Identity, 1900–2000,* edited by Stephanie Barron, Sheri Bernstein, and Ilene Susan Fort, 389–409. Los Angeles: Los Angeles County Museum of Art and University of California Press, 2000.

———. "The Sunshine Strategy: Buying and Selling the Fantasy of Los Angeles." In *20th Century Los Angeles: Power, Promotion, and Social Conflict,* edited by Norman M. Klein and Martin J. Schiesl, 1–38. Claremont, CA: Regina, 1990.

Kray, Ryan M. "The Path to Paradise: Expropriation, Exodus, and Exclusion in the Making of Palm Springs." *Pacific Historical Review* 73 (2004): 85–126.

Kropp, Phoebe S. *California Vieja: Culture and Memory in a Modern American Place.* Berkeley: University of California Press, 2006.

Kruse, Kevin M., and Thomas J. Sugrue, eds. *The New Suburban History.* Chicago: University of Chicago Press, 2006.

Lawrence, Denise L. *The Recreation Gap: How Los Angeles City Recreation Areas in the Central Park Five Area and in Suburban Communities have been Affected by Recent Budget Cuts.* Los Angeles: The Urban Project, University of Southern California, 1984.

Leach, William. *Land of Desire: Merchants, Power, and the Rise of a New American Culture.* New York: Pantheon, 1993.

Lears, T. J. Jackson. *Fables of Abundance: A Cultural History of Advertising in America.* New York: Basic Books, 1994.

———. *No Place of Grace: Antimodernism and the Transformation of American Culture, 1880–1920.* New York: Pantheon, 1981.

Leeuwen, Thomas A. P. van. *The Springboard in the Pond: An Intimate History of the Swimming Pool.* Cambridge, MA: MIT Press, 1998.

Limerick, Patricia Nelson. *Desert Passages: Encounters with the American Deserts.* Albuquerque: University of New Mexico Press, 1985.

Lindsay, Diana Elaine. *Our Historic Desert: The Story of the Anza-Borrego Desert, the Largest State Park in the United States of America.* San Diego, CA: Copley, 1973.

Logan, Michael F. *Desert Cities: The Environmental History of Phoenix and Tucson.* Pittsburgh, PA: University of Pittsburgh Press, 2006.

Luckingham, Bradford. *Phoenix: The History of a Southwestern Metropolis.* Tucson: University of Arizona Press, 1989.

March, Lionel, and Judith Sheine, eds. *R. M. Schindler: Composition and Construction.* London: Academy, 1995.

Marchand, Roland. *Advertising the American Dream: Making Way for Modernity, 1920–1940.* Berkeley: University of California Press, 1985.

Marling, Karal Ann, ed. *Designing Disney's Theme Parks: The Architecture of Reassurance.* Montreal: Canadian Centre for Architecture, 1997.

May, Elaine Tyler. *Great Expectations: Marriage and Divorce in Post-Victorian America.* Chicago: University of Chicago Press, 1980.

May, Kirse Granat. *Golden State, Golden Youth: The California Image in Popular Culture, 1955–1966.* Chapel Hill: University of North Carolina Press, 2002.

May, Lary. *Screening Out the Past: The Birth of Mass Culture and the Motion Picture Industry.* New York: Oxford University Press, 1980.

MacCannell, Dean. *Empty Meeting Grounds: The Tourist Papers.* New York: Routledge, 1992.

———. *The Tourist: A New Theory of the Leisure Class.* New York: Schocken, 1976.

McClung, William Alexander. *Landscapes of Desire: Anglo Mythologies of Los Angeles.* Berkeley: University of California Press, 2000.

McCrossen, Alexis, ed. *Land of Necessity: Consumer Culture in the United States–Mexico Borderlands.* Durham, NC: Duke University Press, 2009.

McCune, Ellis. *Recreation and Parks.* Los Angeles: Haynes Foundation, 1954.

McEvoy, Arthur F. *The Fisherman's Problem: Ecology and Law in the California Fisheries, 1850–1980.* New York: Cambridge University Press, 1986.

McWilliams, Carey. *Southern California: An Island on the Land.* Santa Barbara, CA: Peregrine Smith, 1973.

Meinig, D. W. *The Shaping of America: A Geographical Perspective on 500 Years of History.* Vol. 3, *Transcontinental America, 1850–1915.* New Haven, CT: Yale University Press, 1998.

———. *Southwest: Three Peoples in Geographical Change, 1600–1970.* New York: Oxford University Press, 1971.

Meyer-Arendt, Klaus J., and Geoffrey Wall, eds. "North American Tourism and Cultural Geography." Special issue, *Journal of Cultural Geography* 11, no. 1 (Fall/Winter 1990).

Miller, Ray and Jo Miller. *Catalina!: "...Wish You Were Here."* Avalon, CA: Evergreen, 1993.

Moehring, Eugene P. *Resort City in the Sunbelt: Las Vegas, 1930–2000.* 2d ed. Reno: University of Nevada Press, 2000.

Mohl, Raymond A., ed. *Searching for the Sunbelt: Historical Perspectives on a Region.* Knoxville: University of Tennessee Press, 1990.

Monroy, Douglas. *Thrown among Strangers: The Making of Mexican Culture in Frontier California.* Berkeley: University of California, 1990.

Moore, Patricia Anne. *The Casino: Avalon, Santa Catalina Island, California.* Avalon, CA: Catalina Island Museum Society, 1979.

Morgan, Neil. *Westward Tilt: The American West Today.* New York: Random House, 1963.

Mumford, Lewis. *The City in History: Its Origins, its Transformations, and its Prospects.* New York: Harcourt, Brace & World, 1961.

Nash, Roderick. *Wilderness and the American Mind.* 3d ed. New Haven, CT: Yale University Press, 1982.

Newman, Harvey K. *Southern Hospitality: Tourism and the Growth of Atlanta.* Tuscaloosa: University of Alabama Press, 1999.

Neel, Susan Rhoades, ed. "Tourism and the American West." Special issue, *Pacific Historical Review* 65, no. 4 (November 1996).

Nicolaides, Becky M. *My Blue Heaven: Life and Politics in the Working-Class Suburbs of Los Angeles, 1920–1965.* Chicago: University of Chicago Press, 2002.

Nugent, Walter. *Into the West: The Story of Its People.* New York: Knopf, 1999.

O'Connor, Carol A. "A Region of Cities." In *The Oxford History of the American West*, edited by Clyde A. Milner II, Carol A. O'Connor, and Martha A. Sandweiss, 534–63. New York: Oxford University Press, 1994.

Ore, Janet. *The Seattle Bungalow: People and Houses, 1900–1940.* Seattle: University of Washington Press, 2007.

Ott, John. "Landscapes of Consumption: Auto Tourism and Visual Culture in California, 1920–1940." In *Reading California: Art, Image, and Identity, 1900–2000*, edited by Stephanie Barron, Sheri Bernstein, and Ilene Susan Fort, 51–68. Los Angeles: Los Angeles County Museum of Art, 2000.

Overholt, Alma. *The Catalina Story: Compiled and Edited under the Auspices of the Catalina Island Museum Society*. Avalon, CA: Catalina Island Museum Society, 1962.

Padget, Martin. *Indian Country: Travels in the American Southwest, 1840–1935*. Albuquerque: University of New Mexico Press, 2004.

————. "Travel, Exoticism, and the Writing of Region: Charles Fletcher Lummis and the 'Creation' of the Southwest." *Journal of the Southwest* 37 (Fall 1995): 421–429.

Padilla, Genaro M. *My History, Not Yours: The Formation of Mexican American Autobiography*. Madison: University of Wisconsin Press, 1993.

Pack, Janet Rothenberg, ed. *Sunbelt/Frostbelt: Public Policies and Market Forces in Metropolitan Development*. Washington, DC: Brookings Institution Press, 2005.

Phillips, George Harwood. *Chiefs and Challengers: Indian Resistance and Cooperation in Southern California*. Berkeley: University of California Press, 1975.

Pisano, Ronald G. *Idle Hours: Americans at Leisure, 1865–1914*. Boston: Little, Brown, 1988.

Pitt, Leonard, and Dale Pitt. *Los Angeles A to Z: An Encyclopedia of the City and County*. Berkeley: University of California Press, 1997.

Polan, Donna. "California Through the Lens of Hollywood." In *Reading California: Art, Image, and Identity, 1900–2000*, edited by Stephanie Barron, Sheri Bernstein, and Ilene Susan Fort, 129–52. Los Angeles: Los Angeles County Museum of Art and University of California Press, 2000.

Pomeroy, Earl S. *In Search of the Golden West: The Tourist in Western America*. New York: Knopf, 1957.

Powell, Lawrence Clark. *California Classics: The Creative Literature of the Golden State*. Los Angeles: W. Ritchie, 1971.

Price, Jennifer. *Flight Maps: Adventures with Nature in Modern America*. New York: Basic Books, 1999.

Pyle, Ernie. *Ernie Pyle's Southwest*. Palm Desert, CA: Desert-Southwest, 1965.

Pyne, Stephen J. *How the Canyon Became Grand: A Short History*. New York: Viking, 1998.

Renton, Malcom J. "The SCIC's Third Quarter Century: 1944–1969," *Water Lines*, 3d quarter 1994.

Robinson, W. W. *Southern California Local History: A Gathering of the Writings of W. W. Robinson*. Edited by Doyce B. Nunis, Jr. Los Angeles: Historical Society of Southern California, 1993.

————. *The Story of Riverside County*. Los Angeles: Title Insurance and Trust, 1957.

Rodgers, Daniel T. *The Work Ethic in Industrial America, 1850–1920*. Chicago: University of Chicago Press, 1978.

Rodriguez, Sylvia. "Tourism, Whiteness, and the Vanishing Anglo." In *Seeing and Being Seen: Tourism in the American West*, edited by David M. Wrobel and Patrick T. Long, 194–210. Lawrence: University Press of Kansas, 2001.

Rome, Adam. *The Bulldozer in the Countryside: Suburban Sprawl and the Rise of American Environmentalism*. New York: Cambridge University Press, 2001.

Rosa, Joseph. *Albert Frey, Architect*. New York: Rizzoli International, 1990.

Rosenzweig, Roy. *Eight Hours for What We Will: Workers and Leisure in an Industrial City, 1870–1920*. Cambridge, UK: Cambridge University Press, 1983.

Rosenzweig, Roy, and Elizabeth Blackmar. *The Park and the People: A History of Central Park*. Ithaca, NY: Cornell University Press, 1992.

Rothman, Hal K., ed. *The Culture of Tourism, the Tourism of Culture: Selling the Past to the Present in the American Southwest*. Albuquerque: University of New Mexico Press, 2003.

————. *Devil's Bargains: Tourism in the Twentieth-Century American West*. Lawrence: University Press of Kansas, 1998.

————. *Neon Metropolis: How Las Vegas Started the Twenty-First Century*. New York: Routledge, 2002.

———, ed. *Reopening the American West*. Tucson: University of Arizona Press, 1998.

Rudnick, Lois Palken. *Utopian Vistas: The Mabel Dodge Luhan House and the American Counterculture*. Albuquerque: University of New Mexico Press, 1996.

Rugh, Susan Sessions. *Are We There Yet?: The Golden Age of American Family Vacations*. Lawrence: University Press of Kansas, 2008.

Ryan, Deborah S. "Staging the Imperial City: The Pageant of London, 1911." In *Imperial Cities: Landscape, Display, and Identity*, edited by Felix Driver and David Gilbert, 117–35. Manchester, UK: Manchester University Press, 1999.

Ryan, Mary P. *Civic Wars: Democracy and Public Life in the American City during the Nineteenth Century*. Berkeley: University of California Press, 1997.

Rybczynski, Witold. *A Clearing in the Distance: Frederick Law Olmsted and America in the Nineteenth Century*. New York: Scribner, 1999.

———. *Last Harvest: How a Cornfield became New Daleville; Real Estate Development in America from George Washington to the Builders of the Twenty-First Century, and Why We Live in Houses Anyway*. New York: Scribner, 2007.

Rydell, Robert W. *All the World's a Fair: Visions of Empire at American International Expositions, 1876–1916*. Chicago: University of Chicago Press, 1984.

Sackman, Douglas Cazaux. *Orange Empire: California and the Fruits of Eden*. Berkeley: University of California Press, 2005.

Said, Edward W. *Orientalism*. New York: Pantheon, 1978.

Salvini, Emil R. *The Summer City by the Sea: Cape May, New Jersey; An Illustrated History*. Belleville, NJ: Wheal-Grace, 1995.

Sánchez, George J. *Becoming Mexican American: Ethnicity, Culture, and Identity in Chicano Los Angeles, 1900–1945*. Berkeley: University of California Press, 1993.

Santa Catalina Island Company. "Other Personal Remembrances of Philip K. Wrigley." *Water Lines*, 4th quarter, 1994.

Schama, Simon. *Landscape and Memory*. New York: Knopf, 1995.

Schickel, Richard. *D. W. Griffith: An American Life*. New York: Simon and Schuster, 1984.

Schmitt, Peter J. *Back to Nature: The Arcadian Myth in Urban America*. New York: Oxford University Press, 1969.

Schneider, Robert A. "The Postmodern City from an Early Modern Perspective." *American Historical Review* 105, no. 5 (December 2000): 1668–1675.

Schorske, Carl E. *Fin-de-Siècle Vienna: Politics and Culture*. New York: Vintage, 1981.

———. *Thinking With History: Explorations in the Passage to Modernism*. Princeton: Princeton University Press, 1998.

Schrag, Peter. *Paradise Lost: California's Experience, America's Future*. New York: New Press, 1998.

Schullery, Paul. *Searching for Yellowstone: Ecology and Wonder in the Last Wilderness*. Boston: Houghton Mifflin, 1997.

Schulman, Bruce J. *From Cotton Belt to Sunbelt: Federal Policy, Economic Development, and the Transformation of the South, 1938–1980*. New York: Oxford University Press, 1991.

Scott, Allen J., and Edward W. Soja, eds. *The City: Los Angeles and Urban Theory at the End of the Twentieth Century*. Berkeley: University of California Press, 1996.

Sears, John F. *Sacred Places: American Tourist Attractions in the Nineteenth Century*. New York: Oxford University Press, 1989.

Shaffer, Marguerite S. *See America First: Tourism and National Identity, 1880–1940*. Washington, DC: Smithsonian Institution Press, 2001.

Shi, David E. *The Simple Life: Plain Living and High Thinking in American Culture*. New York: Oxford University Press, 1985.

Sides, Josh. *L.A. City Limits: African American Los Angeles from the Great Depression to the Present*. Berkeley: University of California Press, 2003.

Sies, Mary Corbin. "North American Suburbs, 1880–1950: Cultural and Social Reconsiderations." *Journal of Urban History* 27, no. 3 (March 2001): 313–46.

Smith, Henry Nash. *Virgin Land: The American West as Symbol and Myth*. Cambridge, MA: Harvard University Press, 1950.

Soane, John V. N. *Fashionable Resort Regions: Their Evolution and Transformation with Particular Reference to Bournemouth, Nice, Los Angeles, and Wiesbaden*. Wallingford, UK: CAB International, 1993.

Spicer, Edward H. *Cycles of Conquest: The Impact of Spain, Mexico, and the United States on the Indians of the Southwest, 1533–1960*. Tucson: University of Arizona Press, 1962.

Stansfield, Charles A., Jr. "Cape May: Selling History by the Sea." *Journal of Cultural Geography* 11, no. 1 (Fall/Winter 1990): 25–37.

Starr, Kevin. *Americans and the California Dream, 1850–1915*. New York: Oxford University Press, 1973.

———. *Inventing the Dream: California through the Progressive Era*. New York: Oxford University Press, 1985.

———. *Material Dreams: Southern California through the 1920s*. New York: Oxford University Press, 1990.

Stegner, Wallace. *Where the Bluebird Sings to the Lemonade Springs: Living and Writing in the West*. New York: Random House, 1992.

Steinberg, Ted. *Acts of God: The Unnatural History of Natural Disaster in America*. 2d ed. New York: Oxford University Press, 2006.

Steiner, Michael. "Frontierland as Tomorrowland: Walt Disney and the Architectural Packaging of the Mythic West." *Montana: The Magazine of Western History* 48, no. 1 (Spring 1998): 2–17.

Sterngass, Jon. *First Resorts: Pursuing Pleasure at Saratoga Springs, Newport, and Coney Island*. Baltimore: Johns Hopkins University Press, 2001.

Taylor, Quintard. *In Search of the Racial Frontier: African Americans in the American West, 1528–1990*. New York: Norton, 1998.

Terrie, Philip G. *Contested Terrain: A New History of Nature and People in the Adirondacks*. Syracuse, NY: The Adirondack Museum and Syracuse University Press, 1997.

Thompson, Mark. *American Character: The Curious History of Charles Fletcher Lummis and the Rediscovery of the Southwest*. New York: Arcade, 2001.

Valenčius, Conevery Bolton. *The Health of the Country: How American Settlers Understood Themselves and their Land*. New York: Basic Books, 2002.

Valiulis, Gintaras. "The Southwest Museum: A Community Preserves Indian Culture." *Southern California Quarterly* 66, no. 4 (Winter 1984): 349–57.

Van Balgooy, Mary A. "Designer of the Dream: Cliff May and the California Ranch House." *Southern California Quarterly* 86 (2004): 127–44.

Van Dyke, John C. *The Secret Life of John C. Van Dyke: Selected Letters*. Edited by David W. Teague and Peter Wild. Reno: University of Nevada Press, 1997.

Veblen, Thorstein. *The Theory of the Leisure Class: An Economic Study in the Evolution of Institutions*. New York: MacMillan, 1899.

Walch, Michael C. "Terminating the Indian Termination Policy," *Stanford Law Review* 35, no. 6 (July 1983): 1181–1215.

Waldie, D. J. *Holy Land: A Suburban Memoir*. New York: W. W. Norton, 1996.

———. "Lost in Aerospace: Inhabiting a Future Long since Past." *Huntington Frontiers*, Fall/Winter 2007.

Walker, Franklin Dickerson. *A Literary History of Southern California*. Berkeley: University of California Press, 1950.

Ward, Stephen V. *Selling Places: The Marketing and Promotion of Towns and Cities, 1850–2000*. New York: Routledge, 1998.

Warren, Louis S. *The Hunter's Game: Poachers and Conservationists in Twentieth-Century America*. New Haven, CT: Yale University Press, 1997.

Washburn, Wilcomb E. "The Moral and Legal Justifications for Dispossessing the Indians." In *Seventeenth-Century America: Essays in Colonial History*, edited by James M. Smith, 15–32. Chapel Hill: University of North Carolina Press, 1959.

Weber, David J. "The Spanish Legacy." Chap. 12 in *The Spanish Frontier in North America*. New Haven, CT: Yale University Press, 1992.

Weigle, Marta, and Barbara A. Babcock, eds. *The Great Southwest of the Fred Harvey Company and the Santa Fe Railway*. Phoenix: Heard Museum, 1996.

Weiner, Lynn Y. " 'There's a Great Big Beautiful Tomorrow': Historic Memory and Gender in Walt Disney's 'Carousel of Progress." *Journal of American Culture* 20 (Spring 1999): 111–16.

White, William Stanford, and Steven Kern Tice, *Santa Catalina Island: Its Magic, People, and History*. Glendora, CA: White Limited Editions, 1997.

Wiebe, Robert H. *The Search for Order, 1877–1920*. New York: Hill and Wang, 1967.

Wild, Mark. *Street Meeting: Multiethnic Neighborhoods in Early Twentieth-Century Los Angeles*. Berkeley: University of California Press, 2005.

Wild, Peter. *Desert Magazine: The Henderson Years*. Johannesburg, CA: Shady Myrick Research Project, 2004.

———. "John C. Van Dyke and the Desert Aestheticians." Chap. 6 in *The Opal Desert: Explorations of Fantasy and Reality in the American Southwest*. Austin: University of Texas Press, 1999.

———. *Tipping the Dream: A Brief History of Palm Springs*. Johannesburg, CA: Shady Myrick Research Project, 2007.

Wilson, Chris. *The Myth of Santa Fe: Creating a Modern Regional Tradition*. Albuquerque: University of New Mexico Press, 1997.

Wilson, William H. *The City Beautiful Movement*. Baltimore: Johns Hopkins University Press, 1989.

Wiltse, Jeff. *Contested Waters: A Social History of Swimming Pools in America*. Chapel Hill: University of North Carolina Press, 2007.

Wolch, Jennifer, John P. Wilson, and Jed Fehrenbach. "Parks and Park Funding in Los Angeles: An Equity Mapping Analysis." *Urban Geography* 26 (2005): 4–35.

Wrigley-Rusack, Alison. "William Wrigley, Jr. and Santa Catalina Island, Part I." *Water Lines*, 3d quarter 1986.

Wrobel, David M. *Promised Lands: Promotion, Memory, and the Creation of the American West*. Lawrence: University Press of Kansas, 2002.

Wrobel, David M., and Patrick T. Long. *Seeing and Being Seen: Tourism in the American West*. Lawrence: University Press of Kansas, 2001.

Young, Terence. *Building San Francisco's Parks, 1850–1930*. Baltimore: Johns Hopkins University Press, 2004.

Zimmerman, Tom. "Paradise Promoted: Boosterism and the Los Angeles Chamber of Commerce." *California History* 64, no. 1 (Winter 1985): 22–33.

Zordich, James. "Santa Catalina Island Company: The First Quarter Century." *Water Lines*, 1st quarter 1994.

UNPUBLISHED SOURCES

Crawford, Fred G. *Organizational and Administrative Development of the City of Los Angeles, During the Thirty-Year Period July 1, 1925–September 30, 1955*. Los Angeles: School of Public Administration, University of Southern California, 1955.

Department of Urban Planning, UCLA. *Cornfield of Dreams: A Resource Guide of Facts, Issues and Principles*. Department of Urban Planning, UCLA, 2000. Online at http://www.sppsr.ucla.edu/dup/research/Section1.pdf.

Keil, Andre. *Swimming at the Park Pool: A History of Aquatics in the City of Los Angeles*. City of Los Angeles, Recreation and Parks, 1992.

Spooner, Denise S. "Something There Is That Loves a Wall: Constructing the Landscape of Community in Southern California," Los Angeles History Research Group, Los Angeles, April 10, 2004.

DISSERTATIONS AND THESES

Avila, Eric. "Reinventing Los Angeles: Popular Culture in the Age of White Flight, 1940–1965." PhD diss., University of California, Berkeley, 1997.

Bourne, A. Ross. "Some Major Aspects of the Historical Development of Palm Springs between 1880 and 1938, and in Addition a Continuation of the Historical Changes in the Indian Land Problem and Four Cultural Institutions until 1948." Master's thesis, Occidental College, 1953.

Christman, Anastasia. "The Best Laid Plans: Women's Clubs and City Planning in Los Angeles, 1890–1930." PhD diss., UCLA, 2000.

Culver, M. Lawrence. "Resorting to Tourism: The Town and the Valley of Jackson, Wyoming, through the 1950s." Master's thesis, Utah State University, 1997.

Estrada, William David. "Sacred and Contested Space: The Los Angeles Plaza." PhD diss., UCLA, 2003.

Gibson, Mary Katherine. "The Changing Conception of the Urban Park in America: The City of Los Angeles as a Case Study." Master's thesis, UCLA, 1977.

Hartman, Stella Elizabeth. "A Study of Leisure-Time Habits of Young Men and Young Women in Los Angeles." Master's thesis, University of Southern California, 1942.

Jensen, Thomas A. "Palm Springs, California: Its Evolution and Functions." Master's thesis, UCLA, 1954.

Karnes, David Alan. "Modern Metropolis: Mass Culture and the Transformation of Los Angeles, 1890–1950." PhD diss., University of California, Berkeley, 1991.

Kropp, Phoebe S. "'All Our Yesterdays': The Spanish Fantasy Past and the Politics of Public Memory in Southern California, 1884–1939." PhD diss., University of California, San Diego, 1999.

Okun, Gary Steven. "Avalon, California: Structure and Function of an Island Town." Master's thesis, UCLA, 1976.

Schantz, Eric Michael. "From the *Mexicali Rose* to the Tijuana Brass: Vice Tours of the United States–Mexico Border, 1910–1965." PhD diss., UCLA, 2001.

Shaw, Rachel Dayton. "Evolving Ecoscape: An Environmental and Cultural History of Palm Springs, California, and the Agua Caliente Indian Reservation, 1877–1939." PhD diss., University of California, San Diego, 1999.

Withers, Charles Dinnijes. "Problems of Mexican Boys." Master's thesis, University of Southern California, 1942.

Index